The Correspondence of
BORIS PASTERNAK *and*
OLGA FREIDENBERG
1910-1954

The Correspondence of

BORIS PASTERNAK *and*

OLGA FREIDENBERG

1910-1954

Compiled and edited,
with an introduction, by
ELLIOTT MOSSMAN

Translated by
Elliott Mossman and
Margaret Wettlin

A Helen and Kurt Wolff Book
Harcourt Brace Jovanovich, Publishers
New York and London

Copyright © 1981 by Harcourt Brace Jovanovich, Inc.
English translation copyright © 1982 by Harcourt Brace Jovanovich, Inc.

Library of Congress Cataloging in Publication Data

Pasternak, Boris Leonidovich, 1890–1960.
The Correspondence of Boris Pasternak
and Olga Freidenberg, 1910–1954.

Translation of: Perepiska.
Includes index.
1. Pasternak, Boris Leonidovich, 1890–1960—Correspondence.
2. Authors, Russian—20th century—Correspondence.
3. Freidenberg, O. M. (Ol'ga Mikhaĭlovna), 1890–1955.
I. Freidenberg, O. M. (Ol'ga Mikhaĭlovna), 1890–1955.
II. Mossman, Elliott. III. Title.
PG3476.P27Z53813   891.71'42 [B]   81–48017
ISBN 0–15–122630–X   AACR2

Printed in the United States of America

First edition

B C D E

Contents

Illustrations

Mikhail Fedorovich (Uncle Misha) and Anna Osipovna (Aunt Asya)
Freidenberg. St. Petersburg

Olya and Aunt Asya at the window of their St. Petersburg apartment

Boris Pasternak upon graduating from the Gymnasium. 1908

Olya Freidenberg. St. Petersburg, 1909.
Inscribed on the back: "To the palefaces from the redskin"

Between pages 20 and 21

Leonid and Alexander Pasternak. Merrekühl, 1910

Olya Freidenberg. St. Petersburg

Mikhail Fedorovich Freidenberg

The apartment house on the Catherine Canal in 1975

Aunt Asya and Rosa, Leonid, Josephine, and Lydia Pasternak. Merrekühl

Josephine and Lydia Pasternak in clown costumes

Anna Osipovna Freidenberg and Leonid Osipovich Pasternak

Leonid and Alexander Pasternak preparing an exhibit in commemoration
of Tolstoy's death. Moscow, 1911

Between pages 46 and 47

Olga Freidenberg

Boris Pasternak. 1913

Ida Vysotskaya, Josephine Pasternak, A. Vishnevsky,
and Rosa Pasternak. Kissingen, 1912

Between pages 48 and 51

Olga Freidenberg. Petrograd, 1914

Olga Freidenberg with a wounded soldier. Petrograd, 1914

Boris Pasternak. Tikhie Gory (in the Urals), 1916

Leonid and Rosa Pasternak, Borya and Alexander Pasternak
with their grandmother Berta Kaufman, and Lydia and Josephine
Pasternak. Molodi, 1917

Between pages 72 and 73

Olga Freidenberg

A postcard from Olga Freidenberg. September 15, 1917

The Pasternak family in Moscow before departing for Berlin in 1921:
Leonid Pasternak, Berta Kaufman, and Rosa, Alexander, Boris,
and Lydia Pasternak

Boris Pasternak. Moscow

Evgenya Vladimirovna (Zhenya) Pasternak. Moscow, 1922

Boris Pasternak, Evgenya Pasternak, and young Zhenya. Leningrad, 1924.
Photograph by Nappelbaum

Young Zhenya with his nanny Fenya

Rosa, Lydia, Josephine, and Leonid Pasternak. Berlin

Between pages 116 and 117

Boris Pasternak with his son Zhenya. Abramtsevo, 1925

Evgenya Pasternak with Zhenya

Aunt Asya

Olga Freidenberg

Boris Pasternak. Moscow, 1928

Between pages 154 and 155

Evgenya Pasternak with Zhenya. 1931

Boris Pasternak and Kornei Chukovsky in a conference hall. 1932

Fedor Karlovich (Boris's second cousin), Leonid, Josephine,
Lydia, and Rosa Pasternak. Berlin

Young Zhenya Pasternak. Starki, 1936.
Photograph by Gornung

Boris and Zinaida Nikolayevna (Zina) Pasternak with Adrian Neuhaus.
Odoyevo, 1934

Boris Pasternak. Odoyevo, 1934

Boris Pasternak. Peredelkino, 1936.
Photograph by Gornung

Between pages 188 and 189

André Malraux, Vsevolod Meyerhold, and Boris Pasternak. Moscow, 1936

Young Zhenya Pasternak. Moscow, 1940

Zina Pasternak

Between pages 216 and 217

Boris Pasternak. Chistopol, 1942

Boris Pasternak with S. Tregub at the front. 1943

Introduction

Fo R nearly forty-five years, Boris Pasternak and Olga Freidenberg, cousins, carried on a loving correspondence—he writing from the ancient Russian (and then Soviet) capital of Moscow, she from the imperial capital of St. Petersburg, later Leningrad. Their kinship transcended family ties to encompass a common world of art, cherished cultural values, and the rare experience of a society in revolution. The authors of this "epistolary *contredanse*," as he once termed it in a letter to her, seldom met during their lives, so their letters bound them together. This volume contains the life they shared in letters.

It is quite a common practice to present the "Letters" of a prominent writer as documents, in which the addressee is relegated to salutation and the occasional footnote. Thoughts, feelings, and opinions recorded in the tranquillity and, usually, the privacy of the epistolary form are assembled in a singular portrait of the author. Only occasionally is that portrait at marked variance with the finished, public portrait derived from his works. Letters supplement or complement the traces of autobiography a writer has left in public.

For several reasons, the common practice is ill-suited to the correspondence between Boris Pasternak and Olga Freidenberg. Here, two distinguished authors participate in a correspondence as coequals from the start, even though only one may have drawn our attention to the book. I think the reader will share my conclusion that Olga Freidenberg, a scholar of ancient civilizations with a keen eye for what is concealed in daily life, is as engaging and skilled a chronicler of her experience in twentieth-century Russia as her more public cousin, the poet and novelist. The portrait she creates deserves to be more widely known.

The times in which these cousins corresponded were ones, by and large, when public portraits emerged, if at all, distorted and truncated by the unfreedoms of Soviet life: the will to paint a true portrait was thwarted by the dire consequences that often resulted, and the public means to do so were not easily accessible, even to the bold. Correspondence as a mode of communication emerged from obsolescence in the Soviet Union to assume a new role in the gray area between the proscribed public and the stifled private life. All the more reason, then, to ask for the context in which letters were written.

This correspondence between Moscow and Leningrad also constitutes a rare sort of evidence. Boris Pasternak's and Olga Freidenberg's letters testify to and corroborate a common, anguished experience of life after the Russian Revolution and under Stalin. Textbook dates and events recede, and their consequences come into focus. From Moscow Boris Pasternak wrote to Leningrad in 1933: "I am extremely glad we are at one in our opinions, formed in different towns, in the most diverse circumstances, and without our conferring—my opinions springing from considerations unknown to you and vice versa. This is eminently characteristic of our times. Everywhere an as yet unnamed truth is emerging, be it at Party purges, in the quality of artistic and everyday standards, or in the speech and consciousness of little children. And this constitutes the legitimacy of the new order and its temporary inability to cope with innovations so elusive."

Boris Pasternak and Olga Freidenberg experienced life before, in, and after revolution, so their judgments are couched in a vocabulary different from ours. The letter continues: "It is as if one of the midnight colloquies of the 1890's had gone on and on until it became our present life. Then the very madness was enchanting, wreathed as it was in clouds of tobacco smoke, but how completely mad must the ravings of those revolutionary Russian aristocrats seem now, when the smoke has settled and their conversation has become an integral part of the geographical map—and how solid a part! Yet the world has never seen anything more aristocratic and freer than this, our bare, brutish actuality, still calumniated and deserving of all the groans it has caused." The two correspondents describe the fabric of Soviet life during a period almost completely dominated by Stalinism, and they name aspects of that life which were hidden from public view.

This volume differs structurally from most collections of letters. Its authors had radically different habits and attitudes toward preservation of the materials of biography. In 1955 Pasternak observed in a letter to another Leningrad relative: "Olya was the keeper of family traditions, of letters and mementos. . . . I personally do not keep heirlooms, archives, collections of any kind, including books and furniture. I do not save letters or draft copies of my work. Nothing piles up in my room; it is easier to clean than a hotel room. My life resembles a student's." He believed that a myriad of cultural choices beyond his ken and control preserves what merits preservation. Yet it is precisely Olga's meticulous habits of preservation—of letters, of drafts of her own letters, and of the facts which enable us to understand their lives—that made this volume possible. When her share of the correspondence was discovered after her death, it was accompanied by a retrospective diary of her life, composed in her last years. In the diary she annotates her relationship with her cousin, in effect annotating this correspondence. I have used extracts from that unpublished diary, now deposited at Oxford University, to supplement the correspondence and have added explanatory prefaces to most chapters, as well as footnotes where they seemed necessary. Where there are gaps in the correspondence, one can catch glimpses of the authors' lives from the family photographs included in this volume.

I

Olga Mikhailovna Freidenberg and Boris Leonidovich Pasternak were born in the same year, 1890, she in Odessa on March 28 (Old Style) and he in Moscow on January 29. The Pasternaks, originally Odessans, had just settled in Moscow in 1889. Olga's mother, Anna Osipovna Freidenberg ("Aunt Asya" to Boris), was a Pasternak and sister to Boris's father, the Russian impressionist painter Leonid Osipovich Pasternak. Olga's father, Mikhail Fedorovich Freidenberg ("Uncle Misha"), was an inventor of astonishing versatility whose talents found little application in the lagging industrial economy of imperial Russia. He had designed the first automatic telephone-switching equipment and the hand-operated linotype machine, both marketed abroad. However, business reversals forced him to undertake other ventures as well. For several years he edited and published a newspaper in St. Petersburg, where the Freidenbergs had settled shortly after Olga's birth.

Mikhail Freidenberg and Leonid Pasternak had been fast friends since school days in Odessa. Freidenberg, an abandoned child with a flair for the original, attracted the attention of the talented young Pasternaks. For example, when he designed a passenger balloon to fly over the Odessa bazaar, Leonid Pasternak drew advertising posters, and his sister Asya, later Freidenberg's wife, sold tickets to the public.

Although Leonid Pasternak had received his degree in law at Novorossiisk University, he chose the lot of an artist, completing the course of study at the Munich Academy of the Arts. He married a fellow Odessan, Rozalia Isidorovna Kaufman (Rosa), who had already established a promising career as a concert pianist in performances in Russia and abroad. Together they took up residence at 21 Myasnitskaya Street, in Moscow, the faculty quarters of the School of Painting, Sculpture, and Architecture, where Leonid Pasternak lectured. The apartment was the locus of Boris Pasternak's youth. His brother, Alexander, was born there in 1892. His sisters, Josephine and Lydia, were born in 1900 and 1902.

Austerity was the rule in the Pasternak household in Odessa—the elders objected bitterly to Asya's marriage to the flamboyant Misha Freidenberg —and Asya brought something of that Pasternak asceticism, in an endearing form, to the Freidenberg household in St. Petersburg: strict cleanliness reigned in their spacious apartment on the Catherine Canal. The loss of Asya's first son, Zhenya, to acute appendicitis caused her to abandon her considerable talent for music; Olga's only living brother, Alexander (Sasha), was an unstable, unpredictable boy, as talented as his inventor-father, but shy and awkward. He was to be the bane of Olga's and her mother's existence, though the object of their deep love, for many harrowing years.

Olga's youth was filled with gaiety and mischief. She shared passions and pranks with her girlfriend Elena Lifshits and soon was treated as a member of the Lifshits family. Summer months were spent with the Moscow Pasternaks, first back in Odessa, then at Maloyaroslavets, and later in the Estonian seaside town of Merrekühl—where this correspondence begins in 1910. The cultured atmosphere of Olga's family life—at various times she had private lessons in French, English, Italian, Spanish, Portuguese, and Swedish—eventually brought her to appreciate a Gymnasium education. She graduated in 1908, without, however, the coveted Gymnasium Gold Medal, which alone permitted women to enroll in the "Higher Courses for Women," then the only university education open to them. Nevertheless, she attended the lectures with her friends, mocking the finishing-school attitude fostered by their professors.

Soon, during World War I, Olga Freidenberg discovered a seriousness of purpose that was to be the hallmark of her distinguished career as a scholar. This new dedication coincided with the rejuvenation of Russian universities after the February Revolution of 1917, and Olga Freidenberg enrolled. She studied Old Russian literature, ancient Greek literature, and folklore, focusing her own, quite original research on the *Life* of the early Christian saint Thecla. In 1924, at the Institute for Language and Literature of the East and West, she defended her thesis on the origins of hagiography in the Greek erotic novel and received her first professional degree.

Olga's diary chronicles her academic career in some detail. Having received her doctoral degree, Professor Freidenberg was invited to organize and chair the department of classical philology at the Leningrad Institute of Philosophy, Language, Literature, and History, the home of the former philology department of St. Petersburg University. In 1936 her *Poetics of Plot and Genre* (*Poetika syuzheta i zhanra*) was published, but copies were confiscated by the state only three weeks after it appeared. Thereafter it proved very difficult for her to publish her work; it was only in 1978 that her long monograph *Image and Concept* was finally published in Moscow.*

Stalinism and the ravages of life in blockaded Leningrad during World War II took their toll on the scholarship of Olga Freidenberg. Nevertheless, she left her mark on a number of students who are accomplished scholars today, and her works are appearing anew in journals such as the Soviet *Semiotika* and the American *New Literary History*.†

As Leonid Pasternak observed, there was something "so unmodern" about Olga Freidenberg—a specific application, perhaps, of that asceticism which characterized her mother and derived from the Odessa heritage. In Olga it took the form of an unbending will and, in her mature years, unflinching courage. At times there may seem to be a note of bitterness in her largely self-imposed isolation. "All I ask of Mother Russia is something legal plus something edible—a minimum of each," she wrote to her cousin in 1925, when her first scholarship failed to win her any security in the uneasy Soviet academic world. However, the bitterness, seldom groundless, is accompanied by an optimistic faith based upon a keen appreciation for history and culture. When attacked openly and repeatedly for her *Poetics* at the height of the Stalinist Terror, she stood firm: "One thing and one thing only possessed, supported, and guided me in those terrible days: my unshakable faith in the tradition of scholarship. I knew it existed and that no falsification or destruction of documents could change it. I believed as firmly in its true and unbiased existence as if I could see it with my own eyes. Those in power could do what they would—kill, distort, pervert—but in reality they could not kill or annihilate or diminish the grandeur of human culture. They could only

* O. M. Freidenberg, *Mif i literatura drevnosti* (*Myth and the Literature of Antiquity*; Moscow: Nauka Publishers, 1978).

† The Soviet *Short Literary Encyclopedia* (*Kratkaya literaturnaya entsiklopedia*), volume 8 (Moscow, 1975), entry "Freidenberg," links the accomplishments of Olga Mikhailovna Freidenberg to those of the Russian literary theorist Mikhail Mikhailovich Bakhtin (1895–1975) and the French structuralist Claude Lévi-Strauss (1908–   ). A complete bibliography of the writings of Olga Freidenberg can be found in *Trudy po znakovym sistemam* (generally referred to as *Semiotika*), VI (1973), Tartu, p. 488ff.

build straw houses incapable of withstanding the test of time. However great their power, they had no means of changing history."

Olga studied ancient, distant civilizations. When in the correspondence she turns her attention to her own times, she brings to bear the skills of a scholar of antiquity—a sense of the whole and of the movement of wholes —and a highly individual talent for seeing through the mass of mundane details to the essence of her society. Early on, in 1924, she sensed that Soviet society held little promise for deeply felt, committed creative talent and cultivated a rigid, superficial, almost "scholastic" style: "Heavens, I'm like a provincial actress trying to draw on 'inner feelings' when technique could handle my problems with practically no expenditure of energy." She recognized the all-pervasiveness and anonymity of the Terror: "No one who has not lived in the Stalin era can appreciate the horror of our uncertain position. A person's life was poisoned secretly, invisibly, as witches and sorcerers were hounded in the Dark Ages. Something mysterious was accumulating under the earth and coming to the boil. A person felt at the mercy of an inescapable force aimed at him and certain to crush him." She knew the mechanics of Soviet society: "In our country, logic is installed in the brain as a gadget whose functioning depends not on the object under examination but on the hands of the one who installed it."

Olga's observations on her society at times disrobe political power or brute force to reveal the everyday mediocrity of the Stalinist legacy. From the Russian saying "Money is trouble (*skloka*), but without it, it's worse," she extracted a word and gave it new application to Soviet life: "Wherever you looked, in all our institutions, in all our homes, *skloka* was brewing. *Skloka* is a phenomenon born of our social order, an entirely new term and concept, not to be translated into any language of the civilized world. It is hard to define. It stands for base, trivial hostility, unconscionable spite breeding petty intrigues, the vicious pitting of one clique against another. It thrives on calumny, informing, spying, scheming, slander, the igniting of base passions. Taut nerves and weakening morals allow one individual or group to rabidly hate another individual or group. *Skloka* is natural for people who have been incited to attack one another, who have been made bestial by desperation, who have been driven to the wall. *Skloka* is the alpha and omega of our politics. *Skloka* is our method." Among the many memoirs of Stalinism at its most harsh— most of them from the labor camps—Olga Freidenberg's record of the way it penetrated institutions, homes, and minds nominally "at liberty" is rare and particularly valuable.

II

The youth of Boris Pasternak enjoyed a quality not to be duplicated in Russia after the onset of World War I. In contrast to Soviet reality, he wrote to Olga in 1941, the times of his father were a "nonscholastic era when the natural development of a person's activities filled his life as vegetation fills space, when everything was in motion and each individual existed to distinguish himself from all others." Throughout his life Pasternak often looked back longingly to that era. The quality of these prewar years complicates the early correspondence of Boris and Olga, but the reader's attention to those early letters is promptly repaid with an understanding of the origins and depth of a lifelong relationship.

For the young Boris Pasternak the origin of art was a domestic affair—in the painting of his father, his mother's music, in the compositions and conversations of family friends like Scriabin, Rilke, and Tolstoy. Pasternak's Moscow of the 1900's, with its circles of adventurous poets, musicians, artists, and philosophers, took part in a new age in the history of the creative imagination. In the arts, new visions jockeyed and coexisted —in poetry, it was first symbolism, then acmeism and futurism—while in philosophy, young schools of psychology and aesthetics showed a casual disregard for positivism. Music, art, and poetry spoke the language of the city; the cacophony of politics was an encroaching annoyance.

For Boris Pasternak the choice of a calling—an outlet for one's talents —could be made by trial and error. Lessons first from Yuri Engel and then from Scriabin resulted in his first (and only) musical composition, the Sonata in B minor for Piano (1905). He abandoned music and, upon graduation from the Gymnasium in 1908—with the Gold Medal—entered Moscow University. Philosophy absorbed his attention. He studied with philosophers of aesthetics, such as Gustav Shpet in Moscow, and, in the summer of 1912, with the Neo-Kantians of Marburg University in Germany: Paul Natorp and the head of the school, Hermann Cohen. His essay "On the Subject and Method of Psychology" (1912) and his talk "Symbolism and Immortality" (1913), delivered to the Circle for Research on Aesthetic Culture and Symbolism in Art, are the fruits of this preoccupation with philosophy and his abiding interest in art.

In *Safe Conduct* (1931), an autobiographical inquiry into the origins and nature of art, Pasternak described the transition from philosophy to poetry in his experience. His relationship with his cousin Olga played a role in that transition. In poetry he discovered a voice of his own, captive to none, and it was heard in his first books, *A Twin in the Clouds* (1914) and *Above the Barriers* (1917). It was a voice of the city, as Kornei Chukovsky (1882–1969), one of the finest readers among twentieth-century Russian critics, observed: "Amidst Moscow streets, by-ways and courtyards he felt like a fish in water; here he was in his element and his tongue was purely Muscovite. . . . I recall how his colloquial speech shocked me and how organically it was linked to his whole Muscovite manner. At first it seemed strange to me: after all, of all the poets of his generation he was the most educated, the best read—he read four languages freely, translated German, French and English poets, but no matter how lofty a theme he tackled, those colorful 'low-country' words always crept into his speech. . . ." In 1923 fellow poet Osip Mandelstam noted that "to read Pasternak's poems is to cough, take several deep breaths and purge the lungs; poetry like this has to be a cure for tuberculosis."

In the voice of Pasternak's early poetry there was the assertion of a new and different alliance between man's creation and nature's dominion; he released the two from the isolation to which nineteenth-century literature had confined them. City and countryside found common cause in an urban reality that was Pasternak's Moscow—of his own imagining, to be sure, but also the Moscow in fact alive with the comings and goings of a mixed, variegated population.

In art, Pasternak always sought out the new—not the topical, but life in its passage through the present. His next volume of poetry, *My Sister, Life*, subtitled *The Summer of 1917*, isolated an interlude between the two Russian revolutions of 1917 which would otherwise have been lost in the welter of events that followed: the October Revolution and the Russian Civil War. The book, published in 1922, was an act of precise observation, scientific and historical. In *Safe Conduct* he described the atmosphere of that summer: "I could scarcely tell you of those eternally first days in all revolutions, when all the Camille Desmoulinses* jump on tables and electrify passers-by with toasts to the air. I witnessed them. Reality, like a neglected daughter, ran off half-dressed and presented legitimate history with the challenge of herself just as she was—from head to toe illegitimate and dowryless. I saw summer on the earth, as though unaware of itself, natural and prehistoric, as in Revelations."

The poems of *My Sister, Life* themselves were written in surroundings far from idyllic—during Russia's four-year civil war—yet the book has attained the status of a twentieth-century idyl because it asserts the right of

* Camille Desmoulins (1760–1794): French revolutionary.

spontaneous regeneration in the life of man. In 1922, in a letter to the symbolist poet Valery Yakovlevich Bryusov (1873–1924), Pasternak said: "*My Sister, Life* is revolutionary in the best sense of the word. The stage of revolution closest to the heart and to poetry—the dawn of revolution and its eruption, when it returns man to his own nature and sees the state through the eyes of natural law (the American and French declarations of rights)—all this is expressed by the book in its very spirit, its content, its tempo, the sequence of its parts. . . ." In the same letter he described an interview with Leon Trotsky in which Pasternak defended "true individualism as the new social skeleton of a new social organism."

Pasternak discovered early in the 1920's that "individualism is heresy and idealism is banned," as he wrote to Olga; but it took him several years to acknowledge that there was no cultural alliance to be made with the new leadership. In the narrative poems "A Lofty Malady" (1924), "Lieutenant Schmidt" (1926), and *The Year 1905* (1929), Pasternak persisted in offering a culture unsought-for, alien in origin, and, therefore, increasingly suspect. He justified these solitary efforts to capture the essence of his times in a letter to Mandelstam in 1925: "Everything is corroded, broken, dismantled; everything is covered with hardened layers of insensitivity, deafness, entrenched routine. It is disgusting. . . . The premise of the extraordinariness of the age has been dispelled. The style of the finale (the end of the century, the end of revolution, the end of youth, the fall of Europe) begins to dry up, the water recedes, and it ceases to function. Once again, as before, the fate of Europe (in quotation marks) becomes a matter of choice and good will. Everything is ending that can end, that doesn't carry on by itself. But if one decides to continue something, it will not end. . . . And I, too, am returning to what I had abandoned. Not as a literary figure. Not as one called upon to do so for a finale. No—as a civilian, a natural person, with mixed luck, withdrawn, unknown." The final phrase foretold Pasternak's life under Stalin.

When Stalin rose to power in 1928, Pasternak entered three decades of gradual withdrawal from current events. He noted the change 1928 brought in a letter to Olga: "As you know, terror has resumed, this time without the moral grounds or justifications that were found for it earlier, in the heat of commerce, careerism, and unsightly 'sinfulness.' These men are far from being the Puritan saints who then emerged as avenging angels. Terrible confusion reigns; we are caught up and spun round in waves that bear absolutely no relationship to time." Although he continued to publish sporadically (his book of verse *Second Birth* appeared in 1932, and the volume *On Early Trains* in 1943), increasingly he sought refuge in the anonymity of translation. He translated Goethe, Kleist,

Rilke, Verlaine, Shelley, and other European poets, as well as the poets of Soviet Georgia. His principal endeavor was the translation of eight of Shakespeare's plays. Olga expressed a widely shared view of her cousin's translations: ". . . you have changed the nature of translation, transforming it from a stranger dressed up in a Russian caftan into a fellow countryman with whom one communicates without the feeling of being away from home."

Still, Pasternak was frequently attacked for his writings and for his refusal to yield to Party directives. He well understood the shallowness of humanity that characterized the Terror. In 1936, when Olga was being hounded in the press and at the university for her *Poetics,* he wrote to her: "There are certain miserable and completely cowed nonentities who are driven by the force of their own mediocrity to hail as the style and spirit of the times that trembling, inarticulate obsequiousness to which they are condemned by the absence of choice—that is, by the poverty of their intellectual resources. When such people hear someone asserting that the greatness of the Revolution lies precisely in a person's being able at a time of revolution—*especially* at a time of revolution—to speak out freely and think daringly, they brand such a view counterrevolutionary."

After World War II, Pasternak discovered a new resolve. He ceased to feel the barbs of critics and ignored the intrigues of Soviet society. "Of late," he wrote to Olga in 1947, "I have taken that enormous step in life . . . which brings me to a point where trifles, shadings, accents, transitions, half tones, and other secondary considerations no longer can hurt or delight or even exist for me, a point where one must win or lose on the grand scale—all or nothing!"

The new resolve was associated with his work on a novel, ultimately to be titled *Doctor Zhivago,* the existence of which he announced to Olga in 1946: "Since July I have been writing a prose novel, *Boys and Girls,* which is to encompass the four decades from 1902 to 1946 in ten chapters." Later that year he wrote: "In it I want to convey the historical image of Russia over the past forty-five years, and at the same time I want to express in every aspect of the story—a sad, dismal story, worked out in fine detail, ideally, as in a Dickens or Dostoyevsky novel—my own views on art, the Gospels, the life of man in history, and much more." Since he had no hope of publishing the novel, it afforded him the opportunity to rediscover himself as an artist: "The mood of the piece is set by my Christianity, somewhat different and wider in scope than Quaker or Tolstoyan Christianity, deriving from various aspects of the Gospels in addition to the ethical aspect. All these matters are so important to me, and their varying colors arrange themselves so perfectly on the canvas within the outline I have conceived, that I could not go on living another year unless this novel, my alter ego, in which with almost physical concreteness certain of my spiritual qualities and part of my nervous structure have been implanted, went on living and growing, too."

Pasternak had no pretentions with regard to the formulaic "well-made novel" and made no particular effort to conform his *Doctor Zhivago* to the remnants of a literary tradition disrupted by the Revolution and its aftermath. ". . . I am not even writing it as a work of art," he told Olga, "although it is literature in a deeper sense than anything I have ever done before. But I just don't know whether there is any art left in this world, or what art means. There are people who love me very much (only a few), and I feel that I owe them something. It is for them I am writing this novel, as if it were a long letter to them, in two volumes." Olga was not alone in observing that the novel was a rejuvenation for its author, returning him to the independence of spirit that had marked his early poetry and motivated *My Sister, Life*.

Joy was the keynote of the novel's composition. "I must die as myself," he wrote to his cousin in 1953, after a severe heart attack, "not as a remembrance of myself. . . . I must finish the novel and another thing or two; not that I *must*—the expression is wrong—but that I want to, want to with indomitable will. How do I feel? As happy as can be, for the simple reason that a feeling of happiness must accompany my efforts if what I have planned is to succeed—that is an absolute prerequisite. According to some predetermined pattern, the feeling of happiness comes back to me from what I have written, as in a kind of manufacturing process: the tangible return on an original investment."

The politics of Stalinism was not part of the novel's vocabulary—the central character dies at the beginning of the Stalinist period—and politics in general would have detracted from what Pasternak saw as the purpose of the novel, a revitalization of the spirit of Russia. On the envelope of a letter dated August 21, 1954, from the Germanist Konstantin Bogatyrev, then in the labor camps, Pasternak noted for himself a deficiency in the manuscript to be corrected: "The politically unacceptable barbs not only place the manuscript in jeopardy—but also squaring accounts with the directives of the age is trivial. . . . The novel is opposed to that in tone and scope. So it was in the preceding parts, and so it must be henceforth. There is no need to yield to an open, negative treatment of contemporary dogmas in the characters' dialogues: dogma should be ignored, disregarded."

Although *Doctor Zhivago* did not concern itself with political issues, it did find itself affected by the politics of the age. When it was rejected by the liberal journal *Novy Mir* at a time, after the death of Stalin, when constraints on Russian culture were most relaxed, Pasternak authorized publication abroad. *Doctor Zhivago* was published in 1957. The next year Pasternak received the Nobel Prize for Literature, for his lifelong contribution, in poetry and prose, to Russian and European culture. At home, he was vilified for his achievements.

Olga Freidenberg did not live to see the publication of *Doctor Zhivago*; she died on July 6, 1955, in Leningrad. But before her death she heard rumors that her cousin was a candidate for the Nobel Prize and world renown. He had first been nominated for the prize in 1949. In one of the finest tributes to him, she wrote to Peredelkino, the writers' village near Moscow where he had lived with his wife, Zina, since the mid-1930's: "Dearest friend, never has dynamite led to such happy consequences as your candidacy for the throne of Apollo. What if in Peredelkino you are accomplishing your feat in solitude and seclusion? Somewhere typesetters are supporting their families on the wages they receive for setting up your name in all the languages of the world. You are giving work to men in Belgium and Paris. Presses are humming, pages are being folded, the smell of ink fills the air, while you are having breakfast with Zina in Peredelkino or are complaining of the bars of your golden cage. It is unity of time and action, if not unity of place. . . . Do you not see the great significance of your life in Peredelkino and in the bars, above and beyond which, far, far away, people are talking about the unalloyed you, the unseen you? This, then, is how our fate is determined, without our knowing it."

When Boris Pasternak died, on May 30, 1960, he died "a civilian, a natural person, with mixed luck, withdrawn," but no longer "unknown." He had not despaired of the vision of humanity he had expressed in *My Sister, Life*. In a comment made in 1956 on the times described in that book, he said: "Now I think that it may well be that humanity, throughout long, calm spans of time, always cherishes vast resources of high moral expectations obscured by a deceptive, superficial, everyday passivity, replete with tricks of conscience and acquiescence to falsehood; it nurtures a vision of another life, more vital and pure, unaware and unsuspecting of its own hidden designs."

A NOTE ON THE ENGLISH EDITION

This correspondence was first published, in Russian, under the title *Boris Pasternak: Perepiska s Ol'goi Freidenberg*, edited, with a commentary, by Elliott Mossman (New York: Harcourt Brace Jovanovich, 1981). The Russian edition contains the complete extant correspondence. This English edition omits some few passages from the early letters that are obscure in translation or incidental to the relationship between the principal authors. (Such omissions are indicated by three periods set within brackets.) It also includes substantially more explanatory information for the benefit of the reader not thoroughly familiar with the life and times of Boris Pasternak and Olga Freidenberg.*

Russian names are often bewildering to the foreign reader. Not only do they contain a patronymic—thus, Boris Leonidovich (son of Leonid) Pasternak—but also they are rich in diminutives, usually terms of endearment. Thus, Olga Mikhailovna (daughter of Mikhail) Freidenberg is at various times Olya, Olyusha, Olyushka, and Olechka. In this translation we have retained the diminutives for the principal authors, Borya and Olya; for Aunt Asya and Uncle Misha, Olga's parents; for Olga's wayward brother Sasha; and for Boris Pasternak's two wives, Zhenya (Evgenya) and Zina (Zinaida). Children, like the elder of Boris Pasternak's sons, Zhenya (Evgeny), his second son, Lyonya (Leonid), and his stepson, Stasik (Stanislav), are always referred to in diminutive.

The principals created this correspondence, and Olga's habits saved many of the letters from oblivion and gave them meaning. Still, there are others, in many countries of the world, who valued and preserved the correspondence and the relationship it contains. I gratefully acknowledge the generosity of the Pasternak Literary Trust of Oxford, England, for making these materials available, the irreplaceable contributions of my colleagues Maria Lekic, Arkady Plotnitsky, and Thomas Samuelian, the skill and tact of our manuscript editor, John Radziewicz, the meticulousness of our proofreaders for both the Russian and English editions, Konstantin and Emilia Hramov, the kindness of Marina Liapunov in seeing to many of the technical details encountered in bringing both editions to press, the selfless work of those who typed and retyped the manuscript on

---

* The original Russian of the letters used in the editorial commentary (other than letters to Olga Freidenberg) can be found in the commentary to the Russian edition cited above and in Elliott Mossman and Michel Aucouturier, "Perepiska Borisa Pasternaka" (The Correspondence of Boris Pasternak), *Revue des Etudes Slaves*, LIII/2 (1981), pp. 267–291.

their own time, Diane Flanagan, Ruth Gross, Susan Henick, Elizabeth McPherrin, Kristyne Nicholls, and Patricia Schindler, and the tireless support of my wife, Adele.

To those on other shores I send my thanks for their generosity and fidelity. For what may flaw this correspondence between Boris Pasternak and Olga Freidenberg, I myself retain the responsibility.

ELLIOTT MOSSMAN
Philadelphia, summer 1981

Photographs
1889–1909

Olya Freidenberg's brothers
Sasha and Zhenya.
Odessa, 1889

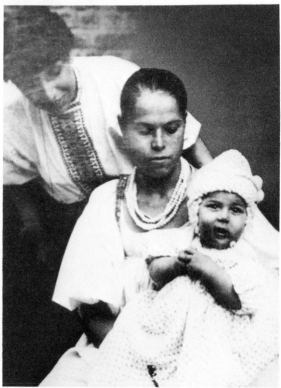

Borya Pasternak
in the arms of his nanny.
At left, Klara Kaufman
(Aunt Klara).
Moscow, 1890

Borya's paternal grandmother,
Rosa Pasternak,
Sasha Freidenberg, and
Borya Pasternak.
Odessa, 1895

Leonid Pasternak
and Osip Kaufman.
Odessa, 1895

Borya Pasternak with his parents. Odessa, 1896

Leonid and Rosa Pasternak.
Odessa, 1896

Berta Kaufman
(Rosa Pasternak's mother),
Rosa Pasternak,
Leonid Pasternak's mother,
and Borya and Alexander Pasternak.
Odessa, 1896

Alexander and Borya Pasternak. Moscow, 1897

Josephine, Borya, Alexander,
and Lydia Pasternak and Olya Freidenberg.
Maloyaroslavets, 1903

Anna Osipovna Freidenberg
(Aunt Asya) and
Leonid and Rosa Pasternak.
Maloyaroslavets, 1903

Sasha and Zhenya Freidenberg, Borya, Olya, Alexander Pasternak,
Aunt Asya, and Rosa Pasternak

Aunt Asya and Olya.
Maloyaroslavets, 1903

Olya Freidenberg.
Maloyaroslavets, 1903

Olya Freidenberg.
St. Petersburg,
September 15, 1903

Sasha Freidenberg.
St. Petersburg, 1903

Alexander Margulius,
Josephine Pasternak,
Mashura Margulius,
Lydia and her mother
Rosa Pasternak,
the nanny,
and Klara Kaufman.
Safontevo, 1905

Aunt Klara, Borya, Alexander Margulius,
Alexander Pasternak, Mashura Margulius,
the nanny, and Lydia and Josephine Pasternak.
Safontevo, 1905

Mashura Margulius. Raiki, 1907

Borya Pasternak with his Gymnasium friends and Josephine and
Rosa Pasternak, the nanny, and Lydia and Leonid Pasternak. Raiki, 1907

Mikhail Fedorovich (Uncle Misha) and Anna Osipovna (Aunt Asya)
Freidenberg. St. Petersburg

Olya and Aunt Asya at the window of their St. Petersburg apartment

Boris Pasternak upon graduating from the Gymnasium. 1908

Olya Freidenberg. St. Petersburg, 1909.
Inscribed on the back: "To the palefaces from the redskin"

CHAPTER I

IN THE SUMMER of 1910 the Pasternak family rented a dacha in the charming Baltic town of Merrekühl (now Mereküla, in the Estonian S.S.R.), near Petersburg. There Boris Pasternak and Olga Freidenberg spent several days together in July. Much of the two cousins' early correspondence revolves around their encounter in Merrekühl, their subsequent trip to Petersburg, and Boris's return, alone, to Moscow.

That same year, Pasternak's artistic talent began to awaken. His letter of July 23, 1910, touches on the theme of "city limits," a theme that derives from walks with Olga in the environs of Merrekühl. Images of city limits —the border between man's creation (the city) and nature's—permeate the early poetry and, much transformed, the later works of Pasternak. The meeting at Merrekühl in Pasternak's interpretation is a lifelong theme in his dialogue with Olga.

Central to an understanding of Pasternak's emerging creativity is his vision of the inanimate, which is linked to the experience of Petersburg he shared with Olga. As he summarized it in his university notebooks: "Personally, I have never found it possible to live other than surrounded by objects; as all do, I live on the basis of the inanimate. And if someone were to suddenly ask me, what do you live by? . . . Oh, I would cite memory. I don't know whether that someone would believe that the past is an inanimate object and that childhood is also inanimate, that it makes demands on you."

The Childhood of Luvers, a tale published in 1922, is an exposition of this vision. Pasternak held substantially the same views in his later years, writing to Stephen Spender in the 1950's, for example: "In my early years I was struck by the observation that existence in and of itself is more independent, uncommon and inexplicable than any striking situation or fact taken individually. The uncommonness of the common caught my attention. While composing music, poetry or prose I always proceeded according to definite outlines or motifs, working out my favorite

1

plots or themes—but the greatest satisfaction came from achieving a feeling of the meaning and sense of reality, when one managed to convey the *very atmosphere of being*, the all-encompassing whole, the all-embracing frame, in which each object you have described is immersed and floats."[*]

It is to claim too much to say that these views, informing the art of the early and the late Pasternak alike, spring solely from his enchantment with Merrekühl, Petersburg, and, foremost, Olga Freidenberg in 1910. Rather, Pasternak's views contributed to that enchantment. For him—and perhaps for Olga, too, in her own way—the enchantment of 1910 is a first love, made more poignant by nature and circumstance.

---

[*] Boris Pasternak, "Three Letters," *Encounter*, August 1960. Pasternak wrote to Spender in English. In the same letter (August 22, 1959) he asked Spender "to translate my gibberish into true English." I have followed that injunction in this quotation.

DIARY

Every winter Uncle Leonid came to Petersburg to hang the pictures for his exhibition, and he always stayed with us. I usually spent my summers with the Pasternaks. Borya used to come and see us; we had been close and good friends for a long time. Intervals between visits were filled with intensive correspondence. All of us wrote one another regularly, except my brother Sasha and Borya's younger brother Alexander, who was too lazy to write. I soon became accustomed to Borya's love and tenderness, his appraisal of me, his appreciation, his exaggerated praise and hyperbolic feeling.

I was twenty when he came to see us in a new key. He was more than attentive—he was infatuated, although our daily pursuits provided no basis for that. In Moscow he lived a full life, studied philosophy at the university, played the piano and composed music, was highly cultivated and had exquisite taste. We all thought he would be a scholar. In everyday matters he was "not of this world"; he would perch himself on hitching posts, was absent-minded and introspective. His Pasternak nature told in the virginal purity he preserved until relatively late in life. Probably his most distinguishing feature was his rare nobility of spirit.

I took him to the Strelka,* where we fell under the poetic spell of the lonely islands. We walked and rode to various places, and he found them all enchanting, following at my side as if tied to me. I took him with me as a brother; he went with me as a lover. In a distant part of town the Lifshitses had a lingerie shop. We put Borya behind the counter and he sold underpants and brassieres—advising, recommending, swearing to the quality, touting for trade at the door. Youth, laughter, the giggles and consternation of the customers! At last Borya went home. In March of that year I went to see the Pasternaks in Moscow. He saw me to the train when I left and sent me the following two cards directly from the station.

Moscow [March 1, 1910]

1. You understand, of course, that I am writing this from a quarantine ward, to which I was taken in a terrible fit of goiter. I writhed on the station platform, murmuring your dear name between convulsions. Then

* A popular promenade along the banks of the Neva River.

I feverishly climbed onto the platform. A gendarme climbed after me and told me it was twelve o'clock. I looked at my watch. Onlookers wept. Kind ladies put balsam on my wounds. The conductor wanted to adopt me.

2. Sheer madness! Fancy one in my financial state wasting eight kopecks on postcards! But to be serious, I really am feeling mournful. So I send you my greetings. Happy journey, and may you arrive safe and sound. There's an old lady standing at my elbow, ready to do me in: I'm using her pencil. Well, what's a platform ticket good for if you can't even borrow a pencil on the platform? Perhaps you think, Olya darling, that all this nonsense is being written after supper in a nice quiet room at 21 Myasnitskaya Street. *Quelle idée!* This card is a masked messenger sent in pursuit of you directly from the station.

St. Petersburg, March 2, 1910

Borya, I had no doubt but that you would be sent to the hospital from the station. You were devouring women students with your eyes so greedily your stomach would have to register a protest.

You can't imagine anything more sickening than my trip. The car was smelly, terribly cold, dark, and gloomy. Only after I threatened to lie down on the rails or swallow a bottle of poison did they yield me one one-hundredth of a seat. The train was packed to the doors. People were sleeping even on the baggage racks (honest to goodness!) and to find yourself on the top bunk was like having a seat in the family circle. A party, with food, wine, and students, was being held in the car where Princess Tarakanova and her suite were traveling. They sang and drank and strummed on the balalaika. One item on the agenda was "a few words" from Princess Tarakanova, which turned into a long and heated speech about goodness knows what. Then the students moved into our car, bringing an animation that had nothing in common with good behavior. One young martyr to science sang hoarsely and at length about black eyes and blue eyes, and this color discrimination incensed me to such an extent that I lustily demanded a song to bottle-green eyes. The voice of prudence kept me from drinking or even fraternizing with the students. In contrast to theirs, my mood was lyrical; I squeezed into a corner with a young girl and recited poetry to her. She was so touched that she addressed me with a line from *The Seagull*, "Come and take my life!" [. . .] and was thrown into a state of despair by learning that my life belonged to me alone and never under any circumstances could belong to another. There's poetry for you!

In the night something you would have enjoyed occurred. A girl who had thus far maintained a studied silence suddenly began to speak. And about what? The battle of Sinope,* no less! I can imagine what you would have done in my place. You would have responded with a tirade on the advantage of wooden furniture over upholstered furniture. She would have retorted with quotations from Andrei Bely or Sasha Cherny.† Wouldn't *that* have been fun?

Or take this. A Fräulein from the suite of Princess Tarakanova, who happens to be a Social Democrat, kept asking for a copy of *The Russian Banner*. No one could supply her with it, and in the middle of the night I heard her murmuring from the top bunk, on which she was sleeping, "My kingdom for *The Russian Banner!*" Very comical.

Today the torture began. I had to tell everyone my impressions. I tried to make wild sounds or just moo, but no one believes I am out of my mind, even when I tell them I spent five days with you. There are some left who believe—and I am not just making this up!—that . . . what do you think? . . . that you are sane! When they ask me how I enjoyed the Tretyakov Gallery, I cut them off shortly with, "I went there with Borya."

Ah, life is so capricious! Here I am again in my room in Petersburg. It is dreadful when dreams come true. Not without reason did Nadson‡ say, "Only the morning of love is beautiful." Neither the satisfaction of desires nor the desires themselves give pleasure, but only the anticipation of their satisfaction. Is there not charm in such a generalization? Take Maupassant, for instance. Desires are always realized in his works, yet there is no sadder, more pessimistic, more hopeless writer. I haven't yet had time to discuss Maupassant with you. If the word "love" were not so conventional and shorn of meaning I would have said I love him, love him desperately. But that's just an aside.

Just think, tomorrow I will go to my courses, where Sipovsky will say, "Thus you see the essence of this drama, gentlemen," and Professor Pogodin will go on for two hours about the necessity of replacing old words with new ones.

Borya, you must come for a visit by all means. I want to tell you not to go in for philosophy, i.e., you mustn't make it your final choice. You would be making a foolish mistake, for life.

---

* Battle fought on November 18, 1853, during the Crimean War (1853–1856), in which the Russian navy defeated the Turkish navy.

† Andrei "the White" (pseudonym of Boris Nikolayevich Bugayev; 1880–1934): prominent symbolist poet. Sasha "the Black" (pseudonym of Alexander Mikhailovich Glikberg; 1880–1932): popular satirist of the period.

‡ Semyon Yakovlevich Nadson (1862–1887): Russian poet.

6

At present I am too tired to write. So many impressions! I must shut them all up inside me and throw away the key. It is disgusting to be so impressionable; better to view life not as theater but as cinema—watch it and then go about your business.

I told my jovial girlfriend about you. The room rang with her laughter.

I haven't opened your book yet—my hands shake, my face blanches. But have no fear, I will read it. Beginning with today I am taking bromides.

Mother looked glum when I gave her your "presents."

I'm going to bed. Good night!

OLGA

I have been to my courses. I gave the girls an imitation of Princess Tarakanova. They shrieked with laughter. [. . .]

DIARY

The Pasternaks spent the summer in the picturesque town of Merrekühl, on the shores of the Baltic Sea.

Merrekühl [July 7, 1910]

Dear Olya,

I cannot write. There are tons of reasons, too many to count, and all so weighty. Three letters, one after another, have been torn up. The purpose of each was to raise to the nth degree the already verbose arguments in favor of your coming here.

For God's sake come, Olya, and as soon as possible. No doubt you are angry with me for not writing all winter, and in general you are averse to accepting such simple truths as the necessity of your presence here. So what am I to do?

A word about my silence this winter. At that time, too, I tore up my letters, long ones—about Maupassant, and *Niels*,* and you. And there were three of them, too (three is my maximum number). But it doesn't matter. Only don't think I was silent. And don't be angry if you can help it. I want to see you so badly it hurts. I'll only be here two weeks, and already three or four days have passed. Not much time left. Can you guess what I'm dreaming of? Long, interesting walks together, you and I; walks that we couldn't take anywhere else. I make myself cross my fin-

---

* Boris had lent Olga the novel *Niels Lyhne* (1880) by the Danish novelist Jens Peter Jacobsen (1847–1885).

gers, but believe me, Olya, it could be heavenly. Hurry, hurry! Leave tomorrow! Mama has such faith in the effectiveness of my entreaties that she has asked me to entreat for her as well. As I tell the beads on her rosary I suddenly recall that you are to bring your own pillow and blanket, and also a pound of mushrooms—white, dried ones, *without* stems—white ones, mind, and highest quality. Be nice if they were without worms. What rejoicing there will be in the kitchen!

Olga darling, surely you understand that even if you harbor antagonisms toward me or anyone else here, you cannot but profit from a trip to this marvelous place with its fabulous living conditions. As soon as the seed of our entreaties sprouts within you in the form of conviction, go and register their germination at the telegraph office. I beg you to wire your arrival date and the number of your train; I will meet you at the station. If you are firmly opposed* to a meeting, sign the telegram "Olga" instead of "Olya." "Olya" will be my password for entering the station. "Olya" will be a thunderous password for many things. Oh, come as fast as possible, Olya dear. The station is Korf. It will be so splendid! I can't believe it possible.

Don't make long preparations. For God's sake, come tomorrow! Then I will interrogate you as to why you are suspicious of philosophy. I have many questions to ask you. Hug Aunt Asya for me. I intend answering her in a day or two, but I do feel a bit sore. After all, her accusation is unjust. *Et tu*, Brother! You are part of the conspiracy and still can smile?

Of course I know this is not notepaper. What do you take me for? I'm not blind. But neither is it what you suspect it of being. It may not have been made for literature, but it certainly was not made for music. It's just wrapping paper issued for the one-hundredth anniversary of the Magnitsky Department Store. The explanation is that my father's snoring in the study has cut me off from access to that nice paper with the Mercury watermark.

Well then, once more, for the last time, and with particular emphasis: Come, Olya dear. I implore you to come.

St. Petersburg, July 12, 1910

Borya, my "acute crisis" has passed and again I want to see you all, talk to you, visit with you. True, I feel rather ashamed when I recall my postcard†—so undeserved after your nice letter.

Of course I could have made up an excuse or hidden the real reason,

---

* Here an arrow points back to the word "antagonisms."
† Evidently Olga had written a rather caustic card that has been lost.

but I am always shocked by untruths, especially in regard to you. I was sure you would not take offense but would apply entirely different standards to me. Consider: of what value is your philosophy and your ego, with all its whims, impulses, etc., if you cannot bear to be told the simple truth, however trifling?

Mama was extremely upset by the form of my refusal: "How could you?!" and so on and so forth. I, however, had not forgotten it was you I was writing to, and you knew it was me who was writing.

Besides, I felt awful and had no inclination to visit any place at all, however "marvelous." I don't like to discuss my feelings and so limited myself to a few words. By the way, a letter addressed to you is lying on my desk this minute, but it is on an entirely different subject. The fate of our letters is an odd one: we write but don't send them off. And that is understandable. One wants to talk, but a real talk is not a dead branch. A thought grows, words are born, a familiar association is found, and one first leaps ahead, then comes back; from between the lines something rises and hovers above the paper. Then one recalls that we love each other on credit and guess more than we know. And so we launch upon new explanations and digressions, or just plunge ahead. This engenders new thoughts; we strain our powers to the utmost, and as a result are only pained by the chaos and the awareness of our helplessness. The letter goes into the wastebasket. In its place we send off a few words, the necessary, the required ones, but far from what we wanted. And how disappointing for the recipient, if he is unaware of the cause of these terse phrases! The fact is that our correspondence is so woeful because we hardly know each other. We wear ourselves out trying to crowd everything into the confines of a letter, a thing that is physically impossible. It is only to you that I find it hard to write. Do I really know you? Do you really know me?

Let me say again that I understand your silence this winter, as I would at any season. And I want to believe that you understand some of my eccentricities, at least those manifest in my last postcard. If we meet and I tell you why I could not and did not want to come, you will understand and forgive. There is so much in life that does not lend itself to definition, analysis, even translation into human language. This has been true of much, very much, of my life in recent years. That is why I am "serenely silent," as you said in your recent card to Mother. Here I am distracted by my thoughts again and beginning to run on. . . . But no, *this* letter must be sent off.

Mama says, "Now Borya will not come to see us, and all because of you!" I can't believe anything so absurd, Borya. Dear God, how sad everything is. But again I'm off on a tangent. Surely you couldn't subscribe to this vulgarity of vulgarities, could you? Surely you will come or not, according to your wish and nothing else. If it was hard for me then, why should I make things worse for myself? Besides, I am going abroad; we will see each other sometime, won't we?

Now I want to come and see you. God knows I've got a strong will; I've taken myself in hand, and now I am myself again. Well, when am I to bring you those white mushrooms? I am willing to do anything if only you are not angry with me for my impudence.

Write me something, anything at all. Who knows? You still may bear me a grudge.

Dear Borya, for the sake of being forgiven I am willing to become the very embodiment of the poetic feeling. . . .

OLGA

DIARY

I made the end of the sheet the natural boundary of my letter.

I went to Merrekühl for a few days. Borya met me when I arrived and accompanied me back to Petersburg, leaving then for Moscow.

My visit to Merrekühl put an end to the relationship that had existed between Borya and me. He was restrained, serious, faultlessly correct in his conduct toward me. We were alone together a great deal, took walks together as he had said he wanted to do. But he behaved without his usual affection and gaiety. We walked apart, and if we accidentally touched he sharply recoiled. He wanted to spend the evenings indoors, whereas I longed to go out under the starry skies, to get away from the family, to feel the poetry of the night. Aunt Rosa watched us with concern. Once when Borya reluctantly stayed out on the porch at my request, nothing poetic occurred. He sat at a distance and waxed philosophical, trying to speak more loudly and dryly than usual, while I felt bored and disappointed. The next day, while on a walk to the outskirts of town, I asked him to tell me a fairy tale, but he did not.

Yet we were drawn to each other by our romantic natures. Usually he would talk for hours while I walked on in silence. I must confess to understanding little of what he said. I was immeasurably less learned than Borya and his vocabulary was unintelligible to me. But the vistas opened up by his new, profound, meaningful words attracted and excited me. A new world rose up before me, unintelligible and alluring, and I felt no need to know the exact weight and meaning of every phrase. I could love the unintelligible; all that was new, sweeping, and rhythmically and spiritually congenial lifted me out of the everyday world and carried me away.

The time soon came when I longed to go home, yet I felt I could not part with him. Though I had been silent most of the time, something had been taking place within me, something inexplicable but deeply significant. Borya did all the talking as usual.

Our trip back brought us still closer. Everything seemed to take on special meaning for us: the people we met, the names of the stations (Vruda, Tikopis, Pudost). Borya's face was full of beauty and inspiration; no other mortal ever resembled him in body or soul. For me he was always perfection itself.

We could not bear to be parted for a moment in Petersburg. When he left for Moscow it was with the understanding that I would go to him there and then he would bring me back to Petersburg. When he was gone I was in a state of distraction. I waited for news of him in a frenzy, bereft of feeling and reason, sat in one spot and waited. And he? He had scarcely arrived when he sat down and wrote me a long letter.

Moscow [July 23, 1910]

Do you still remember that noonday with the screaming dog, when the Engels got lost? Evening crept up on us more swiftly than we ourselves moved; for some reason we were feeling languid. I hope you remember that we turned off that tree-lined street to the left, and it so happened that I was to tell you a fairy tale—that was when the dust had settled and the Engels were gone. If you asked me for it only in fun, it makes no difference; even in fun you were right. I sank deeper and deeper into your debt—a *fairy-tale* debt. At the time I wanted to tell you a tale about the city limits, about the outskirts where I found myself at that very moment, where the street, such a simple macadam street, so used to itself, to being cramped by its crust—where this street, I say, simple and ordinary in the center of town, suffers the shock of having to take leave of the great highways at the town's end, where it waves clouds of dust to the horizon at the far end of a long green leash and, still echoing the town, changes its nature, becoming sentimental in a one-storied, wooden-framed way meant to express extreme tenderness. It is as easy to mistake this for provincialism as it is to mistake tenderness for simplicity or naïveté, but the aristocratic essence of such outskirts lies in the fact that here the din of the town's wrangling streets and squares (music provided by the town's thousandfold, millionfold life) is hushed by satiety, that here silence takes the place of inarticulateness.

But this is of no importance. I have wandered off the path and thank the Lord for it; you will see as I go on how incredibly hard it is for me not to wander. So now I will discourse upon the outskirts of the soul, where streets come together, converging at a boundary line marking the beginning of spiritual spaces unpaved with words, where these streets themselves become something ultimate, staring with their billboards into vacant lots littered with tin cans, descending with their billboards into hillside kitchen gardens to reach the open sky beyond, to reach John the Baptist; I will discourse upon outskirts where all the bickering, wrangling din of great places is enveloped in the tenderness that comes from sharing this same, single outpost. Someday I will surely show you these outskirts, show you what has been, and what is yet to be. I could have told you the tale of the two tops that began to spin and sing the moment they were set loose on the outskirts. But I did not wish to speak and was feeling a bit piqued: I knew that you, so close beside me, so sensitive that one could drown in your sensitivity, were experiencing with me the advent of our surroundings, something that provokes more agitation than beauty does, and that welling up within you was a sense of devotion, almost of dedication, to the advancing footsteps—that you were feeling what we term so briefly "poetry." It was one of those moments when a person feels that he himself is advancing like the footsteps, and he wishes to fall into the rhythm of that approaching fate, which is tranquil and in no way tragic (almost evoking the joy of feeling one's identity with something beyond him). One wishes to pay one's debt for great advents in nature and in oneself. Ours was the same debt, yours and mine, the same debt of joyful devotion—but I was the one who had to pay it while you merely walked beside me and listened, and that was unfair for the following reason: you can never understand how you yourself, expanding, entered into me as a distant, distant debt. There is a name for it; it is a kind of state. You must realize that you were more free than I was; you belonged only to your own world, while I belonged to you, to you as to a soundless event that made demands in monosyllables or just by its presence; you as a presence did not speak and made no demands. And now, today, I want you to know that it was you who told me that fairy tale. It began in the train; it is a tale of rapture, a tale of a four-hundred-mile night spent at the window, with so many places leaping past in the lamplight, with "no-you" felt as a pain now acute, now dull, now piercing, now hypnotizing; it is a tale in which you cannot appear even as an event, in which I can only brood over your absence—considering, reconsidering . . .

And now here am I in this broken, hollow city!

What can I say to you, beloved Olya? Do you suppose this letter that I am sending is the only one I have written you? And why is it any better than the others, in which I told you that at every stop of the train I ran back to the last car, the sleeping car, which stood there as in your dream —remember you said you would dream about it tonight? And can you believe that this car did not reach the station platform at a single stop? At every stop I had to walk the length of the platform and climb down and walk beside the sleeping car along an unpaved path. There stood the water barrels you thought looked so heroic, and there crouched a clump of oil-blackened grass that resembled a coat of arms against the sand. Along the whole length of this last car the earth was rough and broken, extremely unstationlike. And indeed this car was something apart, something from your dream—was, in fact, your dream. In five-minute train stops passengers never walk back to where the last car stands and the watertower rises, where, without a platform, the distance between the ties and the car door is greater than a man's height. And so that is why I, too, was not part of the reality of that night's journey.

And was there not something eerie about the summer lightning? It hovered for some time amid the clouds, then buried itself in them, then fluttered mothlike among them, or polished them along their whole length as if polishing a glazed porch whose panes had sweated into fantastic patterns. Polished them with what? A blue-white flame that shook the guardhouse at railroad crossings with their frayed black threads of gardens and toolchests and guards crossing tracks, but failed to reach the needles of tracks through whose eyes these threads should have been strung. But enough of these rude storm clouds shaking fields and stations. Was there not something just as eerie about the station bells, which, like a band of redheaded hermits suddenly taking over, sent people running out of the waiting rooms hatless, with turned-up coat collars, in crazy postures, while quadrangles of light broke up the crowd into sections, and every quadrangle sent shadows scuttling under wheels and buffers? Ah, that insufferable night swept everything aside, swept everything away.

I wrote you a letter on the train; I threw it in the river at or near Chudovo. Then my condition became so desperate that at one station I went for alcohol to stupefy myself. But even a substantial dose changed nothing, had no effect. I stood at the window, going back to my seat only in the morning, on the outskirts of Moscow. And Moscow? It didn't help me in the least, didn't soothe me; on the contrary, it repelled me just because here the separation from Petersburg reached its apogee (this is a trite falsification). And all these places were made particularly hateful and alien because they knew nothing about you and bore no relation to you (this alone is the honest truth). I had no need to unpack the basket and was not at all upset to discover I had left my key behind. The door was opened to me; I went in and was met by the smell associated with former arrivals and with the music of first encounters with the city in autumn; this familiar smell brought back the past, as on the rollers of what you call the "here and now," and I wished to strain my ears toward this music and record it in lyrical symbols. That is what I am doing now. It turns out a sort of legend. I am astounded by the extraordinary number of intersections and back alleys to be found in my musical improvisations, in the nocturnal city, in the unfamiliar images hovering above your horse-drawn cab.

The driver sorrowfully opens up the crowds at street corners as if they were live padlocks, and shuts and opens the façades of buildings as if moving the thick doors of fireproof safes—fireproof, since the lights and lamps lick out at them with tongues of flame as we go bouncing along from beer hall to beer hall. The driver closes behind him the walls and squares as he floats from one railroad station to the other at the far end of town. And I, only half-conscious, absorbed in my improvisations, direct the music to that same end; and all of this improvisation is like a lyrical transfer to Petersburg, to Izmailovsky Prospect. In a word, I am in search of something connected with you.

I reread the letter you sent me in Merrekühl. In it you mention another letter that is still lying on your desk, one that sings a different tune. It was painful—not just painful but so unbearable that I fled the house—to think that I could have asked you for it in Petersburg and did not do so! Fedya* was not in town; otherwise I would have given him cause for much speculation because of my one-sided story about the summer and you. My misery grew and grew. I went to Sergei's† at the edge of town. He was sitting at his window. Suddenly I had the feeling that everything and everybody in Moscow was dead. I didn't even go in, I just left. I went to a restaurant, a cinema, a bookstore, my own notebooks, but nowhere did I go in. At that moment I was a child and threw myself down on a couch like a child and cried, as helpless as in my childhood summers in Odessa. Slowly, slowly, the time passed, until at last it was late. I was terrified. What was to come? What was my life to be?

Now it is Friday. Good morning, Olya. How are you after traveling through the most terrible twenty-four hours of my life? You were not

---

* Fedya: Fedor Karlovich Pasternak, Boris's second cousin. In 1924 he married Josephine Pasternak, Boris's sister.

† Sergei Nikolayevich Durylin (1877–1954): a poet and, at the time, a close friend of Boris's, who wrote under the name Sergei Rayevsky. He later became a well-known historian of the theater.

absent a single moment. I suppose you want to know now what it is all about. This is what I have to say.

I was telling you about the childhood of our inner world, a childhood that unites us. Perhaps I wasn't telling you, perhaps I was listening to your own recollections. Gradually this experience of the spiritual world, which characterizes childhood and culminates at age fifteen or sixteen, embraces the external world, which until then we merely observed, seizing upon that which was characteristic, imitating it and giving expression to it or not, according to our gifts. Now, at this new stage, the town, nature, and separate lives that pass within our orbit become real and are sharply perceived *for the sole purpose* of fulfilling that function of the soul which enables us to *seem to be part of* these things; they are real just so long as we regard them as given factors of our lives, just so long as they are given to us as part of our lives. If you wanted me to, I could clearly and precisely define reality as but a stage, a phase. But it would require a great deal of elaboration, which is irrelevant here because I only want to clarify for you and for myself this pain I feel for you.

Is it possible that I am dealing with only my surroundings? There are times when objects lose their definiteness, their completeness, cease to be things we have *found the solution for and dismissed*, like a solved problem, things that the common mind and the common life (the life in which Margulius* takes refuge) have solved. Then they, while remaining real to our common sense, become unreal, or rather *not yet* real, because they still have to receive the form of their new reality, analogous to the earlier common-sense form that has found its solution as an object of reality. This new form is inaccessible to man, but he can burst through it to a grasp of its demands (its demands reveal themselves as the poetic sense and are perceived as the idea). Oh, how difficult it is to put this in words, Olya!

Yet, if you remember, it is this that I felt (and you, too, I believe) when we were in Petersburg. As we rode along in the cab, the city seemed to be endless content without a plot, without material attributes— an overflow of the most fantastic content, dark, throbbing, feverish, in frantic search of a plot, a lyrical motif, a lyrical theme it could attach to you and me. If you are prepared to recognize the uniqueness and exceptionality of such a concept of the city and all objective things, and if you keenly feel this uniqueness, then you will understand my saying that the poet, when in such a mood, does not remark that which is characteristic and does not make observations, but merely confirms facts; the verbs and

* Alexander Margulius: railroad engineer married to Klara, Rosa Pasternak's sister. Their daughter Mashura was Olga's cousin and lifelong friend.

nouns of the world you are experiencing, finite nouns and verbs, are transformed into adjectives, into a whirlpool of *qualities*, which must be ascribed to concepts of the very highest order—to things, a reality, inaccessible to us. Not to concepts of the religious experience but rather to concepts of the poetical, of creative joy or sorrow (the two are identical in their pre-eminent sense: the poetical).

As I have already told you, it seems to me that figures of speech serve the purpose of freeing objects from bondage to life or knowledge and turning them into free qualities. Pure art, purged of all other elements, transfers serflike phenomena from one owner to another, frees them from subjugation to the causal connection, destiny, and fate, as these are known to ordinary human experience, and transfers them to another owner; they become fatalistically dependent not on destiny, material objects, and ordinary existence, but on objects nonexistent as such, merely postulated at times when we experience the transformation of the stable into the unstable, of objects and actions into qualities, at times when we experience an entirely different (qualitatively different) relationship to what is perceived, at times when life itself becomes a quality.

To be done with these dull reflections once and for all, let me tell you that just as there are individual moments of creative inspiration, so there are inspired perceptions of the objective world. At such times all those strollers on the Strelka or Izmailovsky Prospect in the evening appear to be forgotten, abandoned, mournful, and consequently legendary qualities abstracted from objective reality. This fantasy without object is doomed, is impermanent, and its causation is rhythm. It comes, is swept away by time, then comes back again, and this over and over. Ordinarily I stood alone behind it all, behind the many people who passed in front of me and on whom I focused my attention (some of them I deeply loved and still love). And two things merged and became one: love, and my feeling for the high romance of qualities. Thus I fell in love with Petersburg and your complicated family, especially your father, and with the fantasy I built up about characters as yet a mystery to me. I spoke of this to you at the time. But you do not know how my tormenting feeling for you grew and grew until it became obvious to me and to others. As you walked beside me with complete detachment, I could not express it to you. It was a rare sort of closeness, as if we two, you and I, were in love with something that was utterly indifferent to both of us, something that remained aloof from us by virtue of its extraordinary inability to adapt to the other side of life.

Well, then, I spoke to you about a kind of activity that takes the place of observation, about experiencing life in a way that turns objects into qualities which eschew objectivity (oh, how boring this is for you, and how difficult for me to give it expression!). But you were feeling much the same thing, were you not? And if so—God, what a sect we made, just the two of us! But now forget it all. I'm afraid I will not soon get used to the idea that I can love all these things and reflect upon them alone. And it makes me quite frantic when I recall that, under the weight of that dedication, of that participation in a life existing beyond the very highest perceptions, dedicated in its own way to the city and to nature, indeed to everything, I am, in such a state, just as feminine, which is to say just as dependent, as you are; and you, in this state, are just as active, aware, and poetically masculine as I am. I cannot be certain that I am right and I should like to hear your opinion. But even if this is all alien to you, do you understand why I am suffering so on your account, and what the nature of this suffering is? Even when a person is in love, he is capable of crossing the road and observing his agitation from a distance, but there is something between you and me that makes it impossible for me to leave you and look back.

Ah me, Olya, what a lot of words I have written! I hoped to use them as artillery defending myself from a misunderstanding that would be very bitter. You might have had quite the wrong impression if I had said nothing but that all the people here in Moscow were as strangers to me, that I trembled on seeing a scrap of Petersburg newspaper on the windowsill, and that I implore you to write to me—anything, even a postcard!!!—and quickly, this very minute, and come to Moscow! Olya, let me know if I ought to write to you *in this way*. And don't be afraid of hurting my feelings. If you are not what I imagine you to be, you must tell me; since I have said so much, it may be easier for you to write. This, it seems, is a declaration. A declaration that I am in love with Merrekühl, our journey, the first evening, Uncle Misha's birthday (when I sought your aid), the Strelka, Petersburg, you as part of it all, the railroad station, everything that immediately concerned *you and me together*—and this last contains the terrible burden of this declaration, the complete declaration.

As you see, I can't write. But I had a lot to tell you and much to ask you; when I began you didn't interrupt, didn't ask any questions, didn't participate in any way. I saw that it could not possibly be of interest to you and quickly put a stop to it. And now I must ask you to forgive me that theoretical proseminarish agitation.

I give your hand a long, long squeeze and kiss you.

BORYA [...]

Moscow [July 26, 1910]

Olya, I know sending a letter like mine requires courage and candor, to say the least. I am happy (you know the story about the Jewish woman who died muttering hurrah to the passing emperor), yes, I am happy that there is no answer from you as yet—perhaps there is still time to warn you. These past few days I have rightfully been torturing myself for the wonderful qualities which I displayed and which euphemisms such as candor and ingenuousness cannot ameliorate. But if I tell you of the true (at least as I see it) cause of such weighty and largely ridiculous verbosity, I will, in the first place, give you an opportunity to ignore my display, to leave unanswered a letter you would probably find difficult to answer; in the second place, I would perhaps later (which is worse than never), and no doubt unconvincingly, try to show you that I do not suffer chronically from candor, rashness, etc., that this letter was an exception, an unforgivable excess, or anything else you like, but certainly not characteristic of me.

Evidently I was too deeply affected by the sudden transition from a mass of diverse impressions, which intermingled with and were strengthened by my unjustified hope that from these impressions, as from a common ground, I could proceed to the expression of my personal reflections and observations, addressed to those with whom I shared that common ground—the sudden transition, I say, from these impressions (after all, you yourself experienced their kaleidoscopic change) to a Moscow that was empty for me, relatively empty, no doubt, empty because at first it represented only the end of a vacation, a holiday whose highest moment was Petersburg, nothing more, represented the end of that paternal atmosphere of Sunday streets when as a schoolboy one went visiting and even the dreary September weather—"today's weather"—was a guardian assuring the success of one's anticipated visit. And suddenly the weekdays were there, the full-fledged schoolday, when everything went against one and no support was to be found in inanimate guardians. That is all. The results of such a transition could not but be felt by even such a balanced and soberly rational nature as mine, exercising as I always do the maximum of self-control. It was the shock of transition that made itself felt in my letter. I hope you will forgive me for it. You gave the correct, the just, the only possible assessment (how could I have hoped for any other?) of the letter when you found it ridiculous or, at best, odd. The one certain and sincere feeling I now have is of self-loathing amounting to physical repulsion. [...]

St. Petersburg [July 25, 1910]

You warned me you wouldn't write from Moscow and I had no grounds to disbelieve you. But I waited for your letter, waited all this time, and only today did certainty take the place of expectation. It wasn't a premonition—I don't believe in that, it always deceives me. But sometimes a kind of enlightenment comes to a person, as if the soul had departed the body, and this can always be depended upon. These are moments of revelation, when everything becomes clear and one sees far, far into the distance. Actually it has nothing to do with me; it is something above and beyond me. I have foretold events to people close to me many a time, and always suddenly, unexpectedly; I know what my fate is to be, what awaits me, and what will never happen to me. It is not premonition but rather a spiritual malady bordering on insanity. Sometimes I fear I will become insane, but then I know that this is not so, that everything will be normal and very natural. These are not empty words; terrible fits of depression are the first symptoms of my illness, groundless depression that completely overpowers me, as if it wished to suck me up, take possession of me, destroy me. I may be going somewhere or leaving somebody when suddenly I am seized by melancholy—but God, what frightful, appalling melancholy! Sense and reason are out of the picture; they operate, and I weigh and understand exactly what is happening, but this is of no help. I have a morbid longing to be home—instantly, this very moment, and I am drawn there as if I knew that some catastrophe had taken place, God only knows what. It is not that I am distressed; there is nothing concrete that I fear and I do not have in mind any particular person or thing. The fact is I am not even concerned with the house, with Mother or Father or Sasha. It is my sick soul that in its groundless depression appeals to my reason, which, having to pick on something, chooses my home, for outside of myself and the world at large, nothing exists for me but home.

Ah, if you only knew what I go through! I enter the house in a terrible state. Everything is as usual, but I see it as if for the first time. Mother! So this is what she's like! . . . I walk through the rooms: everything looks strange, only relatively real, yet the furniture is standing as usual, in the usual places. I remember once noticing the mirror in the drawing room— so that's how it hangs. The chairs are there, frozen in position. Everything, everything—new and strange. Mother is frightened and attempts to calm me. Terrified, trembling, I sit down next to her, and I feel a pain in my heart, which is pounding unnaturally. I am aware of something hardening inside of me, torturing me, threatening me. Depression. Ah, that word, that feeling! The seizure passes slowly, exorcized by affection. There is so much symbolism, so much generalization in this rebellion of the weak human spirit that its meaning cannot be contained in a single word. It is torture. Only the dread of having Mother fear for me (she unconsciously fears for me) makes me summon all my forces to quiet my nerves. Being home does not help in the least. One day I endured a similar seizure when I was far from home and had to return by train. What a trip! Another hour or two and I would really have gone mad.

But why should I have suddenly recalled all this? I began with your letter and my waiting for it. You wrote it at the very time I was expecting it. And I was feeling miserable, of course, because I was here and you were there, walking the streets of Moscow, just as miserable. Do you remember? I wanted to dig myself in somewhere, to hurl myself out of range of myself, to tear loose, to wrench free. I could neither read nor write nor think. You have alcohol (an extreme measure) and I have artificial sleep. But both palliatives only deepen and generalize the misery. You say you wept as when you were a child in Odessa. I have done that, too, but earlier, long ago, before Tonya* came here. Such tears are but tears, they bring no alleviation to the heart's pain and suffering, and the more one weeps like a child, the deeper one plunges into hopelessness.

When you went away and I was alone again, I set out to wander through the streets. I wanted flowers, wanted them passionately. I searched everywhere for them, and when I was too tired to lift an arm or drag a foot, I found them—beautiful, fragrant flowers. I bought as many as I had money for. It was almost ten at night when I got home, all of me in those flowers.

Today your letter came. I opened it, looked at it, held it in my hands, and did not read it. I didn't want to read it with my eyes or hear the words. Only when I had sensed the spirit of it and absorbed all that was spiritual in it, when I had felt through it and thought through it, only then did I read it. Then nothing could startle me: I was prepared to hear anything. Borya, this is your testament, and how very, very much you have bequeathed to me. You ask me, Am I as you imagine me to be? Yes. But I myself would have asked this question without waiting for you to do it. Yes, I am as you imagine me because I dare not say I am not; and no, I am different because I do not wish to give pledges or promises. If I say I am different, I free both you and me, for my saying so bears a note of finality that prevents your approaching me with any sort of standard or demand. It would be too heroic to be as you imagine me. I know life, and be assured I know it well. Do not put your trust in me, I will deceive you; sooner or later, with a single word or even with silence, I will show you

* A childhood friend from Odessa.

that you have been mistaken about me, and this will cause you sorrow, because the desired or the preconceived is never fully realized. Every step one takes is costly; one has to struggle for everything—to suspect everything, scrutinize everything. Allow oneself to be idealized? Oh no, that I shall never do! I am what I am; thank God I am aware of myself and can take my own measure. I have no need to be stretched or shrunken. I fear you bring to me a ready-made mold and hope I will fit into it. That is a great mistake, for, I repeat, I do not match whatever image of me you have created in your mind, and sometime, somewhere, you will see parts of me sticking out of your mold. One thing I can promise you: I will never try to squeeze myself into it and I will never cut myself down to fit it.

But how will you ever get to know me when we live so far apart and see each other only once every few years? Can it be there is only one way—through written conversations? But that is hard for me, Borya. I grew up entirely alone. I needed someone to talk to, was always harassed by problems—after all, I'm only human. But my parents were too busy providing me with daily bread to do anything else; the girls I knew were dull and lived on an entirely different plane. I had no one else. I was too proud to bring my problems to my parents and too alive to accept the ideas of my friends. Everything is trampled upon and reduced to the level of common attitudes; it is, then, only logical that we should

> Jealously hide from friends and relatives
> Our highest hopes and noblest professions
> Under a cloak of disbelief in mocked passions.*

And so I learned never to ask questions; I found out everything for myself. So great was my desire to speak and argue at the time that now I am silent; and so great were my searchings for answers and kindred experiences that now I am withdrawn, finding everything within myself except what is common to all. I am strong, that is true; all, all that is within me is my own, and I have no need to share it. Even when I read, I take the lead and the book follows: I accept what I want and discard what I don't want. There is nothing bookish in me, neither views nor ideas. I have made myself what I am. I am almost incapable of analysis; by nature I lean toward synthesis, and this helps me a lot. In addition, I have endured much suffering of the most real and everyday sort. I am reluctant to speak of it and in fact I never do, but it has been terrible. Where, when, and why—these are mere details; the main thing is that I

* From Mikhail Yurevich Lermontov's (1814–1841) poem "Duma" (Meditation) (1838).

Leonid and Alexander Pasternak. Merrekühl, 1910

Olya Freidenberg. St. Petersburg

Mikhail Fedorovich Freidenberg

The apartment house on the Catherine Canal in 1975

Aunt Asya and Rosa, Leonid, Josephine, and Lydia Pasternak. Merrekühl

Josephine and Lydia Pasternak in clown costumes

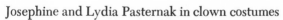

Anna Osipovna Freidenberg and
Leonid Osipovich Pasternak

Leonid and
Alexander Pasternak
preparing an exhibit
in commemoration of
Tolstoy's death.
Moscow, 1911

have suffered acutely. This is fatal in youth and has poisoned my life. By seventeen I was worn out. If I told you everything you would stare in amazement. I am saying this to you now so that you will understand one thing: I have long since forgotten how to talk; words as a means of expressing ideas do not interest me because I find such expression super-fluous. I am hardened and armored in my own silence. Sometimes it seems to me I exist beyond time and space, that I was, am, and always will be—not in the everyday sense but in quite a different one. There is nothing I am afraid of, not even possibilities. I myself am a possibility, and I am not afraid of myself. Besides, I am able to get away from myself when I need to, and that makes me invulnerable. I can live anywhere circumstances demand and become anything I am required to become, but this will be outside of myself; always and everywhere I will remain myself. I cannot, for example, conceive of my meeting catastrophe. In moments of acute suffering I have been able to withdraw and generalize; I have wept and felt pain, but never by so much as an iota have I repudiated my faith and my knowledge. "Nature," "the World," and "I in the midst of them" are not empty sounds or pretty phrases to me. Oh, how I understand and feel them: they in me and I in them! . . .

By all this rambling I have wanted to tell you (1) that if I am silent, it is not an affectation and (2) that you mustn't imagine me to be what I am not. Well, now do you find me "different"?

Oh yes, there is one other thing. You ask whether you can write to me as you did in your letter. Yes. That I can say positively. Don't search for special words for me; use your own words. I know that they are old and feeble (especially when I use them), but it is not the words I am con-cerned with, and therefore don't be afraid to use expressions that sound pompous in everyday usage—that usage has nothing to do with me. I'll understand them differently, very, very differently.

Four o'clock in the morning. Everyone is asleep. Silence. The light coming through the window looks artificial, like stage lighting. The steamboats on the Neva are groaning dully, eerily. My clock doesn't care, it goes on ticking: ticktock, ticktock. Father came home from work and fell asleep. Is he asleep now? Or thinking? If he is thinking, I believe I know what it is about. Father—yes, he is really a father to me. You went up to him, took a long look at him, and instantly were drawn to me. There was something predestined in that, in its being you that glanced into Father's soul, and on this particular trip. Ah, that is a very special province, completely beyond life and words, the province of Father and me, our relationship. Goodness, the night is over; it is morning already. Dawn. How splendid! . . . What do you suppose I shall dream about? And then it will be tomorrow. If only autumn comes quickly, my beloved autumn! I shall go away, I shall save myself from myself. This longing is tearing me to pieces, but I shall not go out of my mind. No indeed, I shall go on living, and there is still much ahead of me, more than I think.

Morning. Forgive me, I hardly know what I am writing, what I am saying. And when I realize you will receive this letter in broad daylight, I know how foolish it is to write at night.

Believe me, I haven't been able to get the picture of those sleeping cars out of my mind for days. How much they mean to me! It was beside such a car that you stood, and it conveyed to me your sufferings.

When you were here, you said, as you stood at the window—remember?—that I was scornful of, or at least indifferent to, things that you held dear. That was a terrrible thing to say and it hurt me. Ah, but what you need are words, questions, remarks! Can't you see that I understand beyond words? Didn't I understand everything at the railroad station?

The letter, your letter. I don't know what to do. I have always been alone, and suddenly you arise before me and begin to speak and want an answer. I should hate to deceive you—such vulgarity would be the last straw. It is important that you get to know me; then you will lose interest in me. I know without your telling me that you are lured by "the enigma of my character." Well, try to guess the enigma; here I am, at your disposal. When you have guessed it you will go away, leaving me to "withdraw and generalize." But all joking aside, I am not afraid; only don't idealize me, please don't do that. [...]

Shall it be "good-by" or "until we meet again"? And will I send this letter or not?

Let us kiss—and I will go to bed.

Things look bad, Borya. . . .

OLGA

Now it is the middle of the day, a bright sunny day. I *will* send the letter and things do *not* look bad.

Oh, damn! I haven't mailed it yet. I will, in just a moment, but I want . . . what? . . . I don't know. Perhaps to keep it with me just a little longer, or perhaps to add something to it . . . but again I don't know what. I only slept three hours last night, but I feel strong and full of energy and in high spirits. How very resilient I am, devil take me! I have always said that about myself. There are earthenware pots that the heat of the fire doesn't affect. I am just such a pot. Sometimes I am sick to death of this endless turbulence going on within me; I long to curb it and settle down, but my spirit is like unto the Wandering Jew.

I could go on writing forever now, and none of it would resemble what I wrote last night. I should love to say something fine, something *yours,* something gentle, something going forth to meet the future. God, what words! How they distort my thoughts and turn them into banalities! You think me strong? I'm very weak. Now I will return to literature and bury myself in it. It was everything to me when I had no one, was all alone. It was in literature that I went through all the experiences of my inner world. Do you understand the romantic poets? I do, too. I love Schiller with a special love, unlike my love for others. There is something so exceptional about him. . . . My love began long, long ago . . . before Odessa, before childhood, before birth even. . . . He is a legend, a spirit, something transcendental. I love him because he is *old*, and I am old, too. . . .

This, then, is what I have said, of all I wanted to say. I am so happy at this moment I scarcely seem to be alive. Here is a kiss for you—and what a kiss!

Moscow [July 28, 1910]

At first I wrote you about how hard (so hard that even my mind and talent rebelled), how hard it was to talk to you after that letter; you cannot possibly imagine how deeply everything you said settled within me. Your words are like vast, calm spaces in which you go about building and constructing. How can I ever forget the measured tread of advancing sorrow as you reconstructed your visit and built *your* testament? Next I wanted to tell you that I am in possession of a special inner ear, of a kind of deep-seated, elementary, ever-agitated attentiveness that has stood by me all my life as I waited for, and as I opened up, hundreds of letters and as many encounters—and what encounters! I opened up the encounters just as I did the letters, and now I know life (you understand, Olya, I am not speaking of what is generally called life, but of my own life); oh, if I should tell you how much of what has been proffered me (things I sometimes wanted, even conjured up) I have opened up, and then yesterday came the one envelope I had been waiting for. Yes, it was your letter I had sought; all others were written in a foreign hand. If this sounds like sheer rhetoric, you must find it vulgar and even base, the syrupy eloquence of a shop assistant. But please try to understand what I am saying and weigh it bit by bit.

What I am saying is that no doubt much that came to me was great, rare, and pure, perhaps even enriching and inspiring. But it *came to me*, whereas here you were calmly and majestically a *companion*; you were *party* to that something from which destiny is ever turning me away. Why in the world did you not stop me when I went on telling you things you knew so well, things that were "yours"? Perhaps then we would have made more headway. But I walked on past those fir trees like a blockhead, telling you about a state in which one lives, as it were, across the street from oneself and looks over to see various things: ah, somebody has turned on the light, somebody wants to write a prelude because that somebody has come home in a certain mood, . . . and then one runs back across the street, dons that somebody's mood and writes the prelude for him. Perhaps this malaise, this paroxysm of rapture, takes place because at such moments the objective "across-the-street" comes to an end and everything is centered in the subject, in that pure concept, that purely spiritual existence which is yours, Olya. But this is unimportant. That you should have had to listen to ideas so familiar to you! Do you understand now how odd it was for me to discover your tolerance? A few days before your arrival I reached out for an envelope which had taken a long time to come and which I highly prized; I wrote much about it.

Then suddenly this happened between you and me. I feel no urge to go to you there, across the street; even if I did, it would be unimportant. The important thing is that you added nothing to what I already have. You did not enrich me as others have done, or perhaps I was prevented from noticing it by that larger thing which, like a mystery, one wishes to follow as one follows music, with a tensing of the vocal muscles, "symbolically participating" in it, by that larger thing which has to be expressed at any cost. Well, then, you did not add one coin to what I already had, but you were the first person to transform that metal into live riches. I was incredibly fatigued by dwelling with you for a week in a realm where I had always dwelt alone. The ability to pass by life and nature without having them touch us, an ability we have in common—*precisely this* (an absolute value) as contrasted with life's banknotes (a relative value) is the ideal and essential condition that brought us together. I want you to understand that if you had contributed a whole heap of gold coins (I see them and am excited by them), it would have been a trifle, would have been as nothing compared to your having made them real, converted them from relative into real wealth. Whether you added a page to the book or not I cannot say; the amazing thing is that out of a leather-bound cube you made a book. As I have already said, I have nothing to offer you of value, of interest, or of meaning, and that is because I was completely overwhelmed by your letter. It was "I" raised to the very highest degree. That "resilience," that "forsaking of life," that "I-myself-am-a-possibility-and-I-am-not-afraid-of-myself," all of it stunned me by its likeness to myself, yet was so much greater than myself. I continuously suffer the pain of wanting to do something dedicated to you, bearing your name. And I wish to carry on, as if I were of your species, a small variety of it, that cannot go forward to meet and merge with you but can only be a continuation, can only elaborate the strain, develop what has gone before as well as what it bears within itself peculiar to the species.

Oh yes, I meant to tell you I had written you page after page full of remorse and endless, exhausting expressions of gratitude. I intended sending it from the railroad station by the midnight express so as to eradicate by morning the impression of that hateful, loathsome letter. Hurriedly, as best I could, I begged you yesterday to try to understand the awful thing. God knows how often, almost constantly, I have had to make a moral curtsy like that disgusting letter, written falsely and with bitterness. I can't bear the thought of being incomprehensible, not out of consideration for my friends or readers—no indeed, for purely egotistical reasons: I am afraid of being thought pretentious or affected, or of trying to be original, etc. And so I told you I live "approximately," coming and going for the sole purpose of living through the ideas that form a perfect skeleton for my feelings, even my most precious feelings, and I tell someone like Sergei my latest "revelation" and watch to see how he takes it; he picks it up enthusiastically but is so commonplace in his inability to grasp the main point that I have but to touch on some subject which is common property to make him go off with the same enthusiasm. So I just put out all the fires: sorry, today is not my birthday, I just fooled you, or perhaps I just imagined I was born a few steps ahead, or I may have read it, or learned it by heart, or maybe I'm sick, dumb, or intentionally made it up—anyway let's change the subject, today's a weekday.

Olya, understand me literally: it is too incredible that our dreams have come true, that we have discovered our unexceptional and insignificant actions to be significant and symbolic, and that while reading meaning into these actions (as early as last winter) we read what another had written into them without adding anything new. You say you understood everything at the railroad station. That means you understood even more: you understood and were convinced that everything could be read in the text of our actions. I only comprehended, only perceived; I grasped everything, everything. I lived in the recognition of its vast significance but could hardly believe it was reality and not a dream. I could not help sending off that "artillery," but once it was sent I realized how absurd it must sound when held in someone else's hands, and those hands yours. And so I made that horrible gesture of denial. Against *your* hands, I sinned against the hands of my dearest sister. Forgive me lest the guilt be passed from one of us to the other. But, O God, how unbelievable that those hands are not a dream! You speak of a false representation. No, no, that is impossible, so absolutely real the whole of you is at this moment! You are exactly as I see you, exactly! It incenses me to think you do not realize the complete incompatibility, the complete incommensurability of you and all that is trite, even outwardly so. I understand your teacher: your letter is like music. I read it in a whisper, its cadence rises and falls. [...]

St. Petersburg [probably July 30, 1910]

I am writing you because you are waiting for my letter, and also because at times it is impossible to remain silent. You are right: last wills and testaments are written only once, and it is hard to say farewell to life and become a dweller in the other world. After writing a will it is usual to make preparations for that other world and to put one's mundane affairs in order. Therefore I wish to talk to you about the most worldly matters. Come to Moscow? I would do it gladly, but I can't say exactly when at present. Next week I am taking mother to Merrekühl; you can imagine my enthusiasm. I am doing it for the same reason that made you visit your friends—remember? Mother will not stay there long, but I will stay on. Grandmother, by the way, is leaving, and I will stay with the girls— that is, if your mother wants me to. Only the presence of the girls makes it possible for me to be in Merrekühl without dying of longing. If only the place were not so beautiful! Again that fullness of joy and that terrible, terrible longing. When will I come to Moscow? Most certainly before your family moves back to town; otherwise they will keep asking all those whys again and make me feel foolish.

I hope to come in the interval between Merrekühl and your family's return, but that is all speculative. Irrespective of this, I do hope you will come to see us in September. I am purposely remaining here that month so as to enjoy one more Petersburg autumn. September in Petersburg means everything to me. I also want to introduce you to some of my friends. I have wonderful and much-beloved friends; they are so uncommon that it will be a pleasure for you to meet them. [...]

Now about your "loathsome" letter. I thought of answering it in a few words, saying, for instance, that I took it to be the result of one of your "transitions"—from what to what doesn't matter. But then I recalled that you must have received my long letter by this time, in which you would find the answer. My mentioning it now is only because I didn't want to pass over it in silence but to speak about it and thereby take the burden of it off your shoulders.

I received another letter at the same time as yours, in which I read: "You've no idea how I enjoy your letters; they're so pithy, so gay, so full of life!" I found it very funny to compare these words about me with yours. When such things are said of me without any ulterior motive it makes me very happy, happy in a special way. It is not that they bring me genuine satisfaction, or that they tickle my vanity—not at all!—but that they take me back to the time when I was at my best, when I deeply believed in myself and my ability to write, when I could take delight in what I wrote. Now that time seems so far away that I often ask myself if I really did have talent, and if I did, how could I have killed it? I killed it, of course, deliberately, but how could it have allowed me to do so? You cannot imagine how dear to me were those simple words, restoring, at least in memory, at least in imagination, the something I once possessed. They were dear by virtue of bringing joy mixed with sorrow. Oh yes, there was a time when I could write—no doubt of it. When I was at my best, when I experienced something so akin to inspiration that I was in love with pen, ink, and paper, to say nothing of the words themselves, at that time of self-abnegation and, simultaneously, of vibrant belief in my creative powers, at that time I *had* to write. How many memories were evoked! . . . And how they all poured forth onto paper. When writing a simple class composition about the life of Lomonosov or Pososhkov,* so much surged up within me that I trembled all over and didn't know how to control myself. When I wrote—in school—about Vladimir's *Testament*,† the teacher held the composition in his hands, turned the pages and said he didn't know what mark to give it; he looked at me in astonishment and said: "You . . . you . . . I don't know, but this is amazing. You must drop everything else and devote yourself wholly to this. . . . I must work with you quite separately." He kept looking from me to the pages in wonder and despair. [. . .]

Ah, if you only knew how bitter it is to have one's creative powers supplanted by tranquillity! No doubt you do know. Hasn't this been your experience with music? At times I long to say to you, Are you sure you haven't made a mistake? Isn't it your first of kin you have forsaken? If so,

---

* Mikhail Vasilevich Lomonosov (1711–1765): self-made Russian scientist, scholar, and poet of the eighteenth century. Ivan Tikhonovich Pososhkov (1652–1726): author of *Books About Poverty and Wealth* and supporter of Peter the Great's reforms.

† Vladimir Monomach: Grand Prince of Kiev from 1113 to 1125. His *Testament*, recounting his military exploits, is an important work of Old Russian literature.

you will be avenged. Never again will you find anything else to satisfy you, and it will be too late—you can't go back.

Goodness me, how I have rambled on! It is autumn outside, cold and rainy. Soon the leaves will turn and fall from the trees. A time for re-membrances—not of events but of emotions; another autumn, another mellowing. "Nature is resplendent; man is shabby."

"The rest is silence."

OLGA

Mother says she wrote to you and mentioned me; I caution you to take Mother's words with a grain of salt. Mother tends to idealize in one direction or another. [. . .]

DIARY

I ought to have gone to Moscow. But I kept putting it off. Then it turned out that I didn't want to go. Everything that took place between Borya and me in July amounted to a great passion engendered by the meeting and intimacy of two people related in blood and spirit. In my case it was a passion of the fancy, not of the heart. Borya was never anything but a brother to me, no matter how warmly and tenderly I loved him. Yes, a brother. Here lay the boundary line. I could never have fallen in love with him. When he fell in love with me, I found him difficult, unpleasant, even repulsive, hard as it is to say so. This was, of course, unconscious, even contrary to my will. It dwelt deep down within me, in the darkness of feelings, in the blood. I was never anything but his passionately devoted, adoring sister.

The fact is that he once warned me against falling prey to a "mis-understanding." I never did.

I felt stifled by his letters and protestations. True, I was in a sort of trance at first, and might have gone on in this lyrical mood had not a round-trip ticket to Moscow brought me back to earth. It cooled my passion. I began to think of practical matters: a dusty apartment, Borya and I alone in six or seven rooms. He would give me tea from a dirty teapot. How would I bathe? What would Aunt Rosa say when she found out? And so forth.

That so many questions should have arisen speaks for the hopelessness of the situation. Of my own choice I had, at times, spent the night and even washed in hovels. Of my own choice I had drunk kvass from a dirty glass in a bar and picked cockroaches out with my fingers. When I have a longing for comfort, it means my heart is empty.

Besides, I never liked long-drawn-out affairs. Passions seek their culmination just as plots do. I wanted an end. I was young and even eternity seemed attractive to me—on condition that it didn't last long.

So I told myself. But it was more simple: I didn't love him. And so, to avoid explanations, I asked him to *tell Tonya* that I wouldn't be coming to Moscow (heaven only knows how I could have been so brutal, so awful). And I wrote it on a postcard showing a view of Merrekühl!

St. Petersburg [August 13, 1910]

Borya,

On the 15th Tonya will be in Moscow. If you meet her, tell her I can't come to Moscow and ask for her Odessa address (she wrote the nicest letter from Elizavetino, but I won't have time to answer before she leaves). Mama went to Merrekühl without me and came back yesterday. Look at these stones. "Mean anything to you, brother?"

Your parents will arrive in Moscow on the 19th, after spending the 18th with us.

OLGA

Moscow [August 14, 1910]

Seriously? Well, I will tell Tonya. Grandmother told me about an anticipated letter from you. How good that you put an end to my expectations with your kind card. Yes, that is truly Merrekühl. I had expected my parents on the 15th. Your note gave me an unpleasant surprise: five more days of solitude. Nothing came of my lessons—terms unacceptable—so I cannot come to Petersburg.* Besides, I've got a toothache. Oh, how it hurts!

BORIS

St. Petersburg [August 16, 1910]

[. . .] I don't believe what you say about the fiasco of your lessons, and the thought that you lied to me offends me more than your failure to come. Today your father sent Mother the letter you wrote her, and I was less struck by your promise to be in St. Petersburg than by the sharp difference in tone between this letter and your postcard to me. Evidently you are again "in transition," and I know exactly from what to what.

---

* Boris had written Olga that he had agreed to teach Latin to a young lady from Irkutsk, to finance a trip to Petersburg.

You had better repent and answer my question about the truth of your words. Say frankly, "Yes, I lied."

OLGA

When a tooth aches, pull it out. [...]

[In a letter to Aunt Asya, written from Moscow probably in August 1910, Boris speaks about his studies. The letter was meant for Olga's eyes.]

The university begins soon. I am going to register for advanced mathematics. I have exams hanging over my head at present. The basic course is logic—terribly exciting. The professor has known me since spring. I will take his seminar on experimental psychology, although he warned me I may be disenchanted since I think too much in abstractions (that was after the philosophy exam). I am telling you this out of vanity.

[He also mentions his teeth:]

As for my teeth—pull them out when they are perfectly sound? It was my wisdom teeth that ached. Just a nervous ache.

Are you catching the signals I am passing through clenched teeth, Olya?

[To which Olga answers, probably also in August 1910:]

How are your teeth? From your letter I had guessed it was wisdom that was ailing—the wisdom of your teeth, of course. I proposed that you pull them out because that is what all healing amounts to, and the sounder the tooth the greater the pain, because the pain of regret and of love for the tooth is added to the physical pain. Yet isn't it better to have it out? You will agree that teeth have a rare and invaluable property: when they ache you can pull them out.

Pure logic, experimental psychology, advanced mathematics—how good it all sounds, and how good that you are in the midst of it all. Even the university itself, the professors, the exams—even they are excellent. Meanwhile I am here completely alone in my room, doing absolutely nothing and unable to read anything but Maupassant—not a thing.

[The last letter of the period from Boris to Olga, written in 1911 after several other attempts that remained unsent, brings this first stage of their relationship to an ambiguous conclusion.]

Moscow [September 20, 1911]

I cannot force myself. To write to you means to make a difficult and unnatural gesture. There would be something artificial about it—a lie, in your opinion—and that would cause me pain. It would not be a letter to you but a manufactured product. But why did my faith exceed yours, and why did you write all that? *You!*

Because *I* needed it. For such a long time and so intensely have I loved your lines written so evenly, with such restraint, almost in a whisper, those profound pages, and the hand that hovered over them. Is it possible that all this will be together here, all three of us, you and I and Moscow, now as it was then? And you dare question it!

Forgive my verbosity. I want to finish my exams before you come. I hope you won't feel offended if I have to go on with my philosophy and seminars.

Oh, how I love peace and quiet and restraint these days! They are so foreign as to require translation, like one of the modern languages.

CHAPTER II

OLGA'S REJECTION left a deep impression on Boris Pasternak. He undertook "a basic self-re-education in order to approach the classical world of Olya and her father," he told his friend Alexander Shtikh. Philosophy was to be the vehicle of that transformation during the next two years, a transformation he characterized as "a retreat from romanticism and boundless creative fantasy, toward objectivization and stern discipline." The transformation culminated in a summer at Marburg University, subsidized by his mother.

Frugality marked his foreign stay. He chose the least expensive room, board, and train fare, reserving his limited funds for fees and books. At first he gave a paper on Leibniz for Paul Natorp, simultaneously auditing the Tuesday and Friday seminars of the leading Neo-Kantian, Hermann Cohen. Then Cohen invited him to give two papers, one on Kant. "Cohen was quite surprised and invited me to his home. I was very pleased. You can imagine," he wrote Shtikh, "how nervous I was in front of all those doctors from the seminar, from all corners of the earth, and their wives."

Olga, too, was abroad during the summer of 1912. She visited the Pasternaks in Berlin, while they were en route to friends in Kissingen (Boris joined them briefly on July 1). She saw Boris in Frankfurt and spent the last few weeks of summer together with the whole family, including Boris, in northern Italy. The two of them made side trips to Milan, Venice, Florence, and Pisa.

DIARY

A year after Merrekühl something happened that greatly changed my life. I contracted pleurisy, which quickly developed into tuberculosis, and our doctor promptly insisted that I be taken abroad to the mountains of the Black Forest. Mama, frightened to death by my illness, left the family and took me to Germany. I was so weak that I made the trip with difficulty. Herr Hofrat, head doctor at the Black Forest sanatorium, after unsuccessful attempts at a cure, sent me off to Switzerland—the French part, of course, since I did not want to go to the German part. So Mama and I ended up in Glion, above Montreux, in the mountains surrounding the Lake of Geneva. We took rooms in a hotel, free to do whatever we liked. The Castle of Chillon was reflected down below in the blue (really turquoise) lake. I quickly regained my strength and, slowly, my health. Three months later scar tissue had formed in my lungs and the tuberculosis was arrested.

A few winters later I went to Moscow. Borya was gentle, as usual, and our old brother-sister relationship was restored. He also came to Petersburg. He became more attached to Mama than to my father, and his warmth, gentleness, and solicitude for me bore the character of close kinship that had bound us since childhood.

This time I was more upset than Borya. I was experiencing a disenchantment. I was sad that everything between us had ended so prosaically. I expected something more—the very something, evidently, that I didn't want. It seemed to me that I had more depth than Borya, that I acquired things with greater difficulty and gave them up with greater difficulty, and that he flitted along, floated along, superficially. Time showed that it was just the opposite and that it was I who was being capricious. My sadness, however, was sincere.

I wanted to go abroad alone, without Mama. Father, an admirer of English upbringing, willingly let me go, specifying only that I spend one month in the Swiss mountains to fortify my health. After that, for the next three years, I went abroad mostly alone. It was there that the war of 1914 caught me.

I fell in love with countries and people, knowing that I would leave them forever. And that made each of my distractions pleasant, superficial, filled to the brim. I had no fear either of accidental friendships or of the ambiguity of meetings and encounters. I flowed with the tide, half-dozing and yet active, open to any impressions or emotions.

Once, while passing through Germany, I purposely detoured to Frankfurt, not far from where, in Marburg, Borya was studying philosophy with the famous Cohen. I stopped there with an artful purpose. I wrote Borya and waited to see if he would respond; if he did not I could leave Frankfurt with dignity, less noticeably than I could Marburg. I wanted to see Borya but I was afraid to intrude, afraid to call on him because, for some reason, abroad I sensed the possibility of new waves of the old feeling.

> [Hotel Deutscher Kaiser und Kaiserhof,
> Frankfurt am Main, June 26, 1912]
> Wednesday

I am two hours' journey from you, in Frankfurt. In such circumstances good relatives get together. Will you grant me an audience? I spent three days in Berlin with your parents and so know all about Leibniz, your Tuesdays, and your Fridays. Please don't think from this that I have designs on the other days of the week. I am free and can come whenever it is most convenient for you—afternoon, evening, or morning.

I did not come to Frankfurt for your sake alone, although for you as well, of course. After Berlin and being with your parents, with their pilgrimages to shops and the Wertheim Department Store, I am immune to strong emotions. I am telling you this so that you will not hesitate to "speak out," that is, to tell me you have neither time nor energy to waste on seeing me. You know that we must be utterly truthful with each other, and your reply must be definite. Reply you must, though; I shall be waiting for it.

OLGA

Whatever the answer, forgive my hesitation.

DIARY
Scarcely had I sent the letter when the answer arrived:

> [Marburg, June 27, 1912]

Good Lord! Only last night I was telling a friend in a café about that autumn and was so disturbed by it that I couldn't get back into the old rut today—and bang! Frankfurt! How is it that we are not astonished by the succession of events? You ask for the day and hour? Not I; I don't ask. I shall live under the sword of Damocles. I won't find you in the hotel? Then I will go to the house that Goethe lived in. Not there, either? Then I will put my ear to the ground. In short, I will have my revenge on you.

Do you understand what it means to have made my way at last to Cohen from the other end of the world, from thousands of days away, and suddenly have myself designated by the word (which, let me remind you, is not a sparrow: once it flies forth it is not to be caught and brought back—even a child, it seems, can understand this)—the word "Pasternak," flying off the lips of the Senior of the seminar in reply to the adored Master's question as to who was to make the report on ethics at next Tuesday's session? There could be no thought of refusing. Considering the terrible tossing to be endured on the journey from Marburg to Frankfurt, do you think me capable of holding, without spilling, the mountain of information required for the report? I may add, my dear, that I cringe at the thought of seasickness. If I turn out to be as stupid as an ox at the seminar, the navigational cause will at least make me an object of envy. I have already put Leibniz in his place and promise to do a mazurka with ethics. But *vogue la galère.*

Shall I leave space on this paper for you to give me a failing grade?

So you don't know what to do with yourself? Nothing. You won't succeed at anything. It's like seeing oneself in a cheap photograph—one never recognizes oneself. But maybe my tone is putting you off? Oh no, I'm not being too familiar. I'm just a slave. And even without your notice —"did not come to Frankfurt for your sake alone"—even without that, I would scrupulously scrape my feet, silently step across the carpet, and, before knocking, thoroughly prepare myself to meet a lively assemblage in your quarters.

By and large I don't understand your cautionary observations. Do I really slip into intimacy so brashly? I suppose the unfortunate tone of my letters may have given you cause to think so. But I rather like the note of seniority that quite unconsciously steals into your letters to me. It is precisely the same note with which you ordered flowers for Alexander. Well, then, I am at your service.

On Friday at about breakfast time I will pounce upon you. That is, tomorrow.

DIARY

Promptly after the arrival of the letter, Borya himself put in an appearance.

I was sitting in the restaurant of my hotel wearing a wide-brimmed summer hat strewn with roses, and eating roast beef *au jus*. Opposite me stood the waiter, with whom I was flirting. By this time I had become accustomed to the grand style of life in Western Europe, to male service, to waiters standing near the table observing one's mouth, one's fork, while satisfying one's every whim and caprice. I was accustomed to ringing the bell and ordering an automobile, theater tickets, a bath. This time the young, chic waiter bent over backward to please me. I loved to drink fine wines and eat well—crèmes, turtle soup, and, best of all, roast beef *au jus*. My young friend assured me that the cook, at his request, would prepare it with special effort.

Suddenly the door opens and a dazed-looking figure walks toward me over the long carpet. It is Borya. His trousers are practically falling down, his dress is careless in the extreme, but he rushes to hug and kiss me. Embarrassed, I hurry to leave with him. We spend the whole day walking the streets, and when I grow hungry toward evening he feeds me sausages in a chophouse. On parting he sees me to the station, and talks, talks tirelessly, while I remain as closed up as a stoppered bottle.

Later he described this encounter in *Safe Conduct*. At the time he was going through a great personal drama: he had just proposed to Vyso-tskaya* and been refused. I knew nothing about it. But somehow I did not like him this time. Not only was I indifferent to him but I recoiled from him, finding him garrulous and unsubstantial. I disregarded his tender-ness and nobility of spirit, indeed did not even notice them.

[Hotel Deutscher Kaiser und Kaiserhof,
Frankfurt am Main,
June 28, 1912]

Despite everything I am very happy that I saw you, even though his-tory will label this meeting of monarchs unsuccessful. I would have wished it otherwise, but I have noticed that in our meetings success and failure take turns, and this variability alone makes me happy. During all the time that you and I have not seen each other a great deal has changed in me, that is, I want to say that there has been a great change in various processes (that is not the word I need, but you understand). Of course I can evaluate all this qualitatively, but I understand it quantitatively, too, so that it is not hard to sum things up. There are periods of greater or lesser intensity. During these past two years much has taken place in me

---

* Ida Vysotskaya: see page 48.

that has not only taken up all of my present time but has also laid claim to a portion of my future.

Why am I saying all this? Here is why. I wanted to say that I expected more of you. Is this because formerly I was less prepared for you and elevated you to a level higher than you deserved? Such a theory would appeal to your taste; you once very wittily called it spiritual reverence. And now here in your letter, speaking of intimacy, which I am supposed to find excessive in you, you make reference to a "certain tone" in your old letters: I wrongly understood it, you say. I don't like that. And I do not want your commentary to those letters, no matter how penetrating it may be. No matter how you defined yourself during that Petersburg period, you cannot overshadow it by subsequent definitions. It is true, I was not entirely prepared for you, but now I am afraid that you are not entirely prepared for me. I have changed very much over this period of time; you have not grown up as much as I had expected. Ah, that was such a difficult, difficult time, when I had to grow up in a few days, at times in a few hours, and saw how things that had once seemed big grew small. The joy of change, advance, and growth was always accompanied by the bitterness of greater and greater loneliness.

Some people have been way stations for me; I saw them from a distance, knew they were still far away, and that I would not overtake them soon. Indeed I didn't believe I would ever overtake them; and so they served me as a goal, something toward which I must strive. After straining forward with all my might, after an unbelievable concentration of will, I discovered I had sped past them without even stopping. Then an ineffable sadness seized me. I was not so vain as to be intoxicated by what I had done; I was only conscious of an excruciating loneliness, an aching, unabating loneliness. In a letter all this sounds easy, but you ought to feel intuitively how difficult it was. What was I to do? Go back? I then plunged into my inner world more eagerly than ever—a quite natural reaction. I abruptly broke off with all my friends and destroyed our relationship with an ordinary three-kopeck stamp.

It always seemed to me that everyone was robbing me of time. I had tutors for Italian and Spanish, and although I needed them I dismissed them both in one day, something I would not ordinarily be capable of. Locked in against the outer world, I spent all my time working on my inner self, and when I opened the door I was different, hardened. There is in me an unusual store of self-confidence and stubbornness. I can always see my flaws and estimate the distance between me and a person standing above me, but I can also look down, without attempting to hide it. That you should enjoy self-flagellation at times, that is nothing—but you also enjoy belittling yourself, and I call that false humility. I have none of that. I know that I have the right to call myself by my right name. At times I have wondered how I would behave the next time you and I met. What way station lures me on now? And in my thoughts I seize on something very far away, so as to observe myself while running and to support myself when I arrive exhausted at the end of the race.

I repeat, I could hold up under the great strain of pursuing your image shimmering in the distance. I would certainly set out after you and—without losing confidence in myself, thank goodness!—I would certainly catch up to you. So there you have it, just as it should be: you are far off in Marburg, and I am at the way station in Frankfurt. Why didn't I talk to you? In Merrekühl—because you miraculously did the impossible! You spoke for me; everything you said was my own. And today—simply because I am worn out. I prepared so much for this meeting, I needed you so many times when you weren't here, that I burned out, like a penny candle.

When I want something badly, I must either get it or be devastated by frustration. How good that you left without drawing yourself and me into this void of silence. How could I have failed to realize that after all this longing for you, after resisting my wish to see you, and after these endless, endless days—that after all this I could be left with nothing but the torment of silence! I am, as you see, fated to live in myself and for myself, and when I don't do what I want for myself, I take revenge on myself by remembering everything, forgetting nothing.

If you turn the map upside down, you will see that it is not you who are far away in Marburg, and I in the way station of Frankfurt, but vice versa. I don't wish to catch up to you; you will have to take the journey back. If you pass through Glion, here is my address: Suisse, Glion, s/Montreux, Hôtel de Glion.

Marburg [June 30, 1912]
How shall I put it? . . . I am disappointed. Of course I will return to your letter, and I will also regain consciousness. Monday evening. Meantime I am disappointed, Olya, that you were so carelessly late with your letter; it should have come in August 1910, when, having returned ill from Petersburg, I was coaxed back into God's world one fine morning by a compassionate friend, and in response to his admonitions that this was not the way to act, that one could destroy oneself by behaving so, and that in such circumstances one must abandon everything and return to Petersburg, I said it was too soon for such a trip. Then with difficulty I con-

vinced him that first I had to change fundamentally, for Aunt Asya reacted to the situation by stating in black and white that I was *not* a man of integrity. That was long before your letter from Frankfurt. So I decided to reform—I am not fabricating this, Olya, I am telling the whole truth—in order to be closer to "Petersburg." True, my purpose did not last long, but my first disciplinary measures determined the further direction of my work upon myself. Other purposes appeared: people who also were, like those from Petersburg, more classical, more finished, more sharply defined than I was. In the end I simply rejected the burden of remorse that was seething within me and seeking expression to please certain people who—asked for it too late. For, curious as it may seem, that same summer, before you arrived, I had heard an entirely different recommendation of my person, also tardy, one that went beyond all my expectations.

I do not know whether you will believe me when I say I was warmed by the inviting look you threw to poor me from such an incalculable distance. I, too, love the poor fellow. So I could not help being touched by your look. I need such things. I'll explain in a later letter.

Don't be angry with me, Olya, but you must admit this is all very disappointing. If only I could turn back time!

Glion [early July 1912]
This is all very boring. Nothing could interest me less than drawing conclusions. I recall how you once said that I was particularly necessary to you when you were taking stock—just when I find it most tiresome. Apparently our relationship has taken an absurd turn.

God only knows into what a sad, dull mood your postcard threw me. Things got so bad I even sat down to write you immediately. Well, you have been away and now you want to see what has happened to your abandoned homeland in these past two years. God, how inexperienced you are! In such cases one takes a round-trip ticket and returns at any time at a reduced rate. You took a one-way ticket and since 1910 have been hopping from place to place. Remember acknowledging, that day in the garden, that you had yet to visit a lot of places that were new to you and obligatory once you had chosen to see them, and until you had completed the tour included in your ticket you would not turn back? And so today it's Marburg. You are leaving, I believe, in a month. For what new scene and for how long?

You have a passion for definitions; you are always politely inviting me to define myself. But that is trite: to define means to limit. That is why I have chosen the lesser of two evils and undertaken to define *you* instead. That, however, is at my own expense. Don't forget that I always examine you from *my* point of view—you as related to me and with respect to myself. That will probably affect you like a dousing of hot water: shocking and scalding! But for all my levity, I really am serious. You and I have a way of being serious while joking, and vice versa. We are constantly joking. That, perhaps, is because being together is too saddening for us. And that, again, is serious. I am always sad in your presence.

You will understand the silliness of my letter when I tell you I have a high temperature and am feeling rotten and so am not to be trusted; I write the opposite of what I mean. Yes, I really am sick and weak. I am, however, so used to doing without health and strength that I would not notice their absence now if it were not for the necessity of holding on to the edge of the desk as I sit and write. It takes strength to do that. For almost two years our differences have remained irreconcilable. I am entirely in command of myself when I have no strength, for then I simply lie or sit and everything is fine. But as soon as I am capable of getting up I become dejected. That, I suppose, is just because my strength has returned to me.

Here are the circumstances in which I am writing: a black night, a storm coming on, a mountain storm with terrible thunder and fiendish lightning. Noise and fire sirens outside. O Lord, how these *citoyens* love those sirens! The alarms don't upset me, because I know that once the sirens sound, Switzerland is in no danger.

I have a calm self-confidence that you will read this letter through. You are not interested in pathology? I seem to recall that you are. After all, you have already begun to study law, haven't you?

So your report came off well? That means Frankfurt had no effect on it. On that very evening I was banished from the hotel: the Germans have a rule about "clearance" (I do like that word!) four hours before the next occupant's arrival, in other words, four hours before the law says you must get out. That is official. In practice, one's bags sit in the lobby and one's self sits in any of the public salons. But I took offense, abandoned all my belongings, left the hotel immediately, and spent four hours at the railroad station. I stood, sat, or drank Apollinaris. My mood was low, and all because I had been unable to speak in your presence, while you spoke well and at length. In order to acquire that surprising capability I drank a great deal of water, including five bottles of Apollinaris. I am not exaggerating—five.

Some Heidelberg students appreciated it. That night at the station they engaged in a drunken debauch, singing raucously and waving their arms in front of the window where I was sitting. I wrote to Kissingen that I wanted to come for Josephine, but there was no answer. Josephine was set on coming with you to see me and spoke of your own visit to Glion with such confidence that one would think the local Catholic chapel with its pews had been turned into a university hall where philosophy was read.

Still I hope Aunt Rosa will let Josephine come if I go to meet her when I recover. If they do not believe I was sick, this letter will prove it. What air there is now, what lightness! Makes one long to sit up and write poetry! But I mustn't sit up, I must lie down. Why is it that one cannot be lyrical lying down?

Finally, don't be angry with me, *quand même*, for imitating your conversation. We will meet again someday. We will go for a walk someday, or to a museum, or to a station to catch the next train. Someday we will write to each other again, and again in leap year. In short, I will mend my ways, and the sooner I do so the faster that "someday" will come. After all, I am delicate: just see what soft paper I write on!

OLGA

Marburg [July 11, 1912]

Dear Olya,

If words were uninhabited islands, and if they were not spotted all over with innuendoes hard to detect because of the mists of the archipelago, I would simply tell you that it is impossible to end things with a letter like that, i.e., verbally impossible. I would write whatever I pleased. As it is, I have to explain to you that my philosophy studies are going well. Cohen was pleasantly surprised with my work. I wrote a second report with still greater success. So my silence is not depression caused by failure at all. I would further explain that I am sure you feel no need of a letter from me. This explanation is made invalid by my sense of my own worth. I suppose there would be other explanations as well.

But if words fell from heaven like inorganic matter and didn't sprout innuendoes, I would just say it's impossible to end things this way. Because that letter of yours, terribly fair and extremely important, was almost my salvation! Was a warning of sorts. In it you spoke of your own rapid development. I am astonished at the insight that allowed you to catch the alien, commonplace, and decadent something that has changed me. You have no idea how I have lost my way. But you make one mistake: all this has come about consciously and intentionally. I thought "my way" had no right to exist. You wrote that formerly I expressed your world, too. Can you now refuse to tell me what has become of that world—mine, as much as yours—in the past two years? I have been away from home, and, steeped in philosophy, mathematics, and law, I have been out of touch with my own self. Perhaps I can return, but I do not contend that you owe me anything. To write about that world means to write about myself. But not as you do: "I have developed," "I have grown up," "I am rushing toward the goal." What half verbs, and with holes in them! You seem to be laughing at me, and at a very hard and serious time of my life.

Glion [mid-July 1912]

Oh, but this is not so dull as it is stupid! Insulted? Without cause? What outrageous words! One must ask you where you acquired this love of verbal fireworks. It is no fault of mine if you have such a fine collection of friends that you can sort my words into groups relating to your friends' words. They may insult you without cause, but I have no thought of inflicting such cruelty. In your card you called your present period "alien, commonplace, and decadent." I think you are wrong. I don't think you are in a decadent period. More likely I am. And you need not have been insulted, because I can only say that even this period is important to you, and you, of course, will get over it. If there is anything disappointing in all this it is disappointment with myself, because without knowing whether you are alien to yourself or not, I know you are alien to me. What do you find insulting in that? I do not touch you. I am even prepared to admit that that's the way it should be. But permit me, when I want to, to step aside and peacefully cross the street. That is what I did do. And so, I repeat, now we can talk about me, not about you. This is thoroughly my business. I didn't even look to see if you were alien or decadent, for I immediately perceived that the commonplace had arisen in you—your word is well-chosen. That was enough. The rest didn't matter to me. The rest mattered to you.

Are you displeased with my writing you? Well, I cannot come to terms with your letter. I don't care whether you wish it or not; not to have answered your remarkable letter would have been worse than to have written it. And my health! You are beginning to be like Alexander Margulius. He advised you to go to Osip's dacha* and drink milk and eat eggs, and he offered such advice when you were visiting us in Petersburg and talking about things of first importance to you! I remember your words in Frankfurt; you have begun to do what you once derided.

* Osip Isidorovich Kaufman: Boris's uncle, brother of Rosa and Klara, a retired doctor who had practiced in the provincial town of Kasimov.

How shall I sign this letter, in formal or intimate terms?

Ah, how stupid when you think that I am saying what your friends have already told you or will tell you. Do you write them the sort of letters you write me? And do they, in the face of the elements, answer them?

That you are going back to Russia is splendid; I envy you. But then you, poor darling, have already been in Kissingen. Spas do not lead to virtue—except that you wrote me such a virtuous letter, the salt of which is good only for the bath. Well, good-by, Borya. I wish you well. Despite everything, I am glad we saw each other.

DIARY

I promised the Pasternaks I would visit them in Marina di Pisa, where they had taken a villa on the Mediterranean.

Uncle's household greeted me with joy. Only Borya was distant. Obviously he had undergone great personal growth, while I—what was I compared to him? He had nothing to say to me. The black Italian nights were filled with extraordinary music; he improvised at the piano while Aunt Rosa, a great and sensitive musician, sat at the dark window and trembled.

Borya and I went to see Pisa: the cathedral, the famous leaning tower —no one can decide whether it is falling or was purposely built that way. I wanted to see things and move on, get impressions and forget them. But Borya, guidebook in hand, meticulously studied each detail of the cathedral, all the figures in the bas-reliefs, each cornice and portal. This drove me mad. My casual attitude irritated him. We quarreled. I walked off. He bent over the book, read, again bent over it, looked, dawdled. We no longer spoke to each other. From that day on, Borya did not utter a single sound meant for me alone. We lived together, next to each other, ignoring each other completely. The family surroundings and the southern, too extravagant beauty of nature fatigued me. I longed to get away. I carried on an extensive correspondence—blue envelopes and telegrams followed me everywhere, and from here, on the outskirts of Pisa, I arranged to meet people on mountain tops and in distant places as nonchalantly as if I were specifying the corner of the Canal and Gorokhovaya Street in Petersburg. Once Aunt Rosa "accidentally" opened a telegram for me that began, in French, "I will be completely alone . . ." and then named a meeting place, day, and hour. I quickly made ready to go. Although the dispatch was innocent—it was from José de Sousa, who expected me back in Switzerland—I seized the opportunity to take offense and leave. At home the sanctity of correspondence was the first commandment, and I didn't believe in "accidents."

They made great fun of me. Alexander called José de Sousa "sauce" and made a fine pun ("no matter with what sauce your telegram is served . . ."), while Borya did not deign to speak to me. From the beginning he had criticized me for meeting and traveling with Vincenzo Perna (I did not hide my adventures), and very wittily called that native of Pavia "your Pavian."* All this was amusing, even if based on false assumptions.

[Moscow, winter 1913; not sent]

I hadn't thought of you once in over a year, but today I did think of you, and in such a way that the memory drove me out of the house, and I returned only for the sake of this letter. I will not begin to tell you about my state of mind, for I do not expect to evoke a similar state in you. Occasionally one feels that time is but a gust of trade winds blowing into the past, and that past seems torn off like a shutter in a storm, swept off into the beyond, into bygone times. It seems only yesterday that I was in that past, and today I have a poignant sense of loss. How could I not tell you of this?

This letter will reach Petersburg and they will forward it to you from there. And indeed it is well that it should spend some time in the city of memories, this "present" letter.

You probably did not understand my summer reproach in the form in which I sent it from Marburg to Switzerland. It was weighty and unrelated to reality. That was but a stylistic shortcoming. Do you still remember? One morning, in the German university town to which I had been brought by the necessity of making a break with quite a different sort of life, which at the time seemed the wrong sort to me, I discovered that that former life was the true one. If prior to the discovery I was suffering merely from the unattractiveness of studies, activities, and interests which were foreign to my nature but which I forced myself to undertake so as to save myself from appearing ridiculous, a sissy, and lonely and to bring me closer to those few people I loved, people who insisted that I make speeches without end and without answers, apparently believing I would acquire a new vernacular in which they could discourse with me—to all this torture has now been added the realization that it was pointless, and that my friends' earlier silence only hid their agreement with me and was a mark of their sharing my thoughts. Yes, that happened in Marburg. I

* *Pavian* is Russian for "baboon."

wandered off with a letter that arrived two years too late and threw my life into utter disarray. It was clear: a new break lay ahead, and I did not hesitate to make it. I wanted to restore much that I had lost. You probably see various picturesque motives behind this and, having put them between you and me, cannot help laughing at the poor figure I cut. I cannot be blamed for that. I must explain myself. One must be just and grateful. Your letter—the long, long, beneficent one from Petersburg, after Merrekühl, in whose depths one could entirely lose oneself, and whose significance in no way diminished when you yourself drew near— perhaps it was this alone I remembered today, and this that wreaked such havoc with me.

You think I am sitting here now digging through old memories and coughing like an old man opening and shutting desk drawers? Actually, I am going over the ways in which I might feel your presence now through painful and almost unbearable memories.

[Inscription in *A Twin in the Clouds*:]

For dear Olya, with love and gratitude
for a certain summer encounter . . .
Until our next meeting on a like page,
BORYA
December 20, 1913

[Moscow, winter 1913; not sent]

Dear Uncle Misha,

At last the occasion has again arisen to write you from that respectful and diffident distance I have always preserved in respect to you. You recall those awkward and futile attempts I made to express my admiration for you when I turned up at your apartment one evening with Olya, who was coming back from a visit with us. Now, taking the liberty of telling you all this straightforwardly, I am aware that I am deliberately exposing myself to the charge of vulgarity. But you rise so uniquely, so like a lone tower in life, and life surrounds you with such alluring shadows, that I am encouraged to break established conventions in addressing you.

I think of you with a certain gratitude. It will be hard for me to explain that to you, particularly if you consider everything I am about to say as a branch of metaphysics unworthy of your regard. Well, I am deeply and extraordinarily grateful to you. Have you noticed how cruelly we must

Olga Freidenberg

Boris Pasternak. 1913

Ida Vysotskaya, Josephine Pasternak, A. Vishnevsky, and Rosa Pasternak.
Kissingen, 1912

pay, on a second encounter with certain people, for the fact that they have become the past, half-legendary figures in our consciousness? It is noteworthy that at the first encounter we could have foretold subsequent disenchantment. It is not a matter of the quality of the people who correspond or do not correspond to our first impressions of them. It may be a matter of a special gift possessed by rare persons, one I would call the gift of time.

Such people are caught up in the present moment, which belongs to no one and embraces them in the general, colorless milieu of a "given time," of reality. A constant stream of new "present moments" approaches, belonging as little to anyone as the chance circumstances that overtake everyone alike. And only the past, apparently, is multiplied to form a personal, individual series. However, I have met certain personalities who, as it were, breathe *their own* time, for whom the evidence of their clocks is but a deference to social order. What is the significance of this? It signifies, first, a certain quality of immortality that permeates their actions. Second, it speaks of their lonely intimacy with their fate. In no way does their fate enslave them. But it is somehow invariably close to them, like a twin—springing from the same source. It is the fate of fate to be their fate. Such people can be examples upon which one bases religious beliefs. The presence of such people fractures reality, and it is impossible to become disenchanted with them; when you speak with them it is as though your memory informs you of them, probably because they have never been part of the indifferent, commonly experienced present.

It is hard to convey my idea in these terms. More rewarding would be the attempt to convey, in life or in art, one's admiration for such people. If this were within my power, it is you I would choose as my model. I would think how, imperturbably and in strange ignorance of it, you embody that chaotic impression, almost visionary, which Petersburg gives of itself, the city as *spirit*. And how, as if fulfilling a dictate of Balzac that has not come down to us, you allow your fantasy full play as you stand over your machines at night, with a bloodless empty expanse extending beyond the window at your back. And how the world of objects surrounding you, the whole mystery of the place and the rooms, is infected by the dramatic way in which you play out your life. Perhaps live personalities are necessary in order to link experience to them. You cannot imagine the ease and freedom my past enjoyed with you. That is what I wanted to thank you for. The trifles* which are enclosed relate to that happy time.

---

* Probably five Pasternak poems published in the 1913 literary miscellany *The Lyric*.

It is sad to encounter these tardy embodiments of something which was ready years ago but which, instead of developing, was cut off by my own thoughtlessness.

Yours devotedly,
BORYA [...]

[Olga's majestic, final rejection, expressed in her letter of June 28, 1912, was followed by a visit to Kissingen on July 1, the birthday of Ida Vysotskaya; Pasternak had earlier proposed marriage to Ida, but had been refused. He described the visit to his friend Shtikh: "The Vysotsky sisters are here, my family, Vishnevsky,* Sobinov,† etc. . . . Do you recall the atmosphere surrounding Natasha Rostova? ‡ That's what I encountered around Josephine and Ida. . . . Delicate, grown-up, dear Josephine, surrounded by solicitude, smiling at Vishnevsky's pranks, and, beside her, tragically beautiful Ida, her every step beautiful, the wind in her hair, against the backdrop of the trees. . . . My sorrow was mixed with reproaches. Olya: 'My God, how boring these disquisitions of yours are. . . .' Ida: 'Try to live normally; your way of life has led you astray. A person who hasn't eaten or slept properly is prone to all sorts of wild ideas. . . .' Josephine: 'Tell me, Borya, have you grown more foolish? Have you become like everyone else?' At least Josephine asked without Olya's and Ida's cold superciliousness, showing sympathy. This evening she was crying. She sat down beside me with the following lament: 'Poor Borya, you are all mixed up in the past and the present; poor fellow, it's very difficult for you now, everything has to be redefined.' "

That summer of 1912, and the encounter in Frankfurt, marked a final turning point in Pasternak's development. To Shtikh he wrote: "She kept silent back then (1910) because a miracle was taking place. I was speaking for myself, for her, for her father, for her life and her city. . . . Back then I was ahead of her and it was hard for her to keep up; now, I have lagged behind and she is farther along than I. . . . My God, if only she had told me all that back then! If only I had not assumed that I had to transform myself through discipline, a process in which everything perished—in an effort to assimilate with the classical and rational! God, if only I had had this letter from Frankfurt to Marburg in hand then!"

Pasternak, barely able to wait out the summer semester, abandoned philosophy, and, upon his return to Moscow, the life of the poet began.]

* A prominent actor with the Moscow Art Theater.
† L. V. Sobinov: a well-known opera singer.
‡ In Tolstoy's *War and Peace* (1869).

Photographs
1914–1917

Olga Freidenberg. Petrograd, 1914

Olga Freidenberg with a wounded soldier. Petrograd, 1914

Boris Pasternak. Tikhie Gory (in the Urals), 1916

Leonid and Rosa Pasternak, Borya and Alexander Pasternak
with their grandmother Berta Kaufman, and Lydia and Josephine
Pasternak. Molodi, 1917

CHAPTER **III**

For almost a decade there is no trace of correspondence between Olga Freidenberg and Boris Pasternak. World War I, together with the Russian Revolution and the civil war that followed, no doubt contributed to the distance they had established between themselves.

August 1914 found Pasternak working as a tutor on an estate near the town of Aleksino on the Oka River. He was exempted from military service because of a crippled leg, the result of a fall from a horse in 1906. He performed his civilian service as a clerk in factories in the Urals, issuing draft exemptions to workers indispensable to defense production.

Pasternak's outlook on the politics of World War I and revolution found expression in his letters. To his parents he wrote in 1916: "Glancing at the newspapers, I often shudder at the thought of the contrast, the abyss which is opening up between the cheap politics of the day and what is just around the corner. The former is associated with the habits of living in a time of war and coming to terms with it; the latter, not billeted in the human brain, now belongs to the new era that I think will soon arrive. God grant it be so. One can already feel its spirit. It is absurd to expect an end to absurdity. Otherwise absurdity would be consequential and finite and would no longer be absurdity.

"Absurdity has no end; it will just break off at one of its absurd links when no one expects it to. And it won't break off because the absurdity has come to an end but because the meaningful has a beginning, and that beginning excludes and annuls the absurd.

"That is how I understand the matter. So I am expecting what you, too, probably expect. In other words, I am not seeking a gleam of light in the prevailing darkness, inasmuch as darkness is incapable of sharing light. There will be no gleam of light because *there will immediately be light*. There's no point in trying to seek it out now in what we know: it is seeking *us* out, and tomorrow or the next day it will flood us with light." This optimism permeated his best-known book of verse, *My Sister, Life*.

The years beginning with World War I and stretching through the period of the New Economic Policy (1921–1928) were extraordinarily productive ones for Pasternak, although many of his works were lost or destroyed. He wrote four books of poetry (those that survived were *Above the Barriers*, 1917; *My Sister, Life*, 1922; and *Themes and Variations*, 1923), several stories, a long novel (only a fragment, *The Childhood of Luvers*, 1922, has been preserved), a lost drama in verse, and two narrative poems ("A Lofty Malady," 1924, survived). Translation became his most reliable source of income: four plays by Heinrich von Kleist, Goethe's "Mysteries," intermezzos of the German Meistersinger Hans Sachs, Swinburne's *Chastelard*, Ben Jonson's *Alchemist*, the poetry of the Belgian Charles van Lerberghe. He also wrote a volume of essays on art and psychology, which was to have been titled *Quintessencia*.

All this activity quickly gained him recognition as a professional writer. He was not, however, in the Bolshevik camp. After the devastating Moscow winter of 1919–1920, he wrote to the young poet Dmitri Vasilevich Petrovsky (1892–1955): "Soviet authority has gradually grown into a sort of grubbing, atheistic sanctuary for the aged. Pensions, rations, subsidies —not doled out to the intelligentsia as yet, and they don't take people out for air in pairs, but otherwise a perfect asylum for orphans. They keep people starving, and make them profess their lack of religious faith while praying for salvation from lice; they make them doff their hats at the singing of the Internationale, etc. Portraits of the All-Russian Central Executive Committee, couriers, business days and nonbusiness days . . .

"Everything here is dead, dead, and the only thing to do is to get out, and the sooner the better. Where to go, I still don't know; that will be determined in the near future. I have lots of orders to fill, many promises with a market value, many irons in the fire, but it is all a professional pastime in the aforementioned asylum without God, soulless, senseless. I was right before, when I refused to believe in it for anything."

During these years of dislocation, devastation, and starvation, it was normal for publishing houses to close suddenly, for manuscripts to be lost at the typesetters, and for publishing houses to reopen under new names, breaching previous contracts. Public support was the only reliable means of subsistence, yet it required a position in, and implied an ideological sympathy with, the new society. Tongue in cheek, Pasternak in 1920 petitioned the Literature Department of the People's Commissariat of Education:

"On the assumption that the following matters fall most naturally within the jurisdiction and competence of the Literature Department, and that one can locate among that department's accounting regulations a rubric that envisions situations such as mine, I respectfully request the Collegium to accord attention to the present petition.

"I am not in Government service, and I subsist exclusively on my professional earnings. In order to convey an understanding of the concentrated labor that this requires and that I have demonstrated in the course of a single year, I submit a list of finished works. The list consists mainly of translations, done to order for the publishing house World Literature and for the Theater Department of the Commissariat of Education. . . . Numerically, the total amounts to 12,000 (twelve thousand) lines of poetry. That constitutes a level of intensity, a form and condition of involuntary labor, whereby its vehicle and agent, first launched on this path by the attraction of a calling, gradually abandons the province of art, then of independent craft as well. Finally, forced by circumstances, he sees himself subjected to an impossible professional involuntary servitude that goes on and on, becomes more and more burdensome, and given the inevitable social inertia, cannot be terminated. . . .

"This spring, the Government came to the aid of people who were not even in my plight. . . . I am referring to relevant promises made to the All-Russian Writers' Union. . . . Circumstances force me to raise the issue not corporately but personally, individually—as perhaps those representatives of the Union did who have been eligible for rations for three months now.

"I am aware that there are two conditions to such a right. One is the presence of real necessity—let's say, need. As best I can, I have demonstrated that. . . . The other basis for receiving an academic ration is the artistic prominence of the applicant. At this point, my application ends. Who might judge that if not the Literature Department—if, in general, such things can be determined."

The times were harsh for the whole Pasternak family. Emigration seemed the only solution, and in August 1921, thanks to the intercession of Anatoly Vasilevich Lunacharsky (1875–1933), the Commissar of Education from 1917 to 1929, Pasternak's parents were permitted to travel to Berlin, ostensibly for treatment of his mother's heart disease. Lydia and Josephine accompanied them, while the two boys remained in Moscow; Aunt Asya and Olga (her father had died in 1920) were invited to occupy the vacant Moscow apartment. It was assumed that the separation of the family would be temporary, and indeed Boris did visit his parents in Berlin in 1922, but the sight of postwar Germany, in ruins, shattered his hopes for a tranquil, productive life there. He returned to Moscow, never to see his parents again.

Boris Pasternak and Evgenya Lurie (Zhenya) met in the fall of 1921. Their relationship developed rapidly, and when, on a visit to Moscow, her brother found Evgenya in love with a somewhat strange poet who seemed slightly otherworldly, she was summoned home to her parents in Petrograd (the name of St. Petersburg during the war against Germany and until the death of Lenin in 1924). They married, and soon a son (Evgeny, "Zhenya" for short) was born. In the spring of 1924, after a harsh winter, the two Zhenyas went to Taitsy, a village of summer cottages near Petrograd. Their deep love, though complicated by the poverty of the times, is evident in the following passage from a letter to Evgenya at Taitsy: "Hail to you, hail to you, my happiness, my wave, washing over my eyes. Stand proud, laugh and cry, show off, pay no attention to me, and don't leave me. Turn away like a goddess, and like a goddess keep watch over me. Turn away, stretched out beside me, undressed by a man with your ring on his hand, but undressed as the hand of your happiest imagining would undress you, or as a warm summer night would, or a memory. Turn away, undressed by me, because the unfathomable turns away, and you are the sublime, higher than the high, better than the best. Lie with your eyes closed, don't look at me, and ignore the fact that I exist, while I worship you and kiss you.

"And always, eternally, be with me, my cold sky, my dreaming nerve, the sleepless vein of the forests and fields when they are in bloom. When we were joined we both ascended to a high place where all is visible, where one cannot be alone, my joy, my joy, my joy!" When Pasternak joined his family for the summer months in Taitsy, the proximity to Olga seems to have offered occasion to renew their interrupted correspondence.

The outbreak of World War I had found Olga stranded in the north of Sweden, in a favorite small town, Elfdalen. After a long and arduous journey through Finland, she arrived in Petersburg on a train filled with refugees. She served throughout the war as a nurse in the military hospitals of Petrograd, attending the victims of Russia's precipitous decline and fall. She became deeply attached to Ivan Ivanovich Dmitriev, a Cavalier of the Cross of Saint George, twice wounded, who later died of tetanus.

After the collapse of the czarist regime, women were given access to the universities. Against her father's wishes, Olga applied. She completed her degree in classics, under the supervision of such scholars as the folklorist A. K. Borozdin and the scholar of Greek antiquity I. I. Tolstoy.

The universities were in turmoil; the prerevolutionary system of advanced degrees based upon a public dissertation defense had been abandoned, leaving no avenue open for young scholars to air their work. The scholarly activity formerly supported by universities was transferred to newly formed research institutes—in the case of Olga's department of philology, to the Institute for Language and Literature of the East and West. After persistent effort, Olga Freidenberg defended her dissertation there, in the Slavic section, on November 14, 1924. The Slavic section was headed by Nikolai Yakovlevich Marr (1864–1934), a leading Soviet linguist in the twenties and thirties, whose "New Theory" of language, raised to dogma in the anticosmopolitan reaction after World War II, was denounced by Stalin in *Pravda* in 1950. Marr was not only a scholar but also an academic and political leader, serving as dean of the faculty of social sciences at Leningrad University, member of the Leningrad City Council, director of the Leningrad Public Library, founder and president of the State Academy of the History of Material Culture (GAIMK), vice-president of the Academy of Sciences, and member of the All-Russian Central Executive, to name but a few of the prominent posts he held during the early years of Soviet rule. A brilliant linguist himself, he developed a since discredited theory of social determinism in the origin and evolution of language, a theory based on a falsely reconstructed "Japhetic" language. Marrism was as symptomatic of the influence of ideology on scholarship as Lysenkoism was in the field of genetics. To the extent of his interest, Marr promoted Olga Freidenberg's scholarly career during the 1920's and 1930's.

Soviet conditions of subsistence were no more gentle for Olga in Leningrad than they were for Boris in Moscow. Life for the bourgeois intelligentsia was impossible without a subsidy from the state, which meant seeking the recognition of the state and its tacit imprimatur on one's work. To promote Olga's welfare, Boris sought to use his own literary ties—with Alexander Nikolayevich Tikhonov, the editor and longtime friend who headed the publishing house World Literature; with M. N. Pokrovsky, the Marxist historian; with Lunacharsky, the Commissar of Education; with S. F. Oldenburg, Permanent Secretary of the Academy of Sciences; and later with Valerian Borisovich Aptekar and Abram Moiseyevich Deborin, Soviet Marxist philosophers of the Communist Academy. Boris achieved little, however, and gave Olga cause to accuse him bitterly of promising too much.

DIARY

At the beginning of the 1917–1918 academic year I entered Petersburg University. The university still looked as it had in the old days. The lectures of its famous old professors were now open to the public. I remember the lecture halls and the professors in their black frock coats reading from the rostrum. A new freedom was born of the Revolution. People from cultivated circles came to listen to anyone they chose. I arrived there battered by the storms I had lived through. If I had been a nun I couldn't have prayed and worshiped more fervently; it was my refuge.

By March I was studying in earnest in the philology department, but I had not yet made a choice of language. I was conscious of the strength that comes with maturity, and this helped me, or so I thought, to penetrate to the very essence of my studies.

The freedom of university teaching marvelously shaped my outlook. The professors were all different, each a distinguished scholar, and they offered courses of their own choosing. I attended all the philosophy lectures.

The year 1919 was a very important one for me. The most important. That year I began studying under Zhebelev in the classics department.

It was then I wrote Borya: "Our two lives cannot be compared. Your tree blossomed forth, nourished by an abundance of sap; my tree had to do with the little nourishment I could suck out of my own fingertips. I had no one to help me. This forced me to become independent and work out a complicated technique for discovering Americas. It also taught me a great many things and developed my 'leg muscles.' And it taught me to study. I study passionately, and everything that brings me knowledge augments the gratitude that enwraps my heart like a coverlet.

"Time's mirror reflects only the classics department, where I stand in a stream of bright light feeling that none of this brightness belongs to me, that a mere flick of the hand may plunge me into total darkness."

And indeed in November I fell ill and took to my bed. We all moved into one room where a little tin stove filled the air with smoke. Mama busied herself in the kitchen, which was the family hearth for her.

My brother Sasha moved in with us. I was in bed. Father, in fur cap and with his coat tied in at the waist (people always tied something around their waists to keep themselves warm that bitter winter; their hungry bodies froze), sat and slept by the feeble warmth of the stove.

Terrible days! Life was empty. Some professors died. Those who remained alive were arrested. The university ceased to function, was gradually covered with dust and mold. Everybody was fighting at home as if at war. What talk could there be of studies!

I lay in bed day after day.

There really seemed to be no hope for me: the flu passed but the fever did not abate.

Just before my illness I had read, at Zhebelev's seminar, about Apostle Paul and Thecla, as told in the Apocrypha. I still had in my possession Zhebelev's book with the Greek text. Having nothing else to do, I made a thorough study of the text. It captivated me. And well it might! The manuscript begins with Thecla's listening entranced to her teacher Paul. The Apocrypha spoke to me. I felt their beauty, their amorous, pagan aroma. Borozdin, Zhebelev, Tolstoy, Bush*—these were my teachers. Everything combined to lead me to Thecla and leave me at her window.

In March I began to walk about but was still very weak. The story from the Apocrypha about Thecla, which had remained in my hands by chance, played a decisive role in my life, as chance things often do. I undertook the study of it.

I worked in the manuscript division of the public library. My task was textological. I examined the manuscript, compared, analyzed; it turned out that manuscripts important to me were in Moscow. When I had accomplished all I could here, I told Bush about it. He was thunder-struck and insisted on my making a report at his seminar.

And what do you suppose? I received a letter signed by the president of the Academy himself—and what a president! Shakhmatov!† Here it is:

May 26, 1920

My dear Miss Freidenberg,

I have the honor of informing you that, on the recommendation of V. V. Bush, the department of Russian language and literature has decided to grant you one thousand rubles to cover the expenses of a trip to Moscow so that you may acquaint yourself with manuscripts containing the apocryphal story of St. Thecla.‡

* Alexander Kornilevich Borozdin (1863–1918): specialist in Old Russian literature, author of a study on the seventeenth-century heretic Avvakum. Sergei Alexandrovich Zhebelev (1867–1941): historian and classical philologist. Ivan Ivanovich Tolstoy (1880–1954): specialist in ancient Greek language and literature. Vladimir Vladimirovich Bush (1888–1934): specialist in Old Russian literature.

† Alexei Alexandrovich Shakhmatov (1864–1920): Russian philologist.

‡ According to R. A. Lipsius (*Acta Apostolorum Apocrypha*, I, Hildesheim, 1959, p. CII), three manuscripts of the Acts of Thecla were deposited at the Monastery of the Holy Trinity in Moscow.

Consider, then, my feelings upon receiving the letter, the money, and the trust, at a time when I was desperately ill!

For in May I had fallen ill again. I coughed, perspired at night, ran a temperature, was terribly weak. I consulted a specialist. After undressing me and declaiming some verses of Homer in Greek, he felt about under my armpits and proclaimed "tuberculosis." He then expounded on the subject of galloping consumption and said that under the circumstances he could offer no advice. Was I to go away? It wouldn't help. He gave me about a month to live. And at just this time came the letter from Shakhmatov!

There could be no thought of my taking a trip. I lay in a state of prostration. The worst thing was that I was incapable of working. My elation, hopes, unlimited prospects, and new-found happiness—blasted suddenly, unexpectedly, once and for all.

Father was seriously ill, lay in bed, did not get up. He suffered from thirst and caprices of appetite that drove Mama mad. It was terrible to see her with two such invalids on her hands and no money and no hope.

On the first of August Papa died. I did not feel any deep and genuine grief. It was swallowed up by the horrors of what we had lived through the past few years, months, days, and by my last encounter with him in the hospital.

Mama broke with Uncle Leonid. She could not forgive him for not coming to see us after Papa's death and for not finding it necessary to come and say good-by to her before he legally emigrated from Russia. True, when he received the letter addressed in Sasha's hand he understood how frightening its contents were and proposed we all come to Moscow and live with the boys (that is, with Borya and Alexander). With what bitter pride we refused that invitation!

In 1921 Petersburg was like an abandoned provincial town. "Petersburg is beautiful in its abandonment," I wrote Borya on May 15, "with its empty streets, with grass and wild flowers springing up in the cracks of the sidewalks. Prolonged misery has made an optimist of me. How odd that desolation should bring freedom, enabling flowers to grow wild in city streets!"

Moscow [probably spring 1921]

Dear Olya,

Mlle. Lifshits will tell you everything in person. When I see you I will explain why I have kept silent so long. If I expanded on the reasons in this letter I would drive it to death as I did the others, and there would be no letter. But you ought to know that it is *absolutely necessary* that you come. It is necessary for us—narrowly, the two of us, and broadly, as a family—to talk about a great many things. It seems to me I could be useful to you in a practical and everyday way. Lifshits says you are again being sent on a research trip and this time seriously intend to reach us. See that you don't change your mind and please carry out this good intention as soon as possible. It would be exceedingly foolish and unforgivable if you didn't. I don't feel like "talking" about anything (to use a figure common to letter writers) in view of our imminent face-to-face conversation. I won't write anything else because I think Lifshits will tell you all that is necessary.

Love to Aunt Asya and Sasha.

Yours,
BORYA

Moscow, 14 Volkhonka, Apt. 9
[December 29, 1921]

Dear Olya,

I still have the letter I wrote this summer in answer to your cruel and mocking one. You didn't understand me then and made brutal fun of me. But because of the way I'm made, and because I am so fond of your Humour* (in English that's a broader concept than the Russian equivalent, isn't it?), I showed it to Papa and my sisters. "Didn't she let you have it!" they said. They enjoyed the way you let me have it, although of course they hadn't read my letter to you and so could not judge the fairness of your caricature. Since you will gain nothing by adopting a more correct view of the matters I had in mind in my letter, and since you are none the worse in my eyes for the opinion you hold of me, we'll drop the subject. But listen: I beg you, now, now, this very minute, to write me how all of you are—Aunt Asya and you and Sasha—how you are living and what you are doing. And for God's sake come down to earth (forgive the crudity). If you don't do it at once I shall be hurt and upset. For God's sake, sit down and write without putting it off. Where have I been all this time, you may ask, that I should be in such a rush all of a sudden? And right you are, I myself don't understand how I could have preferred spending months wishing unwarrantably to hear from and about you, without making a single effort to give warrant to my wishing.

* In English in the original.

Don't be as strict as I was stupid; take it as a measure of your indulgence. And I beg you to let this round of the epistolary *contredanse* conclude by the end of the year (insofar as it is within the power and possibility of the mail). If, however, New Year's Eve falls between greeting and answer, here is a big kiss for you and Aunt Asya and Sasha from all six of us, imparting the sting of a wish whose blunt force defies expression, a wish akin to fate, whose very fatality assures its coming true, a wish that, in the vitality of its sorrow, gives off a convincing froth of optimism, a wish that sees the future belonging to those to whom it is addressed.

Happy New Year, Olechka!

Forgive me for writing only from the heart, without adding any real meat. Forgive my sloppiness. I am writing this in a break between two stretches of deaf-and-dumb inactivity that have become part of my life in recent years. These seizures are, among other things, as idiotic as deaf-mutes appear to be, and I shouldn't like you to be getting letters from an idiot. I beg you, Olya, to sit down and write at once. And don't write a *reply* to my letter, that is, don't enlarge on whether it pleased or disappointed you. Not by a whit must you shorten the real letter by using this as an introductory theme, an assault, an occasion for praise or faultfinding. Do my parents write you from abroad? They have come back to life there, as you know; their letters are younger than those who receive them and than the eyes of those who peruse them, much as I hate to admit it. I won't speak about myself. That will come soon—in my next letter (after yours) or some other time.

I don't want to send another kiss to you and Aunt Asya after my New Year's embrace, which almost prostrated me, so real did it seem. It made my handwriting go soft and my hand shake.

Yours,
BORYA

[Inscription on the title page of the book *My Sister, Life*:]

To my dear cousin Olechka Freidenberg
from her most loving
Borya

June 16, 1922
Moscow

DIARY

Soon after Borya married Zhenya, they came to Petersburg to visit family. Zhenya was an artist, a most inspired creature. She loved us and we loved her.

Whenever Borya came to see us he displayed a strange affection for me, and this brought with it an atmosphere of great kinship, great festivity, great poetic feeling. This particular time he had just been married; he told us all about Zhenya and brought her to our house and was so very tender to her that he made her blush.

Taitsy, Baltic Railroad, Sunday
[probably July 25, 1924]

Olyushka, my dear cousin,

For God's sake don't be in a rush to call me a beast and a scoundrel, just listen. Last Wednesday I was in Petersburg between trains, and it goes without saying that I longed to see you. I could have managed it. I had three hours to wait, but I was not sure how you, and especially Aunt Asya, would receive me. If health, stability, and well-being breathe from these few words, then I simply don't know how to write. There is nothing of the kind. Never is, never was. You know very well that if I had come it would not have been to show off and amuse you. I do not admit the thought that either you or Aunt Asya ever miss me. It would only have been because of my feeling for you. To put it differently, in this great story reaching deep into the past, still going on, even though more slowly for the past ten years, in this grim, this unendurable story that is our lives, you represent the best, the most profound, and my favorite chapters. If I had come, we three would have talked and I would have lived anew with you and for you, as you know. But I was afraid that instead of this I would have found all those Monas and Yashas and Berlins with you, and the talk would have been trifling, unworthy of your rooms on the Canal.

Olga dear, is this what I deserve? In three hours I had no time to send a letter and then come—well, anyway I didn't do it. I just watched with dazed eyes as the city streets flew past the tram, streets of the city that in summer is for me Olga's city—Olga's and no other's.

Remember our coming back from Merrekühl thirteen years ago? Remember the sound of the station names: Vruda, Pudost, Tikopis? We haven't pronounced them since. We've only read them beside the dates at the bottom of Severyanin's poems.* You were telling me about him then,

* Igor Severyanin (pseudonym of Igor Vasilevich Lotarev; 1887–1941): Russian futurist poet.

in a cab, as I recall, on the way from the station. Remember? Remember everything? How Uncle Misha met you? How I loved him that evening! Remember, Olya? I turn my head to one side to gaze into those awesome distances. It's as if a recent gust of wind had swept it all away. Run after it and pick it up!

Just see how extraordinary it all is, how marvelous, if joyless. I am writing you from Taitsy, the station next to Pudost. You are from Petersburg so you find nothing amazing or exciting in the language of the Baltic Railroad. These bewitching Finnic names are newly impressed on your mind, directly or indirectly, summer after summer. But fancy the effect they have on me!

This, then, is how it happened. By spring Zhenya was worn out and exhausted to the last degree. You should know that we have a baby, a boy, also called Zhenya, little Zhenya. Well, big Zhenya is anemic, nursing him all this time; her nerves are worn to a frazzle, and all winter we have been hard up. So she has gone to her mother, where there are also problems, sickness, difficulties. Two rooms on the second floor were rented for her in Taitsy.

I stayed in Moscow to earn money by writing *The Iliad, The Divine Comedy,* or *War and Peace,* so as to put us on our feet for a long time to come. Needless to say I couldn't even rise to the level of Averchenko* in the state I was in, that is, I could do nothing at all. I managed, however, to fall ill with a silly case of tonsillitis that affected my heart. I missed Zhenya terribly but I couldn't get together enough money to pay the several months' rent that was owing, settle some other debts, and join the family. Now at last here I am with them in Taitsy, and this is the explanation of my three-hour stay in Petersburg. My very first thought on arriving was to ask you to visit us, and I would have done this on my knees, meekly accepting all the bad names and insults you heaped upon me in the letter you sent to Berlin. Let me say in passing that I guess you are right: I probably am vile even though I am not aware of it, but you would know better. Yet in my relations with you and Aunt Asya there never has been any neglect or sense of guilt or anything of that sort, only impulsiveness, worry, concern, and devotion. But that's an aside. I intended coming to town yesterday, Saturday, but missed the train. I wanted to bring you here for Sunday. The thing is that on getting to Taitsy I saw that there would be no suitable place for you to stay (you will see this for yourself), that is, you would be crowded, uncomfortable, and get no rest. So Zhenya began looking for a room for you nearby and

* Arkady Timofeyevich Averchenko (1881–1925): Russian satirist.

now there is one in the offing; we will find out for certain in a day or two.

This letter has one aim. To remind you of me and of the fact that a dog does not write letters. It would be painful to begin with that when we met. I will be with you in the middle of the week (Wednesday, Thursday). I would come sooner but, as I have said, I'm afraid to see you until you get this letter.

The real reason why I didn't see you during my stopover is that I couldn't bear to see anyone at all until I had seen my own, so much did I long for them. Now we are together, and when I began this letter I had forgotten that circumstance.

Best love to you, Aunt Asya, and Sasha.

Yours,
BORYA

Taitsy, Monday
[probably August 2, 1924]

Dear Olyushka,

I have a sore throat and a slight temperature (99.3°). Another time I wouldn't pay any attention to it and would arrive at the appointed hour—the more so since it would give me great pleasure and satisfaction to overcome your stubbornness as to a publisher and as to visiting us—but I've had trouble with my tonsils all summer (three attacks that have affected my heart), so now I am ridiculously cautious. Aunt Asya's words about Monday being a bad day have found unexpected application. I will come to town on the next receiving day at the offices of *The Contemporary,** which is Friday, at three o'clock; at least that is my intention today. Don't be angry with me if you have lost two or three hours on my account, and for God's sake don't punish me for the activities of bacteria that are beyond my control. Here in any case is our address: Taitsy, Baltic Railroad, 3 Evgenevsky Lane, Karnovsky Dacha. If you can come before Friday we shall be delighted.

You aren't enough for Zhenya; she wants Aunt Asya, too, and sends both of you her fondest love. Tram 2 goes directly from your house to the station. The stop is on the corner of Sadovaya and Gorokhovaya, as you told me. Here is the plan I had for today. If I had been able to talk you into coming to see us tomorrow (Tuesday), you and I would have taken the nine o'clock train in the morning (city time). To keep me from

* *Russky sovremennik* (*The Russian Contemporary*): A literary journal published in Leningrad, edited by A. N. Tikhonov.

oversleeping and being late, I would have asked to spend the night at your place. Unfortunately the next train leaves after one o'clock (1:40), and that is too late—half the day is lost. Oh, Olya, what a pity I won't see you today! But if two hours ago I still hesitated and had some hope that perhaps I would go after all, now there can be no thought of it; my fever is rising. So, if God grant, until Friday.

Love to you and Aunt Asya, regards to Sasha and his wife.

Yours,

BORYA

DIARY

When I had finished the university and was no longer a student, I lost my "social status," without which it is impossible to live under socialism. I rushed about in search of a publisher for my work. To whom could I appeal?

Marr was not interested in human beings. He lived exclusively in the realm of theory and saw humans only in relation to his theory. He treated me very well, I saw him frequently, he read his works to me—but he couldn't have cared less about me as a human being.

In a frenzy I wrote to Borya, wrote with blood and tears. I implored him to help me. Lunacharsky, of the Commissariat of Education, and Pokrovsky, also of the Commissariat of Education (I don't remember who was what), both knew him well.

Moscow [probably late September 1924]

Dear Olyushka,

Don't think I have forgotten about your affairs. I began making inquiries the very first day, but so far I haven't found out anything that, in my opinion, is worth mentioning. I exhausted all the suggestions you gave me on the third day after my arrival. The Chairman of the Central Commission for the Improvement of the Welfare of Scholars* is not Pokrovsky but Lavrov, a person unknown to me and completely useless to you since, judging by where and on what business he receives petitioners, he is entirely incompetent in scholarly matters, especially in narrow philological ones. I was told he receives in offices dealing with Moscow's municipal and nationalized property; in other words, he deals more with local

---

* Commission for the Improvement of the Welfare of Scholars (KUBU): a governmental agency charged to advance the interests of scholars in the new Soviet state. There was a Central Commission and a number of local Commissions.

squabbles over apartments than with your matter. But since I have undertaken not only to listen to you and follow your suggestions, I prefer not to write anything for the time being. If I have not yet wired you to come, it is because most of the necessary people are on vacation.

I was saying to Zhenya that it would be advisable for you to come now because in casual conversations people show great interest in you, and in general the sphere of my private friends and acquaintances merges gently but certainly with the sphere of those who wield authority and influence. Zhenya scolded me, saying that you and your mother should know you are both welcome here whenever, and for however long a time, you wish to come. That, however, is not the point; the point is, she says, that nothing but extreme necessity could make you leave Aunt Asya. If this is really so, I am very sorry. The prospect of having you here for two weeks, say, would transport me to seventh heaven and I would begin urging you to come this very minute.

By the way, there is an accepted form in which you can register your dissatisfaction with the Commission. You can protest its decision to disqualify. Applications to enter courses for the raising of qualifications are submitted to the local Commission (that is, the Leningrad Commission); you must attach references from two Commission members of at least Fourth Category in the given specialty. But I should like something quite different for you, and while I don't know just what, I am working along the lines agreed upon and hope to achieve something concrete that will bring you joy and be on a scale worthy of you. In a few days I will write and tell you about our journey home. Everything is fine. Best love to you and Aunt Asya.

Yours,

BORYA

Zhenya will be angry with me for sending this off in her absence and without her postscript. But this can hardly be called a letter, and I am writing in haste. We'll have a heart-to-heart talk in the next one. Be assured that every one of my days is partly devoted to your business.

DIARY

The year 1924 was, as everyone knows, the year of the flood. This, too, was a terrible experience. From early in the morning gun salvos announced the rising of the water. A terrifically strong wind howled and raged. The water rose in our canal from within, from the very depths. It gushed forth in waves and churned within the canal's narrow confines.

For some reason everybody ran for the bakeries, and I did, too. The water flooded the yards, flooded the streets. It soon became impossible to approach our house from the canal. With beating heart I managed to reach it just in time from Kazan Street (our yard has an entrance from that side, too). Mother was frantically searching for me in the yard. The canal was overflowing its banks. The city was gradually being converted into a water tank, the water appeared to be surging up from the bottom of the Neva. As we stood at the window we could see the lower stories of houses being submerged. Our horror was indescribable even though our own apartment was on the fourth floor. We thought the water would never stop rising. I imagined that the house would either collapse or be invaded, story by story, by the flood. Mother's concern was mostly about having neighbors billeted with us. I begged her to go to our neighbors upstairs on the fifth floor. It was important to be with people. Down below we could see unfortunates splashing through the water. Later some boats put in an appearance, but not many of them. It was dreadful to realize that people were helpless, that no government in the world could do anything at a time of such disaster.

Never shall I forget the next morning. The weather was heavenly, idyllic. Blue sky, sun, no wind. Nature was calm and blissful. I walked along the street feeling quite limp from my experiences. The harmony now displayed by nature's cruel elements shattered me no less than did their unbridled ferocity. I could not forgive them the torment they had caused. The sidewalks were torn up, the streets were all atremble. Of what violence and treachery that sadistic sky seemed capable.

Moscow, September 28, 1924

Dear Olya,

How strongly and expressively you write! I didn't have to be there—your words enabled me to see and suffer and be deeply moved. A strange coincidence: it happened exactly on the hundredth anniversary of the flood on which *The Bronze Horseman** is based. And this in its turn coincides with the hundredth anniversary of the poet's exile to Mikhailovskoye.

Here we are having an Indian summer as hot and close as a real summer. And through the dust, flying papers, and gray boulevards, I made my way once more to those hot, dirty and frustrating Commis-

* A narrative poem (written in 1833, published in 1841) by Alexander Pushkin (1799–1837), in which the bronze equestrian statue of Peter the Great comes to life during a flood in St. Petersburg. The Neva River overflowed its banks in 1824.

sariats—and you were right: Pokrovsky is the head of the Committee of Experts. But you are very mistaken if you think it means anything for you. On what days does he receive? He never receives. Then on what pretext . . . ? I will tell you approximately, that is, with a permissible degree of approximation. Submit a petition to the local Commission. If it is the Leningrad Commission, all the better; it is highly competent and as authoritative as the Central Commission—all of them are provincial. But that's not what I wanted to say; you just listen, listen. Advise your friends to write to the Committee of Experts here if, as appears from what you say, this is an exceptional matter. Then, according to the degree to which it is exceptional, it may reach Mikhail Nikolayevich Pokrovsky. We shall take it up then.

Why am I writing this? So that you will not be so stubborn in your attitude toward this business, or rather toward one particular aspect of your plans and proposals. Also so that you will know once and for all that there is no fixed procedure waiting to serve you and containing in embryo the possibility of solving your problem. In my vague propositions, which will no doubt take weeks of time and necessitate your presence here, there is more experience, intuition, and knowledge of the situation than you think.

Couldn't you and Aunt Asya both come? Now why is that impossible or so difficult? You would have a room to yourselves. Once here, you and I could throw ourselves wholeheartedly into this business. Why, I might even burst in upon Pokrovsky. But there's no point in bursting in without you. When you are here we can achieve that and a great many other things.

Here we are trying to turn all Central Commission procedures upside down, whereas your coming is, speaking objectively, a much simpler thing, one that only requires a cause, a basis, a summons, and something to hook on to. I implore you to come *without* a summons. Come tomorrow, the day after. Assume the attitude that you are coming to live with us and make the acquaintance of a side of Moscow life that for your own good you ought to be acquainted with. Your opinion of an interview in person, of an unexpected visit, is the correct one. Once you are here, you alone or you and I together can decide whom we ought to call on and when and why; in other words, we would not have to feel our way—everything would be ready. I might even lie to you with the straightest of faces: Pokrovsky, it seems, receives on Wednesdays from two to three. Then on Wednesday morning, at 14 Volkhonka, Apartment 9 (entrance from the yard, Tram 34), the lie would be detected. On Friday evening we would call on Lunacharsky, or perhaps we would not call on

Lunacharsky because before Friday we would have seen somebody else, and this somebody else would have had a brilliant idea, and this somebody else would be a Communist no less, very learned, very informed, and so on and so forth. This scheme presents itself to me naturally, inasmuch as you have forbidden me to recommend or ask favors in the hope of easing a person's lot in some small way, insisting that the matter is its own recommendation and the recommendation of the person concerned and therefore nothing else should be said. At first that was the view you took. Remember your saying what would follow on the heels of September 15? Then everything changed.

By the way, are there any new developments with your dissertation? Tell me, write me the answer in case you don't come and tell me in person. Has Marr come back? When do you expect to defend your dissertation? Or is everything just as it was when we parted? If Pokrovsky is one of Joan of Arc's visions, then of course we can trust him. Such ideas often capture my fancy and I owe much to the force of them. How strange that you have not come yet! And that we should be carrying on this ridiculous correspondence! You must be sure to take a leave of absence of not less than a week. Why don't you convince Aunt Asya? O you of little faith! That we should have forgotten you?! Well, then: Great Konyushennaya Street, second or third house on the left coming up from Nevsky Prospect, municipal office of the October Railroad, second floor, window 21, I believe—get a third-class ticket for a berth on the Moscow *express*. Once you are in Moscow, the stop for Tram 34 is a little to the left of the station exit, across the street from Yaroslavsky Station, which is next to the Nikolayevsky.

Contrary to your expectations, and particularly to Aunt Asya's, we have moved into a new apartment, which is the very quintessence of order, cleanliness, peace and quiet, and this thanks to our neighbors, who don't even wear beards or smell bad, and at a time when the pure swinishness of our species is unadulterated and its character unchanged. To my sinful and still slightly swinish eye, our new apartment is the Lyceum, the Stoa Poikile, a propylaeum as compared with the apartment on Yamskaya Street.

Here a surprise awaited me in a chance and unexpected form, its impact sharpened by contrast with what had gone before. When, my pocket swelling with what was left over from the selling of a medal, plus a contract signed with a Leningrad publishing house for a new book of prose for which I had to write another story (and then all the old ones would be republished), a story I will not write because I have lost all understanding of what it means to write—when, I say, with these comforting things and sensations swelling out my left side, I hopped onto a cart together with ten pieces of baggage and surveyed a Moscow that looked as if the wind had blown it out of a flour sack straight into a fearfully hot September, a gray-white Moscow, with flies and sweat oozing out of it like glycerine drops, I couldn't fathom why I was here and what it all signified. By nightfall the mealy character of the mirage became a mousy one; I succumbed to my exhaustion and had the sensation of headiness and holiness that follows a sleepless night. With all this "languor in my bones," as Tyutchev* put it, it was only natural that I should have been aware of something gone seriously wrong when I met friends and acquaintances who displayed a lot of that "young blood" stuff: some had cooled toward me, others had become openly hostile. (You know the feeling, when it suddenly seems to you that the chapter you had just begun is not only finished but has been read without you, in your absence, and you must begin another—you must, but will it come off?) Well, that was my mood that first evening. It filled me with fear of Sasha's numismatics.† One's downfall in the realm where coins are king can be artfully contrived, and none will understand and sympathize as will one's purse, it being the chief victim. Need I add that my mind naturally turned to reflections on the interdependence of spirit and substance? On how my *moral* state was transformed into practical reality for the sake of two innocent Zhenyas? A nasty and inevitable metamorphosis.

The next morning I learned by telephone that a piece I had forgotten about long ago, the translation of a ten-story, fifty-gallon, hundred-horsepower play, big enough to contain both the houses on Troitskaya Street, a comedy by Ben Jonson, *The Alchemist* (171 pages on my Remington), was accepted for publication by the Ukrainian State Publishers (in Kharkov). My numismatic centers began vibrating again. I set out *sur le champ* for the publishers' representative. The moment I got off the tram my hands flew up to my head. From a billboard *The Alchemist* glared straight at me in two-foot letters. It jeered at me again from the fences. I went up to the bill, swallowing down the disappointment arising from the conviction that someone, somewhere, was staging the comedy I was hurrying to that office three houses away to sign a contract for, and was staging it, of course, as is usually the case, as *must be* the case, in *somebody else's* translation. But oh, how refreshed, how revitalized, did the aforementioned centers become when next to the stage director's name I read my own! How extraordinary that these two things were in no way

---

* Fedor Ivanovich Tyutchev (1803–1873): Russian poet.
† Olga's brother was a zealous collector of coins.

related, that there was no connection between the staging and the publishing of the play, that indeed the one did not know of the other. I am prepared to argue that this coincidence, this absurdity, was engendered during the night by my deep depression, and it was a great mistake for me to take comfort in the billboard. If my depression had not been dispersed on the spot, I swear that the blackness of my mood would have conjured up the name again and again until, in my frenzied effort to exhaust the forms of possible application, the Alchemist would that very day have become a name clapped onto a drink, a smoke, an automobile tire, a film, a postage stamp, a tariff stamp, or would have become a catchword for politicians. Ah, but I was too hasty in taking comfort.

When, for many personal reasons, in connection with inquiries on your behalf, my late sulphurous mood returned with remarkable ease at the dress rehearsal, I found the play sterile and fruitless. I knew now that my Alchemist would fail not only as a name for cigarettes or soft drinks but even as a play; its life in the repertory would be short, its appearances few. It is shockingly dull and foolish on the stage, even though the director turned it into a farce and the actors performed it as one, and not badly. I suppose the fault lies with poor Ben. My translation is good. To the best of my knowledge the director did all he could, too. But the thing is not for the stage. It is the sort of pre-Molière comedy in which all the action boils down to a logical exposition of characters and situations. In that respect it has a certain strength, especially when read.

But I seem to have forgotten I am writing a letter. At this rate I may find myself beginning my introduction to the published play with the words "Dear Aunt Asya and Olya! Does Julius come to see you often? Ben Jonson—contemporary, friend, and literary antithesis of Shakespeare, etc."

Do come to Moscow, Olya; that is all I can say. Come, and I think we will not regret it. I think we will get our meeting with Pokrovsky, especially since you are so sure this is the right way and that you will be able to "stand up" to him. At any rate I will not give up your cause. I will write you again unless you already have a train ticket in your pocket. You in turn must let me know how matters stand with your dissertation, and don't be annoyed if you find my letter lacking in verve and vigor. I am writing at the end of a maddening day. I am tired, and in general I don't know how to write.

Dear Aunt Asya! Thank you for those blessed words. All of us embrace you both and love you dearly.

Yours,
BORYA

DIARY

On my last visit with Borya I begged him to help me, at least with my translation of Frazer.* He took me to Tikhonov, who at that time held some sort of high post. But he introduced me in such a way that Tikhonov paid me not the slightest attention. At the time Borya was in an unproductive period, whining and complaining, with no interest in me or anything else under the sun. A little later I wrote to him: "This business of Tikhonov is all nonsense. I went to see him about Frazer. He was not there; his secretary said that the answer from Moscow read: Nothing can be said yet about 'The Scapegoat'† because it must first be seen how I translate 'something golden.' (As if I applied to translate the entire book.) Try as I would, I could get nothing lucid out of her. The 'something golden' was *The Golden Bough*, but all of Frazer's work is included under that general title, each section with a subtitle. I have not applied elsewhere (except for the application Tikhonov told me to file). Have I been entrusted with the translation of the first book? What am I expected to do? She couldn't explain it to me and I cannot reach Tikhonov. How do you think I ought to proceed?"

Moscow, October 6, 1924

Dear Olyushka,

Why don't you come? Every morning at about eleven we expect to hear a knock at the door—we will open it and you will step in. Your appointment with Lunacharsky is guaranteed, and a person very close to Lunacharsky doesn't advise your seeing Pokrovsky. In addition, I found out that your friend Christy is a great friend of Lunacharsky. At any rate, he will give you a letter for either one of them. So don't put off coming. Zhenya scolds me for your not being here, as if it were my fault. It would be a good idea if you brought a letter of recommendation (or of introduction) from Academician Marr. Now don't get your back up, just listen. The fact is I know these people and I know how *accustomed* they are to miracles on a global scale. That's all they've been dealing with these seven years; that's why they accept the extraordinary as just another classification. They believe and disbelieve you. It seems to you the mere fact of this being a candidate's dissertation‡ is sufficient to make them draw the desired conclusion. They may, however, not wish to draw this conclusion

---

* Sir James George Frazer (1854–1941): eminent Scottish anthropologist.

† Volumes X and XI (1920) of Frazer's *Golden Bough*.

‡ Soviet postbaccalaureate degrees are the "candidate's" degree and the "doctoral" degree, the latter a prestigious degree more significant than the American Ph.D.

on their own, and therefore it might save energy if they were led to draw the conclusion that your work is extraordinary under the pressure of someone else's competent appraisal or, in any case, if the stimulus for the conclusion did not originate with us; we would thereby save our strength to meet all the practical problems that are sure to follow. In addition, you must bring your work with you. After all, it has got to be published. Quite possibly that question will be raised here. The demand for it is obvious and needs no explanation.

Have you got a copy of Frazer's *Golden Bough*? If you have, bring it, too, and your separate copy of "The Scapegoat." I will not write to you about the state publishers or the Commission because I hope you will soon be here, the only thing that could delay you being the defense of your dissertation. Don't be angry with me for not writing sooner; I won't tell you the causes. When you get here you will see for yourself how I live and how my days are spent. Love, and may we meet soon.

Yours,
BORYA

Dear Aunt Asya,

Why don't you make Olya come to Moscow? Unless some happy turn in her academic career is keeping her there, she ought to have left long ago. Before she leaves, consider soberly and objectively just what it is she wants to achieve above all else; then logic, intuition, and life experience will tell you how badly she needs to come. If she comes without her work or without testimonials to her work, she will only cheapen and discredit herself. But I know if I try to talk sense to you I will only be thought unfeeling and disloyal. Well, God be your judge. Thank goodness Olya has only to come here whenever and with whatever she wishes.

And so we are awaiting her. Her room has long been ready. I tenderly embrace both of you.

Yours,
BORYA

Much love to you, Aunt Asya. Olya, come as quickly as possible.

ZHENYA

Moscow, October 11, 1924

Dear Olechka,

What's the meaning of this? Are you and Aunt Asya well? Please answer at once.

Olga Freidenberg

A postcard from Olga Freidenberg. September 15, 1917

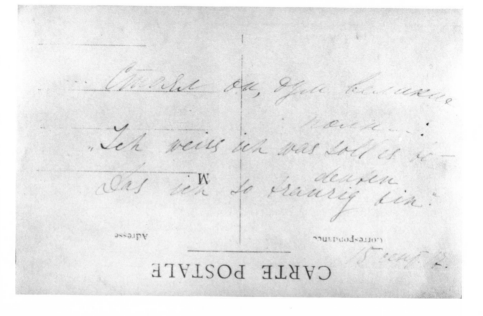

The Pasternak family in Moscow before departing for Berlin in 1921:
Leonid Pasternak, Berta Kaufman, and Rosa, Alexander, Boris, and
Lydia Pasternak

Boris Pasternak. Moscow

Evgenya Vladimirovna (Zhenya)
Pasternak. Moscow, 1922

Boris Pasternak, Evgenya Pasternak, and young Zhenya. Leningrad, 1924
Photograph by Nappelbaum

Young Zhenya
with his nanny Fenya

Rosa, Lydia, Josephine, and Leonid Pasternak. Berlin

[Moscow] October 13, 1924

I really didn't know what else to write, and that ought to have made me send a wire, or at least (and first of all) a money order. Very soon and very well did I understand how vile it was of me to keep sending you letters full of demands, whereas my rightful place in this correspondence about your coming was at the post-office window. But as fate would have it, I have so far been unable to take my place at that window. Today your letter came which, despite its lofty message and numerous surprises, did not surprise me. I concluded from it that in a week or so we will see you—that's the implication of the postscript. In the intervening week or ten days, the horizon here may clear up. I don't wish to add anything else now; I only wish you complete and well-earned success. It is imperative that you come to Moscow, and judging by your closing remarks the day is not far off. The sole purpose of this note is to tell you that in every way and on all points your letter struck home. In a very short time I may possibly communicate something more [page torn] and encouraging. You yourself have no idea what a happy coincidence it is that you wrote that letter and in just that way. It is a document distinguished for its exhaustive clarity and conclusiveness. Its full significance will yet be revealed somewhere or somehow. Well then, till we meet again, or till my forthcoming report (in a letter), which will be all business and no sentimental verbiage.

Humble as are our lives and labors, we have no cause for complaint. We are well and getting on nicely, although the specter of all kinds of possible illnesses hovers above us, all too close to our boy. We've had bad luck with the room I have surrendered to the younger generation. For some days our neighbor's housemaid lay there ill with typhoid fever. She was succeeded by three students, one of whom looked like a deep-sea diver, with his head swathed in towels and his face hidden by bandages because eczema covered his whole body. That room, now furnished with cots and perfumed with a mixture of body odors, cheap tobacco, and carbolic acid, has to be passed through to get to the kitchen, to running water, etc., and it is next to our boy's room. Yesterday, while making inquiries on behalf of a fellow innocently sent into exile, I found myself in a Kremlin apartment where there was diphtheria. Ah well, God in His mercy lets some people slip past, as they used to say in the old days.

Our son has grown quite hoarse from calling out "Auntie Olie" every hour in every key. Strangely enough he has formed a close association between (1) Aunt Asya's photograph on the wall, (2) an apple, and (3) the word "toodle-doodle." He has grown enormously.

Best love to you and Aunt Asya.

Yours,

BORYA

Moscow, November 2, 1924

Dear Olechka,

What's new and how are you getting on? The latter question worries me. How goes your dissertation? But I'm not supposed to speak of this, it seems, until your abstract* comes out. Well, it's not in obedience to you that I've been silent all this while. I wouldn't have broken my silence now but for my concern about you and my desire to know how things are going with you. If I had written, it would have had to be about myself, and that is the last thing I want to discuss at present. Again my life is not what I intended it should be. And it all began so well. I have found work; I won't call it a job only because it's piecework and I am not on the regular payroll. In every other respect, though, it is an honest-to-goodness job. In its own way it is even pleasant. The project is to compile a bibliography of Lenin, and I have undertaken the foreign part. And so I go to the Library of the People's Commissariat of Foreign Affairs, where they get most of the foreign journals, and I dive in and greedily drink up articles, reviews, and publications from ten to four. I don't find much of the stuff demanded of me, but in looking for it I read all sorts of fascinating things, in relation to which "the contemporary West," with its Proust and Satie, is but a reflection in a tiny drop of water. This is how it was until about a month ago, when I compared the demands of life and my personal aspirations with the size of my income, the amount of my leisure, the debts I'd accumulated, and the two contracts that were to bring me money from Kharkov and Leningrad, and I took great comfort in the possibilities and probabilities the comparison presented. I instantly opened *Hamlet* and set about translating it, a task I had been putting off for years. I do not wish to speak of my plans for original work; one's mind is always filled with the vague consciousness of them.

This in no way resembled the dark and passive vacillations of untested potential. On the contrary, as once before, long ago, the translation presented itself as the concrete daily task, as the prospect of constant and

---

* Before a dissertation is defended in the Soviet Union, academic circles throughout the country must be apprised of the contents through an abstract.

regular achievement built up night after night. And then, before Horatio had had time to doubt the reality of the ghost, there came, first from Kharkov and then from Leningrad, cancellations of my contracts, one of which (for *The Alchemist*) was at the signing stage, the other of which (for a collection of stories) had already been signed by myself and the publishers when I visited you; I had but to send in one more story and collect my money. You can well imagine how completely I had counted on this income. What could be more reliable than a confirmed contract?— at least so it seemed until now. Altogether my annual income was cut down to almost nothing. You will have no trouble in guessing that from that day my appearance changed and I began coming home from the library at 9 P.M.; luckily for me the librarians work in shifts so that the reading room is open from 10 A.M. to 8 P.M. It would be a godsend if piecework were calculated on a purely mathematical basis, but I am afraid there exists an absolute ceiling beyond which nothing is counted. I am also afraid that this critical ceiling coincides with the sum suggested to me in advance. I don't believe I shall be able to earn more than 120 rubles a month even if I turn out twice as much work. Since I am incapable of thinking of anything but the treachery of fate when I am at home after 5 P.M., I prefer to kill time reading weeklies, quarterlies, annuals, etc. This, then, is how my affairs stand, and when I come home both Zhenyas are going to bed. Of course I shall do everything in my power to change things and improve my circumstances. I shall have to do this, like it or not, because the bibliography will not even cover my debt to Fenya (Zhenya's nanny)—I owe her 120 rubles, not counting her salary.

Let me put an end to this subject by adding that I have no cause for complaint. I myself am to blame for everything; I ought to have gone to work last winter. And let me also say that, despite all of the aforesaid, I hardly remember a time when I was in finer fettle morally. Having thus answered and disposed of your inquiring glances, let me end as I began. Write me about yourself and your work. Everything that has been said about your coming and all the rest remains in force and has even gained force. What I have told you has nothing at all to do with the plans we made in autumn. The gloomier I am, the more probable it is that your coming will dispel my gloom. The more reasons I have to be indignant at the arbitrariness of publishing houses, the more indignantly I hurl myself into discussions about you and for you. And so farewell for the nonce, as they used to say. Best love to you and Aunt Asya.

DIARY

I defended my dissertation on November 14, 1924. The august event took place on a cold St. Petersburg day in the council hall of the university, which at that time was on the third floor of the main building.

The hall was filled with people I didn't know. It was the first time I had taken part in an academic meeting. Never before had I been present at a gathering of scholars. Never before had I addressed an audience. Never before had I heard the debate following a report.

I preserved outward tranquillity, that lofty sort of tranquillity bought at the price of great agitation.

At the long formal table sat the council members, all the old professors —distant, frightening, unfathomable. They asked me to take a seat in front of them with my back to the audience, facing the presidium and my opponents. It was cold. Everyone wore coats.

Marr, looking very glum, sat in the middle. Next to him sat Ilinsky, the academic secretary, who read out the documents. I said a few words on a purely theoretical topic.

Then the debate began. Zhebelev spoke first—cool, dignified, matter-of-fact. He began by professing ignorance so as to avoid all responsibility. I exposed him, my teacher, rather brusquely. The hall tensed like a balloon about to burst. The second to speak was Tolstoy. He rejected everything, criticized everything I had written.

Tolstoy's objections roused Marr to keen attention. He suddenly came alive, began to breathe, participated with every heartbeat in what was going on. He snickered, winked at me, addressed snide remarks to Tolstoy.

Next Malein began tearing me apart. Viciously and spitefully he accused me of making serious errors. I insisted that he, like Tolstoy, took new principles for errors. By this time the hall was thoroughly electrified.

My official opponents finished. Now the public gave rein to its passions. For several hours the unequal battle raged. When Frank-Kamenetsky took the floor I was terrified. I had not feared the others; he was the only one I feared.

He said, "If I had read this ten years ago all my research would have followed a different path." He spoke intelligently, lucidly, in a scholarly way, wholly supporting me. Marr was a pleased and eager listener, in complete agreement with him.

Suddenly I was aware that here was a friend, that all this high praise was for—me. As a blush creeps over the face, so a hot wave of happiness engulfed my heart. I realized that I had won the battle in a very big and genuine way. Nothing else mattered.

Marr closed the discussion abruptly. He got up and read the resolution he himself had written. In strong terms it said: ". . . considering the completely new and progressive"—I don't remember what, but considering something extraordinarily good—"the academic council had decided to grant . . ."

Before I had recovered my wits, Marr, who had read the resolution standing, usurping the functions of the academic secretary, nodded to right and left, murmured "no objections," and in the twinkling of an eye adjourned the meeting. No one had time to realize what had happened.

[Leonid Pasternak to Boris Pasternak]

[Berlin, October 1924]

Since I wanted to give Aunt Asya something, send her 100 rubles for the present (it is hard for me to send more just now, and besides it would shock her). The best thing would be if it came not from me—if you could say it was from you, that you had been paid for some back work or something of that sort. She will find it hard to accept anything from me, so resort to subterfuge.

[Written on the receipt for a 100-ruble money order]

Moscow [November 19, 1924]

Dear Aunt Asya,

In a subsequent letter I will explain in greater detail how Papa asked me to hide the real source of this money from you, fearing that you would offend him by not accepting it. My intuition told me not to listen to him in this instance. A month or so ago he asked me to sell one of his paintings and we have only just done so. The amount received was divided up and used for various purposes. He asked us to send 100 rubles to you. How are things with you and Olya? I will write soon. Love.

Yours,

BORYA

Moscow, November 20, 1924

Dear Olya,

Thanks for answering so promptly. I read your letter in great excitement. You're a gem for accepting vicissitudes in just the right way. My own experience makes it easy for me to understand how kindly you must feel toward Marr and Frank-Kamenetsky. But what you must have gone through that day! When I mentally compare you with myself I am happy to discover in you a firmness and courageousness which I do not possess in that form and to that degree. If I had faith in you before, and if the picture you draw of the debate (a picture that is normal and understandable as those things go) supports that faith and confirms it, this faith has been greatly enhanced by the manner in which you conducted yourself at that shameful spectacle, as well as by the way in which you recall, judge, and describe the experience. There is something significant and full of promise in your staunchness and enviable devotion to your life's purpose. In this way, and in most cases *only* in this way, are careers with a great future embarked upon; you know this better than I do for you have read more than I have.

Probably you will take a little rest now and make no new plans for a while. I should like to suggest that you spend this time with us, but if you prefer and find it more convenient to stay at home with Aunt Asya, adjusting your visit to us with new plans, so be it. I want awfully to see you; you know how happy it would make me. Zhenya, too.

As for me, I am rarely at home and then only for short stretches, and I feel miserable when, on Sundays, the merry-go-round stops. I love my fast, mechanized, machinelike day, a mélange of my job, of concerns and activities related to it, and of numerous tasks not related to it but connected with the family, with people, with the carrying out of all kinds of requests and missions. I take part in this mad race with enthusiasm, as if I were playing a game, or as if I were a character in a novel, a big fellow, laconic, absent-minded, forever rushing about, in and out of offices, on and off of trams. This is exactly what I meant when we were talking that time. By no means was it a "merging" I longed for; it was just this. I make 150 rubles a month, and if it were not for our debts it would cover three-fourths of our needs. I hope to be able to do some real work in the future. God grant that I am not mistaken in my hopes. Until then I must confess that my day is spent in continuous pleasure, for, let me repeat, I am entranced by the thick mesh of simple, rush-rush trifles that fill the hours. At any rate, this senseless fever is more like the former fever of the spirit that made of me a poet than the enforced idleness of the last two or three years following on my discovery that individualism is heresy and idealism is banned. But enough of this nonsense. Yesterday, at Papa's request, I sent you 100 rubles. He implored me so naïvely, so elaborately, and at such length to send it without revealing the source that it would be criminal on your part if you in any way justified his fears. Sweet, sweet Olya, do take it—that's a dear.

BORYA

You might write and say when you are thinking of visiting us. Much love to Aunt Asya.

DIARY

Oh, how distressed we were to receive those 100 rubles, allegedly from Uncle Leonid! In indignation we swore to send the money back. But we were in such dire straits that it crumbled in our fingers like silk that has rotted with age. I tried to prolong its life, but in vain. Ah, but to accept these alms, this sop, this payment for blasted hopes—no, never! With tears in my eyes I took the last thing we had to fall back upon, Mama's gold chain, and sold it. With what effort, with what a sense of loss did I return to Boris his despicable 100 rubles—the entire amount received for the lovely chain. Under what pressure of temptation, with what tragic regret! In a word, Borya had only increased our woe.

Leningrad, November 27, 1924

Dear Zhenya,

I am writing to you and not Borya because the time has come that we spoke of last summer, and I need *your dependable word* and not his shilly-shally one.

The time has come, I say. The reviews, the debate, the test of strength, the tasting of wine from a poisoned cup—all this is behind me. All is over, all is endured. The time has come to act. And I need your "sacred" confirmation of the summer's pledge, so that I may know whether I am alone or you are with me.

Since that time—you are my witness—not only have I not asked Borya for anything, but I have stopped him and discouraged him. Have I succeeded in quelling his spirits? I doubt it. Here is my whole story of this time. I asked him for information on how to reach Pokrovsky, putting off all the rest till the present, is that not so? Yes, but that is not Borya's story. His is quite different. Borya, despite me, of his own free will, set about doing things and reporting them in empty words. Doing what? And to what end? I don't know and I'm sure you don't. He adopted a mysterious tone, with reservations and great promises. He wrote that he devoted a part of every day to my affairs (I certainly never asked him to) and that he was making ready some great thing that he would presently reveal to me. His letters were like theater bills announcing a coming performance. He gave us reason to await them (and how we waited!), he fanned our growing hopes, he hinted at promises. Zhenya, I know you well enough to be sure you will not misunderstand me. How spiritually unchaste any mere promise is, how flabby the emotion by which it is evoked, how sickening to the strong feminine nature, which knows the passion of ceaseless *action*! Oh well, so he went on promising. And how did it end? In silence. Up to then—tirades as to my letter being an indispensable human document received at a moment designated by fate itself, something great and joyous, and of his "responsible business letter" that was to follow. Then silence. I waited. At last, a quiet apotheosis signifying— nothing.

Who needed this? Did he? Did I? Do you or Mama? How much purer and more meaningful it would have been to preserve a period of waiting with no waste of words. Let me repeat that I demanded nothing of Borya at the time and expected nothing of him. *He himself* insisted on my following him with sharpened attention, *he* made of himself an object of experiment, and I swear to you that neither I nor my love for Borya can be blamed if he assumed, more and more definitely and undeniably, the likeness of Khlestakov.*

Mama took it differently. She always spoiled Borya. And that money! To think of trying to compensate for unfulfilled, torn-to-shreds promises with alms from a relative! How unspeakably tactless! If only you knew what bitterness, what burning pain that 100 rubles has cost us! How Mama wept! How indignant she was! I felt that something fatal had happened. Why this piling up of nothing but woe?

But again one lifts one's head, again one begins to accept life, and this over and over.

After all, when you see life as something heroic, when you ceaselessly defend yourself from its grotesqueness, when you look it straight in the eye, aware of your privations and of your unrelenting obstinacy, oh, how vile and criminal it then seems to have someone let you down! Doesn't Borya understand that my life is already a biography? That its suffering so far exceeds that of the ordinary person as to have acquired artistic value? Tell him my life has become part of an epic, and so to feed me on *promises* is to show the lack of all feeling for literature.

That is why I am writing you rather than him. The time has come for me to act, a time made ready by my labors and brought to highest maturity in the despair of my failures. Oh, do tell me: am I to expect anything or not? If not, have the courage to say so—only for God's sake,

* The main character of Gogol's play *The Inspector General* (1836), a dashing but penniless youth who tries to improve his circumstances by letting the officials of a small town he is passing through think he is an inspector general sent from St. Petersburg. He is dined and feted until the fraud is exposed.

no more promises. I realized very soon that what *I* could not do, *Borya* could not do either. I couldn't find access to the Commission and Borya couldn't help me, I couldn't reach Pokrovsky and neither could he, and so on, and so on. I am done with it all, but I hold Borya to blame for not deflecting my hopes and allowing them to be dashed against the rock of his promises. I no longer put any faith in promises and mystification. My wishes have become limited and for that reason definite. In the first place, I want to publish my work, which the defense proved to be innovative and revolutionary in its scholarly approach; and then I want a position, however modest and ill-paying, that will save me from free-lancing and from leeches like Sasha. I simply cannot go on living a life so full of privations of all kinds, which go on and on and strike out at me from all sides. The Gordian knot consisting of Sasha, free-lancing, and absolute need must be cut.

These are my minimum demands of the U.S.S.R. But even now I have no intention of burdening Borya with requests; I will not pass on to him a single one of my worries. The only thing I ask of him is whether he can arrange for me to meet Lunacharsky or not. I take upon myself the interview, the exposition of the case, and all that. I want only one favor—admittedly an enormous one: his arranging a meeting for me.

I repeat that I am writing to you because your woman's intuition will enable you to grasp the seriousness of my tone and position. You will frankly and honestly answer yes or no.

It will be hard for me to find the money to come to Moscow, but the screws are turned so hard on me that I will have to find it somehow. If you dislike writing, make Borya do it. I will accept the answer as from you.

I will wait impatiently. If you find it possible to arrange this meeting (Borya is in no way responsible for the result), I will come the moment I receive a letter from you or Borya. I will bring with me that miserable money, or, in the event of my not coming, will send it.

I kiss you both.

Yours,
OLYA

Moscow, November 30, 1924

What's this, Olechka? Why have you pounced on Borya so? He begged you to come, couldn't do anything without you. Surely he wrote you of his willingness, of his interest, of his love for you—and that's the honest truth. He took certain measures. But he's like my Doodle, who toddles about the room not knowing where to stop or what to hang on to. Your coming would organize his movements and guide them.

But aside from that you ought to be ashamed of yourself, Olga, and your mother, too. Why should you be so ready to see such vileness in a person? Haven't you looked into Borya's eyes, heard his voice, discerned his concern for you? Why is it that, once knowing you, I could not possibly be offended by you? I would consider it blasphemy. It's the money I'm speaking of now. What connection is there between this money and his promises? I, too, received something from Leonid Osipovich for little Zhenya's needs. Am I to be offended for my own sake, or for Borya's? Am I to look upon the gift as alms? I wouldn't think of it, it isn't true.

Why didn't you throw me out of the house that time when, in the simplicity of my heart, I brought you some fresh eggs? It's exactly the same in this case and you have no right to offend. But forgive me, Olechka and Aunt Asya, and don't think I'm too ruffled. I know what you're going through, I love both of you dearly. I remember the time when you, Olya, came back from seeing a lung specialist and your mother sat there without a word, white as a sheet and full of anguish. Aunt Asya, it would be better if you simply came down on Borya now as you did then: "You're just lying, Borya!" Much love.

Yours,
ZHENYA

Olechka,

So far Lunacharsky has never refused to see Borya, and so he says that to ask him for an appointment might rouse his suspicions. Once you're here he is sure to see you. We are anxiously waiting for you. Before we got your letter saying you weren't coming as yet, there were days when, on leaving the house, Borya would give me orders: "Now if Olya comes, you . . ." Good-by.

Moscow [probably November 30, 1924]

Dear Olya,

Thank goodness. I've asked you to come in every letter, and now I'm very glad you yourself have included it in your immediate plans. The fact is that I take a different view of my letters than you do, and if in any of them I have given you advice about coming, take it. Of the items I remember: be sure to bring your work with you, in two copies if possible.

If you have no objections and it fits in with your plans, ask Marr's advice on what to seek and how, and get a letter from him to Lunacharsky. Only don't fret and despair. The defense of your dissertation was a real fact in real circumstances. Surely you cannot think you are left entirely to yourself in these real conditions. I find myself in an atmosphere charged through and through with sympathetic impulses, harmonious with my views, sentiments, and purposes. The only thing that was and remains in my power is to make you and your affairs independent of me and of what is happening to us. You will find out what this means when you get here. I have, by the way, needed Lunacharsky more than once but have re-frained from seeing him because I was saving him for you. Naturally I was deeply hurt by your letter. The injustice of it was so enormous that its source must have been purely subjective. All the more impatient am I to see you. Lunacharsky will receive us, I guarantee that. Best love to you and Aunt Asya. Happy journey!

Send us a wire and either Zhenya or I will meet you.

Yours,

BORYA

P.S. Olga dear, if it is at all possible, don't put off your trip; I, too, have urgent business with Lunacharsky. Be sure to be here this week. And stop torturing yourself. I embrace you.

B.

Leningrad, December 3, 1924

Dear Zhenya and Borya,

I thank you deeply and sincerely for answering me immediately, and I am doing the same so as not to delay Borya's visit to Lunacharsky.

I am not coming to Moscow. Please don't blame yourselves for this. Indeed I would come if I could afford to, for the sole purpose of embrac-ing both of you and Doodle and proving that I am at peace with you— and then leaving. If you must know, I am worn out by life; I haven't the strength at present to begin a new chapter by making this expedition. That you, Borya, should have advised me to get a letter from Marr perfectly reveals the nature of your patronage. In the first place, I shall never learn to regard a scholar as a source of influence, nor shall I ever bring pressure to bear on a scholar's kindly attitude toward me so as to turn it into cold cash. Never. In the second place, if Marr is so influential that his name must be joined to the treasure hunt, wouldn't it be simpler to concentrate on him alone? You are a queer duck, Borya! If I were capable of asking scholars for letters, how different my life would be! But such is the nature of things: those who take, give nothing; and those who give, take nothing.

Borya, it may seem to you (or already does seem) that I am inordinately conceited. I once spoke to you about modesty, what people call modesty. Now I have become convinced of what pride and conceit are: a feeling of concentration, what Nietzsche so brilliantly defined as "the pathos of distance." But this is seen by the crowd as pride and conceit.

I am so harsh and outspoken for fear you may suspect me of holding something back. I repeat: I have not the slightest feeling that you have offended me or failed me in any way, Borya. When you come right down to it, it was only your temperament that roused my ire, and that is something inherited, involuntary. Was it because your promises couldn't be realized that I was angry? God forbid! That would be crude, or at least inexact. I am too exacting and fed up (vulgarism intentional) to forgive a person I love only potential wrongs; as for other things, we are not talking about them. You are not contained, you are impulsive. One has no right to take offense at that; one can only rebel against it *an und für sich*—which is exactly what I did. Vulgarity must be kept out of our quarrel.

This, however, is not what has dictated my not coming to Moscow, and please don't read things between the lines or look for hidden meanings. The only reason is that the tram route doesn't coincide with mine; it would certainly be easier for me to walk. I am so worn out by life that perhaps I rebelled against you on the rebound. I should like to be a salesclerk in someone's private business, where the owner shoulders all the responsibility, should like to lock up my work in my desk and hide it from mythical publishers; the overdue train carrying my summer plans will not find me waiting. I am weary of compromises, of the charadelike quality of truth, understood by each in his own way, of the slipperiness of words, of cranial partitions and Tyutchev's "sympathy," which comes to us in the form of "benevolence."

The conflict turned out to be more complicated than the scriptwriters would have had it. It is a collision not only of two world outlooks, but much worse: a battle between two opposing camps fought on their own territory.

Hard as the life of man is, the life of the individual is even harder.

To add to everything else, I was overtaken in the street by a professor of Persian studies who kept me there for a whole hour, warming my heart, freezing my feet. As it was, I had a frightful cold—had it before and after (and during) the defense.

My enemies are already teaching the younger generation to hate my book. They roam the university and speak infamies. But the bad gradually evaporates, leaving the hard fact of a candidate's degree intact, so that in the end anyone who shakes my hand will remember my academic degree and nothing else. As for going into their psychology—what tragic consolation! The cards have been reshuffled in such a way that I have envious opponents among those who share my ideas, and sincere well-wishers among scholars of the traditional school. How painful and difficult it all is! Much more difficult than the defense, which went easily for me, like giving birth for the twelfth time. I am pulled in all directions, when all I want is to escape from everyone and everything. The breadth of my specialty also complicates matters. Instead of dozens, I will have hundreds of enemies. So far only the classicists have been vicious, but soon it will be the turn of the orientalists, those very ones who have pressed me to their bosoms. My tragedy also lies in my being as timid as a lamb despite the revolutionary trend of my scholarly thinking. I only want to be left alone. Even so I must admit that the hostility built up at the debate is subsiding, and more and more voices are being raised in my support. But that, too, has its other side: hostility cements scholarly trends better than flaccid good will. I am studying a lot, alone, with the exception of Georgian with Marr, who greatly inspires me. I am making good progress. Now I am finishing the groundwork for Sanskrit and ancient Hebrew and have already begun reading in them. Sanskrit is inconceivably difficult, a nightmare, almost a circus stunt. By Christmas I will begin Assyrian. With the help of the gods this winter I will finish laying the foundations for my next thesis, for which I have already worked out the theme and gathered the material.

I am living "in the beyond." I flee from the evils of this world to find resuscitation there. I come back joyful and refreshed, capable of accepting things easily and in big doses.

Which is what I wish for you. When I have made some money I will come and see you and talk to you in Babylonian. Meanwhile, you bring up Doodle and prepare him to become an academician. Best love to you.

Yours,
OLYA

Don't expect another letter from me soon.

Moscow [probably early December 1924]

Dear Olya,

What have you done! This is the sixth letter in reply to yours. Such talk is not for me—I can't go along with it, do what you will. Analyze, convince, prove? Humbug! Everything is clear as day; for more than three months we knew what was wanted, and suddenly it turns out it was not a matter of you and your work at all but simply that I was the object of a psychological experiment. Well, congratulations. Only you needn't have wasted so much energy on it. From the very outset I would have signed any attestation, yours or Aunt Asya's, as indeed I did do in the end. You cannot live without a rogues' gallery? Good. Now you have added me to it. How subtle this all is, and how like the truth! You have brilliant formulations for everything (such as that which accompanied the money). There were genuine feelings, genuine plans, you were as good as here, we expected you every day, I spoke of it in every letter, you yourself knew and felt that everything hung on your coming and bringing your work with you—but the visit was put off until after the defense. At last there was no longer an excuse and you ought to have either come or made honest confession to yourself and others. Instead you sought a new excuse for not taking the simplest and most essential step. Conveniently you found the excuse in me, in my shortcomings, as if the presence in Moscow of a faultless angel were a precondition to the proper functioning of the Nikolayevsky Railroad or the launching of a scholarly work of exceptional quality. If you were so anxious to become disenchanted with me you had only to come and see me.

It's just this that astonishes me most of all and drives me to distraction. What part do my personal qualities play when you yourself don't wish to do anything and this summer's conversation turns out to have been a crazy misunderstanding? This being the case, why was I taken in by it, and why didn't *you yourself*, Olya, stop Mama or explain to Zhenya that she was not informed in the matter and that you knew Borya could do *nothing* without you, without your tongue, your work, your demands. Olya, Olya, aren't you ashamed to play with the truth that way? This whole affair is known only to me (partly) and you (entirely). You can say anything you like to Zhenya's mother, Zhenya herself, and others; they make a good audience. Only I don't understand why you should want to. Very well, I'm a beast, a windbag, a braggart, a scoundrel, and you are, of course, just the opposite—I accept this without a word. But I imagined it was not of these easy victories and defeats we were talking—and not in the nursery, yours or mine—so why did you not make a timely announce-ment to me and others that negotiations were being transferred to the nursery? Well, listen: you ought to have come here with the alacrity with which you weave fancies. With faith, prepared to come in vain, as any vital person of your age would have done. Instead, our negotiations as to your coming dissolved and changed form like wax in a flame. It was as if you were driving a bargain with me or with fate. Ah, but the lady could not have acted otherwise! I, however, remember *demanding* it, *this very visit.* Since, in the given circumstances, your claims and demands were not formally documented (unfortunately and understandably, as with other people, as with me), we had to go about it in just this way, get things by chance, in passing, over a cup of tea, so to speak, by unpremeditated means.

If you don't want to understand this, what's the sense of explaining it? There's nothing to say. Close as I am to what is going on, I can be sure of only one thing: it was a *genuine* undertaking we conceived. You were to come to Moscow, the country's administrative center, where you would have lived with us, discussed your plans with us (if you wished to), and carried them out, where I could have aided you with my contacts (when I reach this point I don't know how to express myself; you are morbidly proud). It follows that (1) if I express myself vaguely, you see in this empty words, a halfhearted interest in your affairs, etc., and that (2) if I express myself definitely, you push me away and limit my field of action —I am only to find out the exact hours when Pokrovsky receives and you will burst in on him yourself. And burst in you will. As that intention has not yet been carried out, it is the only one that must be carried out. In this respect nothing has changed. *Only* in this light do I see your and Aunt Asya's role in this affair and am capable of thinking along with you in a matter so close to your heart. That is why I am not responding to your mischief: it is a region of mistakes, microbiotics, messy rooms, petty dramas, in a word, a region it is best to keep away from—formless, worthless, miserable, which, once touched, is like a spider's web that cannot be grasped or measured. So let's count everything except your trip here as out of bounds.

Forget it all, Olechka, just come. You and I will laugh at it and set out to see Lunacharsky in better spirits. Just remember that I will not go and see Lunacharsky without you. That's what a scoundrel I am. It would be perfect if you came for Christmas—the best time for everything, including business calls. It was very foolish to send that money, you ought to have used it for your fare; later, when you got an advance from publishers, you could have given it back. For a moment you dropped sharply in my estimation; I considered how I would have acted in your circumstances. One cannot build a career or blaze trails your way. I implore you to come, Olga. You'll get nowhere if a mere trip to Moscow is such an insuperable barrier.

I spoke to Marr and Oldenburg about you. I'll tell you what they said when you get here.

Ah, Aunt Asya, Aunt Asya, how can you see what's going on and not spring to my defense? Shove her off—she's just got to come, and that's that. Papa was right: I overestimated your openheartedness and generosity.

Leningrad [December 1924; not sent]

Two things are true in your letter: that it was not a matter of you but of me, that I lacked the courage to come "with faith . . . as any vital person" would have done. You are also right in saying "One cannot build a career . . . your way." I have already told you that I am touched by your concern over my affairs just because it is someone "not me" *taking my yoke upon him.*

My vital capacities have completely atrophied. At their expense my spiritual capacities have grown, like the liver in certain illnesses. You are also right when you say I myself didn't know what I was trying to accomplish. That Mama should not have to scrub the floors and wash our clothes, in the first place. But that, certainly, is not a demand I can make of Pokrovsky. I was ready for anything, even though I didn't know what. All the more marvelous that you did know. That in vague and tiresome phrases you wafted to me an aroma of hope. That from letter to letter you wove a promising *realizability*—just what I lacked. You took everything upon yourself, by which you, and not I, became the main character. Precisely for that reason—that I lack vitality—words are sacred to me and I swallow them foolishly, like manna from heaven. All the more disastrous is it to be fed empty words. In my lifeless state, words are all that is left to me, but each has a rich kernel. Yes, I have neither the faith nor the readiness to come to Moscow. But is it you who are demanding these things of me? What, if not faith, is the hallmark of lifeless creatures like me? Heavens, I'm like a provincial actress trying to draw on "inner feelings" when technique could handle my problems with practically no expenditure of energy. But when such an actress makes her debut in the capital, is it fair to accuse her of lack of feeling?

Remember the story of David and King Saul? It always upset me. Why should David be so good? Why should he have to be forever justifying himself before the spiteful Saul? Why should life take the very ground out from under my feet, then demand that I restore myself through faith? Have I no right to despise Sasha, to hate Zhebelev, who betrayed me at the defense, and all those other mean, self-satisfied, intriguing people wearing laurel wreaths? Why should I, whose aims and interests are wholly different, accept handouts from this niggardly life and pay them back in small percentages of faith? No, dear Borya, expect neither "faith" nor "readiness" from me. My soul is not that virgin. It has known despair, and that is the same as having been touched by death.

Yes, I have lost my vital capacities. I don't even want to have my work published. That station on my life's road has been reached and passed. Who needs it? What for? Proofs don't prove, facts don't convince, everyone speaks the truth in the language of his own mind. My book is premature. No one will understand it, as they still don't understand the Gospels —that's easy, the magazine *The Atheist* takes care of that. No one will accept my scholarly ideas just as no one in Europe accepts Marr. "How many years have you been fighting for your theory?" I asked him. He replied: "Thirty years. Even though I have a candidate's and a doctor's degree, the faculty will not allow me to teach or even mention Japhetism." And I thought to myself: "Thirty years gone, and the truth of his theory obvious, and he a born fighter, fighting every day in his own defense, and now so old—who has accepted him? Who has understood? Perhaps four people, counting myself."

Mama represents the limit of my capability, of the interests and relationships linking me to ordinary life. My work takes everything out of me, with nothing left over. What will become of us in a month? I don't know and don't think about it. My will is all concentrated on my scholarly ideas, on the second half of my work and a general introduction, and on a separate cycle that is complete in itself and can go on living without me. That is the only reason I go on pulling this cart and don't come to a final halt. My life's work is unfinished and demands all of my effort.

Did I complain to Zhenya and her mother about you? In family discussions it was not so much me as Mama who railed against you. That's all a part of life's program: we have to abuse one another, fail in each other's eyes, carry on a correspondence unworthy of us. Then it will all be erased by time, and the only thing to remain from the moment of our kindred birth will be what we started out with, plus a few small books on various themes and in various forms.

I do not hold any claims against you.

[Leonid Pasternak to Boris Pasternak]

[Berlin, early December 1924]
I must share with you a prodigious dose of abuse (which you, too, Borya, probably received from Olyushka). And in what a form! No doubt you fulfilled my request awkwardly. Ah, the proud, priestly scions of

Abarbanel!* I am not disturbed by it, pay no attention to it, and am happy to have such a fine letter from her, abusive but with the pleasing news of a brilliantly defended dissertation and the receipt of an academic degree. I wrote her the nicest, warmest letter possible, and hope—am indeed sure—it will pacify her. So don't be spiteful or take offense; just the opposite, be good to her and aid the publication of her writings. Don't enter into explanations. Let things be as they are. An exceptional breed of people (so unmodern!).

DIARY

In February 1925, Uncle Leonid sent me a marvelous letter from Berlin, epoch-making for me. It was in answer to a long description of my life for the last six years, provoked by those notorious 100 rubles from Borya; it was proof to Uncle of my spirit and my scholarship. It showed him why the money was intolerable. It arrived when my hopes were at their lowest, and I had to explain everything to him.

His letter was remarkable for its directness, lovingness, and nobleness, qualities conspicuous for their absence in Borya's letters. "Many thanks, my dear, for your letter and for the first opportunity to see you at your full height, so imposing, so beautiful and dignified; to see you, even a small part of you, in the portentous circumstances of these terrible years, unbroken either by carrying the burden of Sasha or wearing the constant chain of the most trying adversities. . . ."

In March I wrote Borya with pride of this letter, full of such faith in life, and added: "My own life has changed somewhat. I haven't been to the pawnshop for two months, having already sold my books and some other things. I am not working on the second part of my book but rather on the introduction, an analysis of the theory of plot structure. Love of research and critical analysis has gained strength in me recently. I now recognize a series of mistakes I made owing to undue enthusiasm and the belief that A equals A in all cases. I have become calm and more settled, and also more concentrated. I am studying physics, algebra, and philosophy, particularly Spinoza. I am continuing my language studies at the university, working on them there rather than at home. My wishes are meager, but irradiated with the hope of being published abroad. All I ask of Mother Russia is something legal plus something edible—a minimum of each. Without a legal document one does not even have the right to residency."

* Isaac Abravanel (1437–1508), the Jewish philosopher.

CHAPTER IV

IN THE LATE 1920's and early 1930's Pasternak stood out among his Soviet contemporaries. From abroad came word that Prince Sviatopolk-Mirsky, author of the standard *History of Russian Literature*, had singled out Pasternak in his 1927 survey of Soviet literature. At home he gained new stature from the publication and republication of his poetry and prose and from frequent poetry readings, such as the evening of poetry organized in Leningrad in October 1932 by Pavel Ilych Lavut (1891–1967), the Russian painter and illustrator. An enthusiastic audience greeted *Spektorsky* and *The Tale* (1928–1930), which attempted to summarize the past decade in poetry and prose; the reworked early verse from *A Twin in the Clouds* (1914, 1929) and *Above the Barriers* (1917, 1929); *Safe Conduct* (1931); *Second Birth* (1932), a new book of poems; and his translations of Georgian poets.

Yet all was not well. For Pasternak, popularity was not a measure of success in art. In 1927, in a letter to the young poet Mikhail Froman, he had written: "I am the son of an artist. I saw art and prominent people from my earliest days, and I am accustomed to treating the lofty and exceptional as I treat nature, as a vital norm. Socially, it has dwelt with my everyday household affairs since birth. As a phenomenon of duplication, I do not differentiate it from the everyday by its craftsman's scaffolding, or perceive it in prominent quotation marks, as it appears to the majority. . . ."

Pasternak was uncomfortable with his fame and dissatisfied with his new works in that they left so much unsaid and distracted from what he knew from experience to be essential, a prose narrative of the history of his generation. Only part of that narrative was written, and only fragments of what he called *A Novel About Patrick* survived.

All was not well in the Pasternak household. Evgenya Pasternak had finished art college and needed a studio for her work, the young Zhenya had his tutor, Elizaveta Mikhailovna Stetsenko, there was a maid—and all

used the one-room Moscow apartment. Domestic disarray made life difficult. Events in Evgenya's life posed further complications: the death of
her mother (A. V. Lurie) after a long illness was a terrible blow to Pasternak's wife, and nervous and physical exhaustion led to aggravation of the
tuberculosis she had contracted during the Russian Civil War. (A trip to
a Black Forest sanatorium in 1931 arrested the progress of the disease.)
The anguish of their family life in the late 1920's and early 1930's is evident in a letter sent in 1928 by Pasternak to his wife: "There are times
when, mastering the difficulties I confront, I take satisfaction in the philosophical sincerity that always accompanies my thoughts of you, but how
alone I am—more than alone—when the thoughts are so far beyond my
strength! Oh, how I fear the moments when I have to seek within myself
aid both from you and against you. . . ."

During the winter of 1929–1930 Pasternak developed new friendships
with the families of Valentin Asmus, a historian of philosophy, and Heinrich Neuhaus, the brilliant concert pianist and a professor at the Moscow
Conservatory, a witty and jovial companion. Asmus and his wife, Irina,
introduced Pasternak to the Neuhaus family—the gracious, hospitable
Zinaida Nikolayevna (Zina) and her sons Adrian and Stanislav (Stasik),
the latter a gifted pianist in his own right. Pasternak spent the summer of
1930 at Irpen, near Kiev, in the light-hearted company of the Asmus and
Neuhaus families. The following summer Pasternak and Zinaida Nikolayevna traveled to Soviet Georgia; after their return, he brought her to
Leningrad to introduce her to Aunt Asya and cousin Olga as his new wife.
Olga was shocked and angered. From experience she knew her cousin's
extreme compassion and cautioned him against living in an unattainable
"fantastic and fairy-tale world."

In an afterword to *Safe Conduct* Pasternak drew contrastive portraits
of his two wives. The painter's eye of his father's son is evident: "A smile
made a round loaf of her chin, suffusing her cheeks and eyes in light. This
caused her to squint, as though from the sun, a filmy squint like that of
the nearsighted or those prone to consumption. The smile spread to her
beautiful, broad forehead, changing her resilient features all the more
from oval to round, and reminding one of the Italian Renaissance. Illuminated externally by the smile, she brought to mind one of Ghirlandaio's portraits. One wanted to bathe in her face. And since she always
needed this illumination in order to be beautiful, she had to have happiness in order to be liked.

"You will say that all faces are like that. Not so. I know others. I know a
face that smites and slashes regardless of whether in sorrow or joy, and it

becomes all the more beautiful the more often one encounters it in situations where another kind of beauty would pall.

"Whether this other woman soars aloft or falls headlong, her startling attractiveness remains unchanged. There is little on earth she needs as much as the earth needs her, because she is femininity itself, extracted whole from the quarry of creation as a rough-hewn block of flawless pride. And since the laws of appearance are most influential in determining a woman's temperament and character, the life and essence—the honor and the passion—of this second woman are not dependent upon illumination, and she does not fear life's distresses, as the first woman does."

The advent of Nazism in Germany compounded the disarray in the dispersed Pasternak family. There was discussion of reuniting the family in Moscow. While the sons in Moscow were not fully able to appreciate the gravity of the situation in Germany, their parents did not understand what unfavorable conditions prevailed in Moscow. On both sides, the need for circumspection in corresponding complicated matters. In 1936, for example, Pasternak obliquely communicates to his parents the perils of returning home: "Ah, this impossible life! Its absurdities here, becoming obstacles for the artist, are unbelievable. But that is what a revolution must be, one that is becoming more and more the event of the century, all the more openly spreading to the very midst of the people, to their very depths. Would there be time for the individual lot here, for lives that justify themselves? History has let loose something unspeakably huge, and that lends dignity. If one can keep that in mind, one can avoid looking over one's shoulder uneasily and drawing sad conclusions. . . ."

On the part of Pasternak's parents, there was a failure to appreciate the harshness of living conditions in Moscow. Leonid Pasternak, his paintings crated and deposited at the Soviet embassy in Berlin in expectation of the expulsion of Russians from Germany, looked forward to a separate apartment with studio in Moscow, but Boris was well aware that the acute housing shortage resulted in intolerably overcrowded dwellings with no concession made to the artist's needs. Thus, invitations to his parents to return made reference to the "kerosene" of Russian daily life, the need to prepare food on a kerosene primus.

Increasingly, there were signs that things were not going well for Pasternak the writer. As he comments to his cousin on October 18, 1933, "the tails have been chopped off all my works." Soviet critics, pressed to develop a Marxist sociological school of criticism, frequently chose Pasternak as their target. Articles by Lezhnev, Pertsov, Postupalsky, and

Krasilnikov (the last in *The Press and the Revolution*) reflect this pressure. Class origin determined literature, in their view, and the burden of disclaiming class origin was on the artist. There was no neutral ground. Principles, of art or life, were denounced as "formalism"—the assertion of a cause higher than, or simply independent of, the state, the people, the revolution, and, most frequently, the Party. The servility of faceless "Prutkovian" writers—a reference to the tradition of pseudonymous satirical verse that began with Mikhail Zhemchuzhnikov and Alexei Tolstoy in the nineteenth century—displaced the sincerity of a Pascal devoted to recording, if only privately, the intellectual history of his age.

Moscow, May 10, 1926

Dear, dear Olya,

You hit the nail on the head. Thanks for your Pythian letter. Fate, which has come up with several cases of acute clairvoyance of late, has, in your letter, provided a paradoxical case within the family. Don't be angry if I tell you Aunt Asya once anticipated it by saying: "I care nothing about what happens to you—you can stop working altogether for all I care. My only concern is for what happens to her." Since this was said in reference to Zhenya and that particular period of her life, I fell under the spell of Aunt's solicitude for the girl I loved, and her words went straight to my heart as an admonition. I do not say that they determined anything by themselves, but they exactly stipulated the self-imposed limitations I had been enduring for two years before the statement, and which I went on enduring for two years following it. There is no one on earth who, knowing me and many of the circumstances, and also knowing the real significance of Aunt Asya's words, would ever repeat them. But other words, no less warm but with quite a different significance, began arriving and accumulating this year (especially in the spring), mostly from abroad. I feel that they are wiser and more generous than those uttered by members of the family. They are for the most part reviews and translations by foreign writers as well as articles published in the best émigré press (by which I mean not the die-hard anti-Soviet press), and many other manifestations of great, lofty, ennobling love dispersed over time and space and purified by this dispersion to a Hellenic, an ideal state of purity. I not only refrain from showing these reviews to anyone but I also live with them uneasily and with discomfort, and all because of the family, for whom such things often bear the stigma of boastfulness. Aunt Asya demonstrates how deep-rooted this prejudice is. That spring when my destiny began to take shape, as it does periodically in the life of every man, and I spoke to you *of that alone*, Aunt Asya assumed that I had come to you to brag and in that sense revive the family opinion of me. Ah, Olya, there is a God; no, rather let us say there is a force counterbalancing earth's gravity, counterbalancing the force of falling, namely, the force of rising, a force drawing self-succeeding, self-destroying form to the Form of Forms. Without realizing what it meant, you wrote that if I fancy my seven years of moral slumber have passed, it is not a mere dream. Yes, Olya, the rest of my life will certainly be like the half I lived through long ago, the one cut off from me by an interval of emptiness.

I shall say no more. There is nothing to say. It is too soon to say it.

What sensitivity you have, Olya! I showed your letter to Zhenya without commentary, in silence. She began to weep, assured that the time will come, that everything will turn out. Don't try to analyze what I say. You mustn't, there's no point in it. I myself will tell you everything in a year or so. The purpose of this letter is to embrace you and thank you for that inherited excellence, that fineness of stock, enabling you unerringly to penetrate the darkness.

The main thing is we are again brother and sister, and you are not angry with me. My love to you and Aunt Asya. Don't go to such lectures. It's disgraceful. That was all done and finished with when even the sidewalks were poets. Since then (seven years!), nothing new or original has taken place.

DIARY

Borya was grateful to me for foretelling the return of his inspiration.

Moscow, October 21, 1926

Dear Olyushka,

Summer is over and gone and we have not seen each other. In good conscience I cannot say how I have spent the time. The windows of our room look out upon the descent to the river embankment. The sidewalk virtually lies upon our window sills. All summer the windows stood wide open, and it seems as though the past three months have been spent in dusting and sweeping the floor. All I remember is the cleaning, plus a few unanswered letters and unread books. I botched the work I had to do. I don't know whether I told you at the time that there is no place for me to work in our apartment, that, as a result of a series of moves, mergers, expansions, and other metamorphoses, I haven't had a room to myself for three years. But that is only half the misfortune. All last winter I worked in Alexander's and Irina's room, often with them in it as well, and when that inconvenienced them I moved into the front room, which serves as kitchen and dining room. For several reasons that possibility was eliminated.

There is an objective consideration making my subjective (and perhaps challengeable) inability to work in the same room with Zhenya, little Zhenya, and little Zhenya's nanny into a decisive factor: I smoke incessantly when I work, and I cannot pour smoke into the room in which my child lives. So we decided to divide the room by putting up a partition.

Isn't it odd that I should be telling you all this just to explain why I am writing you today? Actually the reason is simple: Zhenya brought me a ream of writing paper from abroad and I wanted you to be the first to enjoy it. Remember the room that used to be Papa's studio? Big enough for a riding school. I had to find carpenters and negotiate with them as any amateur would, because Alexander and Irina, both architects, couldn't help me; they are busy from morning to night, he on a site, Irina in the drafting room. The estimate for the partitions came to around 200 rubles. The workmen may be asking a little too much but the real reason for this impressive and terrifying figure lies not in their greed but in the size of the room.

This morning they were to begin bringing materials. When they had left yesterday, I was found in the common kitchen in a state of deep and silent abstraction. The neighbors, who entered some five minutes after I got there, asked me what I was looking for. I replied in all seriousness that I had been consulting Murzilka (a neighbor's cat) as to where I was going to get the money. It had such a depressing effect on Murzilka that she retired behind one of the kitchen tables. I wasn't really speaking in jest, i.e., I had no intention of making anyone laugh. I was the victim of a lamentable absurdity and took no interest in variations on the theme. One absurdity deserves another; the incongruity of seeking a cat's advice is no greater than the incongruity of our undertaking this reconstruction.

There is the question of plastering. The carpenters assure me that given braziers and the constant stoking of stoves, the walls will dry. Some disinterested onlookers say it will take two or three weeks, others a month. In my trancelike state in the kitchen, my mind was filled not only with the rustle of rubles but also with the anticipation of drafts, and wet snow driven through open windows, and hot vapors rising from the gray compresses of plaster on both sides of the partition, their stench augmented by the smell of red-hot iron. Just imagine what it will be like—all normal living suspended while the damp, gritty mess takes over until the day of the housewarming, condemning us to colds and rheumatism and similar joys.

It is not surprising that after such visions I couldn't sleep half the night; I tossed and turned, thinking of everything under the sun. When my thoughts turned to people, I saw you and Aunt Asya first of all. As soon as I got up in the morning I wanted to remind you both how precious you are to me and how I love you.

There is in man an inborn and widespread need directly connected with the music of consciousness, and it is so common, so characteristic of all people, that there must be a name for it; the name has slipped my mind at present, but tomorrow, when I send off this letter, it will be back on my tongue. Years pass, the bases of and adjuncts to one's discontent change, imperfections add up one after another, you dream of perfection in the future, become lost in speculation, and behold!—the best moments of this changeful process of adding and subtracting are probably those when the feelings animating the unquiet answers are of more value to you than the units of which the sums are composed. And so one wants to go back to before the answer, that is, to talk about oneself in such a way that the talk, sad or gay as it may be, the melody of everyday concerns, the human story—even more, the human law—embrace, dominate, and rise above. This need is deceptive. It is rarely satisfied. A person arriving at a railroad station after an absence of many years finds relief from emotional tension by uttering exclamations and snatches of sentences having little meaning. One would not include this in a novel written in the first person. Indeed, such madness obstructs life. The flow of memory does not stop, does not impede the present. This need is a thing of the imagination, yet without its imaginativeness the formula for the soul and its growth would be stripped of meaning and fall apart. Well, then, this need is most fully awakened in me by the image of four windows facing the Canal yesterday, today, and perhaps forever. Why not by the image of my parents and sisters? Because in this case the satisfaction arising from family affinity is laid bare with all its contradictions and is filled to over-flowing with the present. Too great and real is our family closeness.

What a foolish letter this is! But I will not cut it short.

If you think of writing, be sure to tell me how Aunt Asya is feeling, and you, too.

Zhenya's and my differences have receded into the realm of legend. But I do not look upon them as nonsense just because we have begun to forget them. I do, however, think it was foolish of me to have written about them when they were at their worst. Even then I understood the role accorded benign and rational acts of will at a mature age, and the modest significance fate and accident claim for themselves. Certainly fate does not disclaim all importance in this revaluation of values; it merely steps from downstage to backstage. Perhaps it ceases to play a role alto-gether and becomes instead the field of the acting, that is, while seeming to be absent, it takes over the entire stage. The acting itself and its theme are the province of the will. It goes without saying that I did not come to understand this just yesterday. Undoubtedly some of our misunderstand-ings amounted to just this: were we to combine our wills for our mutual benefit, or were we to part? I don't think we shall ever regret the decision we made. God grant it may be so.

They had a wonderful time abroad. Zhenya had a whole month's rest from the child, which she spent alone in a place of which she speaks rapturously and incoherently, somewhere on the shores of a lake near the Tyrolean Alps, with boats, bathing, excursions into the mountains, and the romantic excitement of making new friends. According to Aunt Asya's ideas, I ought to at least frown at this point. I have heard rumors circulated to the effect that I have probably never loved and am incapable of loving. To this are added aphorisms about the creative individual, about solitude and the coldness it generates. My case is really simpler than that. I believe I possess the usual measure of warmth and ordinary human feelings. As for jealousy—is it not, in the long run, around jealousy that all this speculation revolves? Jealousy is an emotion I know too well and too deeply to be caught up in it as in a murky, blinding whirlpool. I like good honest objectivity, and if these words make sense, she will surely respond in kind. It is not her I resent, but all that is inferior to her, all that does not represent her own true self. The place in which Zhenya stayed and the things she did were just that, and the people she met—worthy people, by all accounts—became one with the enormous objectivity of lavish mountain scenery. I am glad that while with me—that is, while I am part of Zhenya's life—she has had, separately from me, an experience she can always look back upon, one that will provide her with inexhaustible memories. It is of just such atoms we ought to consist.

Owing to the number of families living in our apartment and their friendliness, I knew that from the moment of her arrival, from the moment she stepped out of the train, we would be surrounded by people from whom we would be unable to extricate ourselves. And so, to be alone with my family for a little while, I went to Mozhaisk to join them for the last lap of the train journey (a typical Moscow ruse). Well, those *two hours of life* spent with Zhenya and my son in her compartment formed such an oasis by contrast that were I to begin to describe them, the result would be a new and endless letter.

Not long before Zhenya got back, her mother, who had suffered for ten months from a tumor on her spine causing paralysis that was spreading from her limbs to every part of her body, underwent an operation in which they removed five vertebrae. The dangerous and complicated operation seemed to have been successful. But while recuperating, she suddenly came down with something severe, causing chills and fever (up to 103°) and showing signs of blood poisoning and other undiagnosed infections. In the intervals when the temperature is not soaring she has lucid moments. For over two weeks she has been in this almost hopeless condition, a facet as remarkable as it is fearful. I suppose the body, too, has an end to achieve, and a feasible one, judging by the fight it puts up. Her illness presents a mystery to be pondered.

Ah, but I have written not a word of the *genuine* joy I want to share with you both! Father's exhibition in Berlin is proceeding brilliantly and enjoying an enthusiastic reception. In answer to a request I made long ago, he sent me three clippings from leading Berlin papers and a notice actually beginning with an exclamation. An unheard-of success! My spontaneous (that is, elemental) delight in his victory is accompanied by further delight arising from a recognition that he at his age is unbendingly youthful, while I at mine am fatally old, which is to say that I am *voluntarily* gray-haired. What lively *faith in joy*, almost childlike in its spontaneity, he displays, a thing I could not possibly say of myself even when alone with myself. But this simple rejuvenating parallel conceals a lamentable element that can only make one groan and throw up one's hands. The fact is that he has been underrated all his life and is as underrated to this very day as I am overrated. Take pride in your brother and your blood, Aunt Asya, and let us embrace and have a good cry, the three of us.

I embrace you, Olya, and your mother. Toodle-Doodle is a big boy, so charming and amusing that even I begin to be touched by him. To tell you a secret, he always affected me in this way.

Zhenya is not at home; she has gone to the hospital. I shall send this without her postscript. You mustn't expect to hear from her soon, since she finds herself in circumstances that leave her unable to think of anything else.

Yours,
BORYA

Leningrad, September 9, 1927 [not sent]
Fate has decreed that you should receive this letter, too, even though I forgot to begin "Dear Borya."

From it you will find out that Sasha has moved out of our apartment, that I have found tenants for all the rooms, and that this colossal burden is now off my shoulders. You will also find out that, according to today's papers, we have been granted an extra room without any strings attached. Your words about "false perceptions" contain mountains of wisdom. But is it not precisely because we don't trust these perceptions that we refuse to give ourselves up to them wholly? False perceptions are as sweet as one's struggle with oneself, as sweet as betrayal; they are but another way of jumping outside of oneself, of deceiving oneself, only to end up in remote depths. At times of surrender the whole world and all of life are experienced through "perceptions," and whatever we cherish in our storehouse as of more value than experience now seems but a vapor and a dream. Bitterly, bitterly do we beat our heads and hearts with the club of logic, imagining that we are perceptive only at such times. Night times for the most part. Erased by the pale beams of dawning day. How well do I know the meaning of your words, supported as they are by life itself. Their significance makes our trifling apartment problem seem more trifling than ever.

But do you imbibe life as I do? If you wish, take the palimpsest of this event and scrape down to the secret text written in indelible ink. It reveals the same greatness of life, only in different writing. It has been the same with Sasha. Long years of suffering, an endless ribbon. At times I have thought, Is not this the meaning of my existence? Never, never must we fail to seek meaning in the unending content of each day. It exists, it is what we are given; we must treasure its givenness, even though it contains only little things, petty things. Oh, I know now for certain. The idea lies precisely in this, and if it is not mine, it is my biography's. As I look back over my days, I see the single sign under which they have unfolded. Sasha—he, too, is a sign. Its meaning can be read, and then we see the continuity of the work prepared for us by the soul, our encounter with the world, and the stages of this encounter: step by step, upward, like the solving of a vast problem.

Then suddenly—fresh air. You are free. The unachievable is achieved. I am washing dusty window frames, all the doors are open and the place is cluttered with countless things. Am I happy? Here the question touches on love and freedom. In both matters the answer is ready: I don't know; perhaps I am; no doubt I am; somewhere out there, on the periphery of the spirit, lies happiness. But the present moment wields great power, and it is too close to see. I have the same feeling now that I had then—remember our Merrekühl testament?—that the present moment consumes me from top to toe. In a mute and hermetically closed sense of living, with the closed eyes of feeling, I give myself up to what is. Do you suppose I *think* in my work? That I *feel* in my successes? I merely breathe. The process of breathing is like the process of my receiving and responding to impressions. My life is but an impulse. It frightens me to realize how unthinking I am in the intellectual profession of scholarship (I dare not say in the intellectual *sphere*), and I am completely devoid of feeling in matters of love and freedom.

I have rented four rooms of our apartment to three scholars: an Egyptologist, a specialist in Slavo-Byzantine ornamentation, and a specialist in Chinese art. They are so quiet, clean, polite, and ideal in every respect (they do all their own chores without any servants) that poor Mama, as could only be expected . . .

DIARY

At this point "the manuscript breaks off," as they say. The absurdity of our living with Sasha and his false-front wife could not go on forever. I asked him to move out; his wife desired it, too, and the changes in rent made it expedient. Sasha found it very hard to leave his home. He suffered in silence. He could not face the prospect of living with strangers. The day came and he left in deep sorrow. As for me, it was as if the door to life had opened up before me. Now I, a pauper, was "the head of the household," with an enormous apartment on my hands and a large rent to pay. It was spring. I opened up the empty rooms, opened the storm windows, cleaned everything myself, moved the furniture myself, made ready the rooms for their new occupants. When everything was upside down and I was in the act of washing windows, Borya arrived from Moscow, drawn here by our letters and our devotion. I accepted his coming as a symbol. It was the day of my emancipation, of Dante's *vita nuova*.

I instantly perceived he had brought his old feeling with him, and far from reciprocating it I felt repulsion, as one drop of water repels another.

We went for long walks together. At this time discord between Borya and Zhenya had begun, and this made him feel more drawn to me than ever.

I kept asking him to present me with a copy of *The Year 1905*, which had just come out. He promised, but was evasive. On leaving, after he had embraced me, I held his hands and kissed him as a sister. He noticed this and recoiled. When he had left and I went to my desk, I found a volume of *The Year 1905* thrust under some papers. Astonished, I drew it out. I understood everything when I read on the flyleaf "To my beloved." Beneath it he had written my name in a steadier hand. I could not but surrender to the force of his great, if timid, heart. Only Borya could have said so much in the language of deeds and handwriting. It is hard to convey how vividly he had expressed his love for me in that single gesture of hiding his feelings among my papers.

[Inscription in *The Year 1905:*]

To my beloved cousin Olya

BORYA

September 28, 1927

In January of the following year I received a forceful letter from him, evocative of all we had lived through that summer of our youth in Merrekühl.

Moscow, January 3, 1928

Dear Olya,

I read your letter through with tears in my eyes. You cannot imagine how unbearable it is for me to read your sad letters. If you were my wife, the wife I have lived with, of whose love I have taken all, and whom I have abandoned, my grief in all likelihood would not be so permeated with alarm and contrition as it is when I read your letters, whose pages are steeped in proud spirituality and almost passionless, almost soaring suffering (in the sense that it rises beyond needing anyone or anything, not even a rational cause). God, what air you breathe, air beyond my strength, air I ceased breathing long ago! It is not just rarefied but deathly pure, containing not a mote of that relief-giving, compliant pollution which we bring to adulthood in order to bear the paradox of immortality amid corruption and make it thinkable and conceivable. You are dazzlingly flexible and young at heart; even a cousin cannot observe this without being deeply moved by it. You have not always written to me as you did today, but you yourself have always been like that. It was with just this perception of you, your mother and your blood, your room and your gift, your evil genius and your fate, i.e., with such feelings, that I first crossed the threshold of your home. Aware of the restrained authority that protects both of you from any and all loves, understandings, and the like, I put myself at the disposal of you both, no—better and more accurately—at your disposal, Olya, with the greatest passivity of which I was capable, but even this measure of passivity seemed unsatisfactory as soon as I heard Aunt Asya's first words.

Remember telling me that I usually arrived more cheerful and talkative than I did this time? You two must have thought there was a reason for my mood, a reason rooted in me or left behind in Moscow, and that my trip had a practical purpose. Yet I came only to see you, and the only emotion I experienced was agitation. Except for this agitation I felt nothing but a readiness to meet you, as a photographic plate is ready for exposure. That explains the reason for my glumness and restraint. As for any "practical" purpose, I came with no aim but to do everything you requested of me and to follow wherever you led. Those trips to Gatchina and Tsarskoye Selo, which you understood so wrongly, were but the minimum dreams, the delightful anticipations of activity that I brought with me, yet as I told you, I would have preferred even less activity. That I had no one to see in Petersburg save you and your mother I have proved to neither your benefit nor pleasure. My literary friends are half of Leningrad, and it is true I did not see Akhmatova,* or Kuzmin,† or Chukovsky, or the dozen other less dear friends (but why less? perhaps I shouldn't say that about them). The only exception was Tikhonov, but he is practically a younger brother to me.

I don't know how to thank you for not reproaching me for my boorish silence. You know or can easily guess that during the first few days after I got home I was tempted to write you and to thank Aunt Asya for the affection she showed me. But I cannot tell you how many pressing matters swooped down upon me from all directions. At the time of writing, circumstances have taken such an unfortunate turn that these matters have increased tenfold. The fact is that I have been sick practically all this time. I tore the ligaments of my left shoulder and a month was lost on that, i.e., on indescribable suffering and then gradual mastery of the inactive and atrophied arm. Then the rest of the family fell ill. Doodle, as you call him, came down with—imagine!—inflammation of the "kidney bean," as he calls it. At the end of a week-long breather I caught the flu and ended up with a swollen cheek on Christmas Day, so that I greeted the New Year exceptionally pouty. Meanwhile I had to and wanted to work. And so many letters, so many! Olechka, among them there were some marvelous ones about *The Year 1905*. From Gorky.‡ From the best and most independent people of the emigration. Of course you are right, and not Kansky,§ but don't tell that to anyone. I myself talk entirely too much. Of course I had read the article in *The Press and the Revolution* before I came to visit you. A most regrettable article, but I cannot criticize it: the author obviously wished me well and was required to do it in the "terminology of the age." He is from Moscow but I don't even know

---

* Anna Andreyevna Akhmatova (1889–1966): Russian poet.

†Mikhail Alexeyevich Kuzmin (1875–1936): Russian poet and novelist.

‡ Maxim Gorky (Alexei Maximovich Peshkov; 1868–1936): Russian writer.

§ R. B. Kansky: art historian.

him by sight. If these articles cause you sisterly concern (this possibility alarms me in the extreme), then find a way to obtain in Leningrad the July number of the conservative English journal *The London Mercury* for this year (July 1927). In it you will find an article by Prince Sviatopolk-Mirsky on contemporary Russian literature, and although the evaluation he makes of me is undeservedly high, still this is the one evaluation you do not have to "quarrel with Kansky" about. I have told you about Tsvetayeva;* there are surprisingly good things about her there, too. But read the whole article.

I read this article, as well as the *The Press and the Revolution* one, during the summer—I know, I didn't answer your letter. Forgive me. I thank you warmly for everything and kiss you. And your mother. The two Zhenyas do, too.

Moscow [February 17, 1928]

My dear friend,

My letter to you probably seemed obscure and offensively short in answer to your profound and forceful one. You do not take into account the fact that the screws are turned even harder on me than on you. I can scarcely keep myself under control so that things don't slip through my fingers and slither away. It is unconscionably hard for me, dear Olya, because everything depends on memory, on nerves leading into the past, and there is nothing vital now to compensate. I am writing with a request that I am ashamed to make. Having begun to gather clippings with your help, I now collect even words and messages. Someone is sure to indicate the source. Recently the model at Zhenya's art school told her that on Friday she read something in *Red News*. That is your evening *News* of either February 9 or 10. Could you get it, Olyushka? Forgive me and don't laugh at me, and if you love me write *about yourself*. Love to you and Aunt Asya.

Yours,

B.

DIARY

I was in the full swing of writing my *Poetics*,† which I called *Procris*. I wanted to give prominence to my idea about distinctions that in fact

---

* Marina Ivanovna Tsvetayeva (1892–1941): outstanding Russian poet who took her own life in despair at the beginning of World War II.

† *The Poetics of Plot and Genre* (1936).

constitute an identity. In *Procris* I for the first time provided a complete system of ancient semantics. I took images in their variety and demonstrated their unity. I wanted to establish a law of multiple differentiation and the development of forms. The chaos of motif structures, myths, rituals, and objects became a system of specific meanings in my interpretation.

Philosophically I wanted to show that literature can be the basis for a theory of knowledge, just as in the natural or the exact sciences. As far as factual material was concerned, I had many concrete ideas and many new conclusions as to the origin of the drama, the chorus, the lyric metaphor. I was a master at discovering genetic semantics and finding links between the most disparate things.

I was the first to adopt a new approach to the problems of genre and genre formation, freeing them from formal interpretation.

If no one has ever before worked on genre in my way, the same cannot be said of plot structure. Marr's and Frank-Kamenetsky's interest in plot structure was entirely limited to semantics, but for me semantics is the purpose of defining morphology, of discovering the laws of the development of forms.

I dare to assert that I am the first one in scholarly research to discover a systematic world view in literary plots.

In essence it is a question of epistemology. In my view, motif structure bears a purposeful character, directly expressing primitive image (mythical) thinking. It has its laws in the field of the development of form as well as of content, because it is a historically conditioned perception of a world that has developed according to definite laws of formation.

I finished in 1928.

Moscow, February 19, 1928

Dear Olyushka,

Apparently my postcard was mailed at the same time as your letter, and they met in Bologoye. I am ashamed and grateful. Many thanks for the happy news of your work. With all my heart I wish you tranquillity and self-control while finishing your second dissertation. The awareness that it is likely destined for the Academy of Sciences (in general that its future is determined) will be a hindrance to you, and God grant you the strength to cope with the pulsing of a live tomorrow in the concentrated labors of today. I like the title immensely and the wide sweep of interpretation it suggests. Just don't draw final, unsought-for conclusions about yourself *from your work*: they always sting, set one's nerves on edge, and poison one's life. They overlook all the practical intermediate links and convert everything at once into subjectively alarming conclusions involving emotion and fate.

I am saying things you know full well, saying them because I have learned them from my own experience.

My love and congratulations. Love to Aunt Asya.

Yours,

B.

Don't be angry that this is a postcard. I had to answer you as quickly as possible.

DIARY

This is what he meant by the Academy of Sciences. As soon as my manuscript was written, typed, and bound, I brought it to Marr at the Academy of Material Culture.

I asked him to publish *Procris*. He promised to do so. I asked him to accept *Procris* at the Japhetic Institute as a doctoral dissertation. He promised to do so. Despite the usual friendly reception, I left without any hope.

Moscow, May 10, 1928

Dear Olyushka,

I am sorry I was not home when Lifshits called—he spoke with Alexander. I would have put questions to him in my own way, and more. Still, I found out that you are preparing to defend your doctoral dissertation in the autumn and that your reputation is growing with every day.

I have been ill. It began with the flu and ended with an unpleasant complication. Only at that point, alarmed by the strange persistence of headaches, did I turn to a doctor. I discovered it was inflammation of the frontal sinuses (they do exist), i.e., of the cavity above the temporal bone. Thank God I escaped without trepanation and am getting better, otherwise I wouldn't be writing you now. I haven't done anything for more than a month, and even now I sit down to work with great trepidation. What if it again hits my head and starts all over again?

At present we have no money, but I will manage to find some somewhere. When a person settles for the summer in the country outside Moscow, everyone talks about how cheap life is in the Caucasus or the Crimea. They tell how much money they've sunk in summer vacations forty miles from Moscow and swear it would pay the cost of four people touring the Caucasus right down to the Persian border. So by autumn the idea of vacationing in the Caucasus has put down roots, like winter wheat; one doesn't give the idea a thought throughout the cold months, but by spring the seeds have matured to the point at which one's family is as good as settled in Kabarda or Teberda, and one has but to give the hallucination substance.

I was sick a good deal this winter and accomplished little. I have now come to a critical point in two or three works that I have yet to finish; they deal with the past decade, its events, its significance, etc.—not seen objectively, as in *The Year 1905*, but personally, subjectively, recounting what all of us saw and lived through.

I cannot take a single step forward in life or work if I fail to give myself a full report on this stretch of time. To avoid facing the difficulty by working on something else in defiance of my inclination and natural tendencies would mean to rob all future experience of its value. I could do that only if I knew I had two lives to live, in which case I would put off this painful and frightening task to the second, more comfortable life. The task, however, has got to be seen to, and it will be of interest only if it is more or less sincere. That, then, is how things stand.

As you know, terror has resumed, this time without the moral grounds or justifications that were found for it earlier, in the heat of commerce, careerism, and unsightly "sinfulness." These men are far from being the Puritan saints who then emerged as avenging angels.* Terrible confusion reigns; we are caught up and spun round in waves that bear absolutely no relationship to time. We are dazed. I had no expectation of it in the autumn, and so my mood was less gloomy then. I fear that the task of which I have spoken above, the fulfilling of which prevents my completing two works, will bring me trouble and inconvenience if not something much worse. But this is all in the natural course of doing my duty and fulfilling my destiny, not something done as an act of daring or defiance or anything of the sort. And who knows? It may come off successfully. I prefer to believe it will.

May 20

Dear Olyushka,

That's how it always is. My answer has lain on my desk for ten days. I haven't finished it because Aunt Asya's delightful letter arrived in the meantime. I wished to answer it at once, but it raised questions which I expected to have the answers to in a few days. The problems, however,

---

* A reference to the aftermath of the seventeenth-century English Civil War, which brought Oliver Cromwell to power.

have stretched themselves out without bringing forth answers: we still don't know what we are going to do this summer. Probably I will send Zhenya and little Zhenya to the Caucasus for a month, remaining in town myself; then when they come home, we will all go out to live at the dacha. All this, however, is still hypothetical. Whatever happens, wherever we are (even if it is in the Caucasus), you will be a much-desired guest. If, or when, we move to the country, I want you and Aunt Asya to stay there with us for a while.

Much love. Don't be angry with me for not answering sooner. Some of the excuses are in this letter, all of them cannot be counted.

Yours,

BORYA

Moscow, May 20, 1928

Dear Aunt Asya,

You know, or ought to know, how touched I was by your wonderful letter. Since a contempt for sentimentality is among your highest virtues, you will curb any tendency I may show in that direction.

I did not answer you immediately because only last Friday did it become clear whether I would have money and how much; and only yesterday did we go to the town of Kashira on the Oka River, scouting for a summer dacha. In a word, we still do not know where we shall live this summer. As soon as we do I shall ask not only Olya, but you as well, to be sure and join us. My delay in answering was caused by hoping these problems would be solved any day. So far I have been mistaken in my hopes.

I can't tell you how thin Zhenya has become; if she has accomplished anything, it is only to become thinner and to feel worse. This saddens and distresses me. She must put on weight. Objectively, this is possible, but subjectively, i.e., to the extent it depends on her own self, it seems to be impossible. The boy, even though he has a nanny, is being raised as a fat little savage. He is mischievous and at the same time melancholy. Selfish to the point of being heartless, yet as affectionate as a girl. No doubt he is spoiled, but how and by whom I cannot say. Life isn't easy for him in the conditions of contemporary Moscow apartments. These same conditions prevent me from understanding what his shortcomings are and what he is in need of. Life is so crowded and mixed up that it is hard to make out what is going on inside even those who are closest to you, and to attempt to guide them in their ways is as frustrating as to try to tune a piano at the same time that chimes are ringing loudly and out of tune.

The only consolation is that he will grow up along with *his contemporaries,* most of whom are being raised in the midst of the same cacophonous chiming.

You asked about Josephine and the folks. Everything seems to be going well there. Mother was ill for a while but is better now. Josephine is incomparably better. The reason for my not having heard from her so long is that I have not written her for more than six months. I stopped writing as soon as I found out about her illness, and precisely because of her illness. I did not know, and still do not know, what was wrong with her; I learned long ago to steer clear of mystifying things, and the measure of my caution grows in proportion to the nearness and dearness of the people concerned. If I were there I would spare no pains to find out what lies at the basis of the meaningless and pseudoscientific diagnosis "nerves" to which, aping the doctors, my parents attribute everything. My parents don't excel at explaining things fearlessly and with dignity, because they are hysterical rather than philosophical. On occasion their hysteria, so immeasurable that it bursts beyond family boundaries, becomes, by virtue of its intuitive basis, a substitute for clear and concentrated attention. On such occasions hysteria is as self-effacing as wisdom, unsparing of itself because it has no interest in itself. But my parents' hysteria is of the domestic, private-property sort, which means it can come up with nothing in discussion but confusion. I deliberately kept my distance from this lamentable fogginess lest my approach should cause them to increase its density.

Yesterday I saw a live person who had seen all of them only ten days ago, and he gave me a detailed and enthusiastic account of them. Thank God all is well.

But I was greatly distressed by your account of your visit to the oculist. Do you know, Aunt, that Father was told the same thing eight years ago? He is, of course, sobered by such a possibility, but you can see for yourself how hard and how well he is still working.

I will not see them soon. My hope of going there on a visit is as real as ever but is constantly being deferred. At the moment I count on making the journey this winter, but how often have I been disappointed!

I embrace you. I love you deeply and am eternally grateful to you.

Yours,

BORYA

Zhenya read your letter with tears in her eyes. It affected her even more deeply than it did me, if that is possible. At present she is taking exams and has all sorts of other worries.

Forgive these scraps of paper; my supply of both sorts, good and bad, has run out.

DIARY

Among the many adversities of that time, a particularly great one was that Mother's eyes began to fail. It was discovered that she had cataracts (poor Uncle Leonid concealed the fact that he had already lost the sight of one eye—and he an artist!). The news caused me untold suffering. All the doctors agreed that she could not be operated on because of accompanying ailments. For ten years I went about bearing the weight of this enormous, inescapable catastrophe.

Moscow, June 5, 1928

Dear Aunt Asya,

Waiting does not make things easier. Apparently you decided to drive me into a corner with your affection. Well, here I am with my back to the wall. What shall I say? How shall I answer you? Your letter caused me much distress. I could not read it without alarm. With the same alarm Zhenya read and reread it. It was so alive, so like you, that it was as if we saw and heard you. I scarcely know how to thank you for the invitation, and even more for the way it is offered. I find it so tempting that on the very evening on which I received it I accepted it and was as good as there. Actually I cannot promise to be with you before a month and a half. Perhaps in the middle of July I can conjure up some business with Leningrad publishers that will provide me with the means of making the trip, as it has done in the past. This is highly probable. At present I have got to be here. Two hours ago Zhenya left for Gelendzhik in the North Caucasus with our son and his nanny. I remained behind, not only because there was not enough money for all of us but also because the providing of this same money requires that I work and make the rounds of the publishing houses. I shall not write you anything of importance now, nor Olga either, whom I thank over and over again for her letter. Lots of work piled up while I was ill, and even more was occasioned by Zhenya's departure. So I must get busy.

If Olya wants to make sure I will write to her, let her not write to me; the deprivation will force me to communicate. If you can, forgive me this brief note, Olyushka dear. But here I am, answering you. I need not defend myself; I am guiltless.

How am I to form any opinion as to the second plan for the biography when you outline it so sketchily? What a pity that I cannot see you tomorrow and ask you about it directly.

What in the world can be of more importance to me than your peace and happiness?

Thanks for your invitation and hospitality. I hope to take advantage of them both in July. For the present I can but embrace you both. This is an empty letter; I am writing it only to prevent delay, which would be an unforgivable response to such generosity.

Tout à vous deux.

BORYA

Moscow, July 19, 1928

Dear Olechka,

Forgive me for being a swine again. I ought to have answered your greetings from Tsarskoye Selo and the invitation conveyed through Kansky. But oh, my dear, if you only knew how I've been hounded, how I've been rushed! One look at my sunken cheeks would tell anyone that it was not with *you* in Peter* I had spent this past terrible month. It is, however, questionable whether or not I could have accomplished so much without making some sacrifice of health. It would take a long time to tell you what the work was. It included revising old books, such as *Above the Barriers,* which were disfigured by typographical errors (and bad enough without them), and much more. If you wish to take a look at how simply I have begun to write, get number 7 of *Red Virgin Soil,* in which you will find a sequel to one of my novels in verse (but complete in itself; you can read it without knowing what went before). If not this, then take a look at number 1 of the same magazine for this year.

I am leaving in a state of complete exhaustion, and I dearly love you and Aunt Asya.

Gelendzhik, 22 Dr. Gaaz St.

I embrace both of you.

All yours,
BORYA

* A colloquial name for St. Petersburg, now Leningrad.

DIARY

When it was all over, I wrote and told Borya what I had lived through. I wanted him to know at last that I loved someone else, even if unhappily. He answered my letter at the end of October, after a long, cold silence.

Moscow, October 22, 1928

Dear Olya,

I suppose you and Aunt Asya are lost to me, and that is an irreparable loss! You are right in rejecting me for all time and forgetting me, especially since I have nothing to offer in my own defense. I don't know what possessed me at the end of summer and all fall; I was in a strange state that did not lie heavily upon me but in which I would not have answered you even if your letter had consisted of only the first two quatrains, without the third, in which you speak of your "regeneration," as if, having achieved composure, you sought to moderate the alarm aroused by the first part of the letter. Now you see how heinous my crime has been, and I am not sure that you do not regret having honored me with your confidence. All the rest (the excuses for my swinishness) are mere trifles. The fact that we got back on the 16th and your letter lay unanswered, *even if* it was not my fault, so to speak—this in itself testifies to my guilt. And then there was the circumstance of our returning to an apartment upside-down with repairs, a circumstance that always upsets one's sense of time in all respects but especially in respect to one's moral obligations. And, finally, in that period of hopeless exhaustion and blissful negligence, I had committed crimes before I received your letter that were shocking precedents to my neglect of it.

I am writing with no hope of receiving an answer; an answer would shame and confuse me, and I don't want that. I am taking advantage of an opportunity: a gentleman arrived with a full suitcase of presents from our folks, some for you and some for me and some to be sent to other towns. I find them twice blessed since they give me this opportunity to talk to you candidly at last.

Ah, Olya, Olya, it's as if you were unaware of the rule, subject to change neither by time nor by anything else, that makes it inexpressible happiness for me to see you at any time, even though the seeing blights hopes that are still alive. And now let me confess there was a time when I keenly felt the fatal consequences of my long silence. This spring all conversation centered on our taking a country house outside Moscow for the summer and forcing you and Aunt Asya to sign a contract to come and stay with us, or else our going to the Caucasus and sending for you to join us there. Strange that Zhenya did not remember this and tell you about it.

Now as to what you have been through. If you had not insisted that I treat it as a discarded garment, something belonging to the past, I would not know what to say. So far as I can see, you yourself make things as hard as possible. You attribute wholly to fate that which is partly a matter of your own will. Evidently in the farthermost recesses of your heart you do not wish "this," namely, the intrusion of another's life into yours. Who can be your judge or counselor in such a case? It may sound strange coming from me, but I think you ought to blindly surrender to your own *stubbornness*, that is, as to a clock with a long winding mechanism, regardless of whether the clock is old and familiar or new and fancy, so long as it imposes upon you its own surprises. Because this is not a matter of weighing circumstances and coming to reasonable or emotional conclusions, but of preserving the force within you after making a decision and accepting a change—at least in your daily habits, even if your main path remains the same. Perhaps I am breaking into an open door or am altogether mistaken. Because I seem to be talking about some practical step (jumping ahead to conclusions), whereas you, without telling all, spoke to me of feelings, which of course are always immeasurably more important than any practical step.

No doubt you are by this time to be congratulated on finishing *Procris*, that is, on having put the work in its final, traveling, dischargeable form. Have you solved all the problems attendant on giving it to publishers? You made a hasty list of them at the end of the letter. I see and know how tense and difficult are the moments spent at this "last stop," moments that demand neither fresh ideas nor a new upsurge of emotion, but rather a number of shortcomings such as the ability to take things lightly— moments made indescribably hard not so much by passing frustrations as by natural dignity.

Please don't write to me. Give me time to cope with some of my tasks and I myself will write. You will find out that I am living through troubles similar to your own. Do, however, send me a card letting me know how Aunt Asya is. She had a cold, a light case of flu, when Zhenya saw her. Also send me the inevitable, purely mechanical, notice of the receipt of the parcel. You can include news of Aunt's health and your own work in this notice.

I embrace you both and love you dearly. Greetings from all of us.

Yours,

BORYA

Moscow, November 16, 1928

Dear Olyushka,

Forgive me once again, and probably not for the last time. There were many reasons, the most important of them being the death of Zhenya's mother last week. Although all other vicissitudes pale and appear to be trifling in the face of such grief, still the nerves go on recording them and adding them up to a significant sum, however contemptible the heart may find it. So it has been with Zhenya. The shock of her mother's death came to her when she herself had not fully recovered from her trip to Peter and a slight illness she suffered on her return to Moscow. She has done nothing but weep these last few days and is in a constant state of shock and prostration. She is frightened and embittered by the swiftness with which nature and tradition (decay and funeral rites) sweep off the path of life that which *was* life and which *gave* life. I cannot possibly describe it, I leave it to your conjecture and imagination; it cannot be said in two words. For the first time in my life I saw how the Jews bury their dead, and it was terrible.

Like a variation on a horror theme, fate sent Zhenya another ordeal. Surely you remember Fenya, a servant bequeathed to her by her parents; for two years she served as little Zhenya's nanny. We parted with her long ago. For a while she worked for Zhenya's sister (the one who lives here), helping her take care of old and ailing Mrs. Lurie. In time her stubbornness in general, and her refusal to speak in particular, became insufferable even for people who accepted her as one of the family, and they dismissed her. She found another job. Then another. Then she went to her native town but did not stay there. She came back a sad figure, smiling enigmatically. Strange things were happening to her; one misfortune followed another. On a rainy night two days before the death of her former mistress she knocked at our door—dirty, rain-soaked, with definite signs of fever. We took her in and put her to bed, still smiling enigmatically, and she immediately fell asleep, her temperature 103°. In the morning it turned out that a short while ago, while moving her things to a new place (who knows how many that makes!), she dragged her heavy basket out of the streetcar to the sidewalk and, leaving it there with the intention of coming back for it, set off, address in hand (she cannot read), to find her new employers. When, having found them, she returned to the tram stop, of course all trace of the basket had disappeared, and it contained her documents and money in the amount of 300 rubles. Next in her infantile sequence of narration came the story of what followed, something about a friend from home, then of catching cold, then of coming back, ill, to her employers the following evening and not having the door opened to her. We gave her sanctuary. She is terribly slovenly, walks around barefoot with unkempt hair, snatches fishtails from neighbors' window sills, and then, having borrowed five rubles from someone, orders a pastry with whipped cream and treats everyone in the kitchen of this densely populated apartment. Yesterday at dusk she went off to Zhenya's relatives and returned this morning. She doesn't remember the name of the village where she spent the night. She went by tram, which she boarded in the direction opposite to the one she should have taken; it was near some railroad, she watched eighteen trains go by (as she declared with pride), and then acknowledged that if she had had the money she would not have come back, so badly did she want to travel.

At the moment Zhenya has taken her to the psychiatrist, and this morning I began my visits to the various places where one must go in search of things lost and left in baskets, in unknown villages, in the various places she has worked, searching pockets lined with sunflower seeds and smashed eggs.

The worst of it is that for Zhenya two things are involved, both of them agonizing in their uncontainableness, by which I mean one cannot draw limits round them with one's own hands, and one ought to do so. They are the ephemerality of the moral obligation and the ephemerality of the threat to life, which has just shown her such a shocking grimace, immediately after having held up to her the death mask (and such a one!—whose?).

Here I am again: what am I writing? What liberties am I allowing myself? Why should I think of you, why answer you when I know I cannot and ought not to send you letters? Well, it is temporary; you won't have to put up with it for long. I do it because my feeling for you still makes me believe you need my answers, and I bow to this need, although it is high time to know how frail, if not nonexistent, this need is.

The day after tomorrow (Sunday evening) I will do what you and Aunt Asya have requested of me, although I don't quite understand why it ought to be done in that way and wonder whether Struve will not be displeased. That, however, is your business. As I understand it, I am to ask that the museum limit itself to one copy of the book in the hope that they will agree to perhaps twenty-five.

Heaven forbid that you should write Papa about Efros.* He is his archenemy, c'est sa bête noire. In a review of art exhibitions in *The Russian News*, Efros once allowed himself to adopt an outrageous tone in respect to Papa, and so unjustly, so blindly! Papa was and is a very

---

* Abram Markovich Efros (1888–1954): Soviet translator and literary and art critic.

Boris Pasternak
with his son Zhenya.
Abramtsevo, 1925

Evgenya Pasternak
with Zhenya

Aunt Asya

Olga Freidenberg

Boris Pasternak. Moscow, 1928

spirited man, with all the weaknesses of a proud, vital, spirited person who is in the right place at the right time—so unlike me with my "bordering-on-hypocrisy," as my friends put it, i.e., with a trait of character not native to me but a foreign body growing bigger and bigger inside of me, nourished by the influence of the times, the environment, plans, etc., etc. . . . . How affronted he was by so much clarity! Just as I am *dazed* by so much *muddle*.

Dear Aunt, just see what is going on here, and I have not told the half of it because I have not said a word about myself.

Thanks a thousand times for the letter. Tears came to Zhenya's eyes the moment she saw your handwriting. It doesn't matter, indeed it is probably a good thing, that all these misfortunes have come at once. But she looks very bad, is reduced to skin and bone and ought to go away for a month's rest. This could easily be arranged, but she refuses to go; first she must get Fenya into the hospital, then she must begin working again—she hasn't held a brush in her hand for over six months. I really don't know what is to become of her.

Only last evening I was deeply moved by a speech Efros made about a French poet who happens to be in Moscow. It was an excellent speech and he said just the right things. The meeting was entirely devoted to the work of this splendid poet of Romain Rolland's "humane" type. Because of your request I will accept his invitation to dinner on Sunday evening, and he will not know that I have an ulterior motive in being there. Ordinarily I wouldn't go, even though he is a clever and interesting man. I stay at home most of the time.

Superstition made me cross out the results of Fenya's medical examination.* None of the results has yet been confirmed by tests.

Don't be angry when I don't write. You see what my life is like. That is why I am always in a hurry, always trying to save time, always accepting each new day as a gift.

I will tell you the results of my talk with Efros in a separate letter.

Leningrad, December 21, 1928

Dear Borya,

I suppose I must send you the season's greetings and wish you all the best for the new year. You yourself know that our correspondence is such that I can only write you for practical reasons. Such is the present one.

Boris Vasilevich Kazansky, my good friend and secretary of the litera-

* Details of Fenya's illness given earlier in the letter were painstakingly crossed out.

ture department of the Institute of the History of Art, has asked me to convey to you his and the institute's request. The institute is publishing Bukhshtab's* study of your work, and it is their custom to include an article by the author himself at the very beginning. It can be autobiographical (my request: for God's sake, without Odessas, etc.) or theoretical, either about poetry in general or about your own. So they ask you to send them an article, and urgently it seems (I don't recall).

I forgot to insert an epigraph: "May God bless you; I've had no hand in it." I can't refuse Boris Vasilevich his innocent request and I perform it mechanically. There is nothing I can add or subtract from this. B. V. himself will write to you since I refused to take upon myself the more practical functions. Why he wanted me to serve as an intermediary I don't know. Possibly he places too much value on my words and overestimates the force of letters.

We expected Zhenya and at one time were elated by the prospect of her visit.

Love.

Yours,
OLYA

Moscow, December 27, 1928

Dear Olechka,

Ah, if you only knew how bad things have been with me, how inescapably, indefinably hard of late! Since the beginning of spring I have managed to keep us going materially somehow, without writing anything new or vital. I alone am not to be blamed; the times are, too, i.e., the officialdom of our times. At present I can offer no reply to the institute's request, which was probably inspired by you. From day to day I try to get down to work, which is the only thing that can save me spiritually, and only then, when I have recaptured a doomed candor (nobly doomed, and not only now but always), can I determine what I must do and write. It seems to me there is only one thing to write about at this time, in these days—namely, the involuntary, self-imposed limitations of the "fellow travelers,"† limitations that have become as much second nature to them as the distortions in evaluating their historical role.

---

* Boris Yakovlevich Bukhshtab intended to publish a monograph on Pasternak with the Institute of the History of Art. It was not published.

† Russian writers of bourgeois origin who were tolerated until the late 1920's because of their skill and ideological neutrality.

If you know Bukhshtab personally, please ask him to consult me before citing any passage from my *Above the Barriers*. The book is full of typographical errors; it came out without my seeing the proofs because I was in the Urals at the time.

Best love to you and Aunt Asya.

DIARY

A state of extreme nervous tension was brought on by the impossibility of publishing *The Novel* or finding a home for my second child, *Procris*, as well as by all the taboos and "judgments of fools" I had been subjected to. It was while I was in such a state that, wishing to acquaint myself with official dialectical materialism, I found in a book by Deborin (the very Deborin who was state philosopher and dictator of ideas) all the tenets to which I had given practical application in my works. Overwhelmed, agitated to the point of a nervous palsy, and feeling that I had come to the end of my tether, I wrote the following letter to Deborin.

Leningrad, January 4, 1929

Dear Comrade Deborin,

I am turning to you at a very difficult time in my life as a scholar. If you have had to suffer and struggle with extreme despair, if you are acquainted with the thorny path a scholar must tread, you will forgive the note of alarm in my appeal to you. Permit me to disregard for the moment the factual basis for my appeal and come to the point directly: I am requesting an interview with you for no longer than is necessary to summarize the work I have completed and to hear your judgment of it. I am a researcher at the Japhetic Institute of the Academy of Sciences, at the Institute of Language and Literature of East and West, at Leningrad University, etc. I am not a dilettante or a Chaliapin fan and I am a woman, which commands respect even in our society. I do not know whether it would be more convenient for you to receive me in Moscow or in Leningrad, to which you will probably come in connection with elections for membership in the Academy. My financial position permits me to stay in Moscow for one day only. Forgive me for not knowing your first name and patronymic; I know you only as a thinker and the leader of our contemporary view of philosophy.

(Signature)
(Address)

If it would be less trouble for you to answer me by telephone in Moscow, this can be done through Boris Leonidovich Pasternak (14 Volkhonka, Apt. 9).

DIARY

At that time Borya was at the height of his fame, and therefore I thought his name would serve Deborin as evidence that I was not just another one of the countless petitioners who addressed him. Naturally I warned Borya, but things could not have turned out worse. I learned so in an angry card from Borya, who could not understand that the last thing I wanted to do was to burden him with requests for favors.

Moscow, January 17, 1929

Dear Olyushka,

What you warned me of in your postcard just occurred. It was not Deborin himself who called but evidently his wife at his request. She asked me for information I could not give. In general she asked, politely enough, what your case was about and what you wanted. With your card in hand, I told her the only thing I knew: that you apparently wanted an appointment with him, either here or in Leningrad. But since I was led to believe your request was couched in such terse terms that it was not clear (or was represented to be so), I told them all I could about you—who you are, what your work is about, about Marr, etc.

You placed me in an impossible situation. How was I to know what you wrote in your letter to Deborin? You presented the matter as if everything would take care of itself in a way you alone knew and had concocted; I was to be but the intermediary. Wouldn't it be better if, instead of all this, you came straight here? You know how happy we would be. Here you would meet with him, if you must. His wife said he would be in Leningrad in March.

Now you are probably angry with me, but why, pray, am I to blame? The main thing is that you come here.

Love to you and Aunt Asya.

DIARY

I promptly answered him, but my finding that letter among my papers and my not pursuing the request I made of Deborin indicates that I decided to solve my problems myself.

Leningrad, January 21, 1929 [not sent]

Dear Borya,

You are a strange one. As though it is inevitable that someone be to blame, you or I! It is ridiculous to speak of "blame," particularly in our times, when circumstances are so complicated that they often become inextricably entangled. Of course it makes me bitter to realize you are so completely isolated from me; our birthright calls for a greater friendship than this pitiable family parody. But for this at least I am not to blame. Your attitude toward our correspondence makes it necessary to terminate it. To write you confidential letters would simply mean to impose myself upon you.

That postcard must have fallen on you like a meteorite. If Deborin had called Uncle in Berlin, he would have received a complete report, because our friendly correspondence is continuous and Uncle knows all about me. I could hardly have foreseen that Deborin would choose precisely that form of response. You will agree that, having merely asked him for an appointment, the hour and place of it, having given him my address in Petersburg (he knew my official position from the letter) and your telephone in Moscow, having requested that he answer only one brief question, I could not have anticipated that he would ask of the Moscow addressee (not even knowing our relationship) questions about matters the letter deliberately ignored. Even taking that into account, don't think I am so romantic or inexperienced as to write an incomprehensible letter. It was brief, precisely phrased, and to the point, but, true, it was made emotional by the stress under which I wrote it. I spoke in it of a scholarly discussion, declared it was not worthwhile burdening such a letter with factual details, told him the work under discussion was completed and that I would appreciate his opinion of it. My right to this was made clear by the list of academic positions I hold and by the general tone of the letter. Moreover, he is not the emperor of China, and how can he, a scholar, refuse an exchange of opinion with another scholar? That's the whole thing in a nutshell. But his wife's solo part and their questions present the other side of the coin, the bureaucratic side—inevitable, it seems, in the academic world. I have seen it all too often, be it among Red professors or gray ones.* If you keep in mind that Deborin is both a Jew and a politician, there is nothing to be surprised at. Yet I must say in his defense that I am thoroughly convinced he expected to be here for the Academy elections and to see me then to save me a trip to Moscow. That is why he delayed and telephoned you only after he had been blackballed

* Red professors: those teaching Marxism. Gray professors: dull mediocrities.

and saw that the whole business would drag out until March. That is one thing. The other is that at a time of great pressure I could not sit down and describe to you all my affairs and circumstances. Had I done so it would not have been for the purpose of informing you but simply to have a heart-to-heart talk with you. If it interests you at all, I am prepared to tell you. Thank you for saying you would be happy to see me in Moscow, and for that "wouldn't it be better if you came straight here?" Alas, that idyllic time has passed. For me Moscow is now connected solely with business, and even if you had no desire to see me I would come if I had to. You may hear a certain bitterness in that, but the bitterness has already become chronic in every aspect.

Well then, now I shall tell you all. From September to December there was endless red tape concerning my work—its submission to reviewers, the period of having it read, of having reviews written, of having reviews given to Marr, of getting Marr's own review, of having it pass through the hands of secretaries, sections, departments, and so on and so forth. Finally, when all seemed lost (including hope), Marr informed me (on December 13) that my work had been accepted by the Communist Academy and scheduled for publication very soon. In early January I was to take it to Moscow (was given the address of certain individuals at the Communist Academy, etc.). Try to understand my feelings, especially after all I have gone through these past years! I wrote Uncle to pass on the news to Josephine but to keep it from you, giving me the opportunity to surprise you. Marr left for Moscow and I gave a talk on Greek philosophy at the Institute of Marxism with great success. That's how it was. Then the pendulum began to swing back. The Marxists announced "their" conference, at which they declared my name anathema, slinging the well-known epithets at me (behind my back and directly after their applause). That made me raise the issue of *Procris* for the first time and present the Communist Academy with a sheaf of new questions, presaging a new scandal, this time a real one, with consequences, and with the danger of injuring Marr. I cannot describe to you the many roads leading to my despair. Just then Marr arrived from Moscow and said the Communist Academy was evidently afraid to accept responsibility for my work and intended to transfer it to the State Publishing House, but that they would summon me to Moscow to address one of their meetings. At first I was pleased, but then I realized this was a rejection—and Marr was to leave for Paris in February and be gone until summer. Incidentally, Marr read a summary of the talk I gave to the Marxists and found it of interest. What was I to do now? Go to Moscow? Marr was attending a conference in Moscow and would go from there to Karelia.

At this point reviews came of a book published in Germany on the Greek novel, presenting views that coincided with my own. The chorus of misfortune was joined by fresh voices. I found myself facing complete catastrophe. Have you any idea of what I went through? No, I can be understood only by a scholar who has always been persecuted for his individual way of thinking, and who at the same time has had to do battle with the hydra of daily living and vulgarity, and who suddenly learns that his idea, only less inspired and less abused, has come to life in the West, among better informed and sterner judges. This was the last straw; everything within me rebelled. I was aware of the rightness of an intellectual stand that might lead me to the academic stake; at the same time my growing despair tempted me to take extreme measures, and since in my mind I had long ago turned to Deborin, I now sat down (sobbing) and wrote him a short, precise, businesslike letter. What followed is understandable. The very logic of circumstances decreed that I should be left without a reply, for no frustration can compare with the frustration of grief's ecstasy. This was followed by a series of unworthy "sops" to my spirit. I applied myself to a study of Deborin's works, anxious to know once and for all what is expected of us these days—can there be any such thing as a compromise? Gradually I discovered that my *Procris* is an excellent example of dialectical materialism in application.

Marr came back from Karelia. I told him I was holding my own with complete confidence (I was ready to say the opposite after the Marxists), and he promised to find out why I had not been summoned to Moscow. Two days later he returned with the news that I would be published by the Communist Academy! Deborin called you. I decided to go to Moscow at the beginning of February and, with that in mind, began making minor corrections of my manuscript. Now remember your own words, the "instead of all this" wouldn't it be better "if you came straight here" and "you know how happy we would be." I would be just as happy, but I am confident of nothing any longer; the situation as I have described it may change. We shall see. I am thoroughly sick of it all. This cannot be called living. You must understand that I have presented only a skeleton outline; many important things remain to be said in addition to a mass of details that have worn me away like drops of water. For instance, I am threatened with being discharged again for launching *Procris* at the Japhetic Institute instead of at the university. An incredible array of evils, cliques, and machinations.

Do forgive me for involuntarily putting you in an uncomfortable position. Nothing of the sort ever entered my mind. The fact is that I wrote that postcard in the dining room, in the midst of noise and smells, picking up the postcard in one place, the stamp in another, the pencil in yet a third. It was late and the post office was closed, so I took the card to the university to find out Deborin's first name and patronymic; one friend escorted me, we met another on the way, and we were joined by still another in the packed dining room. I knew that if I did not send it off on the impulse of the moment I would not send it at all. Naturally I would like to know what you said about me and whether it corresponds to what I shall have to tell him. At any rate, thank you for your services and your desire to help me.

Best love.

Yours,

OLYA

Moscow, February 8, 1929

Dear Aunt Asya and Olyushka,

I know, I know, both of you are probably angry with me and must have mistaken impressions of my humble existence and the reason for my silence. But that is all beside the point; set my mind at rest as soon as possible by telling me how you are withstanding this accursed cold, and *whether you have enough bread* and how difficult it is to get. Ah, what rumors circulate now and then! Quickly give me an account by postcard of what you are doing in this fantastic ($-40°$) cold. You don't drink vodka, so how do you survive? I know what you will think now. Oh no, I am writing in a frozen, unthawed state, and my excited tone is explained first by the overdue work I have neglected for six months (I wrote you what was going on during those six months): *me tiennent en haleine et encore un pareil mois de plus me rendra fou.* Second, it is explained by certain alarming and foolish stories about Leningrad received from indirect sources. Third, it is explained by my own disbelief in these stories (they came from Paris) and my eagerness to hear your confirmation of their untruth. This third is certainly the most important, if not the only, cause of my excitement. If I did not believe you were all right I would not be excited, but anguished and destroyed.

This is what I can say about myself. My salary and my budget have parted company to such an extent that I am sunk deeply in debt; at present, for example, I am consuming my September promises. You can imagine the rush I am in, and the mood, too, and how much spare time I have. It goes without saying that I cannot be "inspired" sixteen hours a day. And how much I have to read! In addition I have got to refresh my knowledge of languages, which has grown pretty rusty of late. And so all my hours are taken up, to say nothing of those spent on this cursed madhouse of an apartment with its cracks, overpopulation, and the irremediable inability of people to do anything properly (except the purely mechanical) unless provided with minimal conditions, such as a normal income, an outside temperature ranging between 0° and 10°, etc. Oh, if only you knew!

Love and kisses. I shall be waiting to hear from you, and I admit in advance to being a beast and assure you I cannot help being one right up, I suppose, until 1930.

Devotedly yours,

BORYA

DIARY

What bitter laughter Borya's February letter evoked! Fancy his being upset by the cold, by a shortage of bread! With touching emphasis he asked, "Have you enough bread? Bread!" Not a word about my writings, about serious evils and sufferings. It was bread that worried him!

I was getting ready to go to Moscow at the time. An admirer of Marr named Valerian Aptekar was at the head of the Communist Academy. Marr had made arrangements with him about *Procris*.

I made Aptekar's acquaintance in Moscow. He was a portly, outgoing, rather familiar fellow, in a leather coat of the sort only "those at the top" wear. He advanced with a rolling gait as if in defiance of all obstacles. Gaily and self-confidently he acknowledged his lack of education. Uncouth young men like Aptekar come to the city from the country or from small towns, master Party slogans, newspaper jargon, the bare bones of Marxism, and assume the role of bosses and dictators. With untroubled consciences they teach scholars what to think and are sincerely convinced that knowledge itself is not essential to the formulation of a proper scheme of knowledge (methodology).

Borya was not particularly glad to see me. He was suffering from a toothache. Zhenya was in the Crimea. Borya was snubbed by the countless occupants of what had been Uncle Leonid's enormous apartment. They got their meals on fifteen kerosene stoves in the kitchen, they queued up for the toilet, they overran the corridor, the entrance hall, the bathroom. I did not in the least want to stay at Borya's. I told him I wanted to be as near as possible to the Communist Academy. With a little laugh he took me to a window facing the courtyard and said, "In that case this is just the place for you." The Communist Academy was in the courtyard.

That evening I gave my report, and Borya went with me despite his aching teeth and my request that he stay at home.

"Only make it short," he said, completely disregarding the significance the moment held for me, what a great event it was in my life, how long I had awaited it, and how happily excited I felt. Not many people came. Friche, the greatest authority in the field, was in the hospital. The meeting was chaired by Nusinov, his deputy, also a great man, whose every word carried weight. My report was enthusiastically received. I was told all sorts of nice things, and Aptekar became my patron. Nusinov accepted *Procris* for publication.

Borya, gloomy and holding his cheek, hurried me out of the building. On the way home he remarked that I had overlooked the time element in my work. I was astonished at his subtlety. He told me other things that were true but not professional; I saw that he was right but too absolute in his judgments, as are most people outside the field of scholarship.

I spent the night at his place. As in our childhood, we slept in the same room and exchanged views from our beds. There was something here of Uncle's family, of Aunt Rosa, of our blood relationship. The freshness of sheets and the smell of the Pasternak apartment stirred something good within me.

I returned home on the first of May.

At the end of May an academic conference was held in Moscow (I have forgotten the theme of it) to which Frank-Kamenetsky was a delegate. I gave him my *Procris* to take to Aptekar.

Moscow, May 23, 1929

My own dear Olyushka,

I am keeping the provisions you sent—they will come in handy. Thanks. Frank-Kamenetsky came to see me and will tell you about my incomparable boorishness. But, my dear, I did not tell you when you were here how busy I am, and how hurriedly and anxiously I work. It is impossible to judge of my life from the two days of it you witnessed when you were here. Naturally I dropped everything to be with you.

This is how things stand. The appearance of Frank-Kamenetsky reminded me of the paper you had left with me and of your request. Doubtlessly he noted the fright in my eyes on seeing him. The next day I took your paper to the RANION* office but could not find out whether I was too late or not, i.e., whether the three weeks' delay had not spoiled everything for you. Today I set out to be informed, or rather consoled.

* Russian Association for Scholarly Research in the Social Sciences.

Well, you and I never have any luck. A terrible accident stopped me at the very entrance to the RANION office. Two steps away a little boy had part of his foot cut off by a tram. From the office they sent for an ambulance, a crowd surged round the entrance, the child lay on the sidewalk under the windows crying and insisting it was not his fault, begging them to run for his mother, and the pronouncement of the name made him go off into screams of "Mama! Mama!"

An hour later I entered the office and left it without saying a word. I couldn't. I opened my mouth and shut it, knowing that if I tried to speak I would break down.

Love to Aunt Asya.

Moscow, May 29, 1929

Dear Olyushka,

Forgive me for not setting your mind at rest in time as to RANION. Fortunately I have not injured your cause; not a single meeting was held during the time of my neglect, and I turned in your paper a full week before the scheduled one was held.

Things have been going forward in my life, too. At the end of January I began a long novel (in prose) and recently finished the first part (one-fourth of the planned whole). It seems to be turning out all right, but you yourself will have the opportunity of judging. I will let you know as soon as I find out where and when it will come out. My little freckle-face often speaks of you. While his mother was away he managed to catch the mumps and get over them; he's been well for some time now. It goes without saying I didn't write Zhenya about his illness, and it seems I didn't tell you, either. He was delirious the first night, held my hand and gazed into the distance, calling me for some reason Praskovya Petrovna. His eyes were enormous, and I developed an entirely new feeling for him. The greatest things in the world clothe themselves in boundless tranquillity. (One can permit oneself such an aphorism only on the margin of a postcard.)

Love to you and Aunt Asya.

Yours,

BORYA

DIARY

The year 1929 was marked by outrageous litigation over our apartment. Housing conditions were becoming incredibly difficult. It was impossible for us to keep tenants. The government began to support the subdivision of apartments. We wanted to retain two rooms for our own use and partition off the rest. Permission was promptly granted. But the scamps who headed the apartment house management (ZHAKT) wanted our apartment for themselves. Eleven trials! And twenty-two inspections of our apartment by various commissions that broke into our house at any time of day.

Our apartment was turned into heaps of construction rubbish. We lived in dirt and dust amid removed beams and broken plaster. A queue of unknown people who wanted to move in stood at our entrance.

We lost our case at every level. But as if that were not enough, we were sued for such an amount that we not only lost our apartment, independence, and peace of mind, but also had to sell all our possessions and become beggars.

Then suddenly—by pure accident—a change of prosecutors saved us.

Moscow, July 9, 1929

Dear Aunt Asya and Olyushka,

I am writing so that you won't think I've forgotten you. I will have to go back to work again soon, and then there will be no time for letter writing. The interval has been a long one and my neglected work will press hard upon me, so don't be angry if you answer this letter and get none in reply from me. It has been a dreadful interval for the following reason.

You remember, Olyushka, my telling you about the curse of my past five years, about periodic and prolonged pain in my lower jaw spreading over my entire chin, pain worse than any toothache? I finally went for an X ray and discovered it was not neuralgia, as had been supposed; my sensations provided scientifically accurate evidence for the true diagnosis. The X ray showed an enormous cavity under my teeth where there ought to have been bone—the result of bone disintegration that had been taking place periodically over the past five years. And so I had an operation. They removed a huge cyst that had penetrated the bone, and simultaneously they chisled away remnants of bone eaten away by the cyst. You would not notice any change in me now, that is, in my appearance; I have even begun to work again, but I cannot talk at all for the time being. I hope that the only bad effect when the wound heals will be a partial toothlessness. The operation required the extraction of seven teeth, among them all of my front ones. Three months after the healing we can mend that. It was a terribly painful operation, which took an hour and a half instead of the promised twenty minutes. At one point I lost consciousness because the local anesthetic was ineffective—indeed there was nothing to anesthetize in the cavity, and they were afraid that if they administered a general anesthetic they might sever the central facial nerve. While extracting the cyst, they either gave this nerve a jerk or, unable to see it because of the blood, swabbed it with cotton, a misdemeanor I announced by letting out a scream and fainting dead away. Poor Zhenya, who was standing outside the door, nearly fainted, too, but would not let those who ran to her aid take her away. Thank God it is all behind me, but from time to time I recall it and think: this agony was caused by doctors who were trying to cause me as little pain as possible—what, then, must people suffer who are being deliberately tortured? How fortunate that our imagination is too dull to give us a vivid impression of everything!

Good-by for the present. All my love. Be sure to let me know what is going on with you, particularly how both of you are feeling and about your apartment trouble. Let's make arrangements for the rest of the summer. Couldn't we send for you to join us here?

Yours,
BORYA

Leningrad, July 11, 1929

Poor, dear Borya! I shuddered as I read your letter. You can't imagine how sorry for you I am. The only good thing is that it is over. You should have done it long ago and saved yourself from all you have suffered lately. With all my heart I am thankful you are rid of that vicious cyst. Be sure and take a good rest now; you can't do everything anyway.

I would have been delighted to spend a week or two with you. In July I had a pass enabling me to go to the resort in Sestroretsk (a very paradise on earth—if I were you I would take the family there; it only costs 115 rubles a month for food and board, 58 for children, and they have everything a child could wish for, everything for you and Zhenya, too: pine woods, the sea, all sorts of cures for the nervous system—baths, etc.), but in six days I came rushing home, summoned by the latest scandal (a purely "personal" one; I'll tell you about it later), and now I don't know whether I shall return there, or go to Peterhof, or stay here in town. The partitioning of the apartment that was going ahead full steam has been halted for the present. Love to you all.

Yours,
OLYA

DIARY

This was the time of the entrenchment of Stalinism, the ordeal of the peasantry, "dizzying successes," etc. It ushered in the era of Soviet fascism, but we accepted it as a continuation of the revolution, with its thirst for destruction.

At the beginning of March 1930, Frank-Kamenetsky became a member of an antireligious brigade that went to the countryside, where the collectivization of the farms was in progress. He became enthusiastic about the collective farms, built up theories about them, uttered well-meaning stupidities and made public speeches. I waited out this new and foolish infatuation. I could not free my mind of a picture that had once horrified Borya: long columns of peasant families, whole villages of them, whole boxcar trainloads of them, being sent into exile for being what they called kulaks.*

Moscow, June 11, 1930

Dear Olyushka and Aunt Asya,

I have often thought of you this year, often written to you in imagination and never done it in fact, except for one postcard I sent and Olya never answered.

And now I cannot say why I am writing. Happily there is no longer any reason to sympathize with you because of your apartment trouble and litigations, matters of which Papa informed me this winter. I shamefully let the opportunity to congratulate Aunt Asya on her seventieth birthday slip by. There is no reason for writing you now—but one: my fear that if I don't write now I will never have another opportunity to do so. I am practically saying good-by to you.

Don't be frightened; you mustn't take me literally. I am not seriously ill; nothing directly threatens me. But I am constantly haunted by a sense of the imminence of the end, evoked in my case by the most decisive of causes: a contemplation of my own work. It has become caught and held in the past, and I am powerless to budge it. I took no part in the creation of the present and bear it no love.

It is no great revelation to say that every man reaches his limit at some time and that there is an end to all things. But it is hard to face this truth as applied to oneself. I have no future; I don't know what awaits me.

However, this letter is not as unoccasioned as I thought. Intending to

* Allegedly prosperous peasants, considered to be opposed to collectivization.

write you day after day, I gradually forgot the reason for it. This is it: some new acquaintances urged us to spend the summer outside of Kiev, and they rented a dacha for us there. Zhenya, little Zhenya, and his governess have been there since the end of May. I'm afraid it wasn't the wisest thing to do; the first impressions of Zhenya and Alexander's wife (my brother's family has gone there, too) verged on despair; it seemed senseless to have gone so far and with such difficulty. The general opinion, however, is that it will be easier to get food in the Ukraine than here in the north. On the day after tomorrow, the 14th, I'll set out to join them. Will you not come and be our guests—at least you, Olga? I have reason to believe that I will have to return to Moscow in the middle of the summer. Even if I don't, there is room for all of us; the dacha is a big one. If you want to come, Olga, write to me at the following address: 13 Pushkin Street, Irpen, Kiev District, Southwest Railroad Line.

Best love to both of you. Forgive this sad letter.

Yours,

BORYA

P.S. This note paper was given me by an American woman; I didn't use it so long as I could get ordinary paper, but now that is impossible.

DIARY

Hardly had we time to draw breath after the partitioning of the apartment when Mother came down with inflammation of the knee. My old friend Motya Lifshits, an army surgeon, cured her. But before it was completely healed she contracted typhoid fever. The situation snatched me out of my usual routine. I dropped my work, my writing, my friends; I never went out and I ate practically nothing. Day and night I alone nursed the patient and suffered with her all the terrible vicissitudes attending the disease. In the end our doctor told me Mother's stomach muscles had become devitalized and there was nothing he could do about it. Despite his declaration of helplessness I consulted several other doctors. Doctor Waldmann, a German, came—at that time he was just another doctor, but now he has won well-deserved fame and position. He declared she was not dying, but recuperating. He ordered me to feed her three times a day, dinner to be a full meal of three courses (until then she had been unable to take anything but two or three spoonfuls of cereal).

A new phase set in. I worked like a machine, without a moment's free time. I nursed her, kept everything meticulously clean, washed endless linen, invented tempting dishes—all this in an inexplicable surge of energy. I did things I had never done before and had never known how to do.

Mother began to recover.

Kiev, June 23, 1930

Dear Olyushka,

I arrived here yesterday and found your postcard waiting for me. How thankful I am that Aunt Asya is recovering—it always is like a miraculous gift, unexpected relief in whatever circumstances the joyful event occurs. But how sad the rest is, and how dreadful your loneliness! Please let me help you somehow; just tell me how.

I know this is an absurd question, but could it be that you are in need of money? Forgive the asking and don't be angry. After all, I keep going only by allowing the publishers to help and support me; I have long since stopped paying back their loans. God, how hopeless it all seems! And here I was unburdening myself to you at just the wrong time. Or perhaps at just the right time—out of the stifling darkness I wrote to you, wholly unaware that your darkness was even more stifling. Could you not find a servant to relieve you? You can't go on doing all that you described. Not even a young person would be up to it.

Here all goes well and even bears some resemblance to genuine living. Couldn't you come here when Aunt Asya feels stronger? There are rooms for rent. But I know I am asking in vain. I can only wish you fortitude and speedy improvement. Do tell me if anything is needed. I am stunned.

Love to you and Aunt Asya.

DIARY

Procris, of course, was not published. Marr showed not the slightest interest in it. To my complaint he replied, "Why, hasn't it been sent to the printers yet?" Soon thereafter the Communist Academy Publishing House was closed.

At this time Borya and Zhenya were going through a period of strained relations. Each of them was an artist and each had an artist's egotism. Zhenya dreamed of Paris and thought that her marriage to Borya would relieve her of all worldly cares. She was deeply disappointed. He was used to the Tolstoyan standard: a daily life based on lofty ideas and family life such as that depicted in *War and Peace*. Zhenya offered him a Bohemian life. He was not to be tempted by a Puccini libretto or convinced that art required a loosening of the reins. His father was a painter, his mother a musician, he himself a poet. He was convinced of something quite different: that art binds and constrains, concentrates and crystallizes the family.

Aware of Zhenya's suspicions and jealousy, I tried to show the utmost tact as I watched their relationship crumble. I found this particularly difficult on one occasion when they quarreled over the reading of my letter: Zhenya wanted to read it simultaneously with Borya, leaning over his shoulder, and he was exasperated by this attempt to share intimacies.

Irpen, August 21, 1930

Dear Olyushka,

Again I have no intention of writing you a letter, merely of thanking you for yours. How much you put into some of them, and how beautifully you express yourself! It's a pity that such a flow of ideas, caught on the run yet in splendid array, should be sent heaven knows where to heaven knows whom and end up with no more than an acknowledgement of their receipt.

I shall intentionally refrain from mentioning anything of importance in this letter. I will tell you everything when we meet. In order to say a word about my family or myself, about the summer, about freedom of views and a feeling of fatality, I would first have to convince myself that the dining-room table did not stand in the middle of the room, that the sideboard no longer occupied its place against the left wall or the wardrobe in the corner by the window. To begin with, such a melancholy assumption is beyond my power.

My dearest love to you and your mother. I am greatly annoyed in the evenings by foolish moths in shaggy trousers, recklessly circling round and round my lamp and diving headlong into my inkwell or settling on my pen or penholder. A cool night after a stuffy day, a thunderstorm in the distance, a kerosene lamp on our enormous porch (it seems enormous indeed, surrounded as it now is by an ocean of impenetrable black air), and, above all, these midges and moths—what associations all this ought to bring to mind! But, whether owing to revolution or age, I seem to have become immune to the past; the subjective labyrinth does not deflect simple, direct sensations—indeed it is *they alone* (the midges and moths) for whom I feel sorry, instead of for myself, as formerly. I am saddened by the thought that the hot lamp chimney does not *cool* their ardor, not by the remembrance of another hot August night on Bolshoi Fontan,*

* In Odessa.

with the sea in front of us and woods to the right beyond the river, a river illuminated from time to time by flashes of summer lightning. But this sounds like a "landscape painting," and a very commonplace one at that, which in no way fits into my present intentions.

Your explanation of the incident with Aptekar presented the whole matter in a different light, one I knew nothing of. (See this mess? It's all the moths; they made a particularly furious assault on Aptekar.) I gave a different reading to your postcard, a reading that made you more selfish and partial. In matters of this sort we are basically so similar that I would even take a denial of kinship in the spirit that near of kin (in the deepest sense) ought to take it. Explanations here are relatively unimportant because at the very core of our interrelationship lies that which defies explanation, a fact that both of us accept with an equal sense of fatality. In short, if you *could not* have written that postcard, you and I would have been two very different people. Much love.

Yours,

BORYA

P.S. When I began reading your letter, Zhenya leaned over my shoulder to read it with me, a thing I detest. I proposed that she should read it first, just so that we should read it separately. She was so offended that she has not read it at all and doesn't mean to. This is further explanation of why she has not added anything in this letter. You surely know, however, how fond she is of both of you.

Moscow, October 20, 1930

Dear Olyushka,

I was delighted to get your letter. The request and the tone in which it was made enables me to draw vague conclusions that are, nonetheless, reassuring.

I read a hidden rebuke in your exaggerated apologies, but the rebuke, too, is acceptable, although presented in vague form. It goes without saying that in a general sense I am a swine—a swine in the general swinishness of our times. I would have been confounded to discover that your rebuke was based on some definite malefaction on my part. Delinquency in correspondence? Then why don't *you* write, knowing how important it is for me to know all about you in proper time? Or perhaps you are offended that I should have responded to your woeful news on a postcard? But there was some definite proposition I had to make—I've forgotten exactly what at the moment (something about a dacha?)—and expected you to answer at once. It is true, of course (do I deny it?), that the *manner* of my neglect was reprehensible: I waited in listless silence. What can I do about it? It becomes harder and harder to write. Everything is becoming silent. The West has died out of my letters, and so have I myself, after giving due warning.

The summer, however, was divine—delightful friends, delightful surroundings. And my work, the very thing I had sung a dirge to in the letter I wrote you last spring, revived in the sun; it has been a long time since I have worked as effectively as I did in Irpen. Naturally our little world there was isolated and apart, like Hamsun's world of famine,* but it was a robust, balanced world.

I have written my *Bronze Horseman*, Olya—humble, unpolished, but a complete thing and, I believe, genuine. I don't suppose it will ever see the light of day. The censor has begun chopping away at my new editions and, to make up for past neglect, sinks his fangs with excessive fervor into works of mine not yet published.

Do please write to me in more detail. I am afraid to ask about Aunt Asya. Rebukes are rebukes, but *your* silence (under the circumstances) is more cruel than mine. I cannot believe that the effect my silence has on you is as great as yours is on me. So please do write.

Now about Aptekar. I just phoned him and was unable to find out anything more helpful than the following. He will be in Leningrad for two days (November 1 and 2), mornings at the Japhetic Institute and otherwise at the Academy of Sciences, and he requests that you "catch" him (his term) in the morning. I said I intended writing to you and asked couldn't he propose something more closely associated with your problem than "catching" him, especially since the one would have no bad effect on the other. Murmuring pleasantries addressed to you, he put me off as a third party, probably because he did not wish to reveal his ignorance of the Communist Academy business. Now I'm sure you are angry with me, but I swear to heaven I did my best to be nice to him.

Best love to you and Aunt Asya.

A word about our daily life. Since I have not the faintest conception of what the winter will bring, our apartment more nearly resembles a bivouac than ever before: temporary, breathless, unreal.

At least we get enough to eat, thank the Lord, and are in no need of money (I implore you to keep that in mind—do me the favor!). Zhenya is very thin.

* Knut Hamsun (1859–1952): Norwegian novelist, author of *Hunger* (1890).

136

Moscow, December 5, 1930

Olechka, my dear friend, and you, dear Aunt Asya,

Need I say how your letter affected us, Olya, and how you, Aunt Asya, are just the same, not to be changed by anything? I had heard of your last year's troubles but had no idea they were one-tenth so bad.

Your reproach as to breaking off our correspondence (fair enough!) sounded bitter, Olya, and left a bitter echo. It is the echo of my life. It reflects how everything began, how everything took shape. What can be done about it?

Not long ago, when we were spending the evening with friends, Zhenya expressed the sentiment that Leningrad women are exceptional and that all exceptional ones come from there. The remark was inspired by the really exceptional pianist Maria Yudina, who was present. The examples given, besides Yudina, were our close friends Akhmatova, the Radlov sisters,* and both of you. Our hostess reminded us that she, too, was from Petersburg, and this prompted Zhenya to tell about you.

Let me say that I love you as my very own, yet I hardly think I will write to the end of this page. Is that what you call "breaking off our correspondence," Olya? To talk about my own affairs would mean to share them, to present them as food, to offer you a treat; but to do that, one must hold something tangible in one's hands. Is there anything tangible in today's life? Or perhaps I ought to reduce my tale to exclamations, and tell you the following: that at any other time one one-hundredth of the happiness that has fallen to my lot, for some unknown reason, would have been sufficient to buy a huge diamond with which I could begin cutting glass; that again and again I meet people I cannot help loving; that marvelous waves which I in no way deserve break foaming at my feet; that my simple life is strewn with jewels, and that accordingly it is the more bitter that all of this should be in vain. Because it is part of our times, which have reduced life to an immaterial, abstract dream. The miracles of the human heart find no corner here that they can call their own, no stuff on which they can leave their imprint, no water in which they are reflected.

But I am writing to ask a great favor. I beg for your help. I have not given up hope of sending Zhenya and Doodle (as you call him) to my folks abroad. Accordingly I must, for certain purposes, put up a certain sum of money for them. You would be doing me a great favor, one for which I would not know how to thank you, if you agreed to periodically

* More precisely, the Darmolatov sisters: Sarra Dmitrevna Lebedeva (1892–1967), the sculptor, and Anna Dmitrevna Radlova (1891–1949), the poet and translator of Shakespeare. Lebedeva sculpted the tombstone of Boris Pasternak.

send a money order from me (only half of what is sent would be addressed to Papa). Surely you won't refuse. If you do, I don't know why I should go on trying to earn money. And I would know even less what you mean by my "breaking off our correspondence." Because there is no breaking off of correspondence, even in this matter, with my close friends from Moscow or those whom we met in Irpen, and this is the simplest proof of mutual trust. And you could refuse? But the most, most important consideration is that the service you would be doing me ten times outweighs those illusory standards you are always measuring me by. I swear it by Doodle's health! Your refusal would be not only a slap in the face for me but also the annulling of Doodle's future chances. That would be so despicable that I dare not contemplate its possibility. Forgive me for dwelling at such length on such an odious subject, but I am so afraid of you! It is this fear that makes me write to both of you at once. If Olya shows no mercy, do you take pity on me, Aunt Asya. Intercede for me with her, Aunt. I haven't the courage to talk to her alone.

Best love to you.

Yours,
BORYA

Has Papa written to you about Aunt Rosa's death?*

* Rozalia Osipovna Pasternak: Leonid Pasternak's sister.

CHAPTER V

In 1936 Pasternak sought refuge from the politics of Moscow in his newly built dacha in the writers' village of Peredelkino, about eleven miles southwest of the city. Increasingly this haven played the role of an imaginary garden in Pasternak's writings; some of his most evocative poetry draws upon its firs, meadows, streams, and pond. *On Early Trains* (1943) acknowledged his link with the city and its people—he often caught the early train to Moscow, on business or to visit Zhenya and their son.

Pasternak never lost faith in his relationship to nature, be it the nature of Peredelkino or that of the remote town of Chistopol, where he spent several winters in evacuation during World War II. "How indescribably beautiful is life in winter in the woods," he wrote of Peredelkino in 1940, "in the cold—if you have a good fuel supply. Your eyes roam from one delight to another, dazzled with beauty. And the charm of it lies not only in the beholding but also in the minute details of alert, laborious tending. Relax your zeal for an hour and the house becomes so cold that no amount of fire stoking will warm it. Let yourself be caught napping, and the potatoes begin to freeze in the cellar, or mold forms on the salted cucumbers. And all of this breathes and smells, all of it lives and can die. We have half a cellarful of our own potatoes, two barrels of sauerkraut, and two barrels of salted cucumbers."

A reverence for the land and those who worked it well was never far from Pasternak, in European Russia or in those parts that made up the empire inherited by the Soviet Union. In 1942 he wrote to Olya from Chistopol, from a region on the Kama River that figures in the novel *Doctor Zhivago*: "The soil here is miraculous, uncommonly rich, so black that it seems to be mixed with coal dust. If the land were turned over to a hard-working and disciplined population, to people who knew what they could do, what they wanted to do, and what they had a right to demand, no social or economic task would be too hard for them to accomplish; and

in this New Burgundy, art with a Rabelaisian slant or the gusto of Hoffmann's 'Nutcracker' would flourish."

In 1936 the campaign against "formalism" threatened both Boris Pasternak and Olga Freidenberg. As he had done and was to do for others—
Nikolai Nikolayevich Punin and Lev Nikolayevich Gumilev, husband and
son of the poet Anna Akhmatova, and the poet Osip Mandelstam—
Pasternak interceded on behalf of his cousin. Unaware that Nikolai
Bukharin, the old Bolshevik opponent of Stalin and editor of *Izvestia*, had
lost his power and was under close surveillance, Pasternak wrote him to
challenge the mounting newspaper campaign against Olga Freidenberg, a
frequent prelude to arrest. Others—the composer Dmitri Shostakovich,
the playwright Vsevolod Meyerhold, the actor Lebedev, the writers Marietta Shaginyan, Mikhail Bulgakov, Boris Pilnyak, Konstantin Fedin,
Leonid Leonov—some of them Pasternak's new neighbors at Peredelkino,
felt the sting of the mounting campaign. Not long after the campaign had
reached its height, at the Eighth Congress of Soviets, the Secretary of the
Writers' Union, V. P. Stavsky, denounced Pasternak's new poems as a
slander on the Soviet people. Pasternak replied, at the height of the
Terror, in an open letter published in *The Literary Gazette* in January
1937.

The turmoil in his life took its toll on Pasternak's health in 1935, causing
prolonged insomnia and an incipient nervous breakdown. At just that
time, during the summer of 1935, he was forced to attend the Inter-
national Congress in Defense of Culture in Paris. On the way he met with
his sister Josephine in the Berlin railroad station, but despite the anguish
of a fourteen-year separation he did not have the stamina to face his
parents. He returned to the Freidenbergs in Leningrad, his will paralyzed.
Zinaida Nikolayevna traveled to Leningrad and escorted him home to
Moscow.

Moscow, June 1, 1932

Dear Olyushka and Aunt Asya,

How fortunate that I haven't written you all this time! How much nonsense you would have heard, how many troubles already nonexistent you would have read about!

It has been an exceptionally hard winter, especially after Zhenya came back. She suffered terribly, poor thing—she above all, but everyone including me was miserable. How many insoluble problems with the apartment! (Zina, her boys, and I had nowhere to go when the flat on Volkhonka Street was vacated; I would have to write many a page to describe how all these problems got sorted out and resolved.) They all fell on Zina's shoulders—an impossible burden, but as real as the bitter reality of her life as a woman from the age of fifteen. Do you imagine nothing has come of that "fantasy," that "preposterous dream," etc., which you refused to hear of and cautioned me against as sheer madness? Well, of course I am base enough to have stooped even to that, but if you only knew how I worshiped Zina at the same time that I allowed her to make that humiliating sacrifice. I did return to Zhenya for a few days, but so flagrant a violation of life's dictates was doomed to failure. I nearly went out of my mind. Indeed I was in torment during those months, and it was Zina who saved me. Ah, what a terrible winter it was! I moved in with Alexander and Irina, and Zina joined me later. Then began her daily round to her boys and the market, for I turned over my privilege of buying in closed shops* to Zhenya. Zina had several attacks of the flu and in the end, in spring, came down with pneumonia. We were living with Alexander, where Fedya,† too, was sick all the time (at present he has the measles with an ear infection). Zina's boys remained with their father in a neglected apartment because Zina couldn't manage two households; she was, so to speak, a "part-time" rather than a "live-in" mother to them. I wronged her horribly, ruined her health and caused her to age, but after all I was not free to act either: I was bound by my compassion for my first wife. I kept trying all year to give Zhenya a chance to make a noble

* Shops maintained by the government for privileged citizens, usually stocked with goods unavailable to the common consumer.
† The son of Alexander and Irina Pasternak.

gesture, to accept what had happened and forgive, only not as she did—
sometimes grimly and vindictively, sometimes mockingly—but nobly even
if it cost her dearly, and with the disinterested generosity that alone can
give promise of a decent, dignified future. Strangely enough, she is completely devoid of such qualities and laughs at those who show any soft-
heartedness. Well, then, Zina and I were living with Alexander when
suddenly little Zhenya contracted scarlet fever, and I, probably for the
last time and much too innocently, feared for Zhenya. Zina proposed that
I should go and live with them on Volkhonka Street until he got well,
while she herself stayed on at Alexander's. And again Zhenya was told
that I would be living there for a period of six weeks in the capacity of a
friend, and this circumstance presented her once more with an acceptable
and very definite framework, however painful, in which she could have
revealed her better nature. And again nothing came of it. Although I
cleaned my clothes with a brush moistened with disinfectant and met
Zina only in the yard or elsewhere out of doors, I exposed her boys to the
gravest danger, and it is a marvel that so far they have not caught the
disease.

But I'm rambling; I'll try to be more concise. Little Zhenya will be sick
for another week and a half. So far everything has gone well. For the past
week Zina and I have been living in a three-room apartment, as yet
unfinished, on Tverskoy Boulevard, assigned to us by the Writers' Union.
It hasn't been wired for electricity yet and the bathtub isn't connected.
Her charming boys are living with us. She has no one to help her with
them and has to do the laundry and wash the floors almost every day
because building is going on all around us and anyone who enters the
house brings in sand and lime on his shoes. In a week the four of us are
going to the Urals, and there's no sense in hiring a maid for so short a
time. Don't think I have left Zhenya without material support—that I
have, so to speak, deserted her. Little Zhenya has a governess, and Zhenya
herself has an experienced elderly woman to help her. Be fair to her: all
this is done against her will. It is a great relief to me to see her tolerably
comfortable, but every time I attempt to give her money it requires great
and painful effort. And yet (may God be her judge!) there is in her something incomprehensible and completely alien to me. When I think about
her after a long separation I am horrified by the black duplicity and
insincerity of my relationship to her, and in my longing to atone I feel
myself borne back to her on a wave of candor—but as soon as we are
together my only wish is, again and again, to make her happy, and
therefore I must not say what I really think because she cannot bear to be

crossed in anything. This goes on and on and is the more distressing because what I find alien in her contrasts sharply with her outer appearance and, at times, with her inner essence, and all of this is as weird as witchcraft.

I am completely happy with Zina. It seems to me that for her, too, to say nothing of myself, our meeting was not mere chance. I don't know how you regard her. You both wept (especially you, Olya) when we were leaving. Those tears were appropriate, for there was nothing cheerful about my vision of the future. But I don't know which of us you were weeping for.

She is very beautiful but looks much worse when, on special occasions, she goes to the hairdresser and comes back vulgarly crimped for two or three days, until the set wears off. Our visit to you was just such a special occasion, and she came directly from the hairdresser. I don't know how you found her and what your attitude toward her is, but I have already told you *her* impression of *you*.

Several times in December of last year she had an impulse to write to you, Aunt Asya, when suddenly the events you had decried as inadmissible or outrageous swooped down upon us. She turned to you for help in preventing them. She also thought of turning to Papa, but she had good reason to fear that her description of what had taken place might be misinterpreted by those abroad. She suffered greatly, her suffering made incongruous by the complete trust we have in each other and in our own feelings. I kept her from writing to you and my parents for fear it might injure Zhenya. As to the latter, throughout the years of our life together I developed an unnatural, joyless sense of solicitude that often ran counter to all my convictions and made me indignant, for I have never seen a person brought up in such silly, blinding, childishly inert selfishness as she was. The fruits of that idiotic upbringing exposed her to such dangers that I was never free of a superstitious fear for her, a fear that became the more superstitious the more I was repelled by certain of its manifestations. The last instance of my own solicitude, springing from disapproval, horror, and fright, occurred last winter, when, I repeat, I was again ready to sacrifice to her not only my own happiness but the happiness and honor of one very dear to me; this time, however, the very logic of circumstances rose in rebellion and put an end to such foolishness.

If you wish, write to me poste restante, Central Post Office, Sverdlovsk. You know how pleased I would be to hear from you. *You* be the one to write, Olga dear. It would be nice if you both addressed a few words to Zina; she would appreciate them. She is a very simple, deeply loving, and

much-beloved person, and quite naturally, most wonderfully, predes-
tinatedly, my undeserved wife.

Yours,

BORYA

Sverdlovsk
[Received in Leningrad on July 11, 1932]

Dear Aunt Asya,

A thousand thanks for your long letter so full of warmth and sympathy.
Zina will probably answer it, or rather we will both answer it, and do not
think I am sending this card to anticipate the coming reply; I will write as
if the card had never been sent. But now, late as it is, I hasten to correct
your wrong opinion of Zhenya. She persistently refuses to accept any help
from me; this spring she was particularly stubborn and flatly refused to
take any money at all. If she had remained unyielding it would have
killed me. By giving her consent, which I wrested from her with the
greatest difficulty, she rendered me an enormous, an incalculable service;
indeed I don't know what I would have done if she had not made this
concession. My material contribution to her life is always rendered
against her will, and I have to break down her resistance by force every
time. Far from being at the dacha, we are still in this hotel in Sverdlovsk.
But you shall have that dull and unpleasant story later.

I fondly embrace you and Olya.

Yours,

BORYA

[Inscription in the book of poems *Second Birth*:]

To my dear cousin Olya,
on one of my most preposterous visits
October 14, 1932

Moscow [toward the end of October 1932]

My dears,

They say the wine is good, but I don't like the bottles. I am taking
advantage of the kind offer of Comrade Lavut, who is now taking Pan-
teleimon Romanov* to display to your public (as he displayed me not
long ago). He will give you this bottle of Georgian wine.

* Soviet writer (1885–1938).

I called up Tikhonov and told him about the gifts you had sent. He thanks you and will call for them one of these days. I haven't seen him since; he's as busy as ever and so am I.

I found the flat *unrecognizable!* In four days Zina managed to call the glazier and get hold of some glass—all the rest she did herself, with her own hands: made curtains that pull on cords, repaired and reupholstered two broken-down mattresses (making a couch out of one of them), polished the floors, and so on and so forth. She made my room look beautiful, and you would have to have seen it before to appreciate what that means!

When I got back I found a long letter from Papa, which I must answer seriously, at length, giving myself to it wholly, a thing which I fear will be impossible in the next few days; meanwhile he will be finding his own, wholly incorrect explanation for the delay.

Much love to both of you and thanks for everything.

Yours,

BORYA

Don't be angry with Zina for not writing; everything rests on her shoulders all day long. She keeps asking about you. At the moment she is not even home—tomorrow Irina is leaving to join Alexander in the Crimea.

DIARY

"Three Plots" and "The Plot Semantics of the *Odyssey*" appeared in 1929. I sent them to Borya. The capacity to be astonished, a prerequisite for creative work, was born in me precisely when I was working on the *Odyssey*.

That is why this was my first scholarly work in the true sense of the word. It ran at a tangent to my basic occupation and to my future. It was the test of my ability to think independently. Still not believing in the Greek novel and not foreseeing its importance, I kept to Homer: I studied the *Odyssey* in search of an explanation for genre novels. I was struck by Eastern analogies. I sat down and began to write.

In the *Odyssey* my inner eye began to detect a tautology of themes. But what astonished me above all was the almost mathematical reliability of the laws of plot composition (and even of composition): in order to know the content, it is sufficient to know the composition.

In my study "Three Plots, or, The Semantics of a Single Plot," I suggested the following picture: the geniuses of the world holding in their hands the thread of literary continuity, along which they slip the ring of ready-made plots from one to another. From whom and to whom? This is the basic question of so-called development. Genesis, of course, is of no less importance.

In analyzing three plots in succession, I discovered that Boccaccio's plot (Story VIII, Day 3 of the *Decameron*) is analogous not only to the plot of Calderón's *Life Is a Dream* but also to Shakespeare's *Taming of the Shrew*, even though this analogy is presented in essentially different transcriptions: "life is a dream" in one becomes "life is death" in another.

My investigation proved to me that the three plots are actually one. And this one represents an elaborated image of the birth of death.

The image is born of reality, perceived as a counterconcept of this very reality; the presupposition—that sensations and perceptions are not equivalent and that the meaningful content of a perception, its semantics, is determined by the given social ideology. In the diffuse and concrete thinking of the prehistoric period, objective reality is conceived of in images. And for that reason every image represents one or another metaphor of reality, but not reality as such.

There never existed a single plot as the source of my three; the plot is single in that it constantly develops a single image, but it is three (or an infinite number) in that the metaphorization of the image development is threefold.

The great writers of the seventeenth century, in cultivating the ancient plot, did not resort to it as a fortuitous creative device uniquely their own; they adopted it, rather, as representative of the ideology of their times, which demanded just this literary device.

One thing is beyond doubt: the nineteenth century marks the final frontier of the ready-made plot and the beginning of the free plot.

Moscow, October 21, 1932

Dear Olyushka,

How marvelously you write! If only I could do as well! At odd moments and with great absorption I devoured one of your works ("Three Plots"), and I am now reading the other in fits and starts. The ideas you express are very close to my own. How I regret that I do not know and will never know this entire current in its fundamentals. I feel a close affinity for its basic methodology (Cassirer* was a pupil of Cohen), but I have never studied the philosophy of language. It was about symbolism as a principle of every art I was thinking, however ignorantly and ama-

---

* Ernst Cassirer (1874–1945): German philosopher and a founder of modern linguistics. He studied at Marburg University in 1912, but there is no evidence that he and Pasternak met.

teurishly, when I wrote *Safe Conduct,* and for that reason I so enthusi-astically underscore lines of yours such as "There is no such thing as actions in process, there is only their simultaneous existence on a plane," "Unity is revealed only in diversity," "Owing to the law of relationship on a plane, rather than in process . . . ," "The image is born of reality, perceived as a counterconcept of this very reality," and so on. How well you formulate your thoughts! What words you find!

Thank you. Best love. Did you receive the wine?

Moscow, November 27, 1932

Dear Olyushka,

I have been waiting and waiting for word of Aunt's health (her injuries from falling off that chair) and am much worried. Suddenly I remem-bered I had not asked you about it. Do make haste and write me, even if you consider me unworthy of such attention. Surely you and Aunt Asya must admit that I am a live human being, strange as it may seem. Then why should you not go on dispensing generosity in my direction, however futilely? Can it really be of any importance to you whether I write or not? And does it not dawn on you from time to time that my silence may be for professional reasons?

Young Zhenya has begun school and is in raptures. I entreat you to write me about Aunt Asya. Love.

Dear Anna Osipovna and Olga Mikhailovna,

I send you my best wishes and warmest affection. I don't write often because if I did I would exhaust Borya's supply of paper. We are getting on beautifully. Please do write more often and don't be angry with us.

Yours,
ZINA

See that? Even Zina has learned to write!

DIARY

When the department of classical philology was being inaugurated at LIFLI (Leningrad Institute of Philosophy, Language, Literature, and History; formerly the philology department of the university but later made a separate institute), the new director, Gorlovsky, asked me to organize it.

I tried to decline in favor of Zhebelev, Malein, or Tolstoy. Gorlovsky, however, rejected their candidacies and insisted that I accept since my name was rather widely known in scholarly circles and he wanted a combination of the academic school headed by Zhebelev and the new philological teachings of Marr. I went on refusing for some time. I had never taught and felt no inclination to do so, and now here I was suddenly being promoted to a professorship. I had long since reconciled myself to being banished from institutions of higher learning. Hard as I had tried to enter them at one time, I had never been admitted even as a Greek scholar. And now—a whole department!

When I arrived at the institute, Gorlovsky himself came out to meet me. He was still rather young, of pleasant appearance, with rosy cheeks, affable but dignified.

I entered a university classroom in my new role for the first time on December 24, 1932. The enrollment was not large, about 10 persons, most of them specializing in Greek. I myself had to work out the programs of study.

I got in touch with classical scholars all over Russia, inviting them to come and lecture. I made a point of hiring those who had been unjustly victimized by the cruel academic community, those who had been ridiculed by the Bogayevskys and Tolstoys. I brought Berkov and Baranov to the university, as well as the Byzantine specialist E. E. Lipshits, at a time when she had been completely ostracized; it was from this moment that her brilliant career began. Similarly Kleman, Zograf, Ginsburg (a starving translator of Horace), Malozemova, Egunov, Dovatur, Ernshtedt, Shmidt, Zalessky, Kazansky, the schoolteacher Sokolov, and the novelist Bobovich all received work from my hands and got on their feet. I was able to find a place for each of them and was pleased with the breadth of possibilities enabling me to make a break with the usual method of reciprocal benefits and the favoring of friends. It was novel in those days for a department to concern itself with scholarly research; I, however, attributed first importance to it. I read a great deal myself and obliged faculty members to keep up with me. Accordingly we opened up a wide field of serious research.

Moscow [June 1, 1933]

Dear Aunt Asya and Olya,

As soon as I received your card I sat down to answer it with a letter—honest to goodness!—but therein lies the tragedy: the letter led me God knows where and, withering before its time from its own verbosity, remained unended and unsent. Time passes, however, and in that time you have most justly dubbed me a swine. As for the folks, you must have heard from them directly by now. They are alive and well and Lydia has not even lost her job in Munich, which greatly surprises me because a German who recently came from there tells me, citing purely Aryan sources, that the place is truly a madhouse, inadequately described even in our country. Indeed it is not so much the Irish* who are subject to repression and extermination as it is everything of purely German origin that requires knowledge and talent to be understood. The elementary school and average housewife have taken over. True, in his last letter Papa spoke at length about an exhibition of three hundred years of French portraiture to be opened soon. But evidently it is not an easy thing to travel long distances to attend exhibitions. I sent a wire inviting them to come here and later learned you had also invited them. In any event, correspondence has become more difficult. I found it so repulsive to write in German that I tried doing it in French, bad as my French is.

We are all well. We'll spend the summer in Moscow for financial and other reasons. Don't be angry with the ladies for not writing. Zina's time is completely taken up by household cares and chores, and Zhenya is busy earning money—she has been painting portraits of Red Army commanders.

Lots of love.

Yours,

BORYA

Moscow, August 30, 1933

Dear Olya,

Looks as if both of us had an attack of the same psychosis when we wrote our letters. Apparently the folks are not thinking of going anywhere, not even to Paris, let alone coming here. A few days ago Irina (Alexander is in the Crimea) got a letter from my parents that led her to conclude they are staying put. Their departure for the country and the seaside photos which Lydia is sending to her friends indicate that no tragedy is imminent. I have written to them, and the other day I sent them a wire.

The loss of my long letter to them has been confirmed. Another, with the same information but written in a more personal vein, was received.

Greetings, love, and kisses. To Aunt Asya, too.

BORYA

* A conversational evasion of "Jewish" often sarcastically resorted to by Russians.

Moscow, October 18, 1933

Dear Olyushka,

How is it possible that you are a professor and department chairman without my hearing of it in time to congratulate you? All the matters we have congratulated each other on in our lifetime, and to have missed this one!

I've had a terrible headache, was in bed with it until yesterday. I happened to have taken a bath in my friend's hotel room not long ago and, having left my own comb at home, found an old comb in the corner of a drawer, left there by nobody knows who, and I scratched my head with it until it bled. The scratches formed scabs that refused to heal, a circumstance that surprised me, but, having no time to do anything but be surprised, I waited until a high fever put me in bed. The doctor who came assured me it was not syphilis (in the nineteenth century I would hardly have used that word when writing to a cousin), nor furunculosis, nor even eczema, but an infection of the blood and lymphatic system that disappeared in three days, leaving nothing but an ordinary headache like a migraine.

You are quite right about my parents. Two or three times in your letter you expressed my own feelings (your dissatisfaction with their approach to the matter, the weighing of advantages from the point of view of comfort, Fedya's views, etc.). I myself wrote Papa how dismayed I was that he should expect to take a whole year getting ready when everything is so simple. As to his requiring an invitation, isn't that for leaving rather than entering? And isn't it for the sake of taking things out with him or something of that sort that he needs the official invitation? After all, we don't know their laws and restrictions. However, this is only my conjecture and I may be mistaken.

The very thought of moving all those things (or even just the canvases) would make even me lose heart, and I am not seventy years old. In this respect, too, a more radical, or should I say more desperate, approach is required. Is Fedya willing to take responsibility for whatever they leave behind? I seriously doubt it. Perhaps, though, with an official invitation Papa might be able to find support at the Russian embassy. Even this is doubtful in the light of increasing diplomatic tension. One thing is clear: the formula for weighing pros and cons ought to be the one you propose, and it ought to be based on the nearest possible approach to reality instead of on a comparison of "guaranteed" probabilities.

I expect to leave for Georgia on business in a few days, and on my return I will begin a subtle campaign for winning over my parents to our view, even though, following your example, I was inclined until recently to favor waiting. Now, however, I am frightened for some reason and would like to have them here with me as soon as possible, unburdened by "things," in the role of "temporary guests" (let them think so, it will make it easier for them), that is, relieved of an illusory sense of responsibility for their action. Are they right or wrong in taking this step? (As if life were pure mathematics. There it is again, that Philistine recourse to self-torment, a parade of holiness lacking in holiness.)

Oh, I could write reams on this theme based on what I have lived through and thought through, but each time one approaches the main thing, the ready thing (because discovered before anything else), whether in a letter or in one's writings, one is seized by such a Prutkovian melancholy (the unencompassability of the unencompassable) that it is precisely this main thing one passes over in silence. Not because "the uttered thought would be a lie"* or could not be put into words; no, not at all, but because the physical sense of the infinite rooted in any generalization so far outweighs my interest in the generalization itself that I abstain from giving word to it from a kind of inner chill, a fear of the cold that inevitably grips me in that wasteland.

Precisely for that reason I treat of only the secondary; however much I write, the main theme remains unspoken. The tails have been chopped off all my works, each of which, if it had its own way, would turn into a treatise—into something endless about endlessness.

Here, then, you have the watershed dividing genius from talent. The former has no fear of the cold. And so, in defiance of Prutkov, Pascal encompasses the unencompassable and does nothing but write of principles as a matter of principle, and casts his pearls more lavishly and casually than Bunin† describes an autumn day.

Dear Aunt Asya,

My only intention was to thank you and Olya for your letters, but before I knew it I found myself carried away in my letter to Olya.

I am extremely glad we are at one in our opinions, formed in different towns, in the most diverse circumstances, and without our conferring—my opinions springing from considerations unknown to you and vice versa. This is eminently characteristic of our times. Everywhere an as yet unnamed truth is emerging, be it at Party purges, in the quality of artistic and everyday standards, or in the speech and consciousness of

* From Tyutchev's poem "'Silentium."

† Ivan Alexeyevich Bunin (1870–1953): Russian writer, recipient of the Nobel Prize for Literature in 1933.

little children. And this constitutes the legitimacy of the new order and its temporary inability to cope with innovations so elusive.

It is as if one of the midnight colloquies of the 1890's had gone on and on until it became our present life. Then the very madness was enchanting, wreathed as it was in clouds of tobacco smoke, but how completely mad must the ravings of those revolutionary Russian aristocrats seem now, when the smoke has settled and their conversation has become an integral part of the geographical map—and how solid a part! Yet the world has never seen anything more aristocratic and freer than this, our bare, brutish actuality, still calumniated and deserving of all the groans it has caused.

You are right, Aunt Asya—I mean your writing or intending to write Papa about kerosene. Best love to you and Olya. Zina sends hers, too, and thanks you for remembering her.

Young Zhenya is a big boy now, ten years old already. He's lively, absent-minded, impressionable, and, like all the youngsters of our time, stuffed with knowledge gleaned somewhere in between the street and the classroom. Haven't I written you about him? Well, it's a subject that deserves more space than a postscript. Take care of yourself. Once more I embrace you. Do send for the family, but have them come not to you but to me or us, and have them come as Olya would have it, namely, in the spirit of stern fatalism and with the kerosene foremost. This is just as it ought to be, and would be for their good if they accepted it.

Yours,

BORYA

It's late, I am sealing this without reading it. I don't know what I've written.

Moscow [October 30, 1934]

My dears,

How are you feeling, Aunt Asya? And you, Olyushka? It's a mad life— not a free moment. I've been intending to write you for ages and have wanted even more to hear from you. Don't be impatient with me; believe me, I am not lying. Most of all I should like to forget everything and run off somewhere for a year or two. I want more than anything to work, to write at last and for the first time something worthwhile, deeply human, in prose—dull, boring, modest, but with breadth and vitality. Well, it can't be done. I'm the victim of telephone debauchery, always being seduced to do something, as if I were society's kept woman. I resist, I refuse, I waste all my time and strength on these refusals. It is sad and shameful. Last year I translated a great many Georgian poems; the collection will come out this winter. The translation of one of the poets has just been published in Tbilisi in a separate volume.* I don't know how it sounds in my translation, but the original is genuine poetry that moves one to tears. Shall I send it to you? Zhenya is going to Leningrad for a week and asked me to find out about you. Drop us a card, Olechka. Best love to you. Write me about yourselves.

Yours,

BORYA

DIARY

For us, the first clap of thunder was Gorlovsky's arrest. He had been to Moscow and on his return learned that he had been dismissed. He went back to Moscow to plead his case. That was where he was arrested. Nothing more was heard of him.

Gorlovsky was loved, respected, and pitied. Everyone was deeply dejected. Then punitive work began at the institute. A leading article in our university newspaper of January 14, 1935, bore the following headline in big letters: DISCOVER PEOPLE'S SECRET THOUGHTS. "The affair of Gorlovsky and his ilk clearly indicates that Party ranks in our Institute are not what they ought to be. . . ."

It was naïve of me to be amazed by this obvious challenge to shadow and inform. The interregnum and the audacity of the political police caused unrest among the students. This brought on a wave of demagoguery by student leaders and Party dictators. Ida Snitkovskaya, Party Secretary at our institute, assured me that the Party trusted me and therefore was asking me to lower the marks of children of white-collar workers and raise those of the children of blue-collar workers. I refused point blank.

The atmosphere became unbearably charged. Some of the students began intriguing, informing, creating a feeling of secret discontent, fault-finding, and censure. My nerves were constantly strained to the utmost; I was worried and indignant. The incessant ringing of the telephone kept me in expectation of something crushing and unspeakable. Middle-class students complained to me of the intrigues and insults of working-class students, and everything taken together—the rumors, the ringing of the

---

* Vazha Pshavela, *The Snake Eater*, Transcaucasia Publishers, 1934.

phone, the whispered stories, the latest news coming from second- and
third-hand sources—poisoned my life and shattered my nerves.

Demagogic devastation made deeper and deeper inroads. The department began to crumble, to rot at the root.

Moscow, April 3, 1935

Dear Olyusha,

Please let me know how you are and what is happening in your part of
the world. Since I myself have not escaped the ills suffered by certain
Leningrad unfortunates, I am particularly anxious to know that you are in
good health and that everything is well with you.

I do not write to you, Olya, and you do not write to me, and time is
passing. And rather swiftly. But it is not in my power to change anything.
I do not try to, for, considering the elements of which my life is inescapably made up, my life is better and more meaningful as it is than in any
other version. If only you knew what I spend my days on! But what else
can be expected if I have the good fortune to be treated humanely while
others all around me are being devoured?

I want so badly to work. And it would not be a bad idea to pay some
attention to my health if time allowed. Oh, don't think anything is seriously wrong, just passing disorders. I don't lose heart. At present I am on a
strict regimen because, after all, I am writing, in fits and starts, and the
project is a big one. I want awfully to get it done. When I do (in a year
and a half or so) I must change my way of life, at least for a while. It's
impossible to go on living by the clock, half the time by someone else's
clock. The fact is, the longer I live the more firmly I believe in what is
being done, despite everything. Much of it strikes one as being savage,
and then again one is astonished. There is no denying that, taking into
account Russia's resources, basically untapped, the people have never
before looked so far ahead, and with such a sense of self-esteem, and with
such fine motives, and for such vital and clearheaded reasons. At times, in
even the worst of times, everything seems very subtle and astute.

We are all well. Much love to you and your mother. Reassure us by
sending at least a postcard. Indeed a postcard would be best; you would
take less time getting down to it.

Yours,
BORYA

Is there anything you need, Olya?

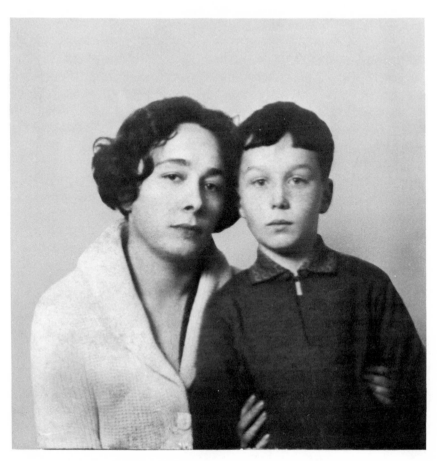

Evgenya Pasternak with Zhenya. 1931

Boris Pasternak and Kornei Chukovsky in a conference hall. 1932

Fedor Karlovich (Boris's second cousin), Leonid, Josephine, Lydia, and Rosa Pasternak. Berlin

Young Zhenya Pasternak.
Starki, 1936
Photograph by Gornung

Boris and Zinaida Nikolayevna (Zina) Pasternak with Adrian Neuhaus.
Odoyevo, 1934

Boris Pasternak.
Odoyevo, 1934

Boris Pasternak.
Peredelkino, 1936
Photograph by Gornung

DIARY

The defense of my doctoral dissertation was set for June 9, 1935. The administration did not wish to post an announcement or send invitations. In front of me lies a postcard bearing the smudged typewritten message:

At 7 P.M. on June 9, in the large auditorium of LIFLI, Prof. O. M. Freidenberg will defend her doctoral dissertation, *The Poetics of Plot and Genre: Classical Period.* Opponents: Academician S. A. Zhebelev, Professor I. G. Frank-Kamenetsky. Administration of LIFLI.

Leningrad [June 19, 1935]

Dear Zhenya,

You made me very happy (with your reply, of course). Let me explain. The thing is that on June 9 Olya defended her doctoral dissertation, and at my request (she herself did not wish to do it, knowing that neither Borya nor Alexander would respond, but I insisted) she sent Borya the abstract and an announcement. That is why I wrote to you to find out whether they were in Moscow or not. Believe me, I am ashamed of them. Olya was a great success, was written up in the papers, received heaps of roses, and to this day people keep congratulating her and ringing her on the phone. The large auditorium was filled, a thing that rarely happens. She was the first woman to defend a doctoral dissertation in that institute and in Soviet times. She became a doctor of classical languages and literatures. Forgive my terrible handwriting.

Now let me get back to Borya and Alexander. They ought indeed to be ashamed of themselves. What cruelty from ones so close to her! Not to send a word, not to make the slightest reply! . . . I cannot tell you how hurt and disappointed I am. Borya must have received her letter; she put the return address on it, so it would have been returned. I shall write my brother about this and tell him I release them from all ties of kinship. Believe me, Zhenya dear, I have already forgotten about my nephews (although I don't hold Alexander guilty; he has long since ceased to exist for me). But Borya?! I can find no excuse for him. None. Ah well, enough of this. They have gone out of my life; true, I have one foot in the grave, but the other is still here.

Young Zhenya did not send me an acknowledgement of the stamps, the ones Grandfather sent him (last winter); did he write Grandfather? My brother asked me about it. That, to be sure, is an atavism.

Dear darling Zhenya, take care of yourself and have a good vacation; we have nowhere to go for a vacation. Olya won't go without me and I cannot go without her, and we cannot both go and leave the apartment empty. In order to take a vacation we need a third person to look for rooms in the country for us, transport our things, and all the rest. I cannot do it; Olya hasn't the strength and is too busy anyway until July 17. A checkup is being made by the institute's trade-union committee, and Olya must be there. Shock workers* are being selected, awards to both students and professors are being decided upon, etc. She hasn't a free minute. She is exhausted. And I've let my pen run away with me. All my love. Thank you a thousand times for your reply.

Yours,
ASYA

Olya sends her love and kisses to little Zhenya.

Moscow, January 14, 1936

Dear Aunt Asya,

They say that someone has already answered your letter, but that doesn't diminish the right you and Olya have to be indignant. I must, however, come to the defense of Elizaveta Mikhailovna, Zhenya's governess. She was ill for a long time, and very seriously. I would also observe that when you and Olya list the many addresses to which you have directed unanswered letters, you touch upon that very complication which does not make my life easier or contribute to my leisure. Olya wrote Alexander that she is *fabulously* busy, underscoring the word. Does that make me a loafer?

That I have not once written to you all these months is of course outrageous and unprecedented. But why is it that when Olya is silent I do not draw drastic conclusions as to her not caring whether I have recovered or not, or whether I am dead or alive? Why is it that only *my* silence means something, and necessarily something bad? But it really doesn't matter; it always has and always will be this way.

It was not because I am a swine by birth that I did not write you, nor for lack of time, but for the same reason that, when I was staying with you, I found it hard to send my family reassuring letters and telegrams that belied the truth. Because, you see, things do not fall into place quickly, and for a long, long time something was happening to me, something very strange, which by autumn ended in my suffering acute pain in my heart and arms throughout the day, and complete disorder of everything that a person ought to have in order. It is only now, at the end of a long recovery effected by *time alone*, that I am again what I once was

---

* Workers who volunteered for additional work to set the tempo for their fellow workers.

and move about and pen phrases to the extent of my strength—it is only now, I say, that I understand what happened to me and what the cause of it was.

Well, at last I am healthy, and again there is such confusion on every hand that I have no time to read a book when I wish to, or even when I need to. What is there to say? You know how I love you and Olya and how I fear you. Both of you are ferociously unfair to me. In your unspoken opinion I am guilty of something, but of *what* I still do not know.

I don't remember whether I sent you my Georgians or not. Half of them are awful rot. It's a pity that the worthy ones are buried in such rubbish. The rubbish was forced upon me by considerations of mistaken objectivity. Read *The Snake Eater* and accept it as a substitute for several unwritten letters to both of you, which of course I did write from the wilds in which I found myself.

Love to Sasha.

BORYA

[Inscription in *Georgian Lyrics, 1935:*]

To my dear cousin Olyushka, from her loving cousin Borya

When you have time, find the patience to look through the entire book because, among the rubbish I was forced to include (not much, to be sure), there is work of genuine talent, an appreciation of which I tried my best to convey.

Don't ever be angry with me.

BORYA
January 15, 1936

DIARY

At the very beginning of May 1936 my *Poetics of Plot and Genre* appeared. I wrote that book over ten years, day and night, while at work and at rest, on holidays and during vacations.

At last it was published and sales began to mount. Three weeks after it came out, it was taken out of the bookstores.

On September 28, in the "bibliography" section of the newspaper *Izvestia*, a review by Ts. Leiteizen entitled "Harmful Gibberish" was published with the following editorial note: "The article we have published about O. Freidenberg's book demonstrates the sort of scholars the Leningrad Institute of Philosophy, Literature, Linguistics, and History is training and the sort of 'scholarly' works it is producing. Freidenberg's book, a doctoral dissertation on literature, bears the stamp of this institute. What is the opinion of the People's Commissariat of Education on all this?"

Izvestia is an official Party newspaper. Its every word has official significance, the practical results of which (or, as was then the phrase, the "organizational implications" of which) cannot be overestimated.

Can you conceive what it meant for one who had gone through such misery, and had just begun to think her troubles were over and that she could breathe freely at last, to suddenly receive such a crushing blow? Oh, the news we were forever expecting in fear and trembling! News that reached one by phone, that overtook one on the street, that came crashing into one's home, that ripped off the door of every refuge!

It is highly improbable that anyone in the future will understand how terrible it was, how sinister and ominous!

Moscow, October 1, 1936

My dear Olya,

I am spending the winter at the dacha. The mail is slow in reaching me and I get no newspapers—but more about that later. Yesterday I was in town and Zhenya showed me the *Izvestia* article. She wept.

In this whole business the *only* thing I worry about is that you are not hardened; it is your first experience of this kind. I suppose the local Leningrad papers have already taken it up; if not, be prepared for it. The thing will be blown up in the same base, mechanical, mindless way, with distortions so transparent as to be self-evident, with preposterous argumentation ("Everyone knows Marx's opinion of Homer"—as if it were Marx you were writing about and you were misrepresenting facts in stating an antithesis, as if your analytical discovery were an indictment, as if Homer were less dear to *you* than to that toady of a reporter, who is tightening the noose round his neck with his own hands; he evidently finds breathing too easy, wants to make it harder for himself).

I cannot come to you now or in the near future, much as I should like to and probably ought to. Couldn't you come here? You would have a separate room and would find yourself in a colony made up almost entirely of victims like yourself.

This winter there was a discussion in the papers about formalism. I don't know whether word about it reached you or not. It began with the article about Shostakovich and was extended to include the theater and literature (with the same sort of insolent, sickeningly unoriginal, echolike, arbitrary attacks on Meyerhold, Marietta Shaginyan, Bulgakov, and others). Then it spread to the artists, and to the best of them, such as Vladimir Lebedev.

When the Writers' Union held open discussions of these articles, I was foolish enough to attend one of them. On hearing what utter nonentities said about the Pilnyaks, the Fedins, the Leonovs (referring to them almost exclusively in the plural), I could not restrain myself and made an attempt to attack precisely this aspect of our press, calling everything by its real name. I was met first of all by sincere astonishment on the part of bigwigs and officials, who could not understand why I should come to the defense of my colleagues when no one had harmed me or even thought of doing so. I was given such a rebuff that, later (again on official instigation), friends from the union—good friends, some even close ones—were sent to inquire after my health. No one could believe that I was feeling fine and was able not only to sleep but even to work. That, too, they took for rebelliousness.

I don't know what you ought to do. One cannot tell from a distance; I must know the objective facts as to how far things have gone, and I must see you. I have known instances when people who received exactly the same sort of slap in the face have tried to elucidate their case, have written letters to the Central Committee of the Party, and when, on their own insistence, they have made the people there acquaint themselves with whatever occasioned the attack (a book, a play, a picture), their position was made not only worse but hopeless by having a second denunciation clapped on to the first. That is what happened to the poet Svetlov* and his play. In all of these instances, as in my own, the injury was solely moral, and, thanks to the ethics of our press, windy and insubstantial, calling forth just the opposite response from all people still in possession of their sensitivity and moral courage.

I don't know what this will do to you, inexperienced as you are. I don't know your friends and acquaintances, your roots in your community, and I am speaking only of things of the spirit, which are the most important things in such circumstances, even if the opportunity to defend ourselves were necessary or available to us. I dare not imagine how you are living through it and how it is affecting Aunt's health. Of this, and for the time being only of this, I beg you to wire me immediately at the address: Pasternak, 48 Writers' Village, Bakovka, Belorussian-Baltic Railroad.

* Mikhail Arkadevich Svetlov (1903–1964): poet and dramatist. The play in question is *Deep in the Provinces* (1935).

Zhenya says I ought to come to your defense in the press, i.e., I ought to write an article about your book. If I did that I know in advance what would happen. If they printed it, I would be laughed to scorn rather gently and condescendingly, but you would be reviled more viciously and, strangely enough, on my account as well.

I have had plenty of experience of this sort; this is what happens every time I speak up for somebody in public.

On the other hand, if it is necessary by private means, i.e., by seeing people personally and persuading them or by appealing to individuals whose names carry weight, etc., I am ready to serve you to the best of my ability, indeed I thirst for battle and only wish to know what I ought to do. As soon as the wire is sent, I implore you to write in detail and send the letter special delivery to the same address.

And now I come to the main thing. I suppose you have long awaited— and been shocked and indignant by not getting—*my* response and opinion of your book, and you are right in finding no words for such an outrage. I might have lied or passed over it in silence had I not known you would have exonerated me if you were here. The fact is that I have not really read it. As soon as I got it (last spring) I went through the entire book superficially, in snatches, but even that was enough to rouse my wonder and admiration for the very virtue which that scoundrel deliberately ignored or insolently misrepresented: the depth and unity of the general conception and its ordered development from chapter to chapter throughout the book. I also read the pages on lyrics which were born of your conversation with me in the kitchen that time, when you explained your idea by showing me photos of late Greek sculpture. I knew *The Taming* from the offprint.

Even at that time I was so afraid I would not have a moment for such pleasure (the book is on the most interesting of themes, treated from a totally inconoclastic point of view, fascinatingly written, and, to top it all, written by you) that I immediately wired an expression of sheer delight (can it be that I failed to send that off, too?). Zhenya was ill at the time, and I had to arrange for her to go to a sanatorium in the south, after which I had to find a rest home for the three of them— Zhenya, young Zhenya, and Elizaveta Mikhailovna—for the entire summer. At the same time the dachas for writers were nearing completion. It was not easy to acquire one, and I had to decide whether I would take the one offered me or not. Then I had to make trips to the country to supervise its completion and go to no end of trouble collecting the money to pay for it. The matter of a town apartment, too, had to be decided financially and in principle in those very months—the building was nearly completed and apartments were being assigned. All these prospects were so obviously beyond my means and so far beyond my requirements (at least three times as much as I required) that ordinarily I would have rejected them or at least half of them and thereby saved time, strength, and peace of mind, to say nothing of money. But it seems that at last our folks are seriously thinking of coming back. Papa has been promised an apartment, but nothing has come of it so far and nothing will. I must keep them in mind in considering my own opportunities. I very much want to live with them, just as I should like you to come and live here. I want this for myself, for my own pleasure, but I am not sure that for their own sakes it is the best decision they could make. All this remains uncertain, so that I live constantly in a state of uncertainty, perhaps spending my money and squandering my energy in vain. The uncertainty about my parents is but a part of the general uncertainty in which I find myself. To live all my life as I am living it now would be the height of madness even if I chose to do so—and their hypothetical coming complicates everything, temporarily fixing me to the spot in which I find myself and postponing indefinitely certain unpostponable matters. But I have no right even to speak of these things.

In a word, I kept putting off our removal to the dacha until one fine day Zina took things into her own hands and carted off all our goods and chattels. I, too, rushed there just as I was, without books or anything else required by my work. As for the latter, I rarely dream of it since the crisis that brought on my last year's illness (and was connected with the fate of my work, just as yours was). I write incredibly little and such unbelievable shit (begging your pardon) that if there were not sufficient other reasons, this alone would drive me mad. But things will not remain as they are; I will pull myself out of it, upon my word I will, and you will see me a different man again, if that matters to you. Indeed for the past two or three days I have been working in fits and starts on intricacies of plot that have stood in my way since 1932 and will stand there until I work them out. It is not only lack of strength that inhibits me but also my furtive glances at objective conditions that make the whole concept of the book impermissible, too naïve in its pretensions. But I have no choice; I must write it. All this, however, is beside the point. I've gotten carried away. What was it I wanted to tell you? Ah yes—well, only yesterday I went to fetch the books I needed, among them yours, which had lain all summer in an inaccessible apartment, empty and cluttered with all the paraphernalia of workmen redecorating it. Can you and will you take the trouble to understand this?

The only thing left for me to say concerns the urgency of hearing from you. Let me put it bluntly: however difficult it may be for you, however slight my right to ask or expect it of you, do find a minute and wire me as to how both of you are—then grit your teeth and sit down and write me in detail. And finally, if it is possible, come and see me (couldn't Sasha stay with Aunt Asya for a short time?). You can have a separate room if you wish, and our neighbors are comrades in misfortune: Pilnyak, Fedin, and others who have lived through a series of wrongs such as you are experiencing for the first time. And now my last word, and a brief one to fill in the space separating me from your wire, letter, and visit: is it for me, an ignoramus, to remind you, a historian, of the inevitable fate awaiting every new word of truth? Had you written a compilation of things read, adding not a single new or original thought, the result would naturally have been quite different. But here you are coming out with a *creative work* expressing your own point of view, adding something to the accumulated inventory, presenting ideas sensationally new. Naturally the geese are furious. There is yet one more factor, inconceivable because at first glance it contradicts common sense. There are certain miserable and completely cowed nonentities who are driven by the force of their own mediocrity to hail as the style and spirit of the times that trembling, inarticulate obsequiousness to which they are condemned by the absence of choice—that is, by the poverty of their intellectual resources. When such people hear someone asserting that the greatness of the Revolution lies precisely in a person's being able at a time of revolution—*especially* at a time of revolution—to speak out freely and think daringly, they brand such a view counterrevolutionary. This is a true observation, but I have muddled it in my haste. If I had expressed it in two words, the absurdity of the situation would have been clear to you.

All my love. I will know no peace until you wire and write. I kiss you fondly, dear Aunt Asya.

BORYA

DIARY

Faculty friends began coming to express their sympathy and give advice. They advised me to make a public acknowledgement of minor errors so as to save the book as a whole. They said it was imperative that I act quickly, while I was still on my feet. But I had already made up my mind.

Recanting was out of the question. Still, I did not wish to be found guilty for another reason, even more serious: I had no wish to involve friends, scholars, and opponents at the institute. Everyone urged me to remember the consequences for other scholars of the campaign begun against me.

As I say, my mind was made up. I wrote to Stalin. Like hundreds of thousands of others, I still sincerely believed in acts of sabotage, the tricks of local scoundrels, and the deliberate distortion of Party instructions. It was said that Stalin wished to do right and that he read all letters addressed to him. I resolved to act in my usual way, by personally appealing to the highest authority, without intermediaries, half measures, and compromises. Disarmed as I was, one weapon was left to me: my pen, my honesty, and my passionate conviction.

The letter was my secret. It was a political secret, which I had no right to divulge.

I wrote it at the beginning of October. Immediately I felt more calm. The time of waiting set in. But the days dragged on, no reply was forthcoming, and the consequences of the defamation I had been subjected to made themselves felt. People avoided me so as not to have to speak to me. My friends ceased calling me on the phone.

One thing and one thing only possessed, supported, and guided me in those terrible days: my unshakable faith in the tradition of scholarship. I knew it existed and that no falsification or destruction of documents could change it. I believed as firmly in its true and unbiased existence as if I could see it with my own eyes. Those in power could do what they would—kill, distort, pervert—but in reality they could not kill or annihilate or diminish the grandeur of human culture. They could only build straw houses incapable of withstanding the test of time. However great their power, they had no means of changing history.

It was this deep emotional and intellectual conviction that enabled me to live, breathe, and keep myself sound. More than that: it inspired me, lifting me high above the daily experiences of persecution.

The period following the publication of the article was filled with an oppressive awareness of dreadful, incomprehensible events, the rumble of subterranean waters, and gathering of storm clouds. Whispers, rumors, intimations, conjectures, the ringing of the phone, of the doorbell. Tongues kept wagging about me. The pack was closing in.

No one who has not lived in the Stalin era can appreciate the horror of our uncertain position. A person's life was poisoned secretly, invisibly, as witches and sorcerers were hounded in the Dark Ages. Something mysterious was accumulating under the earth and coming to the boil. A person felt at the mercy of an inescapable force aimed at him and certain to crush him.

I went on giving lectures and attending meetings at which students despised me and colleagues isolated me in a ring of empty chairs. No chairman would give me the floor, always finding an excuse. In those days I learned to know what cowardice is, what the complexion of baseness is, what mediocrity, servility, and dishonor look like.

I was required to work in such circumstances, and I did work, taking care to give no justification for the accusations lying in wait for me at every step. I grew used to entering doors that had become prison doors for me, and to going about my business as if nobody else existed, accompanied always by a sense of my own dignity and integrity.

The situation at home was very bad. My poor mother, worn out by sufferings and tortures on my account, was in bed with pneumonia. The eminent Soviet physician who treated her, a braggart and egotist, told me there was little hope of her recovery. It took all my strength to keep myself from succumbing to despair.

The holidays* between November 7 and 9 postponed my day of judgment. I had already given up hope of receiving a reply from Moscow.

The date was November 6. A phone call from the university bid me appear there immediately. I hardly need say with what feelings I left my sick mother and set out. I was met—cautiously. A telegram had been received from Moscow and confirmed by telephone saying I was to be sent to Moscow for an appointment with Volin (Deputy Commissar of Education) on November 10. The university would supply me with a ticket for the Red Arrow Express. The rector asked that I report to him as soon as I got back without the delay of waiting my turn.

A phone call to the Commissariat indicated that I was to be received with kindness and esteem. My way was paved with roses.

Volin spoke to me for over three hours, canceling all other business and appointments. He was an old, thickset, square man with unkempt locks of hair and the face and manners of a pugilist. A Soviet censor of the highest standing. I had heard that Stalin thought well of him because he had been his children's tutor.

He greeted me in an affectionate fatherly way, saying, "Come, come, who has offended you?" He went on to say that he had been given my letter to Stalin with the request that he attend to the matter. Later I learned that Stalin had been on vacation for two months and the letter, apparently, had awaited his return. It goes without saying that the erstwhile censor found nothing objectionable in my book. In our country,

* The celebration of the "October" Revolution of 1917—October 25 according to the Old Style calendar, but thirteen days later according to the New Style calendar.

logic is installed in the brain as a gadget whose functioning depends not on the object under examination but on the hands of the one who installed it. It appears he had "studied" my book and found nothing in it contrary to Marx's teachings. He only scolded me in a fatherly way— that's precisely what it was, fatherly—for my difficult language and "scrupulosity."

The most interesting moment came later. When he found out that the book had been confiscated—that is, taken out of the bookstores—his anger knew no bounds.

"Impossible!" he stormed. "I don't believe it! It couldn't be!" The soul of the censor within him burst into flame. "Your book confiscated? What for? You understand I am an experienced censor, I *know* why books are confiscated! Why should yours be?"

Goaded by my own indignation, he got up and in my presence phoned Glavlit.* He spoke sternly, and they seemed to reply with servility. "Freidenberg's book, *The Poetics of Plot and Genre,* when and for what reason was it confiscated? . . . What? . . . Find out at once. . . . It wasn't? And its release wasn't delayed? . . ." After a few more rude and angry remarks, he sat down and turned to me reassuringly. "See? Just what I said, and you didn't believe me. Your book was not confiscated and its release was not delayed."

Try as I would, I could not convince him otherwise by arguments or facts. "Impossible!" he cried. "It's either a misunderstanding or local machinations, absolutely illegal. But it isn't true. The book has been freely sold and circulated. If it can't be bought, it's because it's sold out."

How could I oppose such irrefutable logic? With facts? Only for idealists is existence determined by consciousness. For dialectical materialists it is determined by the pointed finger. I had no grounds for argument. When Volin phoned to Glavlit, my book "smiled at me anew from the window."

In parting he said to me: "You will not be bothered again. If anybody at any time troubles you in any way or tries to impose restrictions on you, write to me directly. You have the right to publish your work freely; your good name has not been sullied in any way."

I spent the evening at Zhenya's in high spirits. Borya and Alexander were there, and Borya saw me to the train.

The atmosphere in Leningrad was completely changed when I got back, and it was as if the former one had never existed. How, from what

* The central organ of censorship.

source, had the news reached them? By what radio? Can radio change the climate?

Everyone was affectionate. Everyone smiled. They came up to me quite openly and expressed their sympathy. They congratulated me.

The rector was anxiously awaiting me at the university. He took my hand in both of his: "I congratulate you, indeed I do! But I congratulate myself first—you second." Then, adopting a serious mien: "I want you to know that while you were in Moscow I reread your book, more attentively this time, more probingly, and I must tell you that I understood exactly what you were saying. Fancy that! And having understood, I appreciated."

That was on November 13, the day of my triumph, of my complete rehabilitation. The day on which I recovered my peace of mind.

On November 14 appeared an ominous notice, in *Izvestia* again, declaring that the patience of the academic community had come to an end, that the administration of LIFLI showed no inclination to understand the significance of its pandering to me, and that the academic community would thus now take upon itself the right to pass judgment. The storm broke. Deputy rector Morgen said to me: "What does it mean? Is this a signal to begin open persecution?" The rector himself behaved as if I had deceived him. It would be hard to overestimate the importance of that newspaper notice. It was sure to introduce forms of torment such as the convening of a meeting of members of the Leningrad academic world to scourge me, the public discrediting of me and my book, and the placing of my name on the black list.

It was expedient that I act quickly, that I counteract the effect of this notice in one day. The notice had been sent to *Izvestia* from Leningrad, which meant that evil forces were operating from here, not from Moscow. Someone from LIFLI itself had written it on behalf of "the community."

Frank-Kamenetsky volunteered to go to Moscow on my behalf. At home he explained that my calamity threatened him as well, since he had endorsed my book. That was true.

We discussed at length to whom he should apply and decided it should be Borya. We also decided to ask Borya to speak to Bukharin, editor of *Izvestia* and a great admirer of Borya's poetry. We could not communicate our decision by letter or phone since letters were opened, phones tapped. I was to write to Volin. Adopting the tone of our interview, I wrote him a short humorous note in which I made gentle fun of the Deputy Commissar's assurance.

Frank-Kamenetsky left that same evening. From Moscow he made a muddy trip to Peredelkino, where Borya was living at the time. Tired and anxious, he found Borya sitting at the dining table with some friends, one of whom was Neuhaus, a professor of music at the Moscow Conservatory, Borya's close friend and the ex-husband of Borya's second wife, Zina. ("That marriage," Borya once told me with a smile, "was just another form of expressing my admiration for Garrick Neuhaus and consequently for his wife.") It was very difficult for Frank-Kamenetsky to get Borya away from his companions and speak to him alone. He found my cousin charming.

Borya told him that Bukharin himself was under suspicion and therefore was keeping to his house. He was practically inaccessible, but Borya wrote him a letter, a copy of which Frank-Kamenetsky brought back to me. Political events that took place thereafter soon made me hide this letter, having first destroyed the beginning and end addressed to Bukharin. I made a copy of the rest, which referred only to me and my work. In expectation of having my apartment searched, I did everything to preserve this historic document without risking mother's life and my own. It reads as follows:

To the Editors of *Izvestia:*

I recently spoke to Zhivov* about Freidenberg's book and Leiteizen's review of it. I know both the book and the author. The review has little to do with the book. Freidenberg's work is an analysis of historical and cultural strata antedating the rich literary heritage of the antique world. As the analysis proceeds, the author shows that what seems a simplicity of plots, forms, and artistic canons in ancient Greece seems so only at a first and cursory glance, that such a glance leads to inconsistencies which may become absurdities if not elucidated. For this, analysis is required, and for analysis, research.

Please don't confound me by demanding that I provide comparisons. I cannot compare the role and significance of the book with anything else because I am no judge, being neither a philologist nor a theoretician. But can you tell me of any study or research that does not begin precisely with this? Does not every problem become evident because of some seeming departure from the norm? Was it not necessary to marvel at a falling apple (what could be more simple?—ah, but there's the catch!) in order to begin searching for the law governing that wonder? Again, without making analogies. Leiteizen quotes Plato as saying that all philosophizing begins with a profession of bewilderment (*aporia*—I believe that is correct; I'm writing from Peredelkino and have no reference books at hand) and, ignoring the saving fact that Plato proceeds to

---

* Mark Semyonovich Zhivov: literary editor of *Izvestia* at the time, later an eminent critic of Polish literature.

give us one dialogue after another, gloats over Plato's simple assertion that a philosopher is one who is fooled more often than others.

All this, however, is beside the point. That same Freidenberg was summoned to Moscow on the 10th of this month by Deputy Commissar of Education Volin, who persuaded her not to leave her job as she intended, assured her that her book would be sold freely, and said that it contained nothing undesirable, even from a Marxist point of view. The only thing he reproached her with was a certain heaviness of style making it difficult to read and for showing bad judgment in having such a scholarly and highly specialized work put out in a large edition for the general public, this latter circumstance inevitably leading to misunderstandings such as that of the good Leiteizen.

Despite this, in *Izvestia* there appeared on the 14th another contribution to the Leiteizeniad, transmitted by telephone from Leningrad.

Where is the coordination in all this?

B. PASTERNAK

That evening Frank-Kamenetsky set out for Leningrad. It was a cold, dark evening in late autumn. Wet snow was falling. When his visit in Peredelkino was over, some people were going back to Moscow by car. Borya pushed him into their midst. Rain, darkness, ankle-deep mud, a roaring motor, a jam-packed car. He plunked down on the seat and before he knew it found two lively creatures of the weaker sex on his knees. They were on their way home from visiting with writers, and from their chirping he discovered that one of them was Leiteizen. He was too exhausted and the world was too like a madhouse for him to properly assess the situation. So on they raced in the darkness, he holding on one knee the very person who was responsible for his exhaustion and misery. The whole of Soviet life was to him a phantasmagoria in which he could not make out why he was being bumped and tossed on a muddy road in a faraway place. Could it be for the sole purpose of holding on his knee a vivacious young lady named Tsilya Leiteizen?

He arrived home to discover that events were grinding quickly to a halt. Fortunately Borya's letter never reached Bukharin; it was lost at some intermediary station, the most likely one in Soviet editorial offices being the wastebasket. Thank God.

Soon we learned that Bukharin was under house arrest (while his case was being "investigated," *Izvestia* continued cynically to carry the name of an editor in chief already condemned to death).

The telephone transmission of that Leningrad newspaper notice had obviously been late. Somehow it was left hanging in the air, which in the meantime had been purified by my summons to Moscow. Clearly it had been written before my summons and its publication had been delayed.

Upon my return its effectivness had evaporated. Volin phoned Morgen personally as soon as he received my letter and gave orders that no meetings were to be called to discuss my case and I was not to be restricted ("squeezed" as we then called it) in any way.

Moscow, October 7, 1936

Dear Olya,

I am amazed by the self-sacrifice Frank-Kamenetsky has shown. The world has never seen anything like it. Ah, but how disappointed you will be in *me* when he tells you about his visit.

I didn't know how to repay him for the selflessness and nobility of his efforts on your behalf. Unfortunately we had overnight guests at the time, so I could not invite him to stay with us. But he will tell you all about it himself, freely and without prejudice, not as a mere emissary but as a judge and observer.

I owe him more than I can say. Surely no letter from you could have brought me as much news (eventually, reassuring news) about you and Aunt Asya as did the four-hour grilling I put him to.

When I asked you to come here, it was not only to try and solve your problems but also because I wanted to see you and talk to you. I wanted you to stay with me or Zhenya; it goes without saying that I found Frank-Kamenetsky a poor substitute for you.

He declined the only help I could offer (arranging appointments and seeing that he had an opportunity to talk to the right people), asserting that this was ineffective and might be awkward for you. He will tell you how I tried to serve you in little ways of doubtful benefit and small worth.

Don't lose heart, Olya! I am confident that, even though cases like yours are as a rule never straightened out and therefore cease in time to be "cases," yours, with a little acceptable compromise, *will* be straightened out. The appointment of a commission to investigate gives me grounds for this confidence.

There is no point in my writing a letter to you now. You will learn from Frank-Kamenetsky more than a letter could convey, sooner than a letter could arrive. Thank him for me again.

Aunt Asya, do please write to Mama and Papa. How will they take it if I, their son, begin dissuading them? I have never done so. Here are the limits within which I invited, and still invite, them to come: I write them that their coming would mean my happiness, that I am ready to share with them the life they find me living when they get here, and nothing could give me greater joy. Deep in my heart I do not believe they will come.

Yours,

BORYA

Leningrad, October 8, 1936

Thank you, Zhenya dear, for receiving my emissary so well. He is quite in love with you. He said that his brain felt like a hot coal before he left, during the journey, and all the time he was with Borya and his own relatives; it was only when he was with you that he had relief from thinking about this problem. In a word, I am delighted. I asked him to go and see you and gave him your address (it was written on the envelope for Borya), but everything flew out of his mind. He had, by the way, intended seeing you before he saw Borya, but the train was two hours late and that spoiled everything.

How do you like this idiotic affair? If only you knew the arguments we have had at home! I was against Frank-Kamenetsky's going to see Borya; I was afraid he would drag him into the mess. But his wife and relatives pushed him into it. Mama doesn't like him. She made us quarrel, set us against each other. When things were at their worst it turned out I had forgotten to pay for the telephone, and it was disconnected. First I would send for him and urge him not to go, then he would come and tell me he was going. . . . In a word, there was no end of fuss. What was the sense of the trip? The only good that came of it was that he made your acquaintance. He could tell us practically nothing about young Zhenya, however eagerly we questioned him.

Borya wrote me that it was you who showed him *Izvestia* and that you insisted on his defending me in the press. Well and good if he weren't my cousin. Such things must not be done by relatives.

I had been dreaming of paying you a visit and seeing young Zhenya. We long to see him! But I couldn't come now, with everything gone sour. And besides, I have no one to leave Mama with. Her sight is failing, poor darling; it gets worse every day. It's hard for her to write and she doesn't read at all.

Best love to you. I understand you.

Yours,

OLYA

Mama says she cannot write. She is terribly worried about the folks and dreads having them come back.

[From the letters of O. M. Freidenberg to I. G. Frank-Kamenetsky]

December 6, 1936

My article on the language of folklore, already in proof, is being sub-jected to the scrutiny of endless editors, who torture it and me to such an extent that I would gladly throw the whole thing over—but I can't, it's too late. I read it again and again, making little changes here and there. "Listen," I say, "what have you got against individual words? The concept is mine and I neither can nor wish to change it." The editor smiles: "We understand the concept, but who else cares about it? It's the words people read."

On the whole, this is no time to engage in analyses. Borya put it beautifully: "Analysis is looked upon as condemnation. Everything must be praised." But that is the province of the necrologist, not the researcher.

December 17, 1936

Malozemova called me up just now and read me what has been printed about Borya in our "family" newspaper, *Izvestia.* The only thing left for me is to write him a warm, sympathetic letter and invite him to come here. Or perhaps someone will come in his stead?

The important thing is to preserve one's identity and go on working. Who am I as compared to him? He is known to all intellectuals in Europe, especially in France; Romain Rolland is his ardent admirer, and so are many others. In a letter from Oxford Uncle writes that Borya told him about my trouble. He is pleased that I take it with a sense of humor and calls me a "good sport." I fear for Borya, I fear much that is in Borya, but I place my hopes in his friends abroad.

December 20, 1936

Oh yes, about my style. It has already made the transition from quan-tity to quality. What hasn't been said about it! True, Shcherba* is one of those who hasn't read my book or even looked at it.

When he said that what we needed was a "simple, realistic, lucid style," I interrupted him; he insisted that I write in another way, but when I said that Boris Pasternak was my cousin I can't tell you how taken aback he was. "Do you suppose he could write in any other style?" I asked. Instantly he surrendered, but he kept repeating: "How interesting! How interesting!" Now he understands. I said it with particular zest because I was holding in my hand the paper with Stavsky's speech in it.

* Lev Vladimirovich Shcherba (1880–1944): Soviet linguist.

Well, now I feel better. My sense of humor has come back. I feel the urge to write Borya a comical letter about "showing off." I remember how he laughed, simply leaped with laughter when I told him what Vladimir Fedorovich* and Co. had said about my book: "The book, of course, is highly original, but . . ." He took delight in the semantics of "originality."

It's absurd to deprive oneself of the air one breathes at home. Were it not for all these meetings and confrontations I could be happy.

---

* Vladimir Fedorovich Shishmarev (1874–1957): Soviet linguist and specialist in Romance languages.

CHAPTER VI

Pasternak's experiences in the 1930's resembled in many ways those of Russia's premier poet, Alexander Pushkin, in the years after the quelling of the Decembrist revolt. In December 1825, liberal noblemen demonstrated in St. Petersburg in favor of limiting the autocracy. The protest was promptly and violently terminated, the leaders executed, and many of the participants exiled to Siberia. Pushkin, in his poem "Strophes" (1826), called upon the new czar, Nicholas I, to show clemency toward the rebels, invoking a parallel with Peter the Great, founder of the modern Russian state, whose early reign was marred by repression. In Pasternak's poem "A century and more ago . . ." (1932), which he regarded as a direct communication to Stalin, Pushkin's admonition is quoted verbatim:

> But let it now be said,
> Comparing different days of pomp,
> "The start of Peter's honored days
> Were darkened by unrest and death."

Clemency, of course, did not mark the era of Stalin, and Peter's example soon yielded to that of Ivan the Terrible. As Pasternak comments to Olga in 1941: "As you know, the atmosphere is thickening again. Our Benefactor seems to think we've been too sentimental and it's high time to come to our senses. Peter the Great is no longer a fitting model. The new admiration, openly confessed, is for Ivan the Terrible, the *oprichnina*,* brutality."

Pasternak imposed an exile upon himself and, like Pushkin before him, sought refuge in the southern republic of Georgia, among its poets. "The people" became the main repository of his hope for relief from the oppression centered in Moscow. In his "Travel Notes" (1936; subtitled "To My Friends in Tiflis") he asserted the duty owed the people:

* The reign of terror under Czar Ivan the Terrible (1533–1584).

> Happy he who, undivided,
> Unadulterated, simon-pure,
> Is of the people with his blood,
> And with his childhood—of the poor.

Such openly "democratic" sentiments were a direct threat to central authority, and the poem was promptly attacked by the secretary of the Writers' Union.

DIARY

Stalin launched a machine of destruction known by the name of Yezhov-shchina. Yezhov was the chief of the secret police. He was always referred to by such Homeric epithets as "The Iron Commissar" and "Stalin's Comrade in Arms." There began a period of dreadful political trials, arrests, and banishments. The trial of Bukharin left an indelible impression. With the bloody hands of the executioner Vyshinsky,* Stalin chopped off the head of the Soviet people: their revolutionary intelligentsia. Every evening, radio broadcasts telling about the bloody and basely conceived trial would be followed by the playing of records of gay folk dances—the *kamarinskaya* or the *hopak.* My soul has never recovered from the trauma of the prisonlike knell of the Kremlin chimes striking the midnight hour. We had no radio, but from the neighbor's room it came booming forth, cudgeling my brains and bones. The midnight chimes sounded particularly sinister when they followed on the terrible words "The sentence has been carried out."

That winter Musya, Sasha's wife, was arrested. She worked at a military plant whose director, a party member of long standing named Bogomolov, had made her his secretary. They had an affair. Musya did not hide it from Sasha, who accepted it thanks to the "unconventionality" of his character. He offered no opposition to her love for Bogomolov. He suffered, but his conservatism, the depth of his devotion, and his pride kept him from leaving his wife. Where could such a queer specimen fit in? He kept what had happened a deep secret from us. His wife had forbidden him to see us, so he visited Mama (whom he loved devotedly) in secret, as if she were his mistress. He loved me, too, but he was uneasy in our company and for some time did not dare tell us about the blow that had fallen. Despite his rudeness and tactlessness, he was a man of great inner pride and sense of honor—even though he could deceive anyone at all.

He never got on anywhere, was always spreading tales and making fun of his superiors—and so the higher-ups hated him, while the workers and poor people worshiped him, literally worshiped him.

---

* Andrei Yanuarevich Vyshinsky (1883–1954): chief prosecutor of the U.S.S.R. from 1935 to 1939.

He was stunned by his wife's arrest. He became meek and thoughtful. As I learned later, one of the techniques they employed in the torture chamber was the following: in the presence of the wife they would call the husband on the phone and request that he bring her perfumed silk underwear to the prison (in Musya's case it was me, a close relative, they called).

With utter disregard for himself at such a fearful moment in political history, Sasha threw all his energies into saving Musya. He rushed about, wrote calumnies, telephoned, prostrated himself before his former bosses. All in vain. Another Stalin hurricane was approaching, indeed was at hand.

I recall that hideous summer at the dacha in Tsarskoye Selo as a nightmare of the distant past. Contrary to his habits, Sasha took us there in a taxi and helped us move in; later he came to see us frequently, a thing we could not have hoped for at any other time. Convinced that his days were numbered, he tried to see as much of his mother as possible. I sympathized deeply and was filled with love and aching compassion for him. Whenever I knew he was coming, I tramped miles through the dust in the hot sun to buy his favorite food at the market.

Alexander came from Moscow with his wife, Irina, and Fedya, his son. Both Alexander and Irina were architects. Alexander, the very image of his father, Uncle Leonid, was building the Moscow-Volga Canal at the time, so he was in uniform and had the expectation of being decorated. He was afraid of the anticipated medal and of his Chekist* uniform. Sasha wasted no time in asking him to slip Kalinin† a petition to have Musya freed when he received the medal from Kalinin's hands. The idea was preposterous and utterly hopeless. Alexander rejected it, of course, for which both Sasha and Mama turned against him, and from that day on Mama disavowed all connection with her nephew and refused to see any member of his family.

Yezhov's fingers were reaching out in our direction. What an unspeakable summer it was! The secret police always began their talks with "matters of deep principle" and ended with arrests. Stavsky's speech about poets rumbled past us. Borya's life was made miserable because of his fine four lines:

* Chekist: a member of the Cheka (Extraordinary Commission), the first Soviet secret police.

† Mikhail Ivanovich Kalinin (1875–1946): member of the Politburo from 1925 to 1946, Chairman of the Presidium of the Supreme Soviet and thus titular head of the Soviet government.

Happy he who, undivided,
Unadulterated, simon-pure,
Is of the people with his blood,
And with his childhood—of the poor.

The lines were deliberately interpreted as being against the masses. The high pathos of the last two was twisted to mean just the opposite. This provided his enemies with a pretext, an invented excuse. The poet was being persecuted for his unwillingness to sign death sentences. They argued with him, they threatened him. Appalling storms were breaking.

The last time Sasha came to see us, he sat out on the porch and slept with his head in his hands. In town, he said, he felt hounded; he fancied he was pursued, that someone was always following him. "But here I feel better," he said. In response to a letter he had sent Stalin he was visited by a military prosecutor named Petrovsky, who assured him Musya would soon be freed, that he, Sasha, made a very good impression on him, and that there was no reason why he should not go on working in peace.

It was impossible to recognize the former Sasha in this quiet man who had grown wise from experience and was suffering deeply. His spirit was calmed by being with us and seeing his mother. Unable to eat (so unlike him), wilted in spirit, full of dreadful premonitions, hounded to death, he would escape by falling asleep on the porch, and this image of him—the image of a kindly old man, tragically persecuted, weary, innocent, with drooping head—is the one that remains in our memories. We can never recall him without the most poignant pain.

He told us he had poison in reserve and would never surrender himself to the hangman. Musya, too, had poisoned herself when she was arrested, and for a long time after that she was in the prison hospital.

In the hope of saving her, Sasha told the authorities about her affair with Bogomolov (who died in jail from heart failure). All of us were told that during an interrogation Musya had confessed her love for Bogomolov and asserted that she found her union with Sasha burdensome. He was deeply wounded. "If only I could see her and ask her one question," he would say. I knew what that question was: Had she really made such an assertion? Twelve years later I learned it was a base lie, told with the express purpose of causing him pain.

"Life isn't worth it," Sasha would moan in fits of depression, and whenever he was left alone he would fall asleep.

While we were at the dacha he took two family paintings to our town apartment, one of them his portrait as a child painted by Uncle Leonid. He donated his entire coin collection to the Hermitage Museum, hoping thereby to save himself.

We decided to go back to town at the beginning of August. Every day Sasha visited our apartment, which was being taken care of by a vigorous woman called Durasikha, an employee of my department at the university and an irrepressible "activist." Sasha was drawn back to the family hearth every day.

It had been agreed that he would bring Mama back to town "if all goes well," as he was now in the habit of adding. I went to town on August 2 to make final arrangements. We met at the kitchen door. I was in an irascible mood.

"Well, are you going for her? When? At precisely what time?"

He grew evasive. "If all goes well . . . If I am able . . ."

"If *you* are able! What about me?" I lashed back. "Does anyone ever consider me? I'm expected to do everything, as if I were obliged . . ."

He was meek and gentle.

"Very well. The day after tomorrow at one o'clock."

"See that you don't forget!"

We said good-by. He stepped out the door, in distraction, I in a flurry of household cares, knowing that the whole burden of life rested on my shoulders.

He did not come. We waited with our bags the entire day. Our indignation knew no bounds. Again I had to do everything myself, and with enormous difficulty.

Our indignation lasted one day, two days; on the third I became thoughtful, on the fourth anxious, on the fifth I almost went mad. Dreadful fears haunted me. Suicide!

Only one thing remained: I had to find out his address and go to him. He had kept his address secret and did not allow anyone to visit him. He lived with his mother- and father-in-law.

In indescribable anguish I went to his home on Krestovsky Island without telling Mother. I was barely able to find the house, an old-fashioned wooden one with a garden gate and columns in front. It was buried in foliage. A wide stairway inside led to a gallery around the upper floor. Outside there was a lawn, flowers, and a vegetable garden.

In a kind of daze I opened the gate and climbed the steps. I'm mistaken, I assured myself. Everything is too peaceful; nothing terrible could have happened.

There was no one at home. I slumped down on the dusty wooden step and began to wait. My heart ached with anxiety. It was bad enough to have come here to learn dreadful news without being kept waiting for it. The anticipation of that first moment—the question and the answer—gnawed at my vitals. Limp, dejected, full of woe, I sat in that silent garden with my head bowed almost to the ground. Suddenly a speckled hen searching for seeds almost bumped into me. She stopped in fright. Cocking her head, one leg still uplifted, she turned a round and startled eye on me. I returned her look with a bitter smile. Good gracious, I thought to myself, how many degrees of fright nature provides! There could hardly be a creature more weak and trembling with terror than I was at that moment, and here was this other one terrified of me! Ah, you fool! If only you knew how much stronger and luckier you are than I am!

Just then Valya, Musya's younger sister, put in an appearance. Quivering from head to foot, I dared not lift my eyes to hers. She kissed me.

"Is Sasha . . . alive?" I gasped.

"He is."

She drew me away where we would be in private and told me the house had been searched and his typewriter and field glasses confiscated as "material evidence" of his being a spy. On August 3, the eve of our removal from the dacha, they had taken him away in the "black raven" (as the police van was called) with nothing but the clothes on his back. I was overjoyed to hear that my brother was alive; everything else was of secondary importance. I rushed home and cried to Mama: "Good news! Sasha's alive! He's only been arrested!"

From that day on I thought of nothing and no one but Sasha. All my life, all my breath was given to him alone. Nothing else mattered. I was miserable when I did not see the Shmidts (Musya's parents) for any length of time. The mother, Olga Ivanovna, was allowed to see her daughter occasionally; she took her parcels and knew all the ropes. It was complicated and sorrowful knowledge. So many people had been arrested on political charges that merely to reach the prison information desk required lining up in the street and awaiting your turn for two or three days in the cold autumn weather. Sometimes Olga Ivanovna would come to us, sometimes I would go to her. No parcels were accepted for Sasha and no visits permitted. At the end of every month we were given a brief account of him, and then we could leave him some money. My whole life was focused on these ends of the month. I waited for them with a concentration bordering on insanity. The thought that I might in some way convey to him news of us and of our suffering on his account was more important to me than the desire to aid him materially. A Chekist of Olga Ivanovna's acquaintance told her he had seen Sasha being led to a cross-examination with his hands behind his back, but he was not blindfolded. (Prisoners were led up and down stairs and through labyrinthine corridors blindfolded and with their hands behind their backs so as to heighten their anxiety.) Sasha, he said, was walking along bravely. From this I deduced that my brother, convinced of his innocence, had no fear of talking to his interrogator.

A severe winter was setting in. I expected Sasha to be released any day. Musya was still in the women's prison and her mother was allowed to see her through the bars.

Soon came days of fierce activity. I had to find warm clothes for Sasha and prepare the last parcel allowed (with or without a personal meeting) to those who were being sent into exile. I ran from one shop to another looking for things that were not to be found and rejoicing whenever I discovered or invented a substitute. Here, then, was the suitcase, into which I put such precious gifts as bread, canned food, paper and pencil, warm clothes, and even a woolen scarf. The preparations took my mind off my troubles and made me almost happy.

Mama, touched and grateful, said to me with tears running down her cheeks: "Surely God will hear your prayers—you are doing this with such love. If only Sasha could see with what love!"

I awaited the end of January 1938 with particular suspense. On January 30 Olga Ivanovna phoned and said she must see me alone, without Mama. I was seized with such terror that I began pacing the floor aimlessly. It was early in the morning, so early that it would have looked suspicious for me to leave the house. I asked her to come to us. The fact is I don't remember in what circumstances we met, but she told me that on January 9 Sasha had been sent off to Chita in Siberia for five years "on suspicion of espionage." We did not tell Mama then, or for a long time thereafter.

Left alone, I threw myself down on the couch. Such helplessness, violence, brutality . . . could it be put into words? Such a thing could not have happened—yet it had happened. I sobbed, I cried out, I lifted my arms and cursed the world, and it was my heart rather than tears that flowed out of my eyes; it was that last ounce of faith without which life is insufferable. The thought that after being locked up in prison for five months he was driven out into Siberian frosts in nothing but summer clothes almost drove me out of my mind.

There was no life for me after this. I could see nothing but my poor Sasha—such a kind, proud, incongruous person—among lice-infested criminals, lying on the floor or on a plank bed, being beaten with his hands tied behind his back, thrown naked into the snow. . . . My God, my God! Without even the right to correspond with us! What fiend but Stalin could invent such torture? The geographical names "Baikal" and "Chita" made my flesh creep.

Such images formed the substance of my life. All hope was gone. Everyone knew the horrors of Stalin's camps and his so-called "construction projects"—working in swamps up to the waist, being beaten almost to death, broken bones, fractured skulls, freezing to death . . .

For some time I felt his suffering eyes turned to us. Then one day I vividly and incontrovertibly perceived that he had reached the limit of endurance. All was over.

Moscow, November 1, 1938

Dear Olya,

Irina told me about her visit to you this summer. Only then did I learn the bitter and shattering news about Sasha. On such occasions human sympathy can get no further than the widening of eyes and deep sighs. For the past two years misfortunes of this kind have been treated in such a way that intercession from the outside can only make things worse.

She told me about Aunt's tears, and about the futile interview, and the anathema hanging over us. What can I say?

Thus have we lived through these decades, separated in space, united in a common, hopeless destiny, practically unable to help each other, keeping silent, each ignorant of what is happening to the other, and this has gone on year after year. Will the curse that has now been pronounced upon us bring some change? It seems unrealistic to suppose so. If we did not look upon separation and ignorance of each other as deprivations before, why should we do so after we have been condemned? And yet the consciousness that from now on you are completely inaccessible to us and that we no longer exist for you is unthinkable and not to be tolerated. How have we deserved it? Could not one of us, either you or I, influence the other's destiny in a way that would break the evil spell and revive our inborn creative forces to take the place of the dull sense of doom increasingly possessing us and everyone else? Who has the power to bring this about?—this or anything else for that matter in our unenviable lives on this earth. The only thing that might bring spiritual relief would be for us to be together. How badly I have always wanted this, and how insistently I have pressed you to come here!

Alas, was it not precisely because of this that I went mad at moments that seemed to have been made for joy and satisfaction? But every enforced approach to the phantasmagoria, from however great a distance (!), ended for me in a general breakdown.

Olya, please write and tell me about you and your mother. What is your telephone number? May I phone you this winter when I am in

Moscow? It would be senseless to talk about myself now, and indeed there is nothing to say. The main thing is that I long to see my parents; the impossibility of doing so casts a shadow on my life.

Embrace your mother for me when she at last forgives me and holds out her arms to me.

Yours,

BORYA

Our address:
17/19 Lavrushinsky Lane, Apt. 72
Moscow 17

Moscow, May 1, 1939

Dear Olga,

Well, thank God! Need I tell you what a joyful surprise your letter was? I hadn't heard the details of Aunt Asya's illness. Absolutely marvelous! Perhaps I am mistaken, but from what you wrote about Sasha I gathered that his neighbor brought you unwritten greetings from him. I think your letter, even in those places where it describes the dramas you have lived through, would not radiate such strength if you did not expect this problem, too, to be solved in the near future.

Many thanks to you and Aunt Asya for your kind feelings. I had two opportunities to come to Leningrad this winter but refused both of them for fear of spending the time to no purpose.

It's very hard to write. There are many things I must ask you. How frightening is everything you tell me! Naturally I didn't know the half of it. Even so I have lived through these two years along with everyone else, and much of it has touched me closely. How closely one cannot surmise; such things are secret.

Yet it was just in these two terrible years that my son Lyonya was born and Zhenya remarried, both joyful events, somehow connected, concurrent, marked with the most extraordinary symbolism. And there were other blessings as well.

As always, you write beautifully; I cannot reply in the same way. But I share your mood: a feeling that this period—probably the equivalent of a whole life span—has reached its end; a liberating, wholesome feeling, gladdening the heart even though little time is left us to enjoy it. [Two lines crossed out.]

We have really got to see each other. There would be no lack of things to say. How marvelous it would be if you came here! Have you not by any chance such a plan in mind? For what, after all, can be said in a letter? See? I just began writing and have already crossed things out.

The main thing is that I love both of you deeply, deeply, and will surely see you this summer if you do not make it sooner.

Yours,

BORYA

Moscow, February 14, 1940

Dear Olya,

I have owed you a letter from the day you wrote to comfort me in my sorrow.* Thank you.

Are both of you alive and well? I know that housebreaking and other evil things are afoot, and I worry about you.

I had hoped to see you in the spring, and this is why: I was translating *Hamlet* for the Alexandrinka†—you no doubt can guess at whose request.‡ Two or three times he and I were to come to Leningrad to see his staging of *Masquerade*, but we kept putting it off.

Then came his catastrophe, followed by the murder of his wife in her apartment. It is indescribable, and all of it touched me closely.

For the past few months I have been haunted by the fear that some contingency might prevent my finishing the translation. It was this fear that kept me from answering letters from Papa as well as from you. As you know, Papa and the girls and their families are in Oxford. A few days ago I turned in the completed translation. The Moscow Art Theater has the rights to its first production. Until the very last day I doubted that the theater would receive permission to stage it. It is to be directed by Nemirovich-Danchenko, that eighty-four-year-old *viveur* in gaiters, with a clipped beard, and not a wrinkle in his cheeks. A translation is no great service, not even a good one. *C'est pas grandchose* [sic]. But it was my happiness as well as my salvation to work on it. Little need I tell you this; *you* wrote the same thing about *The Taming*. To read *Hamlet* aloud, even half of it, without any cuts, is joy supreme beyond compare. For three hours one feels oneself a human being in the highest sense of the word,

* Pasternak's mother died in 1939 in Oxford.

† Now the Pushkin Theater.

‡ That of Vsevolod Meyerhold, who was arrested in 1939 and died in the labor camps. His wife, Zinaida Raikh, a celebrated actress, was murdered in their apartment in central Moscow soon after her husband's arrest.

not a meek, inarticulate, subservient creature, but one full of fire and verve; for three hours one finds oneself in spheres familiar from birth and lasting half one's life. Then, limp from spent energy, one drops down onto an unknown plane, one "returns to reality."

But why dwell on it? Please write and tell me about you and Aunt Asya. Does it make sense *technically* for me to come to Leningrad for a day or two for the sole purpose of seeing you? If so, I will do it when I have the money. Please write, but without forcing yourself, only when you have the time. Be sure to tell me what you know about Sasha—you may do it without fear.

Much love.

Yours,

BORYA

Moscow [May 6, 1940]

Dear Olya,

I was about to dismiss from my mind the idea of coming to see you and meant to write to that effect, but things have taken a turn that makes the trip possible. I may very well see you in the second half of May. In which case it will come off without material inconvenience for you, although I am, of course, coming only to see and talk to you. Thanks for the letter; forgive me for not answering. Love to you and Aunt Asya.

Yours,

BORYA

Moscow [May 14, 1940]

Dear Olya,

I must have expressed myself awkwardly if I created such a wrong impression. Your first words gave me no reason to fear inconvenience; from the very beginning I knew that our meeting would bring both of us joy. I expect to come at the very end of May. Love to you and Aunt Asya. If Mashura and Aunt Klara have a phone, give them my regards.

Yours,

BORYA

Moscow, May 21, 1940

Dear Olya,

This is surely the hand of fate! Just think, five days ago I strained or tore a back muscle and it hasn't healed yet. I intended to give a public reading of *Hamlet* in Leningrad so as to see you and Aunt Asya and give you and me this pleasure, and this had to happen! I postponed canceling the engagement until this very day (it was to have taken place on the 30th), so anxious was I to see you.

But the date is drawing near and I feel no better; and so, clenching my teeth, I am sending a wire today to call it off. The pain in my back is torture; I can neither stand nor sit. Zina is at the dacha with the children; I remained in town because of business with the theater, readings scheduled here, and the intended trip. And suddenly this misfortune!

Love to you and Aunt. If I did not count on the Leningrad reading being rescheduled for the autumn, this letter would be drenched with my tears.

Yours,
BORYA

Moscow [May 28, 1940]

Dear Olya,

I am writing to you from the hospital, where all my proposed trips came to an end. I have a badly pinched nerve. They say the treatment will take long and I will have to be on my back most of the time. What an awful trick of fate! Untimely in the highest degree. I have been so lucky of late, having enjoyed such success! Much, much love to you and Aunt Asya.

It is difficult to write.

Moscow, June 18 ,1940

Dear Olya,

I have been in the hospital and only now read your card. What you foretold has come to pass: it was precisely those painful twinges that grew worse and worse until they put me in a hospital bed for nearly a month with a pinched lumbar nerve, and all because I didn't take the twinges seriously at first.

Can you believe it? Just before the illness I had a card from Papa, perfectly calm, he even discussed *Hamlet*, etc. Not long ago a certain artist told me (he got it from a letter to a third party) that Papa is still painting, that in fact he did an Oxford lady's portrait. Much love to you and your mother.

Yours,
BORYA

DIARY

June 14 was Tamara Nikolayevna Petukhova's birthday. She insisted that I spend the evening with her. The day was overcast and oppressive. I felt dejected. I wanted nothing so much as to stay at home. But I felt I couldn't. Mama pressed me not to go. I must, I said to myself, otherwise I will fall into complete apathy; I must resist. And so, downcast as I was, I forced myself to go. On the way I stopped in at Nord's to buy some chocolates, then waited for the tram on Nevsky Prospect. The tram drew up at the stop. A Soviet citizen pushing his way inside knocked me down. I fell flat on my face, striking my forehead on the stone pavement. Thank goodness the citizen got into the tram. Few people were left at the stop. A person beside me whispered something in an awed voice, but no one helped me to my feet. My first thought was that I had not lost consciousness—then I wondered if I still had eyes. I did. I got up dripping blood. I saw it spattered on the ground. I was afraid to feel my nose and cheeks. They were there. After that I was possessed by one thought: Mama. I must go home, not to the hospital under any circumstances. I set out still bleeding profusely, the drops seeping through my handkerchief onto my coat. I climbed the stairs. I reached the door. I rushed into the bathroom, calling to Mama that I had had a fall. Only then did I see myself in a mirror. Good God! There was a gash above the bridge of my nose exposing the bone.

Quickly losing strength, I collapsed on the bed, hardly able to call the doctor and my friend Lifshits. I was told to go to the hospital immediately. Lifshits took me there. I was given a tetanus shot. They put me on the operating table to sew up the gash.

My surgeon, Doctor Tulkin, proved to be a talented physician and a warm friend. I was in bed for a long time with a brain concussion and was treated by an internist, a neurologist, and my surgeon. My illness was complicated by a series of heart spasms that filled me with terror.

Moscow, June 29, 1940

Dear Olya,

I was stunned by your postcard. How fortunate you are that it didn't end worse! Is there any chance of the cut leaving almost no scar? Dear me, just to think! You probably jumped off in the wrong direction (Zina is always doing that). She sends warmest greetings to you and Aunt Asya. Two more cards from Papa from Oxford, the second dated May 30, which means after Belgium and Holland—both cards as serene as if nothing had happened. Get the May and June issues of Young Guard; they carry my

Hamlet. You won't like it for the shock of its style—simple, prosaic, etc. Nevertheless, give it a try.

Yours,

B.

Moscow, November 15, 1940

Dear Olya,

Your silence fills me with growing anxiety. What's the reason? Is everything well with you? I'm afraid to ask questions; superstition keeps me from putting them in words. Write just a line of reassurance. Surely I have not offended you in any way, have I? I believe I was attacked in the Leningrad papers. Could that have so lowered me in your estimation that you no longer wish to know me? Or perhaps you don't understand the jocularity I bring to our relationship and resent it.

If only you knew how much I miss you! Nothing would please me more than having you come and stay here for a little. How are you feeling after last spring's accident? Is it possible you have heard nothing more about Sasha? I am so worried by your failure to reply that I begin to wonder if you are safe and sound. I even thought of writing to Leningrad University to find out if you still walk this earth.

Oh, how often I need you! Life is passing, may have passed in fact, and, as you wrote last year, we live by isolated bursts of our "seventh youth" (your expression). I enjoyed many such bursts last summer. After a long period of doing one translation after another, I began turning out things of my own. But that's not the main thing. It is astounding that the harvest of this wonderful, vibrant summer played no less a role in our lives than in the life of any collective farmer. Zina and I (on her initiative) made so big a garden that I feared we would not be able to gather in and preserve the autumn harvest. Lyonya and I are spending the winter at the dacha, and Zina is torn between us and the boys, who go to school in town. How indescribably beautiful is life in winter in the woods, in the cold—if you have a good fuel supply. Your eyes roam from one delight to another, dazzled with beauty. And the charm of it lies not only in the beholding but also in the minute details of alert, laborious tending. Relax your zeal for an hour and the house becomes so cold that no amount of fire stoking will warm it. Let yourself be caught napping, and the potatoes begin to freeze in the cellar, or mold forms on the salted cucumbers. And all of this breathes and smells, all of it lives and can die. We have half a cellarful of our own potatoes, two barrels of sauerkraut, and two barrels of salted cucumbers.

And then there are trips to town, waking up before six in the morning, the mile-long walk through fields and woods still dark as night, the lines of the railroad tracks receding in the snow, perfect and austere as death, the flames belching forth from the oncoming train which you almost miss and which overtakes you as you emerge from the woods at the crossing. Ah, how delicious life still is, especially when times are hard and you are penniless (which for some reason we have been for the past few months). How reluctant one is to give it up so soon, how much one longs to hang on!

Can you believe it? The time has come to get little Zhenya enrolled in the university (natural sciences or physics and math), or else he will be taken into the army and forget everything. How time flies! Lyonya is a copy of his grandfather: clever, reserved, sensitive (two years and ten months), and so mixed up in family relationships that he doesn't consider Zina his mother and marvels why young Zhenya has so many fathers (he thinks fathers are things bred of houses—each house brings forth its own).

Most marvelous of all was the news I received from the folks abroad. In the spring and beginning of summer, when I was in the hospital, I took leave in my mind of all I had loved and considered worthy of love in the dreams and traditions of Western Europe. I lamented it all and gave it burial, and this included, of course, the folks. The feeling was particularly keen when I was recuperating, when I realized, after my first serious encounter with medicine, that I was not only destined to live but also was possessed of vast stores of strength of which I had never been aware. And I wondered how and to what purpose I was to expend this strength at a time when the planet was defiled beyond recognition. Then suddenly— wonder of wonders!—I learned that all *this*, all that is wholesome, and the province of all mankind, was slowly coming back, evoking universal delight, secretly and superstitiously guarded, like deep and forbidden love. Ah, the English are bricks, there's no gainsaying it! Of course it's still too soon to rejoice; who knows what is ahead of us? On the other hand it's not too soon, because I know our dear ones are alive and this knowledge rises like the sun day after day above our wintry life in the woods.

This is an odd point at which to break off my letter. I could go on forever, but now it's your turn to write to me and tell me all and everything.

P.S. Don't forget, please, to include everyone—Aunt Asya, Klara's and Mashura's family (do give them my love), yourself and your work. I suppose it's very hard for you now, isn't it? (judging by our own difficul-

André Malraux, Vsevolod Meyerhold, and Boris Pasternak. Moscow, 1936

Young Zhenya Pasternak.
Moscow, 1940

Zina Pasternak

ties). *Hamlet* will begin paying for itself only a year or two after it is staged.

A collection of my translations has come out, an arbitrary selection, half of which I care nothing about, but among them is Verlaine—*most important* for me. Shall I send it to you?

At least drop me a card saying you and Aunt Asya are alive.

Yours,

B.

[Inscription in the volume *Selected Translations:*]

To my dear cousin Olya,
with a relative's natural feelings of
tenderness, guilt, and consternation
in the face of life's swift passage

BORYA

Peredelkino, November 15, 1940

Moscow, December 27, 1940

Dear Olyushka,

Since by some strange coincidence you write your own letters, you must know the measure of their worth and have no need of my ecstatic description. True, but with what delight I receive and read them! What boundless wit and insight you show in those bits about Homer and newspapers and Larissa! How amazingly you write about the essence of translation and how remarkably you express exactly what I deleted from my letter, fearing the theme would lead me on indefinitely and drag the letter with it. And you put it all in a single line!

I can't thank you enough for your swift and priceless reply, bringing me joy in the first place because it is so talented and in the second because it reassures me of your and Aunt's well-being. I have received another wire from Oxford saying everything is well there.

But now I must upset you. Sonya Genikes died in Odessa. Of late she had been leading a hard and impoverished life, but pride kept her from speaking of it; to the end of her days she preserved the humor and grace of a cultivated woman, raised in that consciousness, thoroughly accustomed to it. Of her three daughters, Tasya alone stayed in Odessa, the others moved to one place or another, and all of them are odd, half-educated, wild creatures. They got little attention as children, probably because of their parents' selfishness, and then the selfishness, the only thing they inherited from their parents, increased in them tenfold, nourished by a filial desire for revenge.

Could you find out for me about Akhmatova's health? I know she has been ill, but I should like to know more. It is hopeless to write to her, and besides I don't know whether she is in any condition to answer. You can find out by whatever means you find more convenient—by phoning her directly without hesitating to say who you are, etc., or by inquiring of acquaintances or at the university.

I have a feeling that Sasha will soon turn up. With this hope and faith I end, giving it further expression in my New Year's wishes for you and Aunt.

Best love to both of you.

Yours,

BORYA

Moscow, February 4, 1941

Dear Olya,

No doubt these lines will find you in, or just coming out of, the icicle state you described so beautifully. Don't think I'm saying this to flatter you; you yourself know the worth of your talent and character, so there is nothing surprising in my appreciating every new expression of them.

Well, then, thank you for your letter, which came as a great surprise. I was under the impression I had just *thought* of sending you and Aunt New Year's greetings and asking about Akhmatova but had never really done it. I have no recollection of the letter, and despite your reference to it I have the feeling that you simply read and answered my thoughts.

I cannot conceive how you are managing to live now that everything has become so difficult. Write and tell me honestly (I think I deserve it) whether you are in need of money.

You say I am behaving splendidly, whereas I am on the brink of despair. As you know, the atmosphere is thickening again. Our Benefactor seems to think we've been too sentimental and it's high time to come to our senses. Peter the Great is no longer a fitting model. The new admiration, openly confessed, is for Ivan the Terrible, the *oprichnina*, brutality. These figure prominently in the latest operas, plays, and films. In dead earnest. Of late I have been pursued by failure, and if it were not for the remnants of a certain respect for me in unofficial circles, official ones would see me starved to death. You told Akhmatova I was writing prose.

A fine chance! With the greatest effort I arranged that my nonoriginal writing (which is all that remains to me) should be devoted to something worthwhile, such as *Romeo and Juliet*, instead of translating plays by second-rate writers from minority republics. At best I have not many years of life left. There are things I know, things I can do, things I carry within me. All unexpressed. Forgive me if parts of this letter cause you pain; I promise never to repeat them.

Zina thanks you for thinking of her and sends her regards to you and Aunt Asya. The other day Lyonya was taken to town for his first visit to a barber shop. He asked what they were going to buy there, and when he found out the purpose of the institution he let out a howl and demanded to be taken away. He revealed the same interest in the merchandise when he was taken to a photographer and made the same howl and demand. I will ask one of my acquaintances to take his picture and send it to you; as yet there is nothing to send. He is growing up a savage, albeit a cunning, cowardly, and nervous one.

If Zina has fulfilled my request and been to the post office, you will receive a copy of the magazine with *Hamlet* in it. Do read it if you have time, but don't burden your mind with the notion, always unpleasant, that you will have to write about it later. I would love to think that you and Aunt Asya will like it; yet I know exactly what you will *not* like in it, and while these very prickles and oddities have been ironed out in the version edited by the State Publishing House (but not in the Moscow Art Theater's version) and I could have waited to send you the revised text, I am sending you the first version, which some call *risky* (which naturally I do not agree with) and even a failure. Some of the revising has made for improvement, of course—I was terribly pressed for time toward the end.

But seriously: I will be really distressed if you devote more than two lines to expressing approval or rejection. It will be a sufficient sacrifice of time and energy on your part just to read it through.

Best love to you and Aunt. Do me the favor of answering a question of a baser order, a question as to money. You once reassured me on this matter; how are things with you now?

I am writing this at the height of the cold spell. All day I have been heating the stoves, burning up all my work.

Yours,

BORYA

I have forgotten to express my gratitude for Akhmatova. Many thanks.

Moscow, February 11, 1941

Dear Olya,

What a queer fellow Alexander is not to have told me he was going to Leningrad. And how is it he hasn't been to see you yet? He tried to explain it to me on the phone today (I was in Moscow and called him up), but I understood nothing. It's a strange life that allows people as close as we are not to see one another for years. So you've got the flu again? The weather's taken a sharp turn for the better; it's warmer and probably we'll have no more frosts such as these. I draw this conclusion because the wind is from the southwest, and also because of the following circumstance. I went to town today, and while I was gone I had visitors who brought me gifts of a barometer and an outdoor thermometer. Judging by their appearance, I don't believe they could *ever be of service to anyone.*

So Alexander came to see you during one of the ice ages you described? Why didn't you write me about it? But perhaps I've confused everything in my old age or simply can't get my bearings after sleeping through most of February.

Don't be surprised by this brief and empty letter. I didn't want the unexpectedness of Alexander's trip and my ignorance of it to throw an unnatural light on our correspondence and mix up our relationship. That's one thing.

The other is that Alexander deeply regrets the misunderstanding that has arisen between him and you. But I won't go on about this because I saw him in a rush and we hardly spoke, so I know nothing.

Yours,

B.

Moscow, March 20, 1941

Dear Olya,

Here's a photo of Lyonya, my consolation. I haven't yet thanked you for your letter. I can see you didn't like my *Hamlet* despite your abstruse evasions. Thank you just the same for your affectionate humor and for calling me Borechka.

Recently I went through a trunk full of Papa's sketches, first drafts, all his workaday junk. Apart from the joy and pride this sight always fills me with, I found it devastating. Such things cannot be assessed without an appreciation of the difference between now and the nonscholastic era when the natural development of a person's activities filled his life as vegetation fills space, when everything was in motion and each individual existed to distinguish himself from all others. Olya, Olya, my existence is shameful and pathetic. You can sympathize with my distress because of your own experience. But you are constantly running into obstacles, you are hindered by intrigue. I have no such excuse. I fear that my hands dropped helplessly to my sides long ago of their own free will. From time to time one loses control under the stress of such bitterness.

Forgive me if I break off here. Unnecessary immodesties would only follow.

Better to get back to the purpose of this letter. What I wanted to tell you was that Lydia has given birth to a daughter. She has two boys, and this is her third child. As for Lyonya, he is, of course, the image of Zina, but doesn't he remind you at the same time of Josephine?

Best love to you and Aunt Asya. How is she feeling? Again I thank you for all the trouble you took with *Hamlet*. I am terribly interested in knowing how your struggle with the dark powers at the university turns out.

Yours,
BORYA

Moscow, April 8, 1941

Dear Olya,

Thank you again and again for your priceless letter. No doubt you are surprised, and justly so, that I should have delayed in answering it. The fact is (as I write to Aunt) I was waiting to buy some Estonian paper and wanted to use the first sheet of it on you. By the way, Leningrad should be getting this paper, too; if it isn't sold at the university it may be at the Writers' Union shop. If you wish I will write to the Leningrad Literary Fund and ask them to let you have a ream or so.

Thanks for your sympathy, for the words about Lyonya, for your support, for your kindness. Your letter came on Sunday, the 30th. You ask about young Zhenya. He was staying with me at the time, and on Sunday Zhenya was here, too. In my last letter I began telling you about various intimacies and broke off. Do not associate this in any way with my mention of Zhenya and young Zhenya, but attribute it to the whole tangle of discontentments, the greatest of which is with myself and my wasted life; indeed I was so desperate that I wanted to end everything and begin all over. A month and a half ago I quarreled with Zina and left her. At first I was miserable, but soon I was once more stunned by the noise, the deafening clamor of freedom, its vivacity, movement, color. And this lives beside us. What happens to it when we are not alone? I found myself transformed; once more I had faith in the future. I was surrounded by friends. The most unexpected things began to happen. And this is how it would have continued but for the misfortunes that rained down upon Zina.

In the first place, I never expected her to take it so tragically. I mustn't write or talk about it; it would be indiscreet. But when to her sufferings was added the illness of her oldest boy (who is to be taken to a sanatorium in Evpatoria in a few days), it became impossible, at least for the time being, to stick to my decision. I will help her now; we'll see how things turn out later. I will not give up again something I had forgotten all about and recently experienced anew. I am writing chaotically, omitting some things, scratching out others, the whole sounding quite inhuman. She is a wonderful, hard-working woman who has had an incredibly difficult life and is as much of a crybaby as Lyonya. Well, let's change the subject.

The thought of Greece makes me go cold all over. I fear the situation is again as it was last summer, when they advanced like an avalanche, taking country after country. God grant that I am mistaken. I was delighted with your story about university "ors" (doct-ors, profess-ors). How is it all to end? Will they publish you? Dear me, the same thing over and over, everywhere! Yours was such a fine, rich letter that I can't answer it all at once. Certainly send a telegram to our folks; can't you imagine how glad they will be? A telegram of twenty-five words costs twelve rubles and is marked ELT (Europe Letter Telegram, I guess). Write it in English. Address: Pasternak, 20 Park Town, Oxford. If you change your mind for some reason, let me know what you would like to tell them and I will put it in my wire, introducing your message with "Olga reports . . ." or something like that.

Well, then, in a few days I may be taking one of our boys to Evpatoria. Thank you again. You cannot imagine how I appreciate your support, and if I find within myself the strength to make up for all the lost years, you will see—I will not fail you. Zina sends her regards, and when she gets back from Evpatoria she will surely write to Aunt Asya. Much love.

Yours,

BORYA

Forgive these superficial notes, so insultingly hasty in reply to your deep and thoughtful letter, but it is my curse that I must do everything on the run.

Yours,

BORYA

Dear Aunt Asya,

What joy it brought Zina and me to see lines penned by your hand once more! Thank you for all you said. I do wish you could see Lyonya. He is very like me. He is extremely grave, gloomy, thoughtful, and stubborn; sensitive, touchy, and easily frightened. He can, for instance, be frightened by a moth or a bit of material, or a wisp of cotton wool from the mattress that will rob him of sleep for several nights running. Sometimes he has terrible nightmares. He is very clever and observant. He gets his vivid imagination and timidity from Josephine and my mother.

Sensitive as he is, little Zhenya never had such nerves. You asked about him. In spring he finishes high school and will probably be taken into the army. I hoped he could enroll in the university before that, as young men used to do in my day, and at first it looked as if my efforts to achieve it would be successful. But for this I would have had to push myself forward immodestly and represent him as a child prodigy, which would be both untrue and most disagreeable. Zhenya herself feels I have not shown enough solicitude for him. When I lived in town, i.e., last year, I used to take Lyonya to see them from time to time. They are very fond of him. But they haven't seen each other for nearly a year now. Zina will surely write you, Aunt. Indeed she would have written already, but you must forgive her; she deserves your sympathy. To the winter's exhaustion have been added other troubles, the worst of which is the illness of her oldest boy. He has tuberculosis of the bone in his left foot. At present he is in bed with his foot in a cast, and in a few days she is taking him to Evpatoria. If I find anyone to stay at the dacha I will go along to help them.

I can hardly believe I am writing to you, Aunt Asya. It goes without saying that if I followed my inclination in all seriousness, my letter would be endless. Had anyone told us twenty-five years ago what would happen to each of us, we would have thought it a fairy tale. That is why the writing of a letter to you or Olya or anyone very close to me always leaves me with a sense of having failed, of having missed, of having left a promise unfulfilled. I was so happy to receive Olya's letter, it gave me such joy, that I would have answered it instantly had I not wanted to dedicate the first sheet of that nice Estonian paper to you.

Much love.

Yours,

BORYA

Moscow, May 8, 1941

Dear Olya,

I was in town today, and young Zhenya told me Zhenya was in Leningrad. I suppose she has been staying with you, and that means I will have new reasons for thanking you when she gets back, and for writing you a special letter. But let me write you now, before the advent of those reasons, merely on the strength of this earlier impulse.

For the past two weeks I have feared you would answer my last letter before I got this one off. I have wanted to warn you but have been too busy to do so. You must know that I consider myself too deeply in your debt ever to repay you. I feel rather like a vampire sucking the best juices of your kindness and growing used to this periodic free nourishment. Save your strength—you have your own path in life for which you need it. To put it more simply: you are such a busy person that the only thing I can expect from you is postcards reporting on your health.

Our winter correspondence (i.e., your letters—I put it incorrectly) played a major role in the change that's just come over me. I am not speaking of family affairs; I ought not to have spoken of them in my last letter. I meant that for the first time in fifteen years or more I again feel as I once did; again the day's work seethes within me in all its former freedom, unurged (the only way in which it can come naturally), without the sense of being in the focus "of the whole country," etc., etc. Already I am producing line after line and will go on doing so, which explains why I am writing you in such a hurry.

I wanted to anticipate your letter and beg you not to lavish so much of your spiritual and imaginative powers on me, because your goodness destroys me. What can I offer in return? I wanted to do even more—for instance, much as I love Lyonya, your feeling for him goes beyond all bounds. It must be subdued. I am enclosing this picture precisely because he looks worse in it. They shaved his head, which makes him look more timid and self-conscious than ever, and more like me than in the first one.

But the main thing is Zina's and my request. Please come with Aunt Asya to spend the summer with us at the dacha. Do arrange it somehow —just think how splendid it would be! Perhaps our best friend, Nina Tabidze,* will join you with us in the middle of the summer. For almost four years she has been unable to find out where her husband is. And then there will be Lyonya and us. Do please give it serious thought.

* Wife of the Georgian poet Titian Tabidze (1895–1937), who was executed during the Purges.

Don't judge Zina harshly. In the next few days she is moving out here and will write you; until then she is in town with her other son, busy with countless chores, grieving over her sick son, sewing for all of us days on end, and weeping constantly. Her oldest boy has lost over thirty pounds in one month. His temperature has been high for so long that it cannot be accounted for by tuberculosis of the bone alone.

Well, then, thank you, thank you, thank you again. Best love to you and your mother. Aunt Asya is right in reprimanding me for my handwriting. It is not my hand that is at fault; I write beautifully with a pencil, but I have no luck with pens. I don't remember when I had a nib that didn't split or catch on the paper.

Yours,
BORYA

Moscow, June 8, 1941

Dear Olya,

Many thanks for the precious lines about Zhenya. What you say is interesting, true, and talented, to say nothing about its being generous and affectionate.

I await your Theophrastus impatiently. I am extremely intrigued since I cannot imagine how it is possible to re-create scientific antiquity. No doubt your group has had to adopt its own presumptive terminology? If so, what served as a guide? I suppose you yourself had to delve into the history of science? How really marvelous! My first childhood passion was for botany.

Please don't be angry with me for the fragmentary and belated letters I have sent of late. I cannot begin to describe how complicated and full of care my life is. Half of my "replies" are rush ones, a series of meaningless and reiterated exclamations. Naturally they annoy you.

I had believed somewhat in the possibility of your coming here with Aunt and am chagrined by the view you take of it. On both sides we could have had our fill of looking at each other, and that gives one so much! Our patient is better in that his life seems to be out of danger. Now it is just a usual, if bad, case of bone tuberculosis, which requires long treatment for recovery but is at least without other alarming symptoms.

If you have a spare minute and the opportunity to reach Mashura by phone, please do so. I have forgotten or never knew Aunt Varya's patronymic and would like to write to her (I think the address must be simple: the name of the town—and nothing else). Do you suppose

Mashura would drop me a line? How could I answer her without letting
Aunt Klara know?

Best love.

Yours,

BORYA

Moscow, June 17, 1941

Dear Olya,

Bravo, bravo! My warmest congratulations! I could have said it a week
ago, but it's this wretched life that kept me from doing so. Even now I'm
writing with my tongue hanging out.

Theophrastus is beyond compare. I was far from imagining it could be
so good. I hadn't expected anything remotely like it and devoured it in
one gulp the moment Lyonya handed me the parcel. I read it to my
guests; young Zhenya, who was here Sunday, was delighted. I show it to
everybody, and when I am in town I want to have the philosopher Asmus
read it. It's a pity to bury such a work in a scholarly journal. If Academy
Publishers were still alive, it might have brought your work out along
with something else of the same order.

I find it excellent that you translated literally "strong to do" and similar
things. Naturally I never knew anything like what you know in this field
—the speech about your "Greek scent"—and I have hopelessly forgotten
even the little I once mastered with such enthusiasm. Of the Greek scent I
only remember *apotmetheis tēn kephalēn* (beheaded), and I now see I
have forgotten how to write it.

All my exclamations of delight apply to your introduction no less than
to the work itself. Brilliant, fascinating pages! Particularly notable are
your ideas about the parallelism of ethics and comedy, modifications of
meaning without semantic changes in terms and images themselves, the
history of the shifting of models (gods, heroes, mediocrities), and the
historical and publicistic characteristics of time and circumstances.

I know I will find even more interesting and informative ideas and
surprises in your other work about ancient Greek folklore (how boldly
formulated is the question—of Humboldt-like breadth and tension!), but
I haven't finished reading it yet.

No doubt I have offended you involuntarily by not telling you at once
of my delight. In my opinion, your triumph should be complete. What is
lacking? What can the faultfinders put their fingers on?

I kiss you and congratulate you and thank you again and again. I long
to be free of *Romeo* as soon as possible, but there are complications—

which explains my wilted look and speech. If you have the time and opportunity, ask your students to get you issue 6 (June) of *Red Virgin Soil*. I have a few trifles in it written this spring about last winter and summer.*

Best love to you and Aunt Asya.

Yours,

B.

---

* Poems from *On Early Trains* (1943).

CHAPTER VII

THE GERMAN INVASION of Russia in the summer of 1941 dispersed the Pasternak family across Russia. Olga remained in Leningrad with her mother throughout the 900 days of the blockade. Young Zhenya was first sent along with other students to Smolensk to dig trenches; when he returned to Moscow in August, he and his mother were evacuated to Tashkent. In early July, Zina, her son Stasik, and the three-year-old Lyonya were evacuated with a group of writers' children to Chistopol, on the Kama River. By choice Boris Pasternak remained in Moscow with his Peredelkino neighbors, the writers Vsevolod Ivanov, Fedin, and Leonov. Their presence so close to the German front was regarded with suspicion, and in October 1941, Pasternak was evacuated by air to Chistopol, against his will.

Pasternak was hopeful that the war would at least allow for a reassessment of Stalin's reign of terror and a new candor in the arts. He attempted a series of newspaper essays on the war that were promptly rejected and a narrative poem, "Glow on the Horizon," the first part of which was published in *Pravda* on October 15, 1943, after which further submissions were rejected. He completed an original play about the war, titled *This Earthly Life*, charged with the despair of Gogol's famous phrase "This earthly life is a dull proposition, gentlemen!"

While translation continued to be the mainstay of Pasternak's income (during the war he translated the Polish poet Juliusz Słowacki and Shakespeare's *Romeo and Juliet* and *Antony and Cleopatra*, and he even recorded a BBC talk on Shakespeare), his own play assumed great importance. When read in manuscript by a close circle of Moscow friends it was found so provocative that Pasternak decided to burn it, preserving only two scenes for future use. One was used practically verbatim in the epilogue to *Doctor Zhivago*—the tale of the waif Tanya and her childhood, interrupted by revolution and civil war. The other scene features a character from *Doctor Zhivago*, Dudorov, but has no direct correspondence to the novel. In the play, Dudorov harbors a German army officer from the vengeance of the Russians, ponders the distinctions between Nazi and Soviet tyranny, and invokes the plight of a Hamlet trying to decide between self, family, people, duty, and destiny: "How does it go in Hamlet: 'Now, I am alone. O' what a peasant rogue and slave am I!' That's it, that's it. The expectation of a whole lifetime. And so cold. (Looks down and bends over) A toadstool. (Again looks down) The last, last blade of grass. Burrs, weeds. The last, deathly pale blade of grass, mother-of-pearl amongst drops of melted snowflakes. Today or tomorrow it will disappear under the snow. And I as well, and I . . . Lord, Lord, why do I like your order so. Lord, you will break my heart with the boundlessness of its workings . . . I thank you, Lord, that you gave me eyes to see, and when it is too late to look, to shed tears with. Lead my soul out of this prison to confess in your name. Here we think that life means home, work, peace and quiet, but when some upheaval occurs, how the catastrophe overwhelms us in everything that is close and familiar! Like the return of youth! There is more destruction in our nature than order. Birth, love, death. All these separate jolts are destructive; each step in life is exile, loss of the sky, the fragments of paradise. And always at such times there is no one in sight. Just the snow, the snow, how I have always loved it!" In the atmosphere of Stalinist, wartime Russia and the context of Eisenstein's and Prokofiev's film *Ivan the Terrible*, which substituted a new idol for Peter the Great, Pasternak's play would surely have been grounds for swift response.

In Leningrad the blockade isolated the experience of war: its story could not be told in the terms of strategists or military historians but rather demanded account in the terms of apartment dwellers, neighbors, colleagues, and those chance communities that formed around necessity— the hydrant, the rations office, the telegraph station. Olga's descriptions of Leningrad under siege are a primary historical document.

DIARY

In an idle moment on June 22, a pleasant summer day, I decided to make a phone call. It was Sunday, about noon. I was surprised when a woman's voice said that Bobovich, whom I was calling, could not come to the phone. "He is listening to the radio."

I was still more surprised when the woman added, after a short pause: "War has been declared on Germany. The Germans have attacked us and crossed the border."

It was completely unexpected, almost incredible, although it had been predicted beyond a shadow of a doubt. It wasn't the invasion that was incredible, for who had not expected it? It wasn't even the war with Hitler, for our foreign policy had not inspired confidence. It was the upheaval in our lives that was so unexpected, it was the sudden cleaving of our lives into past and present on this quiet summer Sunday with all the windows wide open. The feeling of buoyancy in my heart, of hope and desire, was like something organically rooted in me, outside of will or desire. And suddenly—war! I couldn't believe it; I didn't want to believe it.

Yet no one could help realizing that this marked the beginning of colossal events and calamities. I understood the theoretical significance of what had happened, but I observed that my only response to this terrible news was shock. What, after all, could compare with the year 1914? My heart remained cold and my only fear concerned our daily lives. What misfortunes awaited us?

It was a pleasant summer day, a Sunday, a day of rest, of open windows, of quiet green trees. I was taken unawares. History was advancing from some dark hinterland. One felt: oh, it's not that bad yet, things will shape up; we must trust life; real trouble is still far away; much will happen before events overtake us and cut into our days. And, indeed, was it not high time for something to happen? "Let it be worse so long as it's different."

At first everyone reacted with confident equanimity; the war reports were read with enthusiasm. But very soon the mood changed for the worse. We were abandoning one city after another. The reports, so avidly, so anxiously awaited, grew more and more laconic. The more each of us worried about the news, the less of it we were given. Rumors began circulating.

The military failures sharply affected morale. People grew angry and reticent, sullen and nervous. They were becoming gloomy. The regime was hated.

In July our gloom was deepened by a succession of defeats. Having seized many cities in Belorussia, the Ukraine, and Bessarabia in one fell swoop, the Germans were moving rapidly toward Leningrad from the south and from Finland.

Moscow [July 9, 1941]

Dearest Olyushka,

Well, how do you like it? I am writing this with tears in my eyes, and yet—imagine—I am writing about our first cause for elation: the eluding of the first terror, the first horror in the series of horrors awaiting us. Zina has been hired as an aide on the train evacuating children (our Lyonya among them) from Moscow. And thus, with God's help, he will not be alone, and he will know who he is and who he belongs to. They are being sent off this minute, which means I am parting with everything for which I have lived and labored.

Zhenya is in the army, in the very heat of action, somewhere in your area.

It may surprise you, but under the most inopportune circumstances, in the midst of tragic conversations in a bomb shelter, I suddenly find myself talking about you and your Theophrastus, which evokes everyone's admiration.

Write to me at my city address: 17/19 Lavrushinsky Lane, Apt. 72, Moscow 17.

How is Aunt Asya's health?

I love both of you. Write to me, remember me, and make use of me.

The children are being sent to a town on the Kama River east of Kazan. What is to become of me I do not know. I dug a deep trench to hide in at the dacha, but Peredelkino is on the road coming from the west. With the family gone it will be deathly quiet and empty there. I don't think I shall be able to stand it.

All my love.

Yours,

B.

DIARY

An air-raid alert sounded on the first night of the war, the night of June 22–23. It terrified me. I was shaken by the very strangeness of an attack from the air, of murder out of the skies. I lay there unable to comprehend, to understand, to accept this strange new life, these strange people, these two tyrants throwing themselves at each other's throats, these factories making explosives, these bombs being thrown into beds where people lie sleeping, children and old folks among them. I was shaken; my heart refused to go on beating.

There were many air alerts after this, but without bombings.

We were terrified by the thought of having to leave Leningrad. After the initial tragic and disorganized evacuation of children alone, parents no longer wished either to leave the city themselves or give up children who had not yet been taken away. Everybody wanted desperately to stay where he was. Neither the intelligentsia nor the broad masses believed in the good things to be found in faraway places, and the very thought of being transported in lice-infested freight cars struck terror in their hearts. Yet organizations were already leaving, taking their personnel with them. The Academy of Sciences was being sent out of Leningrad. My worst fear was that the university would be sent, too.

Leningrad, July 12, 1941

[Received in Moscow on July 21, 1941]

Yes, dear Borya, what a time for us to contemplate meeting! Neither the heart nor the mind can embrace what is happening. One thrusts away the days as if into an already packed suitcase, but they don't fit in. I sat down to write, and it is so hot that my brains are melting. It is 80° in the room.

I would invite you to come and see us, if I had any assurance it was possible with a Moscow passport.* Our spirits are holding up and we are calm. Perhaps with us you would find peace for your daily life.

My heart aches for young Zhenya, our Doodle. Tell his mother that Mama sits here and cries. Tell her we love her dearly. By all means send Zhenya our address. Who knows? He may find himself in Leningrad. Our front is not the worst one. O God, how could the two of them part! How could they say good-by! He is such a tender and inexperienced boy!

How is Alexander? What has Zina done with her sick boy? I am delighted that Lyonya will have his mother with him; separations are terrible, insane.

Klara was lucky; she turned up at Varya's just in time.

* Soviet citizens have always been required to carry internal passports designating their city of residence. Prolonged stay in another city requires registration with the police. No doubt the regulation was more strictly enforced in wartime.

The day before yesterday we underwent a serious crisis when the question arose as to whether we should leave Leningrad with the university or whether I should resign my post. The problem was not, of course, one of work, but of setting out for nowhere. From morning to night friends, acquaintances, and members of the department came to ask advice or take their leave. The departure of the Academy of Sciences, including dozens of friends and colleagues, was a shock. Our own names were on the list of prospective evacuees. What an agonizing problem! But as soon as I had made up my mind I felt relief. We are staying. I haven't the strength to forsake my beloved city, and Mother hasn't the strength to make the trip. Any decision foreseeing the probability of death is an easy one to make. It requires no conditions and no program of action. It is the only merciful one, the only one that presents no other demands. It leaves the soul alive and sound. And it drags the consciousness with it as contraband. I am passionately interested in the progress of the war; in the very first days I volunteered to work in a hospital. But I still buy flowers and write about Homeric similes.

I embrace you, Borya dear. Be cheerful and remain yourself. The promised hour of world renewal will come; the bloodthirsty beasts will be slain. I believe in the destruction of Hitlerism.

Yours,

OLYA

Mother is behaving magnificently. What about Uncle and the girls? Is there news?

Leningrad, August 12, 1941
[Received in Moscow on August 16, 1941]

Dear Borya,

How are you and where are you? I feel a longing to talk to you. I want to remind you that it has been a long time since I received your letter about Lyonya's being evacuated from Moscow. I answered that letter immediately. Since then I have heard nothing more from you. How is Zhenya? Have you received any news from him? Send him our address by all means, although the chances of a meeting are becoming less with every day. We had hoped (as I wrote you) that you might be able to come here on a trip sponsored by the Writers' Union and would be able to get some rest here. We have so many questions: how is our dear uncle, where are Zhenya and Alexander, what is Fedya doing, is there news from Zina? Hurry with your answers. We are alive and well. I am not inviting you until we are fully settled.

Moscow, August 22, 1941
[Received in Leningrad on September 22, 1941]

Dear Olyushka,

Thank you for the letter and the card. Greetings to you and your mother. Zhenya returned from his assignment in due course, was recently transferred, and has now left for Tashkent with his mother. It will be a great miracle and good fortune if this postcard reaches you. I am completely alone; if possible I will go to Kazan in the company of two or three bachelors like myself to visit our wives. Our wives are all well, but, as is natural, they are having a very difficult time.

Yours,
BORYA

DIARY

Disaster was approaching. On September 1 our daily lives suffered their worst setback yet. The so-called commercial stores were closed down. These were stores in which the state sold provisions for inflated prices. The ration coupons that were introduced in July or August did not cause serious deprivation, since all necessities could be purchased at these stores. And suddenly everything disappeared. What would we eat? How would I provide for the two of us?

Disaster came still closer. On the afternoon of September 8 the air was filled with deafening gunfire. One barrage followed another in swift, booming succession, an earsplitting series of thunderclaps, a tornado of sound and fury spelling catastrophe.

Several days passed. By this time we knew what air raids, bomb bursts, and fires were. Now suddenly there is a diabolical addition to the list: artillery bombardment. The house shakes, the windows shriek. We jump up as if scalded. All is quiet. Suddenly another thunderbolt which strikes the house with an explosion that sends everything crashing. People rush about wildly, not knowing where to seek refuge. They fly out into the hall, down the stairs, into the cellar.

This was even more frightening, incomprehensible, and unpredictable than the air attacks, and even more unnatural and inhuman. It is impossible to get used to such horror!

But we did. It went on for nine months, day after day, with scarcely a break. A shell is fired; it approaches with a piercing scream and falls with a deafening explosion. Meanwhile people walk along the streets, as do I; and everyone, like the buildings surrounding us, may be destroyed at any moment.

208

The Germans killed the inhabitants of Leningrad with inhuman pertinacity. During the heaviest bombings of German cities, the English rarely flew more than one mission against the same city in the course of a week. The Germans attacked Leningrad from the air not only every day but many times a day, every hour or two—five to ten raids a day. They killed people and turned five-story buildings into rubble as long as time and the sun permitted. Oh, those heaps of splinters, those bent and twisted iron bed frames from the dwellings of the poor, their pitiful belongings scattered among the bricks and beams! Just as all people become equal when they are naked, so do all houses appear the same when reduced to ruins. Only a gaping skeleton remained of some buildings, while in others we would be shocked to see a door opening into nowhere, half a corridor, or a battered stone partition. The first sound of the air-raid sirens set us all atremble. We would dress ourselves frantically and go out to the stairwell and down to the floor below. This naïve self-delusion reassured us. Oh, the terror, the darkness, the whistle of the German dive bombers, the moment of suspense before the explosion, and immediately thereafter the discharge of death, the shaking of the building, and the dull shriek of the air.

The city was unprepared for air attacks. There were almost no air-raid shelters. People took refuge in cellars, basements, gasproof shelters, and in cold, damp, dreadful caves. Pedestrians were driven into cellars by force, and if the buildings were hit by demolition bombs they would be buried alive.

The artillery bombardments were more terrible than the air attacks because of their unexpectedness and the blindness of their aim. There could be no warning signal. A man might be killed while having his dinner or while walking down the street. Death shells flew into the city from Kolpino, Ligovo, Pulkovo, and Strelna, but where they would fall and explode—on which house, in which street, on which floor—only blind fate knew.

Moscow, September 14, 1941
[Received in Leningrad on October 23, 1941]

Dear Olyushka,

What times, what times! I am so worried about you and Aunt Asya! My heart bleeds for you. The madness of it all defies description! Leningrad is being horribly bombed. We went through the same thing a month ago. I often stood watch on the roof during the night raids. On one such night during my watch, two demolition bombs fell on our building. It is a twelve-story building with four entrances. Five apartments were destroyed in one section, and half of a courtyard wing. The danger frightened and intoxicated me.

I am alone, but I will probably spend the winter with Fedin, Vsevolod Ivanov, and Leonov in one of our dachas. Both Zhenyas are in Tashkent. Zina, Lyonya, and one of her other sons are in Chistopol on the Kama River; the son with bone tuberculosis is in the Urals.

I heard from Oxford; all are alive.

Yours,

B.

Moscow, October 8, 1941
[Received in Leningrad on October 21, 1941]

Dear Olyushka and Aunt Asya,

Zhenya's address: Evgenya Vladimirovna Pasternak, 8 Vystavochnaya Street, c/o Ivchenko, Tashkent. It seems they have no complaints to make. People say young Zhenya has enrolled in the mathematics department of the university and is also doing something or other in the theater. Thanks, dear Olya, for the card and the telegram. You can imagine how happy I was to receive them. Zhenya's former housemaid and I are spending our last days in the country; I intend paying a visit to Zina before the rivers freeze. Everything is quiet out there, although Lyonya has the measles and conditions in the hostel where Zina is staying must be hard. Recently she made the mistake of paying the Literary Fund for the boys' and her own lodgings for three months in advance, even though she is working like a horse in their canteen while the wives of famous prize-winning writers live on loans from the same organization without lifting a finger to support themselves. "Why are so many children born?" is Lyonya's latest *mot* reported in Moscow by returning evacuees.

Moscow, October 8, 1941
[Received in Leningrad on October 21, 1941]

Dear ones,

Just to be on the safe side, here (once more) is Zhenya's address: 8 Vystavochnaya Street, c/o Ivchenko, Tashkent. What good fortune it would be if your paths were to cross! Father and my sisters are well; they sent a cable asking for news about us. Before leaving for Chistopol to see Zina I will send them a cable from all of us. Address: Pasternak, 20 Park Town, Oxford. Of course I miss Lyonya terribly; he told Zina to "have

Papa come so the bombs will stop falling." Zina's requests for me to come are growing more and more imperative. I long to see her. If by some miracle you were to turn up in Moscow, either on the way to some other place or as a final destination, and if this coincided with my temporary absence, there are all kinds of opportunities for you here: an apartment, a certain amount of fuel, some potatoes and cabbage, etc. Zhenya's former housemaid knows about everything (Elena Petrovna Kuzmina, 25 Tverskoy Boulevard, Apt. 7, Moscow, c/o E. V. Pasternak). It is possible that Akhmatova will be living there too, but that should not embarrass you in any way. She is a fine, unpretentious woman.

Moscow, October 8, 1941
[Received in Leningrad on October 21, 1941]

My dearest ones,

Zhenya's address: Evgenya Vladimirovna Pasternak, 8 Vystavochnaya Street, c/o Ivchenko, Tashkent. If you should happen to be in Moscow while I am gone, everything of ours in town and in the country will be at your disposal (the apartments on Lavrushinsky Lane and Tverskoy Boulevard, including whatever supplies of vegetables and wood you find). Elena Petrovna Kuzmina, Zhenya's former housemaid, is in charge of all this (if not at Zhenya's, she may be at her sister's: M. A. Rodionova, 3 Kropotkin Street, Apt. 20, Moscow). Regardless of whoever else may be living there, everything you want will be provided at any time. I told her about you. Alexander will introduce you to her (his address is 8 Gogol Boulevard, Apt. 52, telephone K4-31-50). Should you happen to turn up at Zhenya's in Tashkent, it would be a blessing and a holiday unprecedented. Take care of them in that case. Have them work and make some money—that is what is most important. They seem to be well and without troubles.

DIARY

Beginning in December the hunger and cold increased. Never before had there been such a cold winter. The city was without fuel; neither wood nor kerosene was available. The use of electric stoves was forbidden. Rations grew smaller and smaller. Most of the population was allowed about four and a half ounces of bread per day, but it could hardly be called bread; it was a wettish, suspicious-looking mixture of surrogates that smelled of kerosene. The less bread there was, the longer the lines grew. People stood in line for hours at $-15°$ and $-25°$ in order to receive this miserable ration. By December people were beginning to swell up from hunger. The trolley cars stopped running; there was no fuel and hence no electricity. People were forced to cover enormous distances in the city and suburbs on foot. They walked in silence from one district to another, across bridges, over the ice of the rivers. Behind them they pulled sleds piled high with wooden beams, boards, logs, poles—anything that could be used as fuel.

Suddenly the arrest of academics began. The eminent scholars Zhirmunsky and Gukovsky* were among the first to be taken.

From January 1 through January 20 no food whatsoever was given out. Hungry, swollen people waited in line eight and ten hours in the hope of a food delivery, standing in the searing frost wearing scarves, shawls, and blankets over their quilted jackets and overcoats. Day after day, week after week, people were given nothing to eat. The state, which had taken upon itself the feeding of the population (forbidding individuals to trade or barter), now offered the population nothing at all.

People died in droves. No epidemic, no German bombs or shells could have killed so many people. They fell while walking, collapsed while standing in line. The streets were strewn with corpses. They lay everywhere: in yards, in gutters, in pharmacies, in the entrances of houses, on stairways, on the thresholds of apartments. Yard porters gathered them up each morning like trash. Thousands of dead bodies—livid, emaciated, terrible to behold—were stacked in hospital yards. And still no food was provided.

It is said that three and a half million people perished that winter in Leningrad. More than half of the city's scientists and scholars died, according to Academician Krachkovsky, who made a study of it.

It was forbidden to talk, complain, or appeal for help. The newspapers and the radio screamed constantly about the fearlessness and valor of the victims of the blockade. Oh, we would not surrender the city! Nothing could make us capitulate! There once was a time when fortresses were surrendered when food supplies ran out. We knew that death by starvation of five million people caught in a trap would not diminish the heroism of our well-fed leaders. We often wondered who was more merciless: those who kept human beings locked up in this city of death, or those who shot them down. Not the agony of the living, nor the murder of them, nor the starving of them, could move our heads of state to surrender the city, nor even to open negotiations with the enemy so as to achieve

---

* Viktor Maximovich Zhirmunsky (1891–1971) and Grigory A. Gukovsky (1902–1950): literary scholars.

some small alleviation of the suffering. The law by which man tramples upon his fellow man to achieve his end was in effect here. It was dubbed valor, the heroism of the besieged, the *voluntary* sacrificing of one's life for one's country.

Chistopol, March 18, 1942
[Received in Leningrad on June 6, 1942]

Dear Olya,

My hands tremble as I write your name. Are you and Aunt Asya there, and are you alive? How I hoped you would be able to tear yourselves away and join Zhenya in Tashkent. They waited for you! If you and Aunt Asya had left Leningrad, I feel sure I would know about it. We would have found one another. Send word to me here *without delay*. Then we can get in touch again by letter and determine what to do next. Alexander and his family remained in Moscow. I may return there on business in a month. Answer me promptly and think seriously about leaving. I have heard nothing from Papa and the girls. Lyonya is with Zina, who is working in a children's home. Write as soon as possible.

Love,
BORYA

How is Mashura?

DIARY

I lived from day to day in a monotonous struggle with hardships. The Soviet people displayed limitless endurance and the ability to stretch like a suspender in any direction and as far as necessary. Their indifference to life and death proved to be an enormous weapon. They could die and be resurrected time and again, despite the anemia and exhaustion of the past decades. No longer did they care when or where they lived or died, suffered, ceased breathing, found relief from their misery. No one enjoyed any freedom whatsoever, neither in making a choice nor in seeking deliverance. To be caught in the vise of life was no more desirable than to be caught in the vise of death.

Shortly before New Year's I sent greetings to all my friends, and for the first time in more than five years I sent a telegram to my dear uncle and his family in Oxford. That was a great event. I informed them that Mama was well and that we believed we would meet again.

There were no streetcars and no lights. Telephones were disconnected. Starvation and the terrible cold paralyzed all life.

Pipes froze, drains and sewer systems ceased to function. All life came to a standstill. Newspapers were no longer delivered or sold at newsstands. Pharmacies closed, as did the post office and telegraph. Radio broadcasts fell silent.

People did not undress at night because of the cold; they did not wash because of the lack of water. Acquaintances and relatives crowded together into small rooms filled with the soot of kerosene lamps and the smoke from portable wood stoves. Wearing dirty felt boots and quilted jackets, their faces and hands smeared black, they would chop up boards, furniture, and fence rails on the parquet floors. The pounding continued throughout the day, for the wood stoves required constant fueling. The sharp, stifling odor of the public toilet rose in the stairwell. The floors, pavements, courtyards, snow—all were spattered with yellow, foul-smelling slush.

When Sasha was arrested, it was a pleasure for me to prepare the food parcels we were permitted to take to those waiting to be sent into exile, with or without the right to deliver them in person. I would run from store to store, rejoicing whenever I discovered needed articles of food or clothing, which I stored away for future sending. It was these foodstuffs that kept us alive that fearful winter. As months went by, we opened box after box of Sasha's priceless food.

Mother's morale grew worse. The cruel trials made her nervous and hardened her heart. Like a child, she held me responsible for much that had come to pass and refused to understand the true state of affairs.

It was 25° in our room. The moments of getting out of bed were sheer torment, since we did undress at night, fearing otherwise we would become infested with lice as most people in the city had.

We suffered indescribably from frostbitten hands. Oh, that sharp, intolerable pain in the fingers! Tears came to one's eyes and one cried out loud. We warmed our hands every other minute on the teakettle or a pan. From morning to night we waged a battle against frozen hands and feet.

We enjoyed sitting next to the stove. It was said that "the long-awaited moment has come" when evening descended, the sufferings of the day came to an end, and we sat down to enjoy the stove's heat. It was the moment of crackling wood, of peace and comfort.

Suddenly the sirens would begin their prolonged, mournful wail. This would be followed by a shrill whine, a shaking, an explosion, the chatter of antiaircraft guns. We froze and waited; would we be hit? If not us, our neighbors? Whose lot would be drawn this time?

The radio was dead. There was something terrible in this dead silence that had seized even the Bolshevik propaganda machine. The whole outside world had fallen away. It was terrifying not to know anything—not to know what was going on in the city, the country, the world. In the most crucial hour of their lives, people were artificially cut off from their fellow men; they could neither call for help nor offer a helping hand.

One day there came a knock at the door and Lifshits entered. After the first gasp of surprise, all three of us burst into tears. She had come to see us on foot from the far end of Kamenny Ostrov,* where she and her husband had taken refuge in an office at his place of work. Here we were, the three of us, still alive, at the edge of the precipice, above the abyss of the times and the terror. We had seen each other!

The evacuation of the university began. And so began the agonizing hesitation, the sleepless nights, the shifting counsel, the decisions made and unmade a thousand times. Some advised us to leave this city of death in any way possible, even on foot if necessary. Others smiled and asked why we should consider leaving now after we had undergone so much and when worse conditions of starvation might await us elsewhere. Mother and I lay awake at night rehashing the same thing over and over.

I began having difficulty in straightening my legs. The condition grew worse with every day. The pain was acute in the morning, when my legs had first to support the weight of my body. Oh, those terrible days, which began with cramps in my calves, the indescribable pain of deformed muscles that contracted like the jaws of an angry wolf. On the morning of February 24 the pain became so bad that I was unable to stand, to walk, to hobble. I shivered with chills. My hands grew numb, lost all sensation. This was the beginning of two months of illness. Yet ration cards for March could only be obtained at my place of work—no laughing matter! Water and wood had to be fetched, and the refuse that accumulated in the course of the day had to be carried out.

Mother almost went out of her mind. Here I lay helpless, and there was no knowing how long it would last. There was no diagnosis of my illness —no doctors had been available for months. Three weeks later I unexpectedly discovered our family physician, who examined me and said I had scurvy. It seemed the whole city had scurvy. Vitamin C in various forms and warm compresses constituted the only remedy.

During the summer and fall I continued to work amid falling bombs, constant artillery bombardment, the shriek and explosion of shells. At first

* One of the islands composing the city of Leningrad.

I worked on Homeric similes, an undertaking I finished by the beginning of winter. I then sought a new task that would not require reference books or literary sources. I set about writing my lectures on the theory of folklore.

As I lay in bed I reflected deeply on a theme that had interested me for some time: the problems of realism in ancient literature. My study of Homeric similes was to be the first chapter of this work; the last was to deal with the origins of the intricate plot in literature. While I was ill and in bed I had jotted down my thoughts on Greek realism, the essence of the plot as a realistic view of the world, and a shifting of the center of gravity from religion and the gods to man.

Tamara Nikolayevna Petukhova saved my life by providing me with vitamin C. In the dark and cold of winter nights, down slippery streets, across the ice of the frozen Neva, she brought me jars of "glucose," a sickly sweet syrup with a strong artificial flavor. This revolting concoction sold at the Academy of Sciences for the outrageous price of almost 70 rubles a pound. The vitamin C helped me noticeably. And I was the one who didn't believe in vitamins! Six or seven days later my legs began to feel light and flexible again, and the pain disappeared. On March 29 I woke up feeling well and with confidence that I could soon go to the office again. On the 31st I tried getting up for a bit. Never before had I felt such weakness in my legs! How terrifying it was to get up! At first I walked with a crutch and a cane; then I took to using the cane alone when I went outside.

I was on my feet again! Good God, I was actually walking and no longer had to be waited on!

A bright and sparkling spring had come. The sky was of the deepest blue, of the most brilliant, the most festive blue. Winter had not yet gone for good; there were still frosts and an occasional snowfall. But the sun seemed hot. It beamed, it glowed, it flooded the city with dazzling light. The streets were empty, clean, dry. The city had undergone trans- figuration in the Christian sense of the word. Winter stood silent and spent behind one's back; the shadows of the martyrs were remembered like death on the cross, and the invisible presence of recent sufferings added to the quiet and desolation. There were too few people in the streets. The courtyards were empty.

The evacuation of factories and plants changed the air of Leningrad. It had the freshness of a provincial town, and there was a resonance to its silence. The extremity of our despair was transformed into the ecstasy of spring. The universal cycle of the seasons invigorated and consoled, and it promised a change in human affairs as well.

Leningrad, June 26, 1942
[Received in Chistopol on July 18, 1942]

Dear Borya,

I take the opportunity to send this postcard with someone going to your town. I find it hard to write to you. Can you imagine Dante sitting down to pen a letter while Virgil was at breakfast? What can I tell you that won't upset your nerves? Nothing. Or the following: I was at my wit's end trying to understand why I had heard nothing from you for eight months. I wired Zhenya in Tashkent but got no answer. At last the big day came: in June your letter of March 25 arrived, and with it your address. I didn't realize that Alexander was in Moscow. We exchanged New Year's greetings with Lydia in Oxford; everyone there is fine. In February I received a cable from her in which she expressed alarm and concern about you and Alexander. I answered the poor girl only three months later because I was down with scurvy at the time. Then messages of thanks and best wishes came flying here over the signatures of two different families. Taking a guess, I told them that all of you were well but that I had difficulty communicating with you. I sent an urgent wire in reply to your postcard, but I still haven't received an answer, although it was almost two weeks ago. "The rest is silence."

My department has been evacuated to Saratov, and they insist that I join them. The conditions there are excellent, but I am afraid to drag Mother away; she is eighty-two, you know. Who can say how much longer we will live?

Love to you, Zina, and Lyonya.

Chistopol, July 18, 1942
[Received in Leningrad on August 3, 1942]

Dear Olya,

Your postcard came at a time when I can reply to you without delay. It is Sunday, seven in the morning, and we have the day off. That means that Zina has been with me since last evening and Lyonya will come this morning at ten. The rest of the week they spend in the children's home, where Zina works as an attendant. It is a fresh, rainy morning—to my delight, for otherwise this continental climate would present us with Afri-

Boris Pasternak. Chistopol, 1942

Boris Pasternak with S. Tregub at the front. 1943

can heat. I can't sleep when the sun comes up. I got up at six because the hydrant from which I draw our water often breaks down and, in addition, is accessible only twice a day, at appointed hours. One has to seize the moment. As I lay drowsing I heard the creaking of buckets outside. Every housewife wears a wooden yoke over her shoulders with two buckets swinging from it.

One of my windows looks out onto the road, beyond which there is a large park called the Park of Culture and Rest. The other window over-looks the yard of the People's Court, overgrown with daisies. Here one can often see groups of emaciated prisoners who are being transferred to this local jail from ones nearer the fighting zone. From the court itself one can hear the shouts of the participants when a local inhabitant is on trial.

The road is covered with a thick layer of black mud that oozes up from between the cobblestones. The soil here is miraculous, uncommonly rich, so black that it seems to be mixed with coal dust. If the land were turned over to a hard-working and disciplined population, to people who knew what they could do, what they wanted to do, and what they had a right to demand, no social or economic task would be too hard for them to ac-complish; and in this New Burgundy, art with a Rabelaisian slant or the gusto of Hoffmann's "Nutcracker" would flourish. From my window I watched the postmistress mounting the porch of the People's Court and noticed that she dropped a postcard into our mailbox.

Nothing has interfered with my writing this letter, thanks to the early hour, the quiet, and the picturesque view.

Your telegram came as an understandable shock; I wept with joy. I suppose I did not answer for so long because I was too astonished and intimidated by the magnitude of the sufferings you have borne and still are bearing; I could not write because no exclamations are strong enough to express my feelings.

When I came here at the end of October, I had hoped, for some reason, that you would join Zhenya in Tashkent. I asked her about you. The fact is I did not receive a word of news from her for the first four months; letters began to arrive only at the end of January. I recall having written you either just before leaving Moscow or just after arriving here, and I thought you knew Zina's address (Litfond, Children's Home, Chistopol). What is most important, however, is that deep in my heart I did not accept the idea that you were in Leningrad, any more than you believed Alexander could have stayed in Moscow. And finally, only in March did I learn from my own experience that there is indeed some mail service in and out of Leningrad, despite the blockade. But even then it seemed preposterous to write to your regular address. I had a superstitious fear that your apartment would be found empty just because someone had had the audacity to assume that its occupants would open the door to the mailman as usual. And so I inquired about you through Sergei Spassky* and also through Shkapsky,† a native of Leningrad who is living here now. I thought of inquiring about you through Leningrad University. It was quite by chance that the most *natural* solution dawned on me: why not drop a postcard?

Well, so that's that. The life you know so well goes on as before, save for the changes brought about by the war. While in Moscow I willingly and with an inquisitive mind took part in all the new activities occasioned by air raids and the approaching front. I saw and endured a great deal. There were endless opportunities to reflect, observe, and prove my mettle in work and deed. I attempted to express myself in various forms, each time with that degree of truth and accuracy, perhaps imagined or mistaken, which I consider obligatory for myself. And scarcely one of my efforts was accepted for publication. Meanwhile, one has to live.

I brought with me to this place a feeling of *déjà vu*, of familiarity with all that was taking place, of dissatisfaction with myself, of irritation and perplexity. Once more I had to return to my never-ending translations. I spent the winter productively, preparing a volume of Słowacki's selected works for the State Publishing House and completing my translation of *Romeo and Juliet* for the Committee on Arts. Now I am free. A government summons is required to enable one to return to Moscow, and such summonses are not given willingly. A month ago I asked my friends to try to get one for me. It will probably be another month before I receive it. I am drawn to Moscow by a multitude of natural feelings, not the least of which is curiosity. Until I get there I am free; I have been hastily writing, rewriting, and discarding whole chunks of a modern play in prose, which I have undertaken exclusively for love of art.

For some reason this letter is not turning out right, and I sense (and such feelings never deceive) that you are reading it with coldness and alienation. All my family here and in Tashkent is well, though reduced to skin and bones; they have lost weight to a phenomenal degree. Thank goodness there is an abundance of bread here, but that is about all. Zina's oldest boy (the one with bone tuberculosis) is in a sanatorium in the Urals, and she hasn't seen him for nearly a year; she intends going there

* Sergei Dmitrevich Spassky (1898–1956): Leningrad poet and close friend of Pasternak.

† G. O. Shkapsky: a Leningrad engineer, evacuated to Chistopol.

soon. Today I told Lyonya I had received a postcard from you; he remembers you from last year's stories.

Love to you and Aunt Asya. What are you thinking of doing?

DIARY

With the onset of summer there began a massive and hysterical flight from the city. Everyone everywhere spoke of nothing but evacuation: strangers on the streets, in trolleys, standing in line for bread and rations. This was the sole subject of interest. Everyone was packing bags, tying up bundles. Institutions left the city in the usual muddling haste.

I signed up to go with the Academy of Sciences. Now began the enormous task of sorting out forty years of life lived in one and the same apartment. Its disfigured appearance was actually comforting, since it was easier for me to abandon it.

Friends came and sat amid suitcases, bundles, and general chaos; all of us were in a fever of excitement, all of us were going in the same echelon. There was great joy in these meetings, in the knocks at the door, in the voices and embraces of friends who had survived. Not everyone has died!

The parents of Chistyakova, a pupil of mine who was going with us, offered us an automobile and their help in taking our things to the station.

And so we were going! At last a way out had been found! Life became radiant. The disorder in our rooms grew apace. One bundle after another appeared. Mother baked buns for the trip. Wood, kerosene, flour—God, what bliss that at last we could consume them without the haunting fear of having no replacements!

Sasha was now returning to me everything I had collected for him. There was the suitcase I had bought him, and in it all the small things set aside for him in love and hope: postcards, an indelible pencil (an item no longer available), a warm sweater, underwear, a scarf, a warm shirt, gloves, and what remained of the canned goods we had hoarded for him.

I kept on packing and packing. We had three suitcases, several baskets, and a dozen bundles.

Finally, July 12 came. A storm threatened. Thunder. A heavy downpour. We were met by two vehicles: our baggage went in the truck, we got into the car. Mother stood the trip splendidly. I was depressed.

The four o'clock boarding of the train was a nightmare. We were squeezed into a suburban train, which was to take us to a station not far from Lake Ladoga. The trip was to last two and a half hours, after which we were to board a truck and ride as far as the boat.

We boarded. Inside the train it was a madhouse. The car was filled to overflowing with bundles, which kept falling on our heads.

"Let's go back while there's still time, while it's still possible," I said to Mother. She smiled calmly.

At last we made our farewells. The train set out at 8 P.M. Everything was over. We were on our way.

We traveled a short distance, then stopped, then backed up. We rode in the reverse direction for about ten minutes, then came to a halt. An hour passed, another, and yet another. It grew dark. We were not moving.

They said there was a storm on the lake and so it was impossible to get through. Then, with an air of mystery, they said there was no storm. Those who knew the truth kept silent.

People walked about, jostled one another. I felt ill. With clenched teeth, holding onto the seat with both hands, I tried to hold back a terrible seizure of cramps. I could neither talk nor move.

People spent the night pacing the floor, milling about in silence. I sat and dozed. My bones ached. My whole body ached. No, I could not possibly endure thirty nights like this one! By morning I was crushed and beaten and felt as if I had been put through a press. Mother dozed and seemed not to mind our "excursion."

There was yet another day of waiting. No water, no tea, no prospect of setting out. The day was one of mixed sunshine and rain. Toward evening the weather became increasingly nasty. Meanwhile my condition was becoming unbearable. I resolved to give up this cruel and absurd adventure and return home to die. I perfectly understood the barbaric conditions under which we were being evacuated, and my one wish was to crawl into my own bed. I was ill, but still well enough to make a decision, using my illness as excuse. Nothing could stop me.

I gave my last loaf of bread to the conductor, and she began throwing our things out onto the tracks. Wind, rain. We sat on the rails under umbrellas. We waited for a car. We knew the train had come to a halt near the porcelain factory, which is almost within city limits. It was evening, and we had not been given a thing to eat or drink since the morning of the previous day. People envied us. They looked at us from the train windows with tears of envy in their eyes.

Presently Chistyakov came driving up in a truck. He himself picked up our baggage and loaded it onto the truck.

We were back. Amid the chaos and disorder of the apartment, the trash and scattered bundles, I compared our leaving with our returning.

We had difficulty in reinstating our ration cards. Two days after our return, Mother was suddenly overwhelmed by weakness. Her temperature went up alarmingly. She lay in a coma with a frightful fever, while I myself was still weak from my own seizure. Thank goodness it only lasted two days—what if it had lasted a month?

Our train remained standing in the same spot for four days. Then it departed.

When this wave of evacuation was over, one was aware of a fundamental change. Few people were left in the city, which now took on an air of intimacy. Those who had stayed behind began settling in all over again. I never ceased waiting for news from Borya. All my secret hopes of aid and rescue were tied to his name, my cousin and friend, who did not know that we, though still alive, were in death's clutches. But when I received his letter from Chistopol with a description of the landscape, I knew I had been under an illusion. No, I couldn't expect help from anywhere or anyone. The letter gave proof of spiritual inertia, fatigue, and confusion. Just as at the beginning of the Revolution, the letter spoke of water buckets, and of a spirit worn smooth, like an old coin.

Leningrad, August 7, 1942
[Received in Chistopol on August 24, 1942]

Dear Borya,

How happy I am that I have located you at last. Don't ever again wait so long between letters. If only you had answered my wire immediately! I wired Alexander as well in an attempt to find you but heard nothing from him, either. Your letter took only two weeks to get here. You write that it would make me feel cold and alienated, and that it would fail in its purpose. The letter did make me feel empty and sad, not for myself but for you. You could not and did not wish to write everything. But the form (not literary form, of course) in which you combined saying things with leaving things unsaid brought me as close to you as would binoculars trained on your inner world. Is that the life for you? All you need in life is to express yourself, but the indulgence in self-expression must be put in cold storage until the right season. Difficult and frightening. If one still has any inner resources left, it is frightening because they will dry up from lying dormant; and if one remains silent, it is frightening because this means the end. But I am talking nonsense. You cannot imagine what vitality one's soul has and how hard it is to die—for any creature to die. It is no easier to die than to survive. One needs a bit of luck, the helping hand. Dying is a kind of good fortune. Blood is strong—oh, how strong! You are a donor. After giving of your blood you feel drained, but you lie down and by evening your strength is restored. I cannot boast the strength you have been blessed with. Yet even for me it was not physical death that frightened me. It was the crushing of my soul I feared. But no! One page of genuine art, two or three lines of profound scholarly thinking, and the old gal's herself again. Once more I am passionately involved, and this revolting pseudoreality goes up in a puff of smoke, for pseudoreality has been the mirage, and whether or not it will live on and circulate is a question. My trouble, one of my worst, is of course my optimism; in the long run it will destroy me. It does not spring from theoretical hypothesizing but from a too ebullient perception of life. But putting all optimism aside, he who laughs last laughs best. And we haven't been tossed onto the junk heap yet. And the cover of snow, under which seeds lie germinating, is also beneficent. Chaos: it is significant that all peoples began their struggle to reach the light with chaos, rather than with the devil. Conception has begun. You will see, soon we shall be born. See how much light there is already and how it is spreading! If only we can preserve our souls!

Goodness! This isn't what I had intended writing. Every line is precious, and I have already wasted half the letter.

I was disappointed that you made no comment on the news from Oxford. I had gone to so much trouble to squeeze it into the telegram. I sent them greetings just before New Year's and they replied immediately. Suddenly in February came Lydia's inquiry about you, filled with alarm. I didn't reply for three months—think of it! Oh, what months those were! At last, selecting a day when I could move my legs, and an hour when there was no artillery bombardment, I crawled to the telegraph office. I wired what I could: that you were all well, that it was hard to communicate, that you were in Tashkent (as I believed). The next day I received their thanks, blessings, tears of joy.

Our city is cleaner than any city has ever been. It is a holy city. It has been sterilized. I am taking a course in military training in addition to my regular work. While sitting in my room I can distinguish the shellbursts of twelve-inch guns from those of eight-inch ones. I know how to build Howitzer and machine-gun nests; I do not confuse antiaircraft shells with mortars, nor shore artillery with field artillery. I can tell the difference between the sound of our diving planes and the snake hiss of German ones, and I no longer confuse enemy air attacks with enemy air reconnaissance. Moreover, when the house trembles from the shells flying over it, I can tell from the sound of the explosions whether we or the Germans are attacking. As for the rest, we have become part of the front and have forgotten about the rear. I am afraid of the rear. I am afraid to go there, afraid of the crowds and the crush. We have forgotten how to smile and show affection. We have grown unaccustomed to people and to everyday life, to the market and the menu, to all that is planned and played by four hands. If a city block has water and a working hydrant, we go out to wash clothes or dishes on the corner of that particular street. We read Kotoshikhin* and Olearius† while bending over a ditch underneath a bridgehead and fetching water with pots and pans—noise, shouts, slippery ice, sledges with barrels of water tied to them, a crowd of women in varicolored shawls and blankets . . . But that is in February and March. In summer it's easy to rinse one's clothes outdoors on the sidewalk. We feed on wild herbs and grass; we make our own fires and warm ourselves by burning memoirs and floorboards. Prose, it turns out, provides more heat than poetry. History boils our teakettle for us. A parquet floor makes the best fuel. There is no "tomorrow" for us. I asked when the telegram would arrive. The telegraph clerk replied, "I can't say what will happen to you or me in ten minutes." This is not everyday life, but a succession of grim days and activities, a futuristic composition, which appears to the ordinary man as a mass of falling and colliding absurdities squared and raised to a preposterous power. It is a new concept of space and an unheard-of aspect of time, with a causality that neither Hegel nor your dear friend at Marburg could have dreamed of.

By the way, there is something I wanted to tell you and never did because we never got as far as the theme of death in our letters. World literature offers a competition in describing death. Tolstoy and Maupassant are strong contenders; they stir me to the depths of my soul. But never have I been stirred so deeply as when I read Safe Conduct, in which you describe the death of Cohen. I was stunned by the equation you make, by the simplicity of your statement of zero. With supreme tact and profundity you present the definitive description of death: a blank looking glass. You fill the scene with Cohen, elaborating Marburg to the utmost degree, without hinting what the great philosopher is ultimately equated to. Then, unexpectedly, at the very end: where is Cohen? He is nowhere. He is dead.

I don't have the quotation, but I remember the impression. Shakespeare tried to capture this zero quality in Lear, when there is no sign of Cordelia's breath on the looking glass. A blank glass at the lips—that is the image of death! It is artistic because of its metaphorical quality. But you avoid even the metaphor; you just show "nothing." Cohen is not men-

* Grigory Kotoshikhin: seventeenth-century writer, author of Concerning Russia During the Reign of Aleksei Mikhailovich.

† Adam Olearius (also Adam Oelschläger; circa 1599–1681): author of accounts of travel in Russia, including Reise nach Moskau.

tioned. Where is he? He is nowhere. I don't recall whether you even say that he dies.

Dear friend, with what joy and eagerness I talk with you. The only one left here is Lifshits, because she is a doctor. She lives with her husband, who is almost insane—there are many such people, as is only to be expected according to Kantian causality. I have made several attempts to break away from the ties of childhood. But now a great deal of good and genuine wisdom has appeared in Lifshits. Heroically, she visits us each week, and those are great days for us. As Saadi* once said, "Not a friend have I; no, not an acquaintance." Borya, Borya . . . I tried to shore up Sasha's crumbling life. Like a mason, I gathered bricks—only my bricks were sugar and flour and canned goods, suitcases full of warm clothes, even postcards and stamps. That explains why Mother and I are still alive and why I am able to send postcards and letters. The second year of blockade! That is how we survived from December through February. Then came the agonizing scurvy; the pain in my legs was so terrible I couldn't suppress my cries and groans. I spent February and March in bed. Poor Mother! Can you believe it? Her hands and feet were frostbitten. In the room we slept in, the temperature went down to 25°; the water turned to ice. Her nerves were shattered. She tormented me. And all this happened to people of our constitution, with our painful concern for each other, and to a woman of Mother's age, with her unbending character that permitted no concessions to people or circumstances.

Only on July 12 did we finally leave. Our university had been moved to Saratov. Awaiting us there were a room in a central hotel, special food rations, work, a salary, a normal life. The university left earlier in the winter, during the bitter frosts, while I was ill. They invited me to join them, waited for me, urged me to come. I was deterred by thoughts of Mother. And of leaving everything behind. All my books. The rooms I had lived in since childhood. And there were other irrational considerations. In the end, we set out on July 12 after prolonged physical and emotional preparation. Luck presented us with an officer who sent soldiers and two army vehicles to take us and our things to the station. And here is the upshot. I fell ill at the very outset of the trip. Mother held up splendidly, rose to the occasion like a true gentlewoman. We had to call off the venture and bring me back home to recover. The same officer picked us up in an open field and personally brought us home—and I had set my heart on reaching Chistopol! The apartment doors that had been sealed were broken open; our piles of luggage were dumped inside, and here we

* A thirteenth-century Persian Sufi poet.

have been living ever since, not knowing what to do next. Mother came down with a temperature of 104° but soon improved. Things looked more ominous than ever. The officer left. Saratov was a long way off and a formidable journey from here. To spend another winter in Leningrad seemed suicidal, but here we are.

I don't like Rimsky-Korsakov. He is too academic and too musically correct. I would like to write a new libretto for his *Kitezh*. I would turn it into a sterilized city without a germ of life in it. No pregnant women, no children's voices. It would be a bell jar out of which all the air had been pumped—not air but time. A city of the future. And what about the present? The citizens would eternally await the future, so the present would be futuristic.

On this note I send my love to you and your family. I kiss Zina, Lyonya, and you, beloved Borya. Assume that I am here and write to me here no matter what the circumstances. Just as one's hand gets caught in a chink, so have our lives gotten caught in these days. Will we survive? I worked in fits and starts all the time up to now. I wrote for the sheer love of it. And how I long to work now! But I have neither the strength nor the opportunity: everything is packed up.

All my love.

Yours,

OLYA

DIARY

Many people had hallucinations of food. They saw it, felt it, thought and spoke of it constantly. Oh, will the day ever come when this torture will be over?

Hunger destroyed our nerves, memory, will power. All of us were overwrought and half-crazy. Women in the shops shouted, wept, struck one another, went into fits of hysterics. The jammed trolley cars were a terrible sight; people jostled one another, shouted insults, hurt one another. Then there was the numbness. Many lost the ability to cry even in moments of the most bitter sorrows. Memory was extinguished.

I dreamed of celebrating the New Year, or, to be more exact, of seeing out the old year. For a whole month I denied myself everything in order to save up something for New Year's Eve. I didn't believe any longer in the New Year, but I saw out that terrible year of 1942 and celebrated the victory of life: we had gone through it, and we had come out alive, Mother and I. Death was raging all about us. We had lost dear friends and we had looked death and starvation in the face. We, the living, had been reborn, physically and spiritually. With our last efforts we were crawling out from under the ruins of life, strewn with the stones and debris of a collapsed state. But there was still a glimmer of faith.

Mother and I cleaned up the apartment and changed the linen. We went to bed at eight o'clock, after a supper that took the chill out of our bodies. It was a good night: cheerful, quiet, and warm. It was a night without hope, without grief, without thought.

Now January made its entrance. The water froze in the pipes. It was a nightmare to go with pails and pitchers through that bitter January weather, enter a strange house, climb down into a dark, ice-paved cellar, slosh through the streams that trickled day and night into the ice, then struggle back up the stairs again.

The temperature went down to −18°. Once more that lacerating cold, those numb fingers, those freezing nights under piles of blankets, those endless mornings waiting for daylight to appear.

We had almost come to the end of our endurance. I could not bear to see Mother suffering from cold, hunger, and fear. I suffered doubly: for her sake and for my own.

"You asked for this," she said spitefully. In January the air raids were resumed, and the shelling continued. The two were now coordinated. The newspapers carried nothing about the raids, nor about the starvation, nor about the absence of the most elementary requirements of daily life, nor about the bombardments. It was forbidden to speak about them, to say nothing about mentioning them in letters.

Human beings were being subjected to violence, death, all the horrors of starvation and battling the elements, all the deprivations of creatures abandoned, yet used, by the state.

Events, I saw, were repeating themselves. Spring came, bringing sunny, blue skies intermixed with dull, rainy days. The same holidays came, the same meager handouts, the shameful delays in issuing rations, the same hunger. We had neither kerosene nor firewood. Mother shivered, though spring was here.

Our food supplies were exhausted. Pale, emaciated, haggard, we drank water and ate crumbs of bread. We could not even heat the water—we had no fuel for the samovar. I sat at my desk but was unable to work because of mental exhaustion. Before me lay sheets of paper covered with my handwriting, my *Lectures on the Theory of Folklore*, but my mind registered nothing. Tomorrow would be even worse; there would not be so much as thin soup to restore my powers.

I went out in search of work, since first-category rations were now available only to those who worked as staff members of some institution. I was recommended for work in the archives. I dared not refuse it. I began applying for work in the Senate Building. In late July I was met cordially, but no one could think of how to use me. Finally, it was suggested that I write about the heroism of Leningrad women. The idea of showing how professional women carried on in the besieged city appealed to me.

I was not interested in those Leningrad women whom officialdom had loudly proclaimed heroines. I was interested in the little people. With two of these women I formed a lasting friendship. One of them was Maria Yudina. I had heard of her long ago, at a time when my students Dovatur and Egunov had supplied her with books on antiquity from our department library. Later I learned she was a friend of Borya's and Zhenya's. I had wanted to make her acquaintance.

While a professor of piano at the Leningrad Conservatory, she was expelled because she openly espoused religion, and now she would come all the way from Moscow to give concerts in Leningrad. Her heroism was genuine. One had to have a mighty and unbending spirit to choose to come to our grim city, risk the deadly bombardments, and return to her room on the seventh floor of the Astoria Hotel in the pitch blackness of Leningrad nights. Mother was enchanted by Yudina; she immediately felt an affinity for her that was almost familial.

Moscow, November 5, 1943

Dear Aunt Asya and Olya,

Yudina found you some days ago and gave you back to us again. Last year I sent you several letters and telegrams that went unanswered. From your last letter, Olyushka, I understood that you were about to leave Leningrad but had then stayed on after all. I have heard nothing more from you since then, and all my inquiries were left without reply. But I wasn't the only one in this situation regarding you. The fact that we are close relatives is apparently well known, and it has always brought me the greatest joy. Last year at precisely the time when I was so tormented by lack of knowledge about you, a very nice young woman whom I did not know came up to me in one of the publishing houses and said that she was one of your pupils—Polyakova by name, I believe—and that after your failed attempt to leave Leningrad she had lost all trace of you. Soon thereafter Professor B. V. Kazansky expressed similar regrets to me. In my last postcard I mentioned with pleasure how well you are known and loved here. As a result of your silence I came to several conclusions, one of which was that you must have made it to some Siberian backwater. I was convinced that you weren't in Leningrad and that your house was gone as well (since letters weren't reaching you); it might have been destroyed by a shell. I interrupted my search for you at the end of December. This summer Kazansky advised me to write to the Evacuation Control Center in Buguruslan, but I didn't do that only because there were people here expecting to go to Leningrad and I hoped to inquire at the university through them. You were so lost to me that it was difficult to conceal the fact in telegrams to Papa.

In late December I left these cold regions again to visit Zina and Lyonya in Chistopol for the New Year holiday. Lyonya, as you recall, was born on New Year's Eve. I have come to like that primitive hinterland, where I cleaned privies without revulsion and moved among children of nature at the edge of the forest, where bears and wolves take over. Such elementary things as bread, water, and fuel were available there, in contrast with Moscow's many-storied hives in which all currents stop flowing in winter, like blood in one's veins, and which instill in me a sense of mystical terror. I spent a few months there again and completed my translation of *Antony and Cleopatra*, which is to be published. By Christmas I may be able to send you my last year's work, *Romeo and Juliet*. While I was in Moscow last summer (1942) I found that virtually all our belongings had been destroyed, but what upset me most was the almost total loss of Papa's sketches and drawings, and even a number of the completed works that I had been keeping. I left Moscow in the panic and chaos of the October evacuation. Before we left, Alexander and I went to the Tretyakov Gallery and requested that they take Father's portfolios for safe keeping. But no one would accept anything anywhere, with the exception of the Tolstoy Museum, which was too far away to be reached without horse or car.

Antiaircraft gunners were billeted in our Moscow apartment on the eighth and ninth floors. They turned the ninth, in which they did not eat or sleep, into common ground with doors flung wide open. You can imagine in what shape I found everything when I dropped in for five or ten minutes. Regular army units were quartered in our house at Peredelkino. We moved all our things into Vsevolod Ivanov's house, including a large trunk full of Papa's oil paintings, and soon thereafter the Ivanov dacha burned to the ground. This was my principal sorrow, and it was so terrible that I resigned myself to the loss of the rest of my belongings, once that which was most important, that which linked me with so many memories, was gone. I could not make myself go back to the city apartment, and I spent the autumn and half of the winter without visiting our dacha once—even though I had spent wonderful times there with Lyonya, even though I love the place and worked there with full concentration and in perfect quiet, even though I knew that Lyonya's nanny was still living there and I really ought to go and see her. I drifted from place to place the whole winter (until leaving for Chistopol); I lived for a while with Alexander, but spent most of the time with my dear friends Professor Valentin Ferdinandovich Asmus and his wife. As a matter of fact, I have been here too long and am writing to you now from their place.

In July I brought Zina, her son Stasik, and Lyonya back to the ruins of our homes. Not long ago she went to Sverdlovsk to pick up her eldest son, Adrian, who has had one leg amputated because of bone tuberculosis. She brought him here only half-alive, and with terrible difficulty. He is now in a sanatorium just outside Moscow. It cost us enormous effort to get the antiaircraft gunners out of our Moscow apartment. We succeeded only last week. Zina moved into the empty unheated rooms with genuine heroism and began to make them livable once more. She is there, her son Stasik is living with friends near Kursk Station, I am at the Asmuses apartment near Kiev Station, and Lyonya is with his old nanny—a strange woman, to put it mildly, but one who dotes on him. He lives with her in the kitchen of our empty home in Peredelkino. I hope that the cold weather will drive us all there eventually. When Lyonya steals up to my desk while I am working in order to see whether it bothers me (as one worries a fever blister on one's lip), it affects me in the same way as the presence of music. When you get right down to it, he is my closest tie to life. Besides, how can one better solve the fuel problem than by living in the woods? If we do find ourselves living there, I shall get busy on *Lear*. I have received an order to do a *Selected Works of Shakespeare: Lear, Macbeth* or *The Tempest*, and two of the chronicle plays, *Richard II* and *Henry IV*.

At present things are difficult for us. We have neither a home nor anything to put in a home; we have to begin life all over again. In September I was at the Bryansk front. I enjoyed being with the soldiers (the army was constantly on the move, but even so I got some rest). When circumstances permit, I'll go out there again.

I am sending you a little book that is too slender, too late, and much too unimportant to talk about. In it there are only a few robust pages, genuinely well written—they belong to the cycle "Peredelkino," from early 1941 (at the end of the book). They are an example of what I would be writing now if I were free to do original work. I wrote them just before the war.

You can guess by the handwriting and style that I am scribbling this in a great hurry. I've been working a lot these recent weeks. (Life with the

Asmus family is conducive to work: he has turned over his study to me. I've told them all about you two. Irina Sergeyevna Asmus is my good friend and shares certain qualities with Aunt Asya.) I am working hard. I'd like to do more journalism. I have set about it too late, but I want to provide Zina and Lyonya with a "name." Zina looks much older and is as thin as a rail. Zhenya and his mother arrived from Tashkent. He is studying at the Academy of Tank Construction; he is a lieutenant (twenty years old) and a second-year student, in good standing and popular with his comrades. I am writing, translating, and working on a narrative poem on the war that will be published in *The Banner* and *Pravda*. Papa, the girls, Fedya, and the entire family are all alive and well.

All my love to both of you.

Yours,

BORYA

[Inscription in the book *On Early Trains*:]

To my newly found Aunt Asya and Olya in token of my devotion, and with a request that you forgive these belated trivia and that you not judge them for their insignificance

BORYA

November 2, 1943

Moscow, November 6, 1943

[Received in Leningrad on November 14, 1943]

Dear Aunt Asya and Olya,

Were you aware that last autumn I tried without success on several occasions to find out about your place of residence, after several of my letters to you went unanswered? I am writing this postcard to you as a check. I am sending two to you by registered mail, as well as a telegram. Something ought to reach you. Yudina's messages brought me joy beyond words. I had begun to doubt you were alive. Everyone—Papa and the girls, Zhenya and his mother, and all of my family—is alive and well. Details in my long letter.

Let me know somehow, Olya, about your health, even though Yudina has told me a great deal and reassured me.

[Telegram; November 8, 1943]

HAVE HEARD NOTHING FROM YOU. DELIGHTED WITH YUDINA'S NEWS. WE
ARE WELL AND EMBRACE YOU. WRITE—BORYA

Moscow, November 12, 1943
[Received in Leningrad on November 22, 1943]

Dear Olyushka,

I congratulated Papa and the girls on the occasion of the October
holidays and informed him in the telegram about your health. Received
the following answer: "Thanks often read about you heard transmission
Moscow celebration rejoice with fatherland all well father Pasternaks
Slaters." I just can't go on fighting the tone that dominates in the press.
Nothing is working out; I shall probably give up and go back to Shakespeare.

All my love to you and Aunt Asya.

Yours,

BORYA

Leningrad, November 18, 1943
[Received in Moscow on November 25, 1943]

Dearly beloved Borya,

Thank you for everything (for the poems, the telegram, and the letter).
Until December 1 I shall be *tragically* busy and cannot write to you. Just
one thing now: we are inviting you to come here to spend the winter, get
a rest, and work in peace. You will find the material you need on our
front, the city front, the like of which you can find nowhere else. I have
enough wood and we shall be able to take care of everything else. My
room and our hearts are yours. Mother couldn't restrain her tears as she
listened to your letter, especially about Zina. We embrace you, kiss you,
and weep over what is past and gone.

Regards to Yudina, Zhenya and his mother, Alexander, and Irina.

Yours,

OLYA

DIARY

On November 25 Mother fell down in the kitchen. My neighbor and I
lifted her with difficulty and carried her to bed. She was silent. I was
overwhelmed with terror and cold despair. I wept for Mother, for our

ruined lives, and for all the preposterous cruelties we have been, and still are, subjected to.

There were shadows on Mother's face. My neighbor looked at her and said: "That is the mask of death. There is scarcely a spark of life in her. Another day and it will go out."

But I said, addressing myself in response to my instinct for life: "I don't accept the inevitable. I believe in miracles."

The fact that Mother went on breathing from day to day gave birth to hope. Mother's life acquired the meaning inherent in the ideal concept of "mother." She was given me by nature, and given not for all time, but for a mere life span. I wrote to Borya that I was experiencing the tense happiness of a necromancer. It was as though I were hypnotizing nature with the fierce strength of my will, winning hours and days for this moribund body by means of tearful supplications.

With my customary determination I had now thrown myself into saving Mother from death. It seemed to me that by caring for her, by feeding her and washing her linen, I was erecting a barricade against death, that with my own hands and fervent prayers I was saving her from it.

Leningrad, December 20, 1943

Dear Borya,

I can hardly bring myself to tell you that on the very day when you received our invitation to come here for a rest and a quiet life (November 25, according to the postal receipt), our life collapsed. At about ten o'clock in the morning Mother suffered a stroke that paralyzed her right side and left her speech and mind impaired.

I cannot tell you what spiritual sufferings I have endured. Fifteen minutes after the catastrophe, reason and intuition alike told me that this was a misfortune, but not death. Since that time I have been living a tense deathlike happiness, like a necromancer. Only in a state of well-being can people grieve, despair, feel dejected. In moments of stunning misfortune, life is flipped over like a coin to reveal its true meaning. I have forgiven life everything for this happiness, for every one of Mother's days, for her every breath—each a gift I have done nothing to deserve. She herself no longer has need of such things. She has completed her path of sorrow, and it seems to have brought her to an exalted state of reconciliation unfamiliar to her in ordinary life. On that fatal morning, though her spirit was tried to the breaking point by the cruelties of the blockade, by privations, by all that makes up the sum of our days, she arose in calm spirits, quiet, thoughtful, almost happy. It wrings my heart to see her paralysis and the impairment of her memory and reason. Like the soul in metempsychosis, she is passing through the cycle of her past life. She speaks deliriously of her childhood, then of her family and their cares. And I follow her through the terrible labyrinths of nonbeing. At first I went cold and trembled all over when she would ask, "Where are my children?" and would call me Leonid and insist, with the outrage of a proud mother, that I was not Olya. As soon as the floodgates of consciousness and reality burst, Alexander, Leonid, and Mama (grandmother) appeared—and all this happened in a strictly logical fashion, without delirium. Now I have grown used to being transported back to our childhood, to our family, to a confusion of time and order, without delirium and on a different plane of existence.

And I have grown used to taking care of her, to accomplishing the feat of snatching a victim from under Holbein's terrible scythe. Churchill is not fed better than she is. I care for her ceaselessly day and night—I, and I alone.

At first I was confounded by the pools in her bed. Now I do not shrink from them and have found methods and techniques for dealing with them. The more earthy her odors the better they please me, as does everything warm, physiological, and corporeal that emanates from her, everything that is tangible, like nature itself, or like hard, material proof.

How long will my happiness last? At the risk of tempting fate, I have been hypnotizing events with the passionate will of a necromancer, and Mama is getting better. The Lord lives! Why not trust life? It, too, can be generous.

Her books remain on the table with her eyeglasses on top: Shakespeare, the open pages of Sophocles's *Electra*. She had barely regained consciousness when she related to me in a thick-tongued way an anecdote of Lucullus as told by Plutarch.

*The Death of Tintagiles** passes through my mind like a memory of the distant past. If you only knew how dearly Mama loved you! Her last tears were for Zina. I embrace you. I am crying.

OLYA

[Telegram; January 2, 1944]
CRUSHED BY THE NEWS. WITH YOU IN SPIRIT. HAVE HOPE. ALEXANDER'S MOTHER-IN-LAW HAD THE SAME THING FOR A YEAR AND A HALF AND RECOVERED. ALL MY LOVE—BORYA

* A marionette play (1894) by Maurice Maeterlinck (1862–1949).

Leningrad, January 10, 1944

Dear Borya,

Thanks for the telegram and the sympathy, which in days like these particularly soothe the spirit. Thank you for the *hope*. Mama is getting better, but she is paralyzed and her mind often wanders. I am like the goddess who succeeded in obtaining immortality for her earthly lover but who forgot to ask that he remain eternally young; thus he stayed by her side, but decrepit and overburdened with days.

I received a telegram from Polyakova. She is my pupil, my genuine follower. Unfortunately, I don't know her address. Please give my best regards to Boris Vasilevich Kazansky, my old friend. I don't go out for weeks at a time and there is no one to mail my postcards.

Love to you and your family.

OLYA

DIARY

Mama was improving, becoming more like herself. She had begun speaking, at first in a whisper, then in her natural voice. Soon her periods of delirium were succeeded by periods of clear logical awareness. The wise, wonderful Mama of before was coming back to life. Even her face became such as it used to be: soft, inspired, splendid. Oh, how much love, how much maternal affection Mama gave me! It was as though she were paying me her debt for the days of the siege, and giving me strength for the many days of loneliness lying ahead.

Our experience of purgatory was fading from memory. Wounds were healing.

In early January Mama began feeling pains in her stomach.

At the same time the bombarding became particularly intense. Terrific explosions took place all around us on January 17, shortly after noon. I realized that our turn was drawing near.

I sat down on the edge of Mama's bed. Thunderous shelling. I looked at the clock to check the intervals. Another crash, but this time no explosion. A dud must have hit a neighboring house. Still another crash, and the whole world reeled. We were hit. I looked up to see all the window panes fly out at once. And in flew the freezing January air.

Superhuman powers were born within me. I seized a winter coat, wrapped Mama in it, dragged her heavy bed first into the corridor, then into my own room. One of my windows was miraculously intact, and I stuffed rags into the other one. It seems a human being can endure anything. Time moves on impassively.

That was the last bombardment of Leningrad.

Leningrad, January 12, 1944

Dear Borya,

Thanks for "Peredelkino" (and "The Artist").* My present circumstances are the best test of the authenticity of art. Your books have revived me. I am immensely proud of your artistic "inflexibility," for I know its value, how much it costs, and what it implies. The complexity of your simplicity reminds me of fine fabrics: the simpler the more costly. Your art is real, it is great, and it is lasting.

Mama now qualifies as an invalid—by which I mean she is getting better. She thinks correctly but cannot remember words. For example, she may say, "Leonid found Hesiod," when she wants to say, "Give me my salts." Two unfortunates, Mama and I.

Love,

OLYA

I am writing at night. Taking care of her is very difficult, especially in winter, and such a cold winter at that.

DIARY

By this time, Mama had deep, festering bedsores. Because of the pain it was impossible to turn her over in bed. She screamed and was delirious.

In March her condition became noticeably worse. She lost all appetite and stopped speaking. It was as if she existed only to suffer. It broke my heart to see her suffering. My face puffed up from weeping and I dreaded seeing anyone. In four months I scarcely went outdoors or ate a solid meal. My legs were so swollen I could hardly walk.

Somewhere deep inside me I felt that Mama was made to suffer on my account, that this incredible torture was imposed by fate so that I could and would want to endure the inevitable separation from her. How could I have stood being parted from her if her mind had remained unimpaired and if her wonderful motherly love had not been obliterated by this inhuman, this blind and brutal illness?

On April 6 she kept waking and falling back to sleep after the torments

* Sections of *On Early Trains.*

of the night. With difficulty I was able to give her some sweet tea. Then she fell asleep never again to wake. For four days she slept, and I did nothing but wait for her life to end. I sat beside the bed. Her breathing was dreadful to hear. She had but one task to complete on this earth: breathing. At one moment it was raucous; the next, inaudible. Suddenly I was struck by an ominous silence. I fell on my knees and stayed there for a long while. I thanked her for long years of love, loyalty, and patience, for all that we had lived through, for the fifty-four years of our being together, and for the breath of life she had given me.

Leningrad, April 14, 1944

Dear Borya,

I am alone now. Sometime I will gather the strength to write you, but I don't know when. I am living alone in this big, empty apartment. If only you could arrange to be sent to Leningrad on some mission. You could work and rest with me here.

What I have lived through has been terrible. Mama suffered brutally for four and a half months, but on April 6 she fell asleep and slept until the 9th, on which day, at nine o'clock in the evening, she stopped breathing.

I am not receiving my letters (the fourth floor, mind, and a walk-up!). I probably will get them if you address them care of the yard porter. I am living in the same place (if you should send a wire, use the old address).

All my love,
OLYA

[Telegram; May 5, 1944]

POOR OLYA, I SHARE YOUR GRIEF AND LONELINESS. WITH YOU I MOURN THE LOSS OF MY DEAR AUNT—BORYA

Moscow, June 12, 1944

Dearest Olya,

Don't be surprised that I haven't written. I am surrounded by an execrable number of cares, people, worries, trivialities, hindrances, and difficulties. In between, one has somehow to work, to be ill, and so on. Zina is fearfully busy, torn between the city and our place in the country. It has been a month since I have seen Lyonya. I've been in town all that time—money, money! From time to time one suddenly and by circuitous means gets word of you. For instance, a rumor was brought from Novosibirsk (!!) that your house was hit by a shell while Aunt Asya was still alive. That is how I explained your instruction to address letters care of the yard porter.

I can imagine how empty and lonely it is for you there, my poor Olya! And again fighting has broken out not far from you. Yesterday our taking of Terioki* was celebrated. Much love.

Yours,

BORYA

Moscow, June 16, 1944

Dear Olya,

I left out the most important thing when I wrote you. Come and visit us! We can live at the dacha as if camping. There is no furniture, but there is a garden. We'll cultivate the potatoes, weed the vegetables, pluck worms off the cabbages. If you're here Lyonya will get some sense in that silly head of his. Seriously, think about it. I myself am still in town, but that doesn't matter: I will probably move out in July. You would have a good rest. Write and tell me what you are doing. I am translating *Othello* against my will; I never liked it. I am working with Shakespeare now almost semiconsciously. He seems like a member of a former family dating back to the time when I lived on Myasnitskaya Street. I am oversimplifying him terribly.

DIARY

For the first months after Mama's death I lay in bed with my face to the wall. Then I began walking about. Then I kept expecting someone to come; I would sit waiting, lie down again, wander about the room, go through my things.

I cried unnecessary tears, asking for nothing. I meticulously swept the floor because that is what Mama had done for years. I would go and sit in the room where she had lain. I did not feel at home in my own room; it frightened me.

Now I have so much time. I feel cast away in it. All about me time stretches away to infinity. I want to limit it by doing things, to fill it by moving about in space, but nothing succeeds. No matter how hard I work, time is not diminished. Only late in the evening do my spirits

* Small seaside town northwest of Leningrad.

somewhat revive: another day is over. Relieved, I lie down and for seven hours am blissfully unaware of time. I dream of our family, of Mama, and always of Sasha. Waking up in the morning is frightful—that first moment of consciousness after the night. I am here. I am in time again.

I compare myself to a bombed house: after the ghastly tension of expectation, the bomb strikes, the building shudders, then suddenly, following the crash and the dust, immutable silence sets in.

I am caught in this silence, wherein all things have preserved their visible forms. Complete, absolute silence, and boundless liberation.

This is death. The only ordeal left to me is to pass through time. Time is my only problem now. And time itself is bringing my passage to its consummation. Day by day.

Sometimes I went out to the islands, accessible now for the first time in three years. There I sat by the sea for long hours at a stretch.

I suffered from neglect. I eagerly awaited Borya and my friends as they returned from evacuation. But not one of my colleagues from the institution where I have worked for ten years came to see me. Neither did Borya, and he rarely wrote, and then without warmth, as if it were an effort.

Moscow, July 30, 1944

Dear Olya,

You should be ashamed of yourself for writing such abominable words and sentiments. Did you get my postcard in which I invited you to spend some time with us? Come quickly, summer is on the wane. If you decide to come to Peredelkino, I will make a point of going out there, too, so as to see you in the garden surrounded by green foliage, Zina, Lyonya, the Asmuses (who are living with us), and all the other delights of that place. I am stuck in the city and haven't been to the country even once, and not for any insurmountable reason. The summer has been cool. Zina is in town for three days of each week; she visits her elder son, who is in a tuberculosis sanitorium, and she cooks food for us (me and her other son, Stasik, a piano student at the conservatory) to last while she is away. Then she leaves, loaded down with foodstuffs and other necessities, and spends the rest of each week taking care of the house, working in the garden of her own creating, etc. She hasn't a minute to call her own. I find living in town more convenient for working and seeing to my affairs. I have finished a translation of *Othello* for a theater that kept rushing me and urging me on. In a few days I will receive my *Romeo* and *Antony* from the publishers and will send you copies.

I am driven to despair not by superficial hardships but by the knowledge that I am a writer, that I have something to say, that I have thoughts to express—and there is no literature here now, and under present conditions there will not and cannot be any literature. Last winter I signed a contract with two theaters for an original play, a contemporary tragedy based on the war; I counted on beginning it this fall, thinking circumstances would change by that time, that there would be more freedom. But circumstances show no signs of changing, and the only thing I can hope for is that the staging of my translations will bring in enough money to enable me to write what I like, freely, putting off publication to some indefinite date.

Not long ago I sent a telegram to the folks about Aunt Asya's death. I am both surprised and troubled that they have not wired a reply. Usually they answer promptly. Could anything have happened? Tomorrow I will make another inquiry.

I wanted to write you about many things, but apparently that was a deceptive or misunderstood desire. Probably in reality I want to see you here with us instead, and some of the things I wish to talk to you about I had better sit down and accomplish first.

How are you? Are you in need of money? A short time ago such a question from me would have been purely rhetorical. But in the coming months my financial situation should be much better. But that's not the point. The point is: pack up your things and come.

Love.

Yours,

BORYA

[Telegram; October 1, 1944]

HEARD ABOUT BOMB STRIKE. WORRIED ARE YOU INJURED. WIRE IMMEDIATELY. COUNTING ON SEEING YOU. LOVE—BORYA

[Inscription in *Antony and Cleopatra:*]

To my dear Olya with boundless love

BORYA

November 16, 1944

Peredelkino

Moscow, January 22, 1945

Dear Olya,

Thank you for the telegram. I don't need to have you write me about Shakespeare! Write me about yourself. How monstrous that you are there alone, doing battle, probably winning, but enduring privation and suffering, while I am so idiotically fruitlessly far away! Happily I am coping with all the problems attendant on spending the winter in the country, but at what cost! I am racing through the translation of *Henry IV*, hardly coming up for breath. I haven't a free moment. Not long ago I was sick for two weeks with an abscessed tooth like the most ignorant oaf, but I had no time to go to the dentist. Lyonya is in school. He says, "Papa, I understand this problem, but must I add or subtract?"

Much love.

Yours,

B.

CHAPTER VIII

THE CONCLUSION of the war left Boris Pasternak with a mission that he shaped into the novel *Doctor Zhivago*. First mention of that novel occurs in his correspondence with Olga in 1946. The early manuscript titles disclose some of Pasternak's aspirations for the work: *Boys and Girls*, in reference to the innocence of Russia in 1914; *The Story of a Russian Faust: From the Unpublished Papers of the Zhivago Family*, in reference to the quest of the central character for the essence of his age. "Norms of a New Nobility of the Spirit" was scribbled on the title page— a reference Pasternak explained in a letter to Olga:

"Apart from the revolution, we are living at a time when all basic forms of consciousness are disintegrating, when all useful habits and concepts and all practical skills have lost their stability.

"And so one is late in discovering what one needs; only now have I mastered what I have needed all my life. Well, my having done it at last is at least something to be thankful for.

"And to tell you the truth, I am really happy, not in an exalted way, and not through rationalizing, but genuinely, because I am free in spirit and so far, God be praised, am in good health."

Pursuit of a definition of that new nobility took place in a context of increasing persecution, reinforcing Pasternak's resolve to create a work of art not subject to the vicissitudes of daily life under Stalin. "Often life around me has been outrageously dark and unjust, sufficiently so to justify revolution; this makes me something of an avenger or a defender of its honor, a militantly zealous and keen one," he wrote to Olga in 1948.

"Cosmopolitanism" was the ideological sin of postwar Stalinism. It was colored by Russian nationalism and anti-Semitism. The campaign against cosmopolitans was heralded by a 1946 Central Committee directive attacking the Leningrad journals *The Star* and *Leningrad* and by a speech of Andrei Zhdanov, leader of the Leningrad Communist Party apparatus and Minister of Culture, in which poets and "parasites" were attacked.

Olga Freidenberg and Boris Pasternak suffered alike from the persecution, as did prominent Leningrad literary scholars like Zhirmunsky,
Eikhenbaum, Propp, Tomashevsky, and Azadovsky.

Death and loss set the tone of Pasternak's early postwar correspondence
—the death of Aunt Asya in 1944, the death of her brother (Pasternak's
father) in May 1945, the death of Zina's elder son, Adrian, in April 1945,
and the deaths of two close friends in December 1946: Olga Serova,
daughter of an eminent Russian artist, and Irina Asmus, wife of the
historian of philosophy, a dear family friend and counselor.

Pasternak's translations of Shakespeare and his article "Notes on the
Translation of Shakespeare's Tragedies," true as they were to the spirit of
the playwright, evoked criticism at home but praise in England. He was
not immune to the criticism of erstwhile Shakespearean scholars such as
A. A. Smirnov of Leningrad University. Pasternak had given a radio
interview to the BBC during the war, and Christopher Wren (in an
article in *The British Ally*) and C. M. Bowra both acclaimed Pasternak
for bringing Shakespeare back to life for Russian readers. The link with
Europe, particularly England, the new homeland of his family, played an
important role in the years Pasternak wrote the novel *Doctor Zhivago*.
Dickens's *Tale of Two Cities* was seldom far from his desk.

The seeming apoliticism of *Doctor Zhivago* has unfortunately tended to
support the conclusion that Pasternak's views of art were "liberal," in any
sense of the word. They were far from liberal, as Pasternak states in a
letter of 1958 to the young linguist Vyacheslav Vsevolodovich Ivanov:

"The Platonic train of thought concerning art (and the exclusion of
artists from the ideal society, the notion that 'the majority' should not
cross the threshold of poetry), Tolstoy's rejection of art, and even, as a
kind of rage, the iconoclastic, barbarian ways of the nihilist Pisarev* and
his kind, are all close to me. They are all close to me, but strongly modi-
fied. . . . I could never say, 'The more poets—good ones and varied—the
better!'† because a multiplicity of people working in art constitutes un-
promising, negative grounds for the emergence of someone, no matter
who, someone extremely conscientious and humble, who will redeem
their plurality with his singularity, redeem the broad exposure to their
excesses with the laborious productivity of his suffering.

"Art is not brilliance but disgrace and sin, almost forgivable in its

---

* Dmitri Ivanovich Pisarev (1840–1868): Russian critic and novelist, leader of the
radical "nihilists."

† Quotation from the Russian poet Vladimir Vladimirovich Mayakovsky (1893–1930).

beautiful innocence; it can be dignified and justified only by the vastness of what is sometimes redeemed by its disgrace. . . .

"One should not think that art, in and of itself, is the source of the magnificent. In and of itself, it is a pretension justified only by the future. Any creative activity of a personal, concentrated nature is the temporary reconciliation of imperfect awkwardness and unintentional wrong."

DIARY

June 26, 1945

The apartment is empty. I am sitting and working on *Palliata*. My face has changed. I have become puffy, with a tendency toward angularity. My eyes are growing smaller and have lost their shine. My hands died long ago. My bones have hardened. My fingers are flat and swollen. I have cushions on the soles of my feet. Abnormal metabolism has coarsened my figure.

My heart is dry and empty. It no longer responds to joy. I write, I teach my students (Sonya Polyakova and Beba Galerkina), but I remain cold and unmoved. Only one thought has the power to rouse me: the thought of death. Nothing else is of real interest to me.

I have lost my feeling for family and friends. My friends irk me and I rarely recall Borya. Life has become a mirage, a distant echo, a burned-out fire. My handwriting has changed, as has my gait. My sight is failing.

A long and empty sleep. My days are coming to an end. I have no aims, no desires, no interests. Life has been profaned and desecrated before my eyes. I have survived all that the times have presented me with: moral torture and living death. I have endured unspeakable horrors. Enough. My spirit is dead.

My spirit died not in battle with nature or hardships. It was killed by disappointment. It could not withstand the most dreadful thing in the world: human abasement, human worthlessness. I have looked biology in the eye. I have lived under Stalin. No one could survive two such horrors without the support of love and family. I am left alone. My life has been uprooted.

I resemble the Lavretskys* and the Vronskys† when the novels about them are finished. They go on living somewhere—brush their teeth, dine at restaurants, go to the theater, entertain guests. Outwardly they are like everyone else. But when the story is told, their lives are without meaning. They are empty.

---

* In Turgenev's *Nest of Gentlefolk* (1858).
† In Tolstoy's *Anna Karenina* (1877).

Moscow, June 21, 1945

Dear Olya,

Papa died on May 31. He had had a cataract removed a month before and had begun to recover in the hospital. He came home, but his heart gave out and he died on Thursday, three weeks ago.

Present at the time of his death were Fedya and the girls. He died remembering me. All this from their telegram.

This past winter I wanted to tell him more fully and precisely than I have ever done before how my awareness of his astonishing talent, miraculous craftsmanship, ease of work, fantastic productiveness, and rich, proudly concentrated, well-expended life has been as a guide to me, ever with me, ever before me; I wanted to tell him how, without envy and with nothing but joy for him, the comparison of his life with mine disgraces and destroys me, revealing as it does how diffuse and disappointing are my labors, how uninspired my daily life, how unfulfilled my promise, how few and insignificant my achievements. I wanted to tell him to what tragic heights the public's failure to appreciate his work has elevated him, and how scandalously overrated all my own work is. I wrote all this, better and more succinctly than here, in a letter to him, sent with Ambassador Maisky's* help through the diplomatic mail and accompanied by at least a dozen of my Shakespeare translations, purposely sent as a justification for the letter. They telegraphed me that they had received one book (out of twelve). The letter didn't arrive at all. About two months ago I sent them live greetings through a friend.

I am very concerned about your health. I couldn't comprehend everything at once and regret very much that I did not explain to Chechelnitskaya† in more detail the circumstances of our life and did not convey to you through her our constant and dearest dream: that you would come and stay with us at the dacha for a while. The Asmus family is living downstairs again this summer in the glass-enclosed porch; the upstairs terrace next to us and Lyonya is unoccupied, and you would be very comfortable there.

Chechelnitskaya came at a time when my nerves were completely shattered. It was just before my public reading was scheduled to take place, and the man responsible for it had not done his job; I was afraid that the auditorium would be empty. We had company at the time, and the day before we had just brought from Moscow the body of Zina's eldest son and buried him under the currant bush that he had planted when he was

* Ivan Maisky: Soviet ambassador to Great Britain, 1932–1943.
† G. Ya. Chechelnitskaya: a student of Olga's.

a small boy. He died on April 29 from tubercular meningitis. For the past three months (1) I have been suffering from severe pains in the right arm between the shoulder and the wrist, and so I am keeping my arm in a sling (I am writing the draft of *Henry IV* with my left hand); (2) two or three times a week I develop conjunctivitis from the slightest tension in my eyes; and (3) my liver is enlarged and I ache all over—but I have neither the time nor the inclination to have myself treated. On the contrary, through all this grief and suffering I experience an upsurge of inexplicable good humor, indestructible faith, irrepressible vitality. . . . In other words, I began telling Chechelnitskaya about Papa's death, about Rilke, about Marina (how she hanged herself during the war), and became so overwrought that I couldn't go on for lack of breath.* So please do not draw conclusions about us on the basis of Chechelnitskaya's account. She saw me on an inauspicious day, or rather evening.

Dear Olya, I must stop writing this letter, which I am doing against doctor's orders, with my right hand. The effort has become too painful. I have so many things to tell you that I have barely scratched the surface. Some other time, perhaps. Do come and see us!

Please tell the Lapshovs about Father's death and convey to them both, as well as to Mashura, my tenderest love (and this is sincere—these are not just words) and my joy that they are alive and well. How I should like to see them! Try to get a copy of issue 22 of *The British Ally* if you can; there is a piece there about my Shakespeare translations that you will enjoy. I beg you to take care of yourself. *Please come and see us!!*

Love.

Yours,

BORYA

DIARY

Borya informed me that my uncle had died. I suffered this most recent loss briefly, but very acutely. I cursed the system under which a son did not have the right to correspond with his father, nor the father with his children. And so we took leave of one another at a distance and in silence.

Moscow [July 13, 1945]

Dear Olya,

There is no point in writing letters, because so many of them go astray. Papa died on May 31 and I wrote to you about it, but the letter probably

---

* Chechelnitskaya was working at the time on Rilke and his ties with Russia. Olga requested Pasternak to tell Chechelnitskaya about his acquaintance with Rilke and his role in Rilke's correspondence with Marina Tsvetayeva in 1926.

Olga Freidenberg after World War II

Irina Nikolayevna Pasternak (Alexander's wife), Masha Asmus,
M. N. Vilyam, Lyonya Pasternak, Zina and Boris Pasternak, V. F. Asmus,
and an unidentified person

Boris and Zina Pasternak, Irina Pasternak, Galya Neuhaus, Nina Tabidze,
an unidentified person, and Alexander Pasternak

Boris Pasternak with his son Lyonya. Peredelkino, 1946

Boris Pasternak
with Lyonya

Boris Pasternak. Peredelkino, 1946

never reached you. I am terribly upset by your illness. Please come and live with us for a while at the dacha. I am sure you will be happy here. If I am alive and well (for four months my right arm has been in pain, and I keep it in a sling most of the time), I will try to come to Leningrad this winter on business. It seems that Chechelnitskaya is still here. Do make a point of seeing her when she returns.

Love.

Yours,

BORYA

Moscow [July 28, 1945]

Dear Olya,

I am worried by your silence. I had begun making inquiries by telegraph when I learned, yesterday, that you are alive and have written me. Someone (it is not clear who) asked Aseyev* my address, as Zina heard by chance when she was in town. If you are well enough to write, send your letter care of House Superintendent, 17/19 Lavrushinsky Lane. With that address I will get them; otherwise, I will not. My mood is excellent; I am madly busy; my life is hard, uncongenial, more than I can bear. *Please come.*

Love.

Yours,

BORYA

Did you read the article about Papa? Did you read Grabar's article on Papa in *Soviet Art*, issue 28 (960), for Friday, July 13, 1945?

[Telegram; August 1, 1945]

KAZANSKY HAS GIVEN ME YOUR LETTER. MANY THANKS. LOVE. TRY TO COME—BORYA

Moscow, November 2, 1945

Dear Olya,

I flew to Tiflis for two weeks and twice—once on the way there, once on the way back—flew over the Black Sea, carrying bags full of dark grapes that I bought for almost nothing in Sukhumi and in Adler. I thought of you at the time. From the air the Black Sea is the most

---

* Nikolai Nikolayevich Aseyev (1889–1963): Soviet poet, contemporary of Pasternak.

beautiful color in the world, one that can neither be named nor recalled: quiet, refined, opaque, gray-green, like some types of clay. Life in Tiflis was like that breath-taking beauty. Strange that I should have come back. Just before my departure we had news from England. Poor Lydia's husband has left her, and she is now alone with four children. But more about that another time.

Love.

Yours,

B.

[Inscription in *Selected Verse*, 1945:]

To my dear Olya, with best wishes for the New Year—1946
From BORYA
December 23, 1945
Moscow

Moscow, December 23, 1945

Olya, Olya, Olya, what is this, anyway? When will it end? I have not written you because I have had no time. I am being driven not by life or its difficulties but by less noble and more asinine motives. Now that the scandal and the misunderstanding about me have taken such deep root, I wish to become a human being in the full sense of the word. Dolt that I am, I hope to clarify and rectify all my imperfections and the insinuations made against me. For the first time in my life I want to write something deep and true. Oh, Olya, you can't imagine the immeasurable debt I owe to life, which has been so generous and merciful to me. But how little time there is, how much I must catch up with, how much I must make up for!

You and Alexander must live long and be near us. If only I could think of some part of me to send you that would make you feel less lonely! You really ought to have come here. You could either have stayed on with us or have taken something home with you that would have made you feel better, more cheerful, for my own life is *exceedingly* easy (not materially easy, but extraordinarily easy)—a much better life than I deserve.

Forgive me. For all I know you may misunderstand me and take what I have said as an outburst of rude, insultingly commiserating boasting.

What a misfortune! How am I to explain it all to you, especially in such haste?

I love you. Try to arrange it so that we can be together next summer if, God grant, we are still alive.

There is no rupture in my life any more, no pressure of any kind. Suddenly I am wonderfully free. Everything around me is wonderfully my own.

I feel this most acutely at the dacha, in summer. Alexander, Irina, and the Asmus family are living with us. Young Zhenya is here from time to time as well. He is being sent to Leningrad and will come and see you.

B.

Dear Olechka,

Come and stay with us this summer without fail. I will be delighted to see you. Am hurrying off to a concert that my eldest son, Stasik, is giving and therefore am not writing more. Much love. I look forward to seeing you here in the spring.

Yours,
ZINA

There is a great deal of news. You will get it from Chechelnitskaya. Once more, best wishes. I would very much like to see Aunt Klara and her family.

Yours,
BORYA

Wouldn't it be a good idea for me to inscribe a book for Aunt Klara and Vladimir Ivanovich? You could give it to them if you thought they would like it. If not, tear out the page with the inscription, let them do without it.

(I am not sending one to you since you have it already. If you want a copy, let me know and I shall send you one.) I'm sending the book.

Moscow, February 1, 1946

Why do you never write, Olya? Am I really such a blackguard in your eyes that I don't even deserve a kind word? How difficult it is at times, and how unexpectedly hurtful! And, in general, what a set of unfortunate circumstances of time, birth, and other classifications! How they all contradict the essence of things, the way pointed by destiny, the dialogue we ought to be carrying on with the world! How can one wrest oneself loose? Wish me fortitude, Olya, fortitude that will keep me from drooping under the weight of fatigue and boredom.

I have begun a long prose piece in which I hope to express the ideas most important to me. That explains my present exuberance. I am hurrying because I want to finish it before you come here this summer so that I can read it to you.

Did Chechelnitskaya give you the note?

Yours,

B.

DIARY

The doctor who examined my heart found that it was "petering out" and that my nervous system was completely exhausted. Indeed it has been nine years since I have had a vacation in the fresh air—and *what* a nine years! On the one hand I gradually became used to my heart problem, and on the other the addition of sugar to my diet strengthened my heart muscles. The doctors kept theorizing, trying this and trying that, when actually all I needed was to begin eating again and regain my strength, and the heart restored itself.

I have developed some major ideas about prose. This has now become my sacred task: to define what prose is. It seems to me that just as a poet turns to prose only in maturity, so a scholar can allow himself to attack a problem of this dimension only toward the end of his intellectual career.

Despite traditional views, I have never admitted the existence of independent forms in antiquity, such as the short story and the novella (*logos*). At first there was lengthy and complex prose of paratactical composition. I clearly discerned that the development of ancient thinking was from the complex to the simple, not the reverse.

Moscow, February 24, 1946

Dear friend Olyushka,

What a joy it was for me to get your letter today. Zina thanks you, too, and sends you a kiss. No, in the letter written in pencil from the islands you said nothing about your heart. How upsetting and frightening! But don't be alarmed. There were two periods in my life when they told me terrifying things about my own heart.

You write wonderfully well; you are to be envied. But I'm sure you must realize this yourself. I can well imagine on what a solid foundation of questions your interest in the analysis of prose is based, and how deeply you will delve into it. You will, no doubt (in juxtaposing it to a hypothetical nonprose), draw a parallel between two cultures or systems, the soul of one being continuity and form, and of the other—innovation and revelation.

Your words about immortality were just right. This is the theme, or rather the primary mood, of the prose I am now writing. I am writing in a very scattered manner, not the way writers do, as if I were not writing at all. If only I have enough money to finish it, since it has put a temporary end to my regular earnings and has upset my plans! But I am in the same high spirits I enjoyed more than thirty years ago; it's almost embarrassing. Lots of love, dear Olga.

Moscow [May 31, 1946]
Dear Olya,

It's summer again. Although I don't allow myself to believe it can happen, I am again inviting you to visit us. Deep in my soul I nurture the hope that you may come this time, and therefore we have the Asmus family living in the sun parlor and are saving a room downstairs for you, or for Alexander and Irina, or for somebody else.

I am still in town. I must and want to write a general introduction to the Collection of my Shakespeare translations (the ones you know plus *Othello* and *Henry IV*). Instead of doing that, I find myself overcome by drowsiness most of the time. God willing, and if I am still alive, I will definitely make a trip to Leningrad in October or November.

I can't tell you anything new: the relations between the various aspects of my life remain the same as before. I am extremely happy—no one more so—so far as my inner life is concerned, but my outer life requires, less for my own good than for Shakespeare's (if he is to reach the stage), that I be exalted to the rank of *Kammerjunker*, an honor I shall never be awarded and my need for which so surprised you. But things would take a different turn for me and I would probably do a lot of new things if the theaters were to begin producing my work.

How is your health? I don't expect a long letter from you, and I understand how difficult it is to write when one realizes that one *has* to write. It would be best if you could come here for a visit. Lyonya is already at the dacha; Zina spends time both here and in town. Young Zhenya is graduating from the academy. Forgive me for these wilted lines. I had nothing particular to tell you; I just wanted to remind you that summer has come.

Lots of love. I would be very grateful for a postcard just the same. Zina is looking forward to seeing you, just as I am.

Yours,

B.

Leningrad, June 29, 1946

Dear Borya,

Forgive me for not having replied to your kind letter. I have fallen to pieces from the heat, the squabbles, and an inner numbness. In a few days the academic year will be over. It has consisted not so much of academic activities as of my getting myself disentangled from the snares I was forced into by associates—the informers and intriguers, such as Tolstoy. The phrase from *The Seagull* burns before my eyes: "You diehards have gotten the upper hand in art and consider only what you yourselves do to be legal and legitimate; everything else you repress and stifle."

I will write when I feel more rested. Best love to you and Zina.

Yours,

OLYA

DIARY

The new academic year began with a meeting of the entire faculty, who were preached to and admonished by the doctor. In August the Central Committee issued a directive concerning the journals *The Star* and *Leningrad*. The statement became well known for its overt cynicism, typical of the police, and showed the whole world that art in our country is created by direct orders from on high. Everyone was eagerly awaiting words of wisdom.

When the rector appeared, he was wearing a peasant shirt under his jacket, open at the collar. That symbolized the change in the political course and a shift of ideology in favor of the "great Russian people," away from "obsequiousness" toward the West. He spoke of the directive of the Central Committee, of diplomatic war, and of the antagonism of the two worlds. He uttered the following phrase: "Unfortunately many Soviet people have been abroad. That has caused them to be blinded by the ostentatious culture of the West. We must now expose these people and their wrong views. The most careful selection of persons is essential, and the most careful examination of all that goes into print."

The university no longer means anything to me. The last sap has dried up in this tree of mine. My face is heavy and leaden-hued. Seeing myself from a distance, I was struck by an impression of deathly, crushing dejection. I tried to find a word for it. None would do—not "depression" or "dejection" or even "broken" can describe this state of coldness, of stoniness. After Zhdanov's speech the last spark of life was snuffed out. Now anyone who in any way shows respect for European culture is dubbed a toady. A new wave of holding eminent scholars up for public opprobrium is rising. One finds it all the more sickening when one knows that the victims are mostly ailing old men, half-dead, with heads shaking with palsy, whose loving wives try to hide from them the "critical" attacks they are being subjected to.

Moscow, October 5, 1946

Dear Olya,

How are you? How is your health? This summer Zina and I cherished some hope, however slight, that you would come. We had many guests the whole time. Alexander and Irina were here, as were various young people, yet we always kept a room or the upstairs terrace ready for you.

Forgive me for not having written before. I have been working with rare success of late, especially during the spring and summer. I had to write an introduction to the collection of my five long Shakespeare translations, and I didn't believe I could get it done. To my surprise, I did. In thirty pages I was able to say what I wanted about poetry in general, about Shakespeare's style, and about each of the five translated plays, as well as several matters connected with Shakespeare: the level of education in those times, the authenticity of Shakespeare's biography. A copy of the article is to be found in the editorial offices of one of your ill-fated journals, either *The Star* or *Leningrad*, with either Sayanov or Likharev as editor. If you happen to have any acquaintances, try to get the article. I would like you to read it. I have asked Akhmatova and Olga Berggolts* to do the same.

Since July I have been writing a prose novel, *Boys and Girls*, which is to encompass the four decades from 1902 to 1946 in ten chapters. With intense absorption I have already written one-fourth or one-fifth of what is planned. This is a very serious work. I am already old, I may soon die, and I must not perpetually put off giving free expression to my true thoughts. My activities this year are the first steps in that direction, and they are new for me. I must not live endlessly at thirty, at forty, and at fifty-six by what an eight-year-old child lives by: passive indications of one's abilities and the good will of the people surrounding one. Yet all my life I have been forced to adhere to such a restricted regimen.

At the beginning of the summer I remained untouched by the "current events" taking place in my own literary sphere. I sat in Peredelkino and worked with complete absorption on the third chapter of my epic.

---

* Olga Fedorovna Berggolts (1910–1975): Soviet writer and memoirist.

But more and more often Zina returned from town looking grim, miserable, pained, and aged because of a feeling of wounded pride on my account. Only in this manner, through my alarm for Zina, did the distressing events force their way into my consciousness. For several days at the end of September, a cloud seemed to hang over our lives and future (mostly a threat to our material well-being). We moved back to town uncertain of what the year would bring us.

Now, however, I believe everything will turn out all right. The sense of happiness and trust in happiness that filled me to overflowing all last year has returned in full. And so, before returning to my interrupted work (today I resolved to go back to it), I wanted, while I still had free time, to let you know how we all are.

No doubt the "campaign" has struck at you as well and multiplied your misfortunes. Is this so?

How stale and stupid it is, and how sick of it I am!

Your quotation of Treplev's lament from the *Seagull* was well chosen.

Love from me and Zina, who asks to be remembered. At the last minute I decided to send you my last, dog-eared, almost indecipherable copy of the article. If, after you have finished reading it, the letters are not completely effaced, pass it on to somebody else to read.

So here we are again: Lyonya, Zina, her helper Olya, and I, in various combinations.

Yours,

B.

Let me know how you are. Do you have my translation of *Othello*?

Moscow, October 13, 1946

Dear Olya,

No sooner had I finished writing you than I came down with a sore throat; I was in bed several days.

I'm in a very bad frame of mind at present. It's just another one of those bad times that occasionally cut across my life for extended periods. But this time it is combined with old age and the fact that in the past five years I have become so used to good health and success that I look upon happiness as a constant and indispensable part of existence.

In one thing I will try to take myself in hand: my work. I have already told you I am writing a long novel in prose. It is, in fact, my first real work. In it I want to convey the historical image of Russia over the past forty-five years, and at the same time I want to express in every aspect of the story—a sad, dismal story, worked out in fine detail, ideally, as in a

Dickens or Dostoyevsky novel—my own views on art, the Gospels, the life of man in history, and much more. For the time being I call the novel *Boys and Girls*. In it I will square accounts with Judaism, with all forms of nationalism (including that which assumes the guise of internationalism), with all shades of anti-Christianity and its assumption that there are certain peoples surviving the fall of the Roman Empire from whose undeveloped national essence a new civilization could be evolved.

The mood of the piece is set by my Christianity, somewhat different and wider in scope than Quaker or Tolstoyan Christianity, deriving from various aspects of the Gospels in addition to the ethical aspect.

All these matters are so important to me, and their varying colors arrange themselves so perfectly on the canvas within the outline I have conceived, that I could not go on living another year unless this novel, my alter ego, in which with almost physical concreteness certain of my spiritual qualities and part of my nervous structure have been implanted, went on living and growing, too.

The package containing photographs, the article, the books, etc., was dispatched not by me but by our postmistress, so when you get it don't start up a long letter in response. Just drop us a card saying how you are and what you are doing.

Love. I'm in a blue mood.

Yours,
BORYA

Leningrad, October 11, 1946

Dear Borya,

You are the only one in the whole world I can say "dear" to. You are my only remaining relative: Sasha and Uncle are gone. I am completely alone. Somebody at some point asked me who I am living with, and I answered, without noticing, "I have no relatives." I said it easily, but the sound of it hurt me. The phrase made me suffer, as from something worse than the actual loss of relatives. You are so generous! It's so like you. The package was like a Christmas stocking full of all the most precious things. Including yourself. Beloved faces, poetry, spirituality, and thought.

Happily you cannot imagine how overwhelmed I was by the family photographs. My first reaction was to run and show them, but suddenly I realized there was no one to show them to. Mama is gone.

How terrible is this, our first encounter; I dreaded it. Perhaps for that reason I did not come to Moscow. I am afraid to embrace you with empty hands. And you, with Zina and Lyonya, do you not see that there is nothing behind you, as if you were standing with your backs to the void? I used always to kiss you for Uncle as well, breaking through time and distance. It is terrible to be a relative without relatives, to kiss those beyond the grave. And indeed I doubt that one who is all alone can have relatives.

You have changed. There is an unfamiliar gravity in your face and thoughts—a gravity, I would like to add, that sounds great depths of gravity. One gets the impression that you have sworn to put aside all that is chance and fortuitous and concern yourself with fundamentals alone. A chill went down my spine as I read Shakespeare presented in the worn, scarcely legible letters of your old typewriter. That typewriter spoke to me in a tongue as unknown to Gutenberg as a typesetting machine was to an ancient slave. A whiff of eternity rose from the pages. There is something in this from the chronicles of history. Your thoughts on Shakespeare might be a document from the archives of eternity— preserved, of course, in manuscript. Today the printing press has become something imperfect and obsolescent. Your worn typewriter is vastly more eloquent and loud-voiced; it outvoices radio and lithography.

I could easily reach Sayanov, if that old sot is capable of doing anything at all, let alone returning a manuscript. I don't know whether to send this (your) copy back, or only Sayanov's. If this one, too, I shall have a copy made.

Everything in your article is interesting, exalted, and fearfully serious. I have the feeling that you are speaking out, no matter the cost. But I am not really the reader for you.

Can one impartially read one's cousin? I find myself instantly immersed in an atmosphere of family encounters, of the embraces and exclamations that were exchanged by good people on the shores of the sea at Mer-rekühl, under the leaning tower of Pisa, inside Moscow Station, on Myasnitskaya Street or the Catherine Canal. It all boils down to a copy of a photograph that I study with the eyes of two families. What I see is kindred, is of my own blood, and gives me the feeling that you are obliged to speak for all of us.

That which is new in your personality is new in your vocabulary. It is hard to believe that it is *your* vocabulary—that is, that you are capable of speaking in the most ordinary words and constructions. I loathe such language. I find no excuse for it. What right has it to make anyone carry such a burden? The entire weight of ideas should be expressed in ideas alone, without the help of language. It may do for passing an exam but not for creating a style.

All the greater, then, is the virtuosity you show in your chosen medium. Let him who so desires buy it for cash; he who has ears, let him hear.

In so short and popular an article your views are macrocosmic. One is aware of great thoughts breaking through into history. Shakespeare is a part of all of us, especially all of our family. To examine Shakespeare is to give an account of one's own life, to revive one's youth, to declare one's poetic and philosophical credo. All this you did in a popular article. Very good indeed did I find your feeling for scholastic logic, the scholasticism typical of Shakespeare's thinking, the conjugation of events in all tenses, the bits of biography in the tavern, whispered love in solitary places, the shorthand of metaphor. Your interpretation of *Hamlet* and *Othello* is the same as mine. The former is a colossal drama of what they now call "single-mindedness" rather than of scattered pearls. And your understanding of the scene with Ophelia corresponds to my own. What I find really splendid is your conception of the religiosity of Othello's brutality. You are right—he pitied Desdemona. Antony and Cleopatra are beautifully revealed. Lasciviousness and debauchery according to the world outlook of Shakespeare's day. But I will reread your article again and again.

I was astounded to find you placing *Victoria** next to *War and Peace*. True, *Victoria* is a great work.

I find your translations of Baratashvili† admirable. I devoutly hope he is worthy of such beautiful verse.

It is as if I have made the acquaintance all over again of Zina, of the new you, and particularly of Lyonya. He is a sensitive boy, "subtle" and oval-faced. Who knows what he will become? Yes, I said "oval-faced" because I neither like nor trust the round-faced type. He is a good and beautiful child. How sad to think that he will never see his grandmother and grandfather, and that they never saw him. He appears to me to be of the same mold as our dear departed Zhenechka‡—the same oval face and high brow.

How splendid that you are writing, that *your own* censor has passed you. That is the most important thing. Yours is a genuine and marvelous happiness. My only regret in the circumstances is that you will not come here. But I never doubted your ability to make yourself do what you ought to do.

The length of this letter will tell you that I have attained my prescribed

---

* Novel (1898) by Knut Hamsun.

† Nikoloz Melitonovich Baratashvili (1817–1845): Georgian romantic poet.

‡ Olga's brother Evgeny, who died of acute appendicitis in his youth.

norm for subsistence. I did not write this way for three years. I have attained, so to speak, the morphology of a norm. More than once have I told you that my life is but a passage through time. I prepared myself for a long voyage, boarded the ship, and mastered the skills of a stoker, who doesn't care a hoot how many miles lie ahead. So be it. I didn't die.

I cured my heart ailment with sugar. In summer I suffered from neuralgia that culminated in sciatica. I didn't work or leave the house. I am losing my hair as a result of the scurvy, and my eyesight is failing. I can't concentrate. At one time I was barren of ideas for but brief spaces at a time; now it is the ideas that appear only for brief spaces at a time. My students only imitate and distort. Nothing is published. In August I considered resigning my chairmanship of the department and taking a light load of teaching hours. I dread the winters. I did not, however, resign. I feel drawn into a state of nonbeing, and that frightens me. Under the influence of friends I have again tied myself down to responsibilities as a kind of anchor. This spring I was tormented exceedingly; they drank as much of my blood as they dared. My students were getting ready to defend their dissertations, and that was looked upon as an unforgivable offense. I conducted myself with calm firmness; when the department council rejected my candidates, the university council accepted them.

I am working hard but unproductively on Greek lyric poetry—a kind of charade. I don't seem to be getting anywhere, there are no chances of my being published, and my mind's a blank. I read a lot. To deaden my senses, I have taken on more teaching hours. No one, of course, can compete with me in lecturing on Greek literature because I have done intensive research in all major works. For two months I have been expounding the *Iliad* and there is no end in sight. I was hauled over the coals by *The Leningrad Pravda* and at various meetings, but very quickly they made their peace with me. They call me Father Avvakum.*

Today I am at home, feeling unwell. I received your package last night.

What are Zhenya and young Zhenya doing? What is he like? Where is Fedya? Do you have any news about Josephine or poor Lydia?

I visit the Lapshovs sometimes. Thank God, they are alive and active (knock on wood). Vladimir Ivanovich called this morning unexpectedly at 8 A.M. and—what do you suppose?—invited me to dinner.

They wrote to you last summer. I will give them news about you. Best

* Avvakum Petrovich (1620–1682): Russian archpriest and heretic, a founder of the sect of Old Believers; author of *Life of the Archpriest Avvakum, Written by His Own Hand* (1672–1675).

love to you and Zina. Take care of yourselves. I don't expect a speedy reply, but don't forget me.

Yours,

OLYA

Moscow, October 15, 1946

Dear Olya,

Thank you for such a prompt, lively, and generous response. I am sorry that you wasted so much energy on me. I don't need the articles, but if you could get Sayanov's copy from him, I would be glad to have it. What you said about my gravity, and that there is no one to live for now that the folks are gone, is profoundly true. But of late I have conquered my grief over their loss. I regret having sent you another letter, a rather gloomy one, I fear. Don't take it seriously. I now see that I was depressed for no good reason. Everything will be all right. Regards to the Lapshovs, and give Aunt Klara a kiss for me. Shall I send you my *Othello*?

DIARY

Papers read at the annual academic conference are guaranteed publication. For that reason I had welcomed the opportunity to make such a presentation. But I have never attached importance to abstracts and extracts, which I always deliberately separated from concrete proof; for that reason I have always reacted negatively to preconference publications of the intellectual essence and most interesting aspect of a work. Scholarship has its own style, its own composition, and its own exposition. How rough, how contemptible are abstracts and extracts that precede rather than culminate research work!

The study I made of Homer's similes, which I now planned to present in extracted form, was carried out in the midst of the bombing raids of October through December 1941.

[Inscription on an offprint of an article entitled "The Origin of the Epic Simile, Based on Examples from the *Iliad*"; *Papers Presented at the Jubilee Academic Conference*, Leningrad State University, 1946:]

To my dear Borya, as testimony to life's manifestation

OLYA

260

October 30, 1946

An analysis of similes from the *Iliad* shows that the second element of a simile (the plant, animal, cosmic, or everyday-life image, to which the first element is compared) is the one that is extended, independent, and realistic.

Animal comparisons are used to express rage, belligerence, and violence; cosmic comparisons express darkness, death, and destruction. Similes from the *Iliad* do not present images of sunlight, only of storm and tempest.

Moreover, in every extended simile the mythological plane provides the basis for that which is being compared, and the realistic plane provides the basis for that to which it is being compared.

The mythological concept of a simile is based on the idea of a struggle taking place between a totem's two phases: action and nonaction. Both phases are presented concretely and in images as the usual mythological opposites: when the evil force triumphs, it is represented as merely a likeness of the true totem, as its aggressive twin; when the good force triumphs, the false chthonian totem is vanquished and is temporarily silenced (as was the good force in the other instance).

Mythological thinking knows no similes because a simile requires purely conceptual processes of abstraction. Mythological thinking has recourse only to personification, animated by the idea of struggle.

Conceptual thinking revises that which has been handed down by tradition without creating anything new, subjecting the material not to a mythmaking consciousness but to a realistic one. Realism is not the mere portrayal of everyday life; the portrayal of everyday life becomes part of the picture as a result of realistic thinking. Realism affects the conception of time, representing it as durational in contrast to the mythological representation of time as spatial and static. Flat and confined space now becomes three-dimensional. Relationships assume a causal quality. A transition is made from the perception of only single concrete phenomena to the recognition of associations and the making of generalizations. The object becomes separated from the subject, the active from the passive. Similes are the involuntary result of the realistic consciousness, involving as it does conceptual thinking.

The extended epic simile (the oldest form of all) was created before the category of quality evolved. As soon as this took place, the simile became a comparative. "How" was transformed from an indication of likeness into an indication of quality: "what kind?" From this viewpoint a simile might be called a "prequality" category.

Dear Borya,

It is highly significant that the paper I wrote under a rain of bombs and artillery shells, utterly exhausted, expecting the end of the world, I later read on the highly festive occasion of the university jubilee. It seemed to me that it was not I but Saint George holding up the dragon's head. And I gave my paper on the most terrible day for me—exactly one year after Mother's death.

Now all those festivities are forgotten. I was not allowed to give a brief introductory statement of the sort I have just written to you. The idiots don't understand one thing (a thing that fills all your poetry): the semantics of time.

I am no longer sensitive to the high pathos of history—or of immortality, either. I still believe in the history of scholarship; this for me is no longer a bright flame, however, but a mere postulate. You, on the other hand, are a great monument of culture. Your trust in the grandeur of illusion is the very foundation on which you stand.

I received your second letter and the postcard. I wanted to ask you about one other thing. Should I let anyone read your article? You realize that it will be plagiarized immediately, disguised by scholarly "apparatus." The greedy ones will leap at it. It is full of brilliant passages. Let me know your reply when you have the chance.

I also wanted to ask you about Bowra. Chechelnitskaya told me he was a critic and translator of your poetry. Is that right? Is he the same person who wrote *Greek Lyric Poetry*? Do you pronounce his name "Bavra"? There is much that is fresh in his book. In his interpretation of Alcman* he, the scoundrel, published some things that I had been keeping for my own *Origin of the Lyric*. Answer me when you have time.

I haven't forgotten about Sayanov. I shall ask him for the article at Katerina's nameday party (Katerina is his wife). I am preparing for the annual university conference. I shall make a preliminary report on the origin of the Greek lyric. At present I am working on Sappho, and she presents one of the most difficult problems in all of ancient literature. Anxiously awaiting *Othello*.

Love to you and Zina.

Yours,

OLYA

---

* Founder of Doric lyric poetry in the seventh century B.C.

Moscow, November 12, 1946

Dear Olya,

I hasten to reply to you with this postcard because lack of money and too much work make it impossible to say when I will be able to write as a human being. What I found to be best of all in your "similes" was the part about the second element (that to which the first is compared), about its realism, its independence, and its presenting the entire essence, so that it is for the sake of this element alone that authors write (the best example being "the image of a boiling pot in which pork is being stewed"). But in Part V (too specialized for me—I prove to be an ignoramus when it comes to "totemism" and all that) not everything is clear; sometimes it seems to be forced, heavy, recondite. In Part VI it evens out again, and the flow is resumed (the path of the simile toward the category of quality); I find it excellent. On the whole, it is terribly like my own way of thinking: in its strength and weakness, in the lively freedom with which you shift from theme to theme, and in the sins (I'm speaking of myself here . . . sins!) of false profundity and "perfectionism." I will write you later about my own sins in Shakespeare, by way of illustration. But on the whole—good girl, Olya! It is wonderfully fresh, daring, and valid (in the parts I have mentioned).

Soon I will write you about Bowra and the rest.

The main thing is that it is youthful, strong, and proud, with a consciousness of its own worth. After reading a work like this, one wants to read, reflect, study. Only it seems to me that elements such as Part V slow it down. When I find this element in myself, I see it as something negative, as an alien tendency toward analysis that gets nowhere in its efforts to attain universality. But, I repeat, I am talking about myself.

Bowra* is a professor of ancient literature at Oxford who knows Russian as well as ancient Greek, and who translates Akhmatova as well as reading lectures to his students on Sappho. Yes, he's your man. I don't know the book of his which you named, *Greek Lyrical Poetry*. He has written a great deal (*From Virgil to Milton, The Heritage of Symbolism*), compiled an anthology of Russian verse, translated a great deal of Blok,† and, indeed, is one of those who causes me embarrassment by showing me so much attention.

I love you very much, Olya, and send you a kiss. Zina loves you so much it frightens me.

---

* Boris's Cyrillic transcription here indicates the proper English pronunciation.

† Alexander Blok (1880–1921): the foremost Russian symbolist poet.

Leningrad, November 24, 1946

Dear Borya,

Thanks for *Othello*. You're probably sick of hearing what a marvelous translation it is. You translated not only language but also ideas. For the first time, Shakespeare's simplicity, a simplicity common to every genius, has appeared in Russian. No Greek tragedy has been translated in this way. To find language for the simplicity of grandeur is beyond the strength of a mere translator; it can only be done by a great poet.

Perhaps I have acted foolishly in giving copies of your work not to the Lapshovs or Mashura but to other people, for whom they are the greatest of gifts. These people know you and appreciate your work in a sensitive way. After all, it is a gift of the spirit and not of the blood.

Thank you for your reflections on my similes. But in scholarship there exists only context. One must keep in mind that there is much invention here and that until the present *nothing* has been said about extended similes. But I don't like either polemics or assertions of originality.

I am suffocating from being unable to publish. The members of the editorial board publish only themselves ("Once Again Concerning the Question of . . ."). It is not only because they don't publish *me*—they don't publish anyone but themselves. And I write one book after another. Like the Wandering Jew, I am the itinerant pharmacist peddling extracts. Oh, this tragedy of summaries and abstracts! And even they exist only under the best of circumstances. All my love.

Yours,

OLYA

Borya, Sayanov is no longer connected with *The Star*, and I have no access to Druzin.

I've written my new address on the back. Our house is now closed on the canal side.

Moscow, January 24, 1947

Dear Olya,

How could I have failed to greet you on the New Year and wish you the old clichés: money and health, the two things from which all other blessings flow? Please let me know you are still alive, and anything else that you can squeeze on a postcard.

Why haven't I written you? Because I have been torn between the usual demands of the day and the task that is my final happiness and madness: the writing of my novel in prose which, like everything else, does not always go smoothly.

What else is there to say? Only the same thing I say in every letter to you: come and see us. Do something about your Leningrad apartment for the summer (find someone to take care of it for you) and come and share our life and its daily commotion.

Once this is said, the question is not why I have been silent but why, having nothing new to tell you, I have suddenly sat down to write.

More and more often rumors reach me that Prof. A. A. Smirnov (and perhaps many others) are attacking my Shakespeare translations. I suddenly recalled that this is taking place at the university, and since you are there you may be offended or upset. Let me hasten to reassure you that this is of no significance whatsoever and would still be of no significance if the attacks were to increase a hundredfold. It would mean nothing even if they affected more than my purse, or even if what Smirnov says is true (and perhaps it is).

Of late I have taken that enormous step in life, be it a game or a drama (or perhaps I only fancy I have taken it, but that makes no difference), which brings me to a point where trifles, shadings, accents, transitions, half tones, and other secondary considerations no longer can hurt or delight or even exist for me, a point where one must win or lose on the grand scale—all or nothing!

What, then, is Smirnov to me, when my (and Smirnov's) worst, most dangerous enemy is I myself, my age, and the limitations of my powers, which may not hold up under all that is demanded of them and may crush me.

So don't be sad on my account, if ever you are inclined to be. Little do you know how undeserving of pity and how disgustingly self-assured I am!

In this matter I seriously worry about you, as I do about Zina when (as in the attack on me last autumn) I feel that in some indirect way I am injured and sullied just because she is pained and insulted on my account, and I tolerate it and do not avenge myself by hurling back a double insult.

In the last days of December I lost two close friends in one week. Olya Serova (the eldest daughter of the artist) and Irina Sergeyevna, Asmus's wife, both died.

Love.

Yours,

B.

Leningrad, January 31, 1947

Dear Borya,

It is amazing. I don't know whether you sense my intentions or I yours, but our letters, rare as they are, always cross in the mail. I had just been thinking about you and had been looking for a free moment to write . . . almost without a reason. "New Year" is nonsense; I don't have "new" years of any kind. I didn't notice that you had not sent me a New Year's greeting and it doesn't matter in the least.

Here is what I wanted to tell you. In January I read a paper at the annual conference at the university—the one tradition I still observe. The conference was postponed three times: from November to December, from December 1946 to January 1947. I am sending you the abstract. In the paper I pointed out several peculiarities of the ancient Greek metaphor. In order to show this properly I chose, as an extreme example, your artist from *On Early Trains*, the line, you remember, "There's a glass half empty on the table"—that whole passage is so remarkable. The audience listened with the greatest attention (only my friends know that you and I are related). In a sense, then, I was able to comprehend the classical poetic metaphor through you. We must talk sometime about the difference. I very much want to do an article on the theory of metaphor; I have a great many new ideas about it and they are purely my own, based on my own studies over many years. I am writing a book about the origin of the Greek lyric and have written a great deal recently about Sappho, things that have not been noticed up to now. How timely such a publication would be! But there are no prospects whatsoever. I can't even publish a brief notice. The possibilities that exist are only for those who sit next to the pie. So life is not easy for me.

I know about Smirnov. He gave a vile speech, malicious and utterly vile. But it failed to please. Even in these days and under these circumstances, everyone disapproved.

I have known Smirnov for about fifteen years. We work side by side. He is a complete nonentity. There is nothing to say about his scholarly profile because it doesn't exist. But he is an interesting type. An inveterate debaucher in the past, he maintained a villa in the south for purposes of illicit "experimentation," for which he became notorious. Later he married a wealthy lady. In lieu of vodka, he speculates in literary translations, is a kind of "capitalist" in the publishing business, buys translations and fleeces the poor translators for all they're worth. In appearance, he has a drooping lower lip, his head tilts to one side, and his glance is plaintive. He crawls about. But on the teaching faculty he is a very lion. He speaks of "hedonism" and "aestheticism." He played without success on the theme of religion and medieval mysticism; then shifted to Shakespeare, where he took it on the chin. He is now masquerading as a Shakespearean scholar and is doing his best to become a speculator in that field as well.

In 1937 he was frightened to death. He explained to everyone he was not an aristocrat, not Alexander Alexandrovich, not Smirnov, in fact, but Abram Abramovich, the illegitimate son of a banker and a housekeeper— a democrat, body and soul.

Sayanov was very nice and promised to return the article. He should do it very soon now. He is your devout admirer. Love to you and Zina.

Yours,

OLYA

I was shocked to hear of the death of Asmus's wife. I believe she was still quite a young woman. For some reason her untimely death shocked me.

DIARY

As early as September we were required to turn in the abstracts of our papers for the university conference. They were snatched out of our hands in such fearful haste that we had no time to properly consider. This time I decided to expound my genuine theses, since this is the only proof of authorship one can claim for unpublished works.

I ought to have finished my study of the lyric long ago, because I do not feel at home in Greek lyric poetry. I never studied it or was interested in it. I knew very little about it. It was always something very remote from me, this genre without myth, plot, or semantics. What sort of "unclassical" phenomenon was it, anyway?

At last I decided to take refuge in the ultimate haven, the one that for me has always been the most reliable: I sat down and began writing. And suddenly, while plunged in complete self-oblivion, I began discovering things that surprised even me.

Lyric poetry represents a great change in social consciousness and one of the most important stages in the cognitive process. It marks a shift from figurative to conceptual thinking, from a mythological to a realistic view of the world. It is in lyric poetry that the universe is inhabited for the first time by people in a social world, and all functions of the elemental forces of nature are now applicable to man.

The separation of subject from object represents a lengthy process; the birth of the author in the seventh century B.C. is a reflection of this process. The lyric author is in no way like the lyric poet of more recent times; he is a singer of songs. The myths about gods and heroes become the biographies of poets; cult themes become the themes of the lyricists. A poetic metaphor is an image functioning as a concept. In Greece metaphor building was not an artistic function; it was a reflection of the change in social consciousness, not a poetic entity. The Greek poetic metaphor derives its figurative meaning from its own concrete meaning. Modern lyric poetry stands in diametric opposition to this. Compare Pasternak's

> What is honor and fame to him,
> World renown and instant praise,
> When words are linked to words
> By acts of breathing fusion!
>
> For that he'll burn the furniture,
> And friendship, reason, conscience, life.
> There's a glass half empty on the table,
> An age unused, a world forgotten.*

The metaphor of the glass that has not been emptied stands beside metaphors for the lifetime that has not been lived to the end and the world that has been forgotten. The metaphor and the real meaning have been split, and between them there is limitless freedom. In Pasternak's poem there is a new microcosm, but there is no mythmaking. He removes old, conventional semantics and introduces a multilevel system of images. The Greek lyricist takes his metaphors not from a reality that has been contemplated freely; he still sees with the eyes of ancient models.

Moscow, February 16, 1947

My own dear Olyushka,

What a dog I am for yapping out replies to you on postcards or in brief notes, when naturally I want to reply like a human being and in detail.

The three pages of your outline represent a matter of the greatest profundity and presage a revolution, rather like the Communist Manifesto or the Epistles. How characteristic it is of you to see things in their true, pristine freshness!

Here are the Herculean pillars of that outline:

2. Lyric poetry represents a great change in social consciousness, a stage in the cognitive process, a shift in the world outlook. The universe is inhabited for the first time by *people in a social world*.

3. The myths of the gods become the biographies of poets.

* From the cycle "The Artist," *On Early Trains* (1943).

5. Personification becomes metaphor by transferring the objective to the subjective.

6. The fact and the moment are everything. It does not resort to generalizing repetition.

11. It arises simultaneously with a newly developing philosophy. All this is strikingly true and unusually congenial to my way of thinking and to what I am writing now in the novel (where there is a certain reflective, unfrocked priest from the literary circle of the symbolists, along with his notes about the Gospels, about the image, about immortality). You couldn't have known about this. Some of the expressions are directly from there.

Good girl! But how sad, and at the same time how marvelous, and how similar!

I'm fearfully busy at present. To top off the overall rush, I have accomplished a task the very thought of which I had always dismissed as something too vague, undefined, and unrealizable: a revision and reworking of *Hamlet*. It had needed some kind of revision, but what exactly? I couldn't figure it out. But now it is being reissued by The Children's Publishers, and so I put the novel aside, read the play at one sitting, and set about lightening and simplifying the text. The very same thing needs to be done with *The Year 1905* for a new edition.

Thank you for the return of my article. I just received it. And for the letter and the package. (It is not your handwriting on the package; you probably gave it to someone to mail.)

If I can spare a minute I will send to one of you three (you, Olga Berggolts, or Akhmatova) the poems from my novel (how much simpler they have become!), so that you can know at least something about me. You can copy them or give them to the others to copy. Most likely I will send them to Akhmatova, the foremost martyr, and I will ask your namesake to make a copy for you.

Much love. You cannot imagine what pressure I'm under!

What about the summer?

Yours,

B.

Moscow, March 2, 1947

Dear Olya,

We were delighted to hear you are coming this summer. See that you keep your word!

It is clear that you don't want to become involved with my "literary ladies." Your postcard reply arrived faster than a telegram. Unfortunately I had already written to Anna Akhmatova with the request concerning you. I can't guarantee you absolute immunity, but on the other hand, Akhmatova is so lazy about replying and carrying out requests that that joy may easily pass you by. Zhenya is now a graduate student in the military academy; he finished so brilliantly that they asked him to stay on. You should be ashamed of yourself for passing on to me as "rumors" what I myself had told Chechelnitskaya about my prose, and which she, in turn, had told you. I am exhausted from lack of sleep as I write to you, and yesterday I smashed and bloodied my nose on the corner of the kitchen sink. Love.

Yours,

BORYA

March 9: Forgive me for waiting so long to mail this letter.

Moscow, March 26, 1947

Dear Olya,

I have been sick with the flu and have not been out yet. Lyonya fell ill at the same time I did and is also still in bed with a minor flu complication (a slight ear infection). But I feel fine and my mood is as cheerful as ever, despite the increasing number of attacks on me (such as the article in *Culture and Life*). [. . .]

Of course I am prepared for anything. Why should it have happened to Sasha and everyone else and not to me? I write no protests and say nothing when addressed. It's no use. I never try to justify myself or get involved in explanations. I suppose my pocket will suffer from it. I write this to you so that you won't be worried or upset. Perhaps everything will smooth over. There really was much foolish confusion in my early work. But my new-found clarity will prove to be much less acceptable.

Love,

BORYA

All this has nothing to do with your coming to see us. On the contrary, it is more important than ever that you come.

DIARY

My birthday is March 28. I asked friends not to stir up old memories. To emphasize the ordinariness of the day I went to the store to buy salt in the afternoon. When I got home the thought occurred to me: "It's a bad omen to buy salt on your birthday."

It was a dull day. I lay down, comforted as always by the approach of oblivion and the unfailing contact with my family that dreams bring. On the preceding night I had listened to a radio program about Beethoven, who did not give up even when he became totally deaf. I didn't understand why this musical genius should not have given up and why his not doing so was considered so great a virtue. What if he had spit in the face of life—his executioner? Would that have been less worthy? Suddenly the announcer said, "Despite his sufferings, Beethoven fulfilled his human destiny." I stopped, shaken. This I understood. It was not virtue, not the will to live, but pride that motivated him. He followed his given path to the end. He remained himself despite everything. It was as if he said: "I will do what I must, according to my lights. Nothing else concerns me. Strike me down if you will, but I will still be a human being."

Why then was I unable to go on?

Only a living soul can rise up; dead souls are not resurrected. Deaf as he was, Beethoven heard the harmonies within him.

From childhood I have been a perfectionist—in love, in life, in my idea of God, and what I consider real values. The tragedy of my life is that the Leningrad blockade killed this in me. I push away all the thoughts, sufferings, and actions of those days, including my own; they don't bear contemplating any more than Sasha's days of torment.

Inner deafness! Did Beethoven plumb the ultimate depths of despair?

Leningrad, March 28, 1947

Dear Borechka,

Best love to you and Zina, and may you remain strong of heart. If I don't write it is only (but that "only" covers a multitude of things) because the epistolary genre has gone out of fashion. It is not keeping up with the times, doesn't fit into one's frame of mind, let alone one's emotions.

You and I are not like your father and my mother were. They enjoyed writing regularly and unburdening themselves to one another.

Don't ever torment yourself about not being able to reply to me. Of course it is more pleasant for me, as a cousin, to learn about you from you directly rather than from newspapers and magazines, but I understand how precious your time is. Hurry and work; all conventions such as letter writing are sheer nonsense.

Yesterday I heard a statement over the radio about Beethoven that has stayed with me. Despite the blows of fate and unspeakable sufferings, the radio said that "he fulfilled his human destiny." How well the air waves said it!

Today is the saddest of all for me. I was born exactly fifty-seven years ago. For fifty-four of these years my birthday was celebrated by our family, which has been withering away like a man approaching old age. And it was on this day exactly three years ago that Mama kissed me for the last time.

But I am not sad and add nothing to the bare facts. This is only what all people call life.

So let's live it. I am also writing a book. About Sappho. Everybody has fun in his own way.

Much love,
OLYA

DIARY

In the ordinary passage of days, one may suddenly be overwhelmed by the realization of something one has long seen and known. This winter it was the sudden realization of what my own life had become that made me choke and gasp with indignation. I no longer believe that anything can change it. Like a bleeding wound in the side was the knowledge that I shall never see my work published.

The idea of keeping archives is an idea conceived by history itself. My sympathy has always been with what is beyond the individual and the epoch. The keeping of archives makes me a member of the universal brotherhood of humanity.

As I look back over the course pursued by my family, I see that all the things by which I live came from them. And I think to myself, Here were these great and exceptional people—my father and mother—and nothing but myself remains of them. But it was they who created for me the things I live by so that their lives should find consummation in me. That is the only thing that lends meaning to my present existence.

I have always been immensely aware of history as an objective process. In this lies my faith, my absolute reverence for the objective process above and beyond human beings—my materialistic outlook, if you will, which sees individual lives as an integral part of the whole. I am speaking, of course, not of written history but of history as a world process. In this process nothing is discarded or forgotten. The ideas about heaven, immortality, and the other world, conceived by the peoples of the earth, are all true—not as heaven or paradise or Valhalla, but as history. It is impossible to deceive history no matter how documents are falsified or facts distorted and concealed.

Moscow, April 9, 1947

Dear Olyushka,

Thank you for the letter. I believe I had the flu when I received it. I say "I believe" because, as you quite justly note, everything flashes by so quickly that it is soon forgotten. I still have written no complaints or entered into explanations with anyone. So far as I can tell I am still breathing. Nothing has happened. But my constant hopes that Shakespeare would be staged and bring me premiums have not been justified, owing to the all-prevailing uncongenial atmosphere. I shall have to turn to translation again, as in all these other years. There is a chance that I will be given the first part of *Faust* to translate, but no agreement has been reached so far. On the whole I have no reason to complain. As for what fate holds in store for me—that is the marvel, the mystery.

Love,
B.

The radio words about Beethoven were remarkable!

Moscow, April 24, 1947

Dear Olya,

For three days it has been so warm that Zina is talking of going out to the dacha. I would like to know *whether you have made up your mind* about visiting us. You are already living here so vividly in our consciousness that Zina has you in mind when she turns down others who would like to visit us. I have never played cards or gone to the races, but now suddenly in old age my life has turned into a gambling game. It turns out to be very interesting. I feel fine and spend most of the time working, but without compensation. It is boring, horribly boring, as though I were dumped on a desert island.

Love,
B.

DIARY

In summer I underwent a transformation. I was intoxicated by the sun. I reveled in the sun. The tanning of my skin made me a different woman. With all of nature, with all of the universe, I walked with my face turned away from the damp earth, up to the sun. Again a rebirth!

I wanted to break loose from my chains, to go somewhere far away from my dull and monotonous friends. I thought of visiting Borya, who had invited me so insistently. I wanted to set out, shake myself loose, and forget everything.

It was rest I wanted, a vacation, a break from the squabbles at work and its disappointments, an oasis! My whole attitude changed. I basked in oblivion.

Borya bombarded me with invitations to come. Evidently things were bad for him. They kicked him whenever they could. Art, like scholarship, resembled a convict denied permission to write letters. And Borya was a man of art.

I let him know indirectly that I was ready to come.

Then I had the feeling that I was being smothered. I didn't dare write to him. All personal correspondence was read by the censor. I waited to hear what his response would be.

Moscow, May 20, 1947

Dear Olyushka,

The most important thing is that you have made that joyful decision, and as far as coming is concerned—well, you can come tomorrow if you like. Your comforting intention is just as pleasing to Zina as it is to me, but since she has been busy all week moving us from the city to the dacha, she asked me to express joy on her behalf and to thank you for your good wishes. As for the best time to come, I think it would be in July, when Alexander and Irina will be here. Those two or three days you speak of—we'll discuss the length of your stay when you get here. Just to be on the safe side, here is how to get to the dacha: Kiev Station (there's a subway stop there), Kiev Railroad; the stop is Peredelkino (about eleven miles), Writers' Village, Dacha 3, Pasternak. If I can't meet you, Alexander will.

May 20, 1947

This is a continuation of the card. Get in touch with Alexander, who will be staying in the city until July, and have him meet you at the station and bring you to our place. His address: Moscow, 8 Gogol Boulevard, Apt. 52, telephone K4-31-50.

You know our town address. The telephone is V1-77-45. But we will rarely come to town, and only for a few hours at a time. I have grown too old to translate, but since circumstances have taken a bad turn of late I have with aversion had to make several offers of this sort. Even these were turned down at first, upon which I susbstituted one proposal for another, and suddenly all of them were accepted. As a result, this summer I must translate *Faust, King Lear,* and a narrative poem by Petőfi* called *The Knight János.* But I will keep on writing my novel—in the twenty-fifth hour of each day. In general things seem to be straightening out. Usually the Zhenyas (both he and she) turn up in Peredelkino in July.

[Telegram; July 15, 1947]

WHY SILENT? WHY NOT COMING? EXPECTING YOU DAILY. INFORM BY POSTCARD OF HEALTH AND PLANS. LOVE—BORYA

Moscow, September 8, 1947

Dear Olya,

What goes on and how are you? I growled out something unkind and unfeeling in response to your decision not to come. It's this doglike haste that is at fault for everything. This sort of work doesn't tire one out so much as it ruins one's character. One forgets how to relax, to be joyful, to understand what pleasure is. I always want something badly but I don't know what, and so I don't know how to appease the desire: is it cheese I want with my tea, or do I want to go to Moscow, or do I want to see somebody, or do I want to be reassured that I will *not* see anybody? I suppose it's just a secret longing to have my youth back without selling my soul to get it.

It's a shame you didn't come. Alexander and Irina lived here, as did Zina's son and his wife; Zhenya came for a brief visit and Nina Tabidze stayed longer. There were many others besides. You would have enjoyed yourself; you wouldn't have been bored. Lyonya and Zina would have taught you to play cards and mah-jongg.

God knows what mischief I've been up to—a barbarous and unforgivable orgy. In five weeks I translated 2,500 lines of Petőfi's lyrics (among them a narrative poem of 1,500 lines), and I translated *King Lear* in a month and a half. There was a time when I translated well, but it got me nowhere. The only way to avenge this is to do the same thing badly and unconscionably fast. The novel, or rather the world, in which I took refuge last winter (an indulgence I allow myself and have a right to allow myself because it is bearing fruit!) is so far removed from, and so incom-

* Sándor Petőfi (1823–1849): Hungarian patriot and lyric poet.

mensurate with, the daily grind that what do I care about *Lear* or whether I translate him well or badly—that is, *how* badly. Damn it all, it really makes no difference to me any more.

Smirnov wrote me in the spring about Shakespeare and wouldn't I agree to revise parts of *Romeo and Juliet*. I replied in a light vein but firmly, so that he would know with whom he was dealing, very *sans façon*, and ended good-naturedly by saying that although he had ruined my Shakespeare through lack of understanding, I really had taken no notice of him, spoiled and thick-skinned as I was and with an innate dullness of understanding that made it impossible for me to take any unpleasantness to heart. My only regret is that I didn't send the letter by registered mail; ordinary letters sometimes get lost.

I am scribbling this to you after having just finished the final draft of *Lear*. Tomorrow I will take it to town to be retyped. It is for a children's edition for school libraries. Zina and Lyonya are already in town; his school has begun.

This summer (speaking of my work) marks the first steps for me along a new path; it is very difficult, but it is the first undertaking I have ever been really proud of. I am living and working on two planes: part of the year (in a great rush) I spend on earning enough money to last the entire year; the other part goes to myself, for serious labor. Don't forget I have a big family that I have taught to live well, which means I must turn out new work to the tune of from ten to fifteen thousand a month. Now don't gasp and throw black looks at Zina. She too is working without respite. You can't imagine what a contribution her garden makes!

Again I haven't really told you anything. Let me know how you are. Are you carrying out the plans you told me about? Is the book progressing?

All is well here. I will probably be moving back to town, too. I'll dig up the potatoes and go. I have made a commitment to add *Faust* to my outrages. But before that I shall finish writing the first book (?) or first part (?) of the novel. I have only the chapter on the first imperialist war (1914) to do.

Love,

B.

Moscow, October 14, 1947

Dear Olya,

Mashura came to see us as she was passing through Moscow yesterday and told us some very alarming things about your health and that your eyesight is failing as a result of your work. Are you still alive at all? Why haven't you uttered a single sound in reply to my inquiries? Are you angry with me for my sharp retort when you declined, or rather expressed your inability to accept our invitation? Have you broken off relations with me entirely? Nothing has changed here, i.e., externally all is more or less in order. My summer income-earning period was too long an interruption of the work on the novel, and now it has been hard to get going ("well begun, half done") or to collect my thoughts and re-create the necessary mood. What is Mashura's last name? I have her address, but it was awkward to ask her her name.

Love,

B.

Moscow, June 29, 1948

Dear Olyusha,

How bitter it is that our family dramas keep repeating themselves! Now you are punishing me with your silence, or even by wrenching me out of your heart because of my egoism, because my feelings are only "words, words, words," "literature"; if they were real, I would have proven my love in deeds and not in sighs recorded on paper.

October 1. My Olya, this is the introduction to a letter I began in the spring. It breaks off after two words because of my feeling it would accomplish nothing, and also because of my eternal haste. At that time I was living alone in town (Zina was at the dacha), and now I am living alone in this huge, cold dacha and Zina is in town.

At that time I was finishing the first book of my novel in prose and at the same time editing and re-editing seven of my translations of Shakespeare's plays according to the wishes of countless editors sitting in various publishing houses.

In the same mad hurry I am translating the first part of Goethe's *Faust* in order to earn the opportunity and the right to continue and perhaps to finish the novel this winter, an undertaking that is completely unselfish and profitless because the work is not even intended for current publication. Furthermore, I am not even writing it as a work of art, although it is literature in a deeper sense than anything I have ever done before. But I just don't know whether there is any art left in this world, or what art means. There are people who love me very much (only a few), and I feel that I owe them something. It is for them I am writing this novel, as if it were a long letter to them, in two volumes. I am happy that I have brought the first volume to completion. Would you like me to send you a copy of the manuscript for two weeks or a month? Only I'm afraid you will be offended by reading my summation of antiquity simplified to the point of caricature (for the purpose of making the essence of Christianity stand out in more striking relief).

Be generous and forgive me if I have done anything to hurt you. Write me about yourself or ask someone else (perhaps Mashura) to do so. I love her not a whit less than I do you, and it would be as wrong to attach meaning to my writing to you rather than to her as it would be to draw reasonable or factual conclusions from my erratic and many-sided behavior. Do have someone write and tell me if you're alive, if you're well, if you're in need of money. I, who work year after year like a dog, could weep with pity for all of you—Zina, you, Lyonya, and a number of your namesakes and nonnamesakes. It is as if everyone else were unhappy and I alone allowed myself the privilege of being happy, thereby becoming a burden to all of you. And indeed I am madly, unutterably happy in my free, open, all-embracing acceptance of life, an acceptance I ought to have known—or at least I would have been better off for knowing—at the age of eighteen or twenty, but then I was constrained, then I had not yet grown up to basic things and did not know, as I have since learned to know, how wonderful is the language of life, the language of earth, the language of heaven.

All of us are alive and in good health, including the two Zhenyas and Alexander's family. Everything here goes well.

Be so magnanimous as to write me a line or two (don't waste time on writing much). For some reason I am terribly alarmed about you; somebody must settle my doubts (are you still at the university?), and yet I fear to have them do so.

Love,

BORYA

Regards to Aunt Klara, Vladimir Ivanovich, Mashura, and all the others.

DIARY

Political clouds continued to thicken. The persecution of learning took on the form of poisoning the lives of scientists and scholars. Malevolent criticism by the "gendarmes," which had begun in such organs of defamation as *Culture and Life* and *The Literary Gazette*, spilled over into institutions of higher learning and scientific institutes. At last a meeting of the philology department was called to "discuss" persecution. A similar meeting had been held at the Academy of Sciences and the Institute of

Literature on the eve of ours. All the professors were put to shame. Some, like Zhirmunsky, endured it elegantly and with flair. Eikhenbaum made an attempt to shield himself from being denuded morally by heroically concealing his private parts. He was alone in this. Propp, who was mercilessly tortured for being a German, lost the sense of dignity he had defended so long. Others did whatever was required of them. Upon the completion of the ceremony two events occurred that didn't, as a matter of fact, attract the slightest attention. Professor Tomashevsky, a well-known Pushkin specialist, is a man of cool temperament, not yet old, not even elderly. A caustic wit, I should say, very calm and lacking in sentiment, he walked out into the corridor of the Academy of Sciences after his moral execution and fainted dead away. Professor Azadovsky, a specialist in folklore, already weakened by a heart disease, lost consciousness during the meeting itself and had to be carried out.

Any reference to works by foreign scholars was dubbed "cosmopolitanism," a term fraught with dire police (political) consequences.

I found myself in a state of deep depression. Impressions of the cold clouds in the low gray sky, the icy corridor, the semitwilight that filled the wintry rooms, and the cold gray thoughts that hung in the air merged indistinctly in my mind.

I fell ill. At first it was just a cough and a tightening in the throat accompanied by a heavy sense of spiritual decline. I would have given anything not to have to return to that place, that accursed quagmire. The illness smoldered, manifesting itself in chills and tremors. I wrapped myself up in blankets. My throat became worse. I moved a small table up to my bed, boiled water in my electric teakettle at sunrise (the electricity was turned off later in the morning) and buried it in wrappings to keep it warm. There I lay all day long without thinking, without moving, just lay there as part of the darkness, with no desire for anyone or anything—not for friends or food or life or thought.

For a month I was home and in bed. The department grew anxious. They phoned me, they expressed displeasure, they dropped warning hints. But my temperature did not fall. In order to have the right to be sick I summoned a doctor from the university polyclinic. She discovered I had a chronic infection and sounded the alarm. Without further ado she took me to the clinic to have a bagful of pus removed from my throat. Then I was ordered out of the city and into the fresh air. I made the radical move of going to Terioki. Terioki was horribly expensive, but at least I enjoyed the freedom of life in a hotel—a hotel that was a confiscated Finnish home.

The scenery was austerely Finnish. The sharp air of spring was fragrant with new buds. Trees and plants were just awakening. The place was deserted; the sea was cold and empty. I had but one task: to breathe. In a state of deep apathy I sat and breathed. In nine days I recovered my strength and went home. I still had a temperature and heart murmur, but I gave up all further treatment.

A summer of rest revived my spirits, but I shuddered at the thought of having to go back to that torture chamber, the university. Resolving to leave the department, I went to speak to the rector. He was a new rector named Domnin, a man endowed with the charm of modesty and simplicity. I could hardly believe such a miracle, but I came to appreciate it. In desperation I asked his help in accelerating my release.

With the new semester the forces of destruction set to work again in our department. The atmosphere was one of slander, gossip, and lies. I was spied upon; my every move was checked. I found myself in a quagmire from which I could not escape. Vague dissatisfactions, complaints, and squabbles among students were being encouraged. The air was rank with subtle, indefinable decay. Much as I wanted to escape, it was beyond my strength. Something hung over me that reached out to threaten me, grab me, entangle me in a secret net. At my feet flowed a noisome, amorphous stream that swelled with every hour. Anxiety was deliberately created. At the most unexpected moments, and from the most unexpected sources, blows were struck at my nerves and my brain.

In response to my request the rector said: "We have decided to ask you not to leave the department at such a critical moment. We have decided to request that you keep on working as long as you can—so long, of course, as it does not threaten your health."

I vacillated. I suggested that my health would not be threatened if the situation in the department were not so difficult.

"So incredibly difficult," he concurred in a sad little whisper.

Leningrad, October 9, 1948

Dear Borya,

You will have seen Mashura before receiving this letter. She will be returning from Kislovodsk and will telephone you. You will learn from her, probably, about how I am getting on, although what she knows belongs to the Stone Age of my life.

After Fedya left last February I fell ill with a throat disease that became a chronic infection. I did not work the entire second semester. In early May I witnessed the birth of a glorious, gleaming spring in Terioki.

The powerful sea air, the Finnish pines, and the healing aroma of the young buds brought me back to life.

My illness coincided with certain well-known events in the field of literary criticism. A number of shocks came simultaneously. I withstood them honorably but at the cost of my health, which I used as a reason for asking to be released from the department. They declined to release me, although you would think they ought to have been glad to let me go.

Rest and fresh air were prescribed for my summer, but I was so happy to have any vacation at all that I remained in town and found excursions out to the islands a sufficient restorative.

Beginning with the new academic year I have renewed my request. I now find myself in a period when I must face all of these matters point blank. I have been placed in impossible conditions, from which I must free myself at whatever cost and at the price of giving up the department that I myself created and directed for sixteen years, the only one of its kind in the U.S.S.R. and the biggest undertaking of my life.

Our new rector is an exceptional man, a sensitive human being, who will not allow them to trample me underfoot. After my students spoke with him, he was even more adamant in refusing to grant my request.

Now that is all fading in my memory. My thoughts are occupied by something else: my *belle-soeur* is coming to visit me from another part of the world! And how much her visit recalls from the past! I see Sasha and Mama in my dreams every single night. A student of mine is planning to go to Moscow and she can bring me your novel. This is your good fortune. How well I know it! It is the inexpressible happiness of a hand that is writing and a heart that can hardly keep up with it.

Now I have become clever and artful, and that is a sign of old age.

I am closer to the Lapshovs than they and Mashura are to one another. I love and treasure this sliver broken off our family, I, who am alone. Happily you are unable to understand it. Klara's eternal youth delights me (knock on wood), as does the vitality of her feelings.

So there, I have written to you. And I keep thinking of my sister-in-law on her way here from such distant parts.

Love,

OLYA

Moscow [mid-October 1948]

Dear Aunt Klara, Olya, Vladimir Ivanovich,

Olya, you wrote so beautifully in your letter about Aunt Klara and

Vladimir Ivanovich that I suddenly saw her the way she has always lived in my memory, young and ageless, and I was moved to write to her, as often happens when one has been in love with somebody; and then Mashura unexpectedly called us up this morning. I am sending this manuscript to all of you. You can read it in whatever order you wish, but perhaps it would be better to let Olya begin so that she can write to me that much sooner when she has finished. If possible, read it quickly; I may have need of it.

This first book is probably written for the sake of the second, which will encompass the period from 1917 to 1945. Dudorov and Gordon will remain alive; Yura will die in 1929, and after his death a notebook of poems will be found among his papers by Evgraf, his half brother. The poems that have already been written are enclosed here. The complete poems, in proper sequence, will make up a chapter of the second book.

In terms of plot and conception, I see the second book better than I did the first at this point in its development, but in order to earn a living (remember that this novel is not intended for publication at present) I have to occupy myself with translating, and as a result the work on the novel has been interrupted. Now I am hurrying through Goethe's *Faust* (Part I) as well as a Hungarian classic in the hope that I can have them both completed by Christmas. Even so I am bursting with ideas and projects and I long to work as never before.

Apart from the revolution, we are living at a time when all basic forms of consciousness are disintegrating, when all useful habits, and concepts, and all practical skills have lost their stability.

And so one is late in discovering what one needs; only now have I mastered what I have needed all my life. Well, my having done it at last is at least something to be thankful for.

And to tell you the truth, I am really happy, not in an exalted way, and not through rationalizing, but genuinely, because I am free in spirit and so far, God be praised, am in good health.

I love all of you and embrace you fondly.

Yours,

BORYA

Too bad I'm such a scarecrow. If I were as handsome as our aunt, I would have myself photographed every day. However, since we haven't seen each other for so long, here are two or three pictures to bring you up to date.

Leningrad, October 31, 1948

Dear Borya,

Please don't take my silence for rudeness. I know what a precious gift you have sent me. But naturally Mashura had it first, then it went to Aunt Klara, and I will get it only in a week or so. True, I'm up to my ears in work. But I will write you immediately.

Here's a kiss for the "already" and another for the "to follow."

Yours,

OLYA

Moscow, November 6, 1948

Dear Olya,

Thank you for the postcard and the earlier letter. Don't make your life miserable by reading the manuscript, and you needn't write me anything if you don't have the time or it is difficult. But eventually I shall have to know who has the manuscript in order to get it back or pass it on to someone else. When you no longer have need of it, you can give it to anyone you like to read. I warned you about my ignorant exposition of antiquity (Rome). What did the Lapshovs and Mashura have to say? Does anyone still remember me? Who is that *belle-soeur* of yours— Sasha's wife? Has *she* arrived? I am translating the first part of Goethe's *Faust*—for money and on commission.

It turns out (and this is natural since it was led up to by everything that went before) that much of what is most powerful in the works of Lermontov, Tyutchev, and Blok has come directly from Goethe. I am surprised that such continuity should have escaped Fet and Bryusov when they translated *Faust*. One translates *Faust* into Russian *involuntarily, impulsively*.

Love.

Yours,

B.

Leningrad, November 29, 1948

Dear Borya,

At last I have read your novel. What is my opinion of it? I'm at a loss. What is my opinion of life? This is life, at its broadest and greatest. Your book is beyond judgment. What you have said about history as a second universe applies to your book. It conveys something enormous. Its novelty is particularly new (fortuitous tautology), and it is not a matter of genre or plot, and certainly not of character. I can't define it; I would like to hear what others have to say. It is a special version of the Book of Genesis. Your genius shows its full depth here. I held my breath as I read the philosophical parts, afraid they would reveal the final mystery, which one bears within oneself and always hopes to reveal or to have revealed in art or science—yet dreads the revelation of, since the mystery should always remain a mystery.

You cannot imagine the sort of reader I am: I read at once the book and you and our common blood, and so my opinion is not that of the ordinary reader. This book must be possessed rather than read, as a man does not read a woman but possesses her. For that reason, slipshod reading makes no sense at all.

The realism of the genre and of the language does not interest me. That is not what I prize. The novel has a grandeur of an entirely new sort, more overwhelming in scope than in idea. But I must tell you that the final impression on closing the book is a terrifying one *for me*. I perceive that you are afraid of death, and this explains your passionate preoccupation with the idea of immortality that you are constructing with your life's blood. I am wholeheartedly with you in this, but it pains me as a member of your family—some are gone, others distant*—and also as one who subscribes to Tyutchev's "As I await my fated end. . . ."† The shock I got was similar to what I experience on an escalator when, standing perfectly still, I suddenly find myself at the bottom instead of the top.

There is in the book much that is dear and close to me, that is wholly my own, as well as much that is of our family in its great and small demands on life, ranging from abstract categories to solutions of personal problems. In saying "the dear" and "of our family," I have in mind "the great" applied to individual instances (and not concrete trifles per se). But don't let me hear you saying anything so foolish as that everything you accomplished before this was as nothing, that only now, etc., etc. You are a unique phenomenon and your entire path lies open to view, as in the

---

* A reference to Chapter 8, Stanza LI of Alexander Pushkin's (1799–1837) *Eugene Onegin* (1833):

> Some are gone, others distant,
> As Saadi said once upon a time.

The quotation from Saadi's *Bustan* also appears in the epigraph to Pushkin's "Fountain of Bakhchisarai" (1824). Generally, the first clause is understood to be a reference to Pushkin's young student friends from the Tsarskoye Selo Lyceum. The second clause is thought to be a reference to Pushkin's friends exiled to Siberia after the unsuccessful Decembrist revolt of 1825.

† The final line of Tyutchev's "My brother, who accompanied me so long . . ." (1870), dedicated to his brother and closest friend, Nikolai Ivanovich Tyutchev, who died in 1870.

picture of a road in perspective, showing the great depths into which it recedes. The poems attached to the novel are an integral part of it and of all your other poetry. They are splendid.

I haven't written anything like all my impressions. The best way for me to respond would be not in a letter but by giving you a long kiss. How well I understand the things that are all-important to you!

Thanks for the picture, although I didn't get the best one. I got the one with the big jaw and the arched neck.

I have an awful lot of work. Ah, yes: what am I to do with the manuscript? I'm waiting for a chance to send it to you with someone; I don't trust the post. I expect such a chance to turn up soon.

With gratitude, I send you all my love.

Yours,
OLYA

Moscow, November 30, 1948

Dear Olya,

What a magnificent letter you wrote me!

Your letter is a thousand times better and means more than my manuscript. So it touched you? It is not a fear of death but a consciousness of the futility of one's best intentions and achievements and of the best guarantees, and of the consequent effort to avoid naïveté and make the right choices. If anything at all is to be lost, let it be free of error and not the result of one's own error. Don't worry your head over what I've just said. If it is unintelligible, that is as it should be.

You often speak of blood ties, of the family. Consider, though, that that represents only the proscenium in the performance, just the place of greatest concentration in the whole drama, essentially a harmonious drama. I am overawed by Papa, by his brilliance as an artist, by his complete mastery of form, by his vision—more perceptive than that of most of his contemporaries—by his perfect ease of craftsmanship, by his ability to playfully throw off several works a day, and at the same time I am shocked by the disparity between all that and the lack of recognition accorded him. Then suddenly I feel it (the shock) in respect to the fate of Tsvetayeva, an extraordinarily talented, daring, and educated poet, who passed through all the vicissitudes of our times, a person dear to me, who came back from a great distance only to hang herself at the beginning of the war in complete obscurity in some remote backwater.

Often life around me has been outrageously dark and unjust, sufficiently so to justify revolution; this makes me something of an avenger or

Evgeny Pasternak
("young Zhenya").
1947

Boris Pasternak, Heinrich Neuhaus, Lyonya, Sviatoslav Richter,
and Galya Neuhaus. Peredelkino, 1947

Zina Pasternak,
Nina Tabidze,
and Boris Pasternak

Boris Pasternak

a defender of its honor, a militantly zealous and keen one. My efforts won me a good name and made me happy, but in essence I was only suffering for *them*, getting even for *them*.

Thus Rilke died several months after I began corresponding with him; thus I lost my Georgian friends; and you yourself stand for something of a loss—you, our return from Merreküll in the summer of 1910 (Vruda, Pudost, Tikopis), and something in your life that signifies permanent evidence of my wrong.

I wronged all of you. But what was I to do? So you see, the novel is a part of this debt of mine, proof that at least *I tried.*

Forgive me for carelessly burdening you with so much nonsense, true only as an approximation. For that reason, strictly speaking, I ought to have begun a new letter and torn this one up, but when would I have written it?

I am amazed by the immediacy of your understanding and its affinity to mine—instantaneous, developing parallel to mine, always confidently guiding you; only that same Marina Tsvetayeva understood me so well, and occasionally Mayakovsky, but with his tendency to falsify reality and meaning. It is surprising that I even mention him.

You can lend the manuscript to anyone you wish. When *your* need for it passes, send it back in the way you propose.

I thank you that, despite your busy life, you read it. In your conditions, even if the manuscript glowed in the dark and gave off heat you would be within your rights to view it as an intruder and wish you had never seen it.

In similar conditions and with those same sentiments I am now working on *Faust.*

All the best to you. Love and kisses. I will always remember your striking theory of the simile. *This is of the same order.*

Take care of yourself.

Yours,

B.

CHAPTER IX

T H E "moral and intellectual pogroms," as Olga characterized the campaign against cosmopolitans, continued. Pasternak's origins became an obstacle in postwar Stalinist Russia, but he drew strength and a new happiness from his work on the novel *Doctor Zhivago*. Echoing a poem from the novel, "Hamlet" (1948), he wrote Olga: "No longer does my life belong to me. It is a role that is set and fixed; I must play it out with dignity. With God's help, if I live, I will finish the novel. I will finish everything."

"A new, deep attachment" was to complicate Pasternak's life in the late 1940's and 1950's. Olga's "namesake," Olga Ivinskaya, entered Pasternak's world in 1946. She was arrested in November 1949 and was "transported to a place similar to the one where Sasha was," as Pasternak hinted in his letter to Olga of December 9, 1949. The romance of Olga Ivinskaya and Boris Pasternak, described in her memoirs, *A Captive of Time*, has no particular bearing on this correspondence.

Stalin's death in March 1953 soon put an end to "the daily and indiscriminate disappearance of names and people," as Pasternak put it in his New Year's greetings to Olga. The end of Stalin's rule brought a short-lived breathing spell to Russian life: "There came a break in that wearisome voyage, captainless and rudderless, on a shoreless sea of our making; something resembling fresh, life-giving air was wafted our way, enveloped us, and restored form and outline to our lives. It became easier to work. By its very existence this element of definiteness, be it but a promise of definiteness, made it possible to know where one begins and ends, what one wants, why one should have such strange wants, and what one should do about them."

During that interlude, several of the poems from the novel *Doctor*

Zhivago were published in the journal *The Banner*. Yuri Zhivago's poems were next published, in part, in the Soviet Union in 1980. By that time, the author had attained the status, world-wide, he ascribed to himself in a 1949 letter to Olga: "Boris Pasternak without any epithet, as though the name meant something in itself."

DIARY

In November of 1948 I saw Sasha's wife, Musya. There had been little news of her prior to that. During the blockade summer of 1943 the "mainland" (as they spoke of the Russia lying beyond the blockade zone) vanished from our horizon. Letters and telegrams did not get through. Once in a while a crumpled letter sent to a now-nonexistent addressee would fall into our hands. We would gaze at it in awe, like illiterates, then read and reread it dozens of times, take it to our friends, read it to our neighbors, beginning with the janitor, who, it would turn out, had been the first to read it at his own dinner table, among his friends, who had discussed it and shed tears over it.

One day I miraculously received a telegram, return message prepaid, from distant Siberia. It was from Musya, entreating me to wire her as to her parents' health. I had no doubt that they were no longer among the living (her father was very old, her mother wasted and ill), but I could not wire such terrible news without verifying it. What was I to do? I had not heard a thing from them in a long time. Musya's mother had occasionally dropped in to see us at the beginning of the war. I had not seen them since. She had not answered my New Year's card. Of course they were dead. Otherwise they would surely have sent word in the course of the years. Nonetheless, I had to go to Krestovsky Island and make inquiries.

I was a long time choosing the day. It was hard to make myself go to that ill-fated spot. Besides, there was artillery fire, my weakness, the trouble with my legs, the unreliability of the streetcars. But the day arrived and, sorrowfully, I set out.

Here I was on the island—Krestovsky. Once again blue sky, the blue Neva, the same bridge, the same unwinking sun.

I moved slowly, shuffling along, and searched a long while for the tragic dacha where Sasha had once lived. I couldn't find it. As if in a dream, I rubbed my eyes, returned time and again to the same spot, inquired of passers-by. Finally the truth emerged. The dacha no longer existed. It had been razed, broken up, and converted into firewood. The spot where so many people had lived and so many lives had passed was a wasteland without any trace of life. So there it was, that awful place where Sasha had suffered, where I had awaited news of him in a state of mortal fear, where a frightened hen had looked at me in terror out of the corner of her eye.

I was already aware that life, like a stage director, cleared the stage of actors and settings at the end of each act. But a blank space overgrown with weeds in place of a living, human habitation was a disturbing sight. There was no past. Nothing remained of Sasha's life. A vacant lot overgrown with weeds.

I answered Musya that her family had been evacuated to a place unknown to me. She was clever, she guessed the truth.

November 1948. A ring at the door. Covered with wet snow, Musya tumbles in and hangs on my neck. She laughs, lets out little cries, and hugs me. With her is a man in the uniform of the MVD, the secret police. He has the face of a degenerate, of a beast. I think to myself: Is she under guard? A keeper? Someone coming back from the same place? It turns out he is her husband, the head of her former camp; she works with him in the MVD and is proud of it.

God, how happy she is to be back in Leningrad! How she laughs, how life bubbles in her! She is drunk with happiness. She wants to sing, shout, kick up her heels.

"I want to get drunk, Olenka!" she says, intoxicated with joy. "Drink up; here's to my happiness!"

Sadly I raise my glass (they have brought food and wine). My heart sinks. In place of the brilliant Sasha, here is a secret police officer, illiterate, with an ugly animal face. And where are the rest? Sasha, Musya's mother weeping in my presence in fear for Musya's life, her father, my mother—all gone. How dead I was as compared with Musya! Does the camp in which I find myself exterminate life more effectively than hers? No, that's not it. She had hope and a goal before her, and that sustained her. I have nothing before me.

Life, life! In life everything is possible, any paradox. At my table sits a member of the secret police, and I feel warm and friendly toward him. I consciously bless him for protecting Musya, loving her, supporting her. With all my heart I identify with this strong young woman who has gone through such enormous trials, with this martyr who has had to suffer so terribly because she dressed well and worked at an arms factory. This muslin countess, this spoiled touch-me-not, underwent a penal servitude of which I am incapable of speaking. Musya's life was mutilated, like the lives of millions of others. Now she is faced with returning to Kolyma in the forests of the far north because she has been deprived of the right to live in any big city. Why?

To me she is Sasha's wife, and I know that Sasha would have accepted her new husband and would have wanted me to do so. Musya said: "No, no one, absolutely no one can understand my happiness, the fact that I'm here, I'm alive, that I triumphed over everything. . . . Only one who went through what I did could understand!"

They were both from the other world, the world of Soviet reality, the Soviet underground—from Kolyma, a legendary land of torment and slavery. I didn't ask the martyr a single question. Horrendous things arose like chilling vapors from her boots and overcoat, from her unwitting stories of how she walked some eighteen miles to "freedom" across a peat bog, at times in water up to the waist, her feet sunk so deeply in mire that she could hardly pull them out—and when she arrived, exhausted, it was not to be freed as she had hoped, but to be thrown into a labor gang. Or how one night in a violent snow storm—lost, frozen, her strength spent—she stumbled along beside a drooping nag with no road or landmark to be seen in the utter darkness, certain that she was about to meet her end, but her determination to hold on to the last enabled her to survive even that ordeal. She panned for gold, tended gardens, drove horses, dug ditches, felled trees, gathered peat, carried weights beyond her strength, and did filthy, servile jobs. Now her laughter and rejoicing were punctuated by glimpses of interrogations at which she underwent torture and humiliation. She was tempted into betrayal, but she "did not sell herself" for wine and candy.

I arranged for Musya and her husband to stay in another apartment, since it was illegal for me to house a returned convict (her passport had a secret mark on it known only to the police—and Musya's husband). They both spent the night in an excellent room, which they could have occupied for a whole month. But they disappeared early the next morning. Where, why, and for how long, I do not know.

Strange as it may seem, our brief encounter left me with the warm feeling of having been close to Sasha; I wanted the ex-wife of my poor brother to live near me.

Moscow, August 7, 1949

Dear Olya, my very own Olyushka,

How am I to thank you for your letter? One thing I didn't understand: exactly when did poor Aunt Klara die? I always remember her wearing a headdress like the ones village wet nurses wore, as Papa painted her more than fifty years ago (I have written this to Vladimir Ivanovich). Papa painted her more than once, using her as a model for various heroines in his early genre paintings, at the time of the Peredvizhniki.* Such she remained all her life—tall, graceful, strong, trustingly impetuous. I had hoped to see her sometime soon and anticipated much pleasure from the meeting.

Another thing I didn't understand was your accusing yourself of rudeness for returning the manuscript with someone coming here, without including in it a note of thanks. Can you have forgotten the amazing letter you wrote me after reading the manuscript? Didn't you ever receive my answer?

I was particularly struck by the coincidence of your letter coming at a time when I was feeling anxious about you and felt a strong urge to write to you. I seem to recall that you were expecting a visit from your sister-in-law at the time. Who do you mean, Olya—not poor Sasha's wife? Where is she? Is she with you now?

I prudently resist the desire to unburden my heart to you, for I must not do so. I formed a deep new attachment, but since my relationship with Zina is a genuine one, sooner or later I had to sacrifice the other. Strangely enough, so long as my life was filled with agony, ambivalence, pangs of conscience, even horror, I easily bore it and even took pleasure in things that now, when I have made peace with my conscience and my family, reduce me to a state of unmitigated dreariness: my aloneness, my precarious place in literature, the ultimate pointlessness of my literary efforts, the strange duality of my life "here" and "there," etc.

I was then writing the first book of the novel and translating *Faust*, encountering obstacles on every hand, working without full concentration, constantly plunging from carefree ecstasy to deepest tragedy, but I didn't care a hoot and imagined I would succeed at anything I put my hand to.

Now I have had to shut myself up at home, in part as a consequence of having exhausted my funds. In the past three or four years I have run through all the money I received for translations of *Henry IV* and *King Lear* and for two volumes of Shakespeare translations now being published by Art Publishers. In two or three months I will have to ask for a contract to translate, say, the second part of *Faust* (which I dislike) just to earn money. In the meantime I have hastily begun the second book of my novel. I want to finish it for my own sake; in this part, too, I want to express my ideas clearly and definitively on matters of life and the times.

* "The Wanderers," a movement of artists between 1870 and 1923, organized into the Society of Wandering Art Exhibitions. Members included I. N. Kramskoi, V. I. Surikov, V. E. Makovsky, A. M. Vasnetsov, V. D. Polenov, I. I. Levitan, and V. A. Serov.

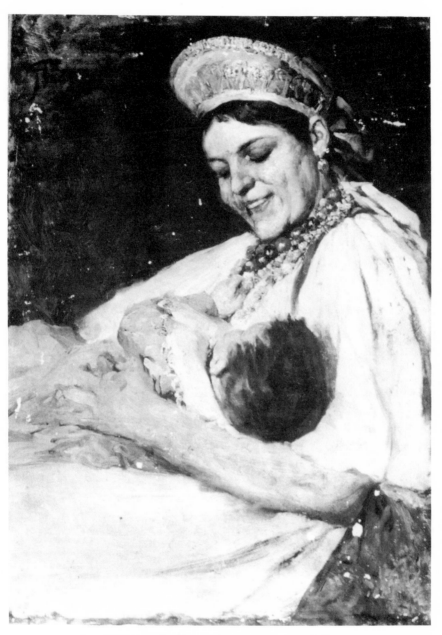

Aunt Klara in the dress of a wet nurse, with Borya.
Painting by Leonid Pasternak (1890)

Boris Pasternak. Moscow, 1948

But the further I go in this work, the more foolish and contradictory seem my aims, and the more mediocre my powers, my gifts, my status and circumstances.

I was shown the *Oxford Book of Russian Verse* (second edition) with Russian texts and Bowra's translations, and Bowra's book on Apollinaire, Mayakovsky, myself, Eliot, and the Spanish poet Lorca. In anthologies published abroad, Pushkin, Blok, and I are accorded more space than anyone else (I blush to say it). It becomes clear from notes and introductions that collections of my poetry in translation (these alone are mentioned) have passed muster on the market. They must have, if another publisher is putting them out in a new translation. And they speak not of "the best" or "the foremost" Soviet poet or anything of the kind, but of Boris Pasternak without any epithet, as though the name meant something in itself, as, for instance, we once published Verlaine or Verhaeren without any epithet.

Five years ago, when facts such as these were not discrediting (even subjectively, for one's own self) as they are in their new context, they could give satisfaction. Now their effect (I am still speaking for myself alone) is quite the opposite. They only serve to stress the disgrace of my failure here (both official and, apparently, with the public). In the final analysis, what am I worth—and indeed can I be of any worth, however slight, if the obstacle of blood and origin remains unsurmounted (the only obstacle that had to be surmounted), and what a pretentious nonentity I must be if I end up with nothing but a small, surreptitious following of Jewish intellectuals, and the most harassed and unfortunate of them to boot? Oh, if so it must be, then I would rather have nothing—what can I make of myself and why bother with me when heaven itself turns away so easily and completely?

Once before, during the war I believe, when Aunt Asya was still alive, I turned to you in a fit of despair and you comforted me. I wouldn't allow myself to "stand naked" before you now if I had not, without asking you, assumed you would not object. This letter is monstrous in its unbridled egotism, but allow me to make a feeble attempt to justify it. (1) A person has to be the victor in art, and since art is my enforced, unflagging, and inescapable labor and means of earning a living, I must be forgiven for being infected by the egotism of all those who practice it. (2) In speaking of affairs of the heart, I wrote of myself alone and not of another, not because of momentary blindness but because on this subject I am not free to speak, and even the little I said violated the pledge of silence I owe Zina.

P.S. Suddenly I am uncertain of Vladimir Ivanovich's address. Would you mind slipping this note into an envelope and sending it to him through the local mail?

If you should happen to answer this letter, I naturally beg you to make no mention of the romantic theme.

I love you very much, Olya. For some reason my heart is heavy. No longer does my life belong to me. It is a role that is set and fixed; I must play it out with dignity. With God's help, if I live, I will finish the novel. I will finish everything. It is important, and I must see that those near and dear to me are happy. Thank goodness they are all well. Again things are plentiful, beautiful, and marvelous here at the dacha. Despite the rain. The two Zhenyas are in Koktebel.* Stasik, Zina's son, is a good pianist and will probably enter the Chopin Competition in Warsaw. Love and kisses.

Forgive this callous letter.

DIARY

I began to work on Sappho. No matter how I gnawed at it or tried to take the problems by storm, nothing helped. I worked long and hard, with no results. I didn't accept the common conception of Sappho. It contradicted all the rules. The Lesbian theory seemed to me the height of vulgarity. Sexual excesses could not find realistic expression in the classical genre, which drew its themes from inner rather than outer sources. The masculine element is found in Sappho's songs, and it is expressed in typically matriarchal forms that make it difficult for modernizing researchers to recognize it. Sappho's songs cannot be dated precisely. But one thing is certain: Sappho, like Homer, belongs to folk art. The direct implication of the breakdown of genres is a breakdown of the social consciousness. The changed social outlook, in which the main role is played not by gods and nature but by man and society, created the lyric. Sappho's lyrics are on the border between thinking in images and thinking in concepts. The mythical picture of the world is edged out by a realistic, social picture.

Out of a variety of themes and personages arises the author. Sappho appears now in the third person, now (less frequently) in the first person. She is both the object and the subject of the theme. Like her characters, Sappho moves among the gods and merges thematically with the goddesses, who bear mythical names.

* A seaside resort (now called Planerskoye) on the Black Sea in the Crimea. It was earlier a well-known haven for Russian writers.

Moral and intellectual pogroms have spread like a plague through the cities of Russia. People in intellectual walks of life have finally lost faith in logic, have lost all hope. The purpose of the last campaign has been to cause concussion of the brain, with accompanying vomiting and dizziness. Intellectuals with Jewish names are subjected to moral lynching.

One should see the pogrom as carried out in our department. Groups of students rummage through the works of Jewish professors, eavesdrop on private conversations, whisper in corners. They make no effort to conceal their purposeful vigilance.

Jews no longer receive an education, are no longer accepted at universities or for graduate study. The university has been devastated. The finest professors have been dismissed. The murder of the remaining intelligentsia goes on without cease. Students, teachers, doctors, and professors are overloaded with senseless work. Everyone is forced to study, to take political examinations, men and women alike.

They strike at scholars with whatever means they have at their disposal. Throw them out of work, force them to retire, condemn them to nonexistence by banishment. Professors who survived last year's pogroms are dying one after another from strokes and heart attacks. Eikhenbaum is a complete invalid. Propp recently fainted in the middle of a lecture and was taken directly from the university to the hospital. A few days later Bubrikh,* hounded by *The Literary Gazette*, died at work. Bubrikh was a courageous, honest, humble man. Most cynical are the elaborate funerals with thousands of floral tokens given to these men. The Soviet authorities know how to honor their scholars.

The department is in complete disarray. Members keep baiting me, at the same time refusing to let me leave. The devil only knows what is going on—totally unchecked! An abstract of my Sappho has come out at last. It has broken through! The collection in which it is printed was held at the publisher's for three months before they dared let it out. But its hour came. It appeared. I am glad and sad.

[Inscription on an off-print of "Sappho":]
To Borya, my dear cousin

OLYA
November 27, 1949

* Dmitri Vladimirovich Bubrikh (1890–1949): Soviet linguist.

Leningrad, November 27, 1949

Dear Borya,

I am sending you the sediment rather than the wine. Even so, the epigraph ought to read, "Life asserts itself everywhere." This, at least, has pushed its way through to the light of day. In the original the stress is on textual analysis: I discover masculine images beneath the feminine ones. Philological subtleties make it a difficult work, the first of its kind in philological studies. I believe it is my swan song. I am growing weak, I am petrifying. In January I intend to retire (under a new law).

I have been very busy with Father's affairs. The Moscow Academy of Sciences sent a man to see me, and I am giving them some rare documents for study. The Museum of Communications here has already taken over Father's private archives. I have succeeded in achieving some recognition for him, the tragic failure (like our whole family). He was a great inventor. I recall how you alone appreciated this when you were young, in Petersburg. Do you remember?

I have been rummaging in the past, in photographs. A very painful occupation. I am writing Father's biography. It is a complicated and difficult task, tragic and inspiring. Man and history! Antipodes! But there comes a moment when the two merge. I am dazed by his ideas and flashes of insight.

Letters can no longer be used for conversation. I thought of coming to Moscow and I ought to do so, but my arms are like rubber, my head hangs, my legs dangle.

I understand you, but you are making a grammatical error when you conjugate yourself in the past tense only. It's nonsense that your only following is among "somnolent"* Jews. Who knows better than you that history is a chronicle not of the past but of the eternal present? Time will never make an old man of you because that which your name stands for does not age. You will go on writing splendidly, your spirit will remain alive, you are and will continue to be the pride of a vast following in your own country and not of a mere handful of the "somnolent" or of Jews. You are a man of the shifting tide rather than the even flow. The Greeks were wise: they taught that without intervals there could be neither music nor rhythm. Ah, how much there is to say! I will end by just giving you a hug and a kiss.

Yours,

OLYA

---

* Olga misread the Russian for "harassed" (*zagnanny*) as "somnolent" (*zaspanny*).

DIARY

I sat in a state of deep depression, reflecting on my own life. Those close to me had departed. Faith and conscience had gone. Maturity had come. Creativity had disappeared. Work, the last thing that kept me alive, had also gone. Huddled in Father's dilapidated old armchair, I suddenly began to feel palpably my debt to him. I must write about him, make him part of the history of technology. I am the last survivor. With me, the chain breaks off.

Somewhere, I recall, there is a thick, unwanted bundle of patents of his inventions. Sasha, fearing his arrest, brought us his portrait as a child, his savings book, and this packet. In a state of great agitation I found the dusty packet, put it on the window sill, and opened it with trembling hands.

Patents. One, two, ten; English, Russian; for an automatic telephone exchange, a typesetting machine. There is a document concerning the 1881 balloon flights, old play bills, an article on the history of the first theater in Evpatoria. And suddenly a thick manuscript: *The Memoirs of an Inventor*, typed by Father himself.

I read it from morning till late at night, not daring to interrupt this sacred task for food or rest. It was as if time itself were speaking. This lonely, neglected man, no longer counting on help from any source, was addressing the future. The bitter tale of stifled genius. Boundless faith in history. Foresight. Faith in one's ability to defend oneself, and strength of spirit unshakable in its purity and innocence. This manuscript was meant to lie undiscovered until I had matured to the point of appreciating its deep significance, and until this dark Russia with her hatred of mankind should begin to take a greedy interest in anything that could be traded— among other things, discoveries and inventions of universal interest for which Russia had the priority.

I understood now the meaning of "what has been written." What has been written creates; what is unwritten brings chaos and separation.

The discovery of Father's memoirs was a kind of miracle for me. I alone of the entire family was destined to find the manuscript and take out a patent on Father's life.

Moscow, December 9, 1949

Dear Olyushka,

I am writing in a fearful rush (a constant refrain). But this time really don't expect anything of my letter and don't "flatter yourself with hopes."

Your article was as sharp, impulsive, and succinct as usual, and rightly so. I was struck most of all by your old idea that the rise of the lyric was concurrent with the formation of a differentiated society and that "the soul of the lyric is a realistic outlook." Lack of time is the *only* thing that keeps me from expanding on Sappho.

Everything you wrote in this and the preceding letter about Uncle Misha is astonishing, astonishingly interesting, but what amazed me most is your courage and resolve. I for one could never have retained your clarity of vision in the face of the exhaustion and disillusionment caused by your past sufferings and your immersion in the great works of antiquity that have become part of your life. I am no less amazed by your ability to keep fresh the memory of one who was not so much your father as a victor who did not live to taste the fruits of victory, one who raises your spirits heroically; that you never lose sight of this is indeed astonishing.

New for me and fascinating were details I had never known before: the diversity of the inventions, stretching to the utmost the possibilities of "the given," so to speak, in a way almost prophetic, foretelling the course technology has actually taken. And about Thompson, of course. You are right—I did recognize Uncle Misha's pre-eminence intuitively, but I am surprised you should have remembered.

Now as to the "somnolent . . ." (could I really have used that word?— how odd). The letter must have been written in a fit of genuine, unfeigned despair lasting perhaps several hours. But that is not likely; I am too sure of myself. That I should have inflicted upon you—you, my beloved, talented, guileless cousin—the onerous task of encouraging me with your criticism in the hope that I might hear some flattering objective observation such as I could not anticipate, oh, how unspeakably base of me!

I was indeed a swine in those days. A great misfortune woke me up and set me almost straight again. My friend and your namesake, about whom I wrote you not long ago, fell upon bad times and has been transported to a place similar to the one where Sasha was.

I am working furiously, everything at once—my own writing and translations of both prose and poetry. I am burying myself in work.

Love.

Yours,
BORYA

What a pity you don't come! *It is of prime importance.*

Moscow, August 1, 1950

Dear Olyusha,

Irina has been telling us about you pleasantly, beautifully, and in detail: how you met on the street, how you saw her off at the station with meat pies and food supplies, about your hospitality, how you were dressed, about your friends, how much they love you, of your popularity with your neighbors. It was as though I had been with you and had steeped for a while in the ennobling atmosphere of cleanliness, coolness, spiritual elevation, and clarity that you create.

Too bad that you didn't come with Irina. It was a very convenient opportunity to have both a traveling companion and to visit us here. But we can easily renew this lost opportunity. Telegraph Fedya; he is in the city and will meet you and bring you to us.

It's quite possible you lost nothing by remaining true to your principle of staying at home, except one pleasure: that of seeing the joy your company brings me every minute we are together—and that's always pleasant.

That's all. I just wanted to say that I love you and see you in my mind's eye. The rest is silence.*

Yours,

BORYA

Dear Olyushka,

After a letter like this from Borya it is hard to say much. I can only repeat what I wrote on my last postcard to you. Irina's arrival with stories of you only makes us want to see you the more. Love, and I hope you will come soon.

Yours,

ALEXANDER

Peredelkino, August 1 (already!)

Leningrad, November 7, 1950

Dear Borya,

How do you like my bad luck with Zina's visit? We didn't even get to see each other! On Thursday, when she arrived, I had a full day of lectures at the university and private lessons in the evening, and on Friday I didn't go to work. The doctors think I fell ill because I had a tooth pulled the day before, causing a "disturbance of the blood." What a

* The final sentence is in English.

wretched creature I am! As a consequence of having had scarlet fever three times in my life, I keep getting nose and throat infections more and more often as I grow older. This charming state of affairs is really a chronic sepsis that breaks out on the slightest provocation. I don't know how I shall last out the winter. I have never been sick so often and so early in the season.

I don't go out on winter evenings, so I didn't get to hear your Stasik's concerts. But I did hear him play on the radio (I have a very good radio). Whether a pianist plays well or badly doesn't decide the question in my opinion. But Stasik has his own relationship to the music, and that's the important thing. He plays like one "in authority," the truest sign of real talent. Here's a kiss for Zina and you. I dream of a proper visit. Do listen to Zina's admonitions and promise to behave like a grownup. Take care of yourselves.

Yours,
OLYA

Moscow, December 20, 1950

Dear Olya,

Thank you for the letter and thank you for forgiving me my silence. Of late I have been communicating with you through the medium of word pictures and impersonations supplied by Moscow travelers to Leningrad (Fedya, Irina, Zhenya, and Zina). Thank you for the tone in which you supported the two-hour telephone conversation with Zina; she told me about it. Zhenya adores you, but you know that yourself. Zina may reward Lyonya with a week in Leningrad if he brings home good grades in the second quarter. He studies well but is often absent because, like you, he is very susceptible to colds. If they (he and Zina) do come, it will be in the first days of January, from the 1st to the 8th; they will phone you. So at last you will see him, born so fair and grown so dark.

Forgive me again for not writing anything of substance. What is there to write? Everything is well excepting that which is ill.

Love,
BORYA

Leningrad, December 25, 1950

Dear Borya,

Your news that I would soon be visited by the family gave me great joy, but I should warn you that I am seriously ill. Our "family" stomach ailment has struck me. I can't digest food; only with artificial assistance, at certain times, can I eat the most innocent fare. Loss of weight accompanies it.

I am impatiently awaiting the end of the first semester so that I can give attention to myself early in January, first of all by having a series of X rays taken. This requires certain procedures for which I have no time until January. Since I live alone, the way of life dictated by my illness is hardly one to be shared by others.

The diagnosis they give me in mid-January will either require me to put my personal affairs in order quickly or to go to the Caucasus for treatment, since I can neither live nor work in my present state.

I would not have written you this were it not for the news just received from you. By the way, of the two possible outcomes I would *sincerely,* without any affectation, prefer the worse one.

My love to all of you.

Yours,
OLYA

Moscow, December 30, 1950

Dear Olya,

Your letter frightened and distressed me. Yesterday, the day I received it, I wanted to call you, but they could put through a long-distance call only after one o'clock in the morning. I didn't want to add to your illness by frightening you and disturbing your sleep, so I gave up the call.

Here is what I wanted to tell you. I have had colitis and various other things of the same nature several times, as probably you have, too. The attacks dragged on, reached monstrous proportions, and took on the character of chronic illness only in periods of relative idleness, when I had the opportunity to pay attention to my health and began taking treatments for the pains, always poorly diagnosed because they are compounded of the sickness itself, the complications induced by the treatments, and the bother involved.

But even if you look upon this as words, words, words and haven't the patience to read such nonsense, surely you know that even the most terrible afflictions of the entire alimentary tract can be successfully treated surgically; I know many such cases quite well.

I don't remember whether I wrote you that Zina and Lyonya would not trouble you even if you were in the best of health. If all goes well, they will be in Leningrad between January 2 and 8 and have promised to inquire into your condition by telephone from the hotel.

My New Year's wish is that all will come right of itself, without the intervention of doctors and X rays.

Love,

BORYA

DIARY

The "free discussion" of Marr* going on in the newspaper *Pravda* took the form of cunning mystification. Stalin, the conjurer, the circus magician, assumed the role of a humble, ordinary reader defending the freedom of personal opinion.

Never before had he done anything so insidious. The impression created by his articles defies description. A bomb burst! Stalin annihilated Marr, a scholar he himself had created and encouraged. In good times he had demanded that the Central Committee of the Party turn the teachings of Marr into irrefutable dogma, thereby shifting all blame from himself to the executors of his will. Just before the articles appeared, innocent people were persecuted and killed as never before for criticizing Marr, and this on Stalin's orders. The whole thing was a scandalous and revolting betrayal. It was not, it seems, the government, nor Stalin, nor the Party that had founded academies and institutes for the study of Marr's teachings, not they who had awarded him the highest official decorations and held public ceremonies in his honor. It was . . . who? You. I. Ordinary mortals. The man in the street.

An unprecedented furor was created. Academies, universities, scientific research institutes, began shouting that their pundits had never caught so much as a glimmer of the truths Stalin had revealed. Of course they had not, for what Stalin asserted was unsupported by a single scientific institute or scholar, whatever his views. Scientific research, it turned out, had been completely in error, all scholarly works had been erroneous, and all the scholars specializing in this field were discovered to be simpletons. Ah, but not He. He alone, with no special training whatsoever, perceived

---

* The " 'free discussion' of Marr" of 1950 culminated years of turmoil in linguistics. During the anticosmopolitan repression that followed World War II, Marr's "New Theory" was forcibly imposed by Stalinist authorities as part of the campaign for ideological purity. Opponents were reviled at academic meetings and in the press, as Olga describes; many, including full members of the Academy of Sciences, were removed from their posts, or worse. Beginning on May 9, 1950, some two dozen linguists contributed articles to *Pravda* defending and denouncing Marr's theory on linguistic and Marxist grounds. On June 20, Stalin came out against Marr's "distortion" of the Marxist category of class and put forth his own formulation of Marxist linguistics, which in turn was raised to dogma in all social sciences until well after his death in 1953.

the truth and used administrative measures to see that it was accepted. In our country Marxism is neither a philosophy nor a scientific method. It is a bludgeon. It falls into the category of police power.

It was a sad summer for me. The sun never shone. The sepsis in my throat subsided, but my general state did not improve. I expected evil consequences for myself from the devastation of Marr. The teachers on our faculty ran about in a flurry of excitement, denouncing Marr and pointing fingers at one another. At meetings lasting all day long, yesterday's followers of Marr beat their breasts and confessed to having violated their consciences by teaching Marr's theories, the falseness of which they had been aware of all along. I did not attend any of these penitential orgies.

On the last day of the academic year one such ordeal took place at which I was the accused. While Marr was still revered, people shouted themselves red in the face trying to prove that I had nothing in common with him. Now they tried to prove that he and I were one.

By that time I felt nothing but revulsion. Once again I was torn between the longing to retire and the fear of retiring. No one did this voluntarily who was not dying or under the threat of arrest or dismissal. Such an action was unprecedented and always politically suspect. To leave was to make a break for freedom. But there is no such category of retired individuals in our country.

Moreover, I felt at times that I could not bear to give up the department whose creation had been my life's work, and which had become part of my mind and my heart. I had made it, I had given myself wholly to it. I had taught, guided, and perfected its staff, not allowing them to become prejudiced and bigoted. Now it offended me to see it turned into a battleground where people were pushed off the scene by factionalism and favoritism.

I did not keep silent, but I fought and realized that nothing would restrain my protests and indignation. People feared me as always, but they avoided me; they ignored my complaints and did nothing to prevent the ruin of the department.

Wherever you looked, in all our institutions, in all our homes, *skloka* was brewing. *Skloka* is a phenomenon born of our social order, an entirely new term and concept, not to be translated into any language of the civilized world. It is hard to define. It stands for base, trivial hostility, unconscionable spite breeding petty intrigues, the vicious pitting of one clique against another. It thrives on calumny, informing, spying, scheming, slander, the igniting of base passions. Taut nerves and weakening morals allow one individual or group to rabidly hate another individual or group.

Skloka is natural for people who have been incited to attack one another, who have been made bestial by desperation, who have been driven to the wall.

Skloka is the alpha and omega of our politics.

Skloka is our method.

Moscow, October 11, 1951

Olya! Where are you and how are you—that is, how is your health? Last winter you complained so of your innards that you frightened me and were frightened yourself (or just the opposite—you fearlessly awaited the worst). How are you now? Have you recovered, as I was sure you would?

All this last year the very act of writing has caused sharp pain in my left shoulder and part of my back and neck. That's why I haven't written even to you, limiting myself to writing for money to meet my obligations.

How is Vladimir Ivanovich?* How is Mashura, her husband and family? Give them my greetings and write me about them and about yourself. Assure Mashura that these are not mere words or an evasion; *you* have no need of such an assurance.

Best love.

Yours,

BORYA

Greetings from everyone—Zina, Lyonya, Zhenya (young Zhenya is in Cherkassy†), Alexander, Irina (Fedya is working in Novorossiisk; they have a daughter), Rosa (Fedya's wife), et al. All are safe and well.

Leningrad, October 17, 1951

Dear Borya,

I am very grateful to you for the letter, and for remembering me and not holding a grudge. I have thought of you so often lately that you must have been aware of it.

Zina probably associated my silence with our last meeting and the topic of discussion. But you must understand that it is quite the reverse; I was sparing not myself but you. I have had a series of disappointments that I did not want to impose upon you.

What can I say about my health? In early spring I was so bad I had to

* Klara Kaufman, Rozalia Pasternak's sister, married Alexander Margulius; their daughter is Olga's and Boris's cousin Mashura. After Margulius's death, Klara married Vladimir Ivanovich Lapshov.

† A city in the Ukraine.

go to the country outside of Leningrad for two months, where I spent an enormous amount of money on creating sanatorium conditions for myself. I had just begun to emerge from my prostration when trouble found me out and brought me back to the city, to the university. Two difficult months succeeded in erasing the barrier between treatment and suffering.

I am now retired, on pension. Please do not react to this lyrically, either in poetry or prose.

This spring Mashura and I became very close. It is a source of strength for both of us. She has a lively mind, an open and sincere nature, and her mother's temperament, and she is a person of real cultivation. Unfortunately they learned recently that Pavel, her husband, has a serious vascular disease.

I thank everyone for their greetings and you in particular for the imaginary cure effected by your devotion. I am brave; I won't allow myself to sink. I work, I live. I go to the theater often. I am again having trouble with my stomach, and not with it alone. But that is not the main thing.

Both Mashura and I send our sincere love.

Yours,
OLYA

Moscow, July 16, 1952

Dear Olya,

How odd that your letter should arrive just now. The strangest coincidence! Livanov* and his wife had just been trying to persuade Zina and me to go to Leningrad with them (the Moscow Art Theater is going there on tour); they had convinced us, had sent scenic designer V. M. Khodasevich for us, and had secured the cooperation of the theater administration in reserving a hotel room for us and a room in the house set aside for the actors in Terioki. And I declined.

But Leningrad remained a topic for discussion for a time, and a few days ago Zina and Lyonya did go to Leningrad with the wife and daughter of the Georgian writer Leonidze.† They left directly from town; I remained as usual at the dacha.

Yesterday, the 15th, I was in town and wondered whether Zina and Lyonya would see *Romeo and Juliet* on this trip. We hadn't mentioned it when they left; I didn't see them off and had forgotten to remind them of it at Peredelkino.

* Boris Nikolayevich Livanov (1904–1972): leading actor of the Moscow Art Theater.
† Georgy Nikolayevich Leonidze (1899–1966): Georgian poet.

I think they will be back on Friday the 18th. Perhaps I will hear from them that they ran into you on the street or that some other coincidence brought you together. I know that, if Zina has difficulty in getting hotel reservations (because she is not on an official visit), she will not seek aid from the publishers or the Writers' Union or anywhere else but will do something about it herself, just as she undertook the trip herself. As far as I know, she did not take a single Leningrad address with her and had no intention of looking up even Mrs. Livanova, who had invited us to Leningrad and who will certainly be as hurt as you will be if, for some unforeseen reason, you do not see each other.

How youthfully and with what clarity of mind you discuss the theater, the cinema, the change of artistic forms and their purposes, and how unerringly you identify the structure of theoretical phenomena and their counterparts, and with what a talent for philosophy!

I noted several such passages in your letter. They struck me as being very close to my position and my way of thinking, but your terse clarity is far superior to my manner of dealing with the same subjects. This is all very good, but in order to avoid turning my letter into a tract I will resist the temptation to make citations and footnotes.

Even if you singled out Livanov because you know that he is my very best friend, it still gives me pleasure to see that our attitudes toward him are similar. One cannot call him a failure or say that he is not understood or sufficiently appreciated, but his breadth of vision, his cultivation, his many interests, and the fact that he has not limited himself to being a character actor allow his confreres to frown upon him under many pretexts: that he is undisciplined, that he suffers delusions of grandeur, that he is not sufficiently professional and still shows signs of dilettantism, that he is a drunk and a rowdy, etc., etc.

July 19

Zina returned yesterday. Of course everything happened as I predicted. She did have trouble getting a room and only with difficulty managed to stay at the Hotel October. On one of their sightseeing expeditions they went to Terioki but didn't bother to find out Mrs. Livanova's address and made no attempt to see her. Thank you again for a brilliant letter, bursting with vitality and intelligence. At the end of the letter you have the sentence (you are explaining the absence of any reference to your daily life, health, etc.) "But long ago I lost you and Alexander as brothers." If this is a reproach and written in a tone of regret, then the loss is very easily rectified. The very moment you find yourself in need of those brothers for any reason whatsoever, you will discover that you haven't lost them.

If those words were meant in an entirely different sense, referring to a plane of existence above family relationships, then I understand you very well and in this case, too, all is well.

Love.

Yours,

BORYA

Leningrad [January 3, 1953]

Dear, darling Borechka,

I am overwhelmed by Alexander's letter with the news that you have fallen victim to the fashionable affliction.* I cannot tell you how upset and distressed I am, how it has quickened all my feelings. I had thought those "family relationships" of which you wrote—that you stood above them. But that is nonsense when we come face to face with that one great and serious circumstance that dominates our lives. They exist, these family relationships; they are strong, and perhaps they alone are of genuine value. One is made keenly aware of it at times like this.

Borya dear, fancy my not having received Alexander's first letter telling me of your illness! The news just reached me. He says you are already out of bed. Thank God!

I relived everything from the beginning, as though it had just taken place. I relived it for myself, for Mama, for Uncle Leonid and Aunt Rosa—for the whole family, through all the decades.

I embrace you, dear cousin, and weep with you for what you have suffered.

I am surrounded by friends who have had coronaries, the most remarkable of them being Boris Eikhenbaum, who has had three very severe attacks yet is now well and happy, as fresh as a cucumber.

God willing, all will pass and you will be none the worse for it. We all go about with our "vessels" in a precarious state. What else can be expected?

I embrace you tenderly, warmly, and am with you heart and soul. I hope you will be well in the new year, will recover and regain your strength. This summer I will certainly see you.

Yours,

OLYA

Mashura asked me to give you her heartfelt greetings.

---

* A heart attack in 1952.

January 3, 1953

Dear Zina,

You poor darling, how much anguish and anxiety you must have suffered! Don't be angry with me, Zina. Believe me, life in all its wretched simplicity is extraordinarily complicated, and what we criticize or take as bad usually has its justification. Differences in character and way of life often put people at a distance from one another, and sometimes completely alienate them. But is that so important? At our age, confronting as we do the great, the inevitable, everything else shrinks to nothingness. You are close to Borya, he is my cousin, and the rest is of no account. Believe me, I have lived through a great deal, and if life had placed us in a different relationship you and I would have seen each other in quite another light. Our natures, as you know, respond to people and events differently, but that doesn't mean that I harbor bad feelings toward you. If the beginning of our family acquaintance was a trial, there was good reason for it; and if now, after being with you, Borya should fall in love with another woman and I should transfer my allegiance to that other woman, I would be acting despicably. Is it surprising that the thought of his wife, whom Borya had brought to us first as his fiancée, then as his wife and the mother of his son, should have made me feel ashamed and embarrassed for him? Now that you are his wife and also mother of his son, you should understand and not ascribe what was then my unfriendliness (to speak frankly) to your personal qualities, but accept it as an involuntary and legitimate moral reaction. Is it not true that when you became part of Borya's life I wanted to love you and be a sister to you? You may find the gravity of my character uncongenial, and time may have raised a barrier between us, but believe me when I say (and I say it sincerely) that I stand before you with a pure heart and harbor no enmity toward you. Trifles mean nothing to me. If only you could feel toward me as I do toward you, I would be very grateful.

Give me your hand, Zina, and don't be angry with me.

I love you, sincerely sympathize with you in your anxiety about Borya, and wish both you and him only the best.

Kiss Borya for me.

Yours,
OLYA

Moscow, January 20, 1953

Dear Olya,

Your letter was waiting for me when I got home; I was discharged from the hospital the day it was received. The sight of it alone gave me great satisfaction: the energetic flow of your bold, confident handwriting, as it was before the war and earlier.

Thank you in particular for your words to Zina. She is not in the least angry with you and has never felt that anything complicated your relationship with her.

Everything that I write to you is for Mashura as well, but I cannot write her a separate letter because it is still difficult (for which reason I am writing in pencil). Thanks to her and to you for taking my illness so much to heart. Show her this letter or send it on to her.

They have charged me to be careful. I don't know to what lengths I must carry it. The fact that I have a heart inside of me makes itself felt constantly and in various ways, none of which causes me discomfort except for the anxiety of not knowing whether the signals are dangerous or not.

This mode of existence in enforced inactivity (they say I will have to consider myself ill for six months to a year) is similar to my former inactivity caused by an overabundance of strength and health; it was that stretch which prepared the way for this one.

During the early moments of danger in the hospital I accepted the thought of death with calmness and a feeling almost of bliss. I was conscious that I would not be leaving the family without funds to tide them over the initial period, and I knew they had good friends. I looked back on my life and found nothing accidental in it—rather, a sequential logic operating from within, which promised to perpetuate itself.

The force of this logic told even in my moods at those moments. I rejoiced that on being brought to the hospital at night I was put to bed in a corridor overcrowded with a miscellany of mortals at death's door, and I thanked almighty God for having created me an artist, capable of being moved to tears of triumph and ecstasy by the contemplation of form in all its manifestations—the city rising outside the windows, the juxtaposition of light and shadow, of life and death.

Much love.

Yours,

BORYA

Give my greetings to Eikhenbaum, if he remembers me and if you see him. Here is an astonishing fact: just ten minutes before my heart attack I was walking along Bronnaya Street and on the opposite side I saw Eikhenbaum, or a man very like him, coming toward me. If it was Boris Mikhailovich, he must surely have responded to the glance I fixed on him. I vaguely remembered that he had been very ill, and the thought occurred to me that a person can never foresee what is going to happen to him. Ten minutes later . . .

Love.

Leningrad, January 25, 1953

As I walked home along the wintry street the other day, I reviewed my life for the hundredth time (it has become a habit with me of late). Naturally you figured in it. It was with thoughts of you in my mind that I caught sight of your letter in the mailbox.

Thank God I again see your handwriting and hear your voice.

Let me tell you about Boris Mikhailovich. He was touched and flattered by your greetings. It was not he on Bronnaya Street, but the strange coincidence is to be explained by your extraordinary sensitivity. To your question ("if he remembers me") he answered: "Not only do I remember him, but the name of Boris Pasternak has a special ring for me. It signifies much that is great, and it is impossible 'to remember' or 'not to remember.'" In any case, Boris Mikhailovich is a rare specialist on heart attacks. He asked me to tell you the following: (1) Recuperation really does require one full year. One must do no work in that year, but when it is over, one feels renewed. Boris Mikhailovich cannot believe that he was as good as sentenced to death. He is perfectly healthy now and fully able to work. (2) Coronaries are dangerous between the ages of forty and fifty. At your age they are more easily cured. (Boris Mikhailovich is sixty-six years old.) (3) If you do not suffer from hypertension or angina pectoris, you will forget in time that you ever had a coronary, so successfully does it heal.

I felt that I had to tell you these three things—this by way of apology, because I don't want to draw you into a correspondence. Pray don't think you have to answer. I understand perfectly that you need rest, especially rest from writing.

No doubt you are already at a sanatorium. At any rate let me remind you that an hour's ride from Leningrad brings one to the village of Komarovo (the former Kellomäki, near Terioki), a place with a divine climate and comforts. They say the air there has no equal. The Writers' Union has a house there, a kind of hotel for writers, with separate, comfortable rooms and special food. That is where Eikhenbaum recuperated.

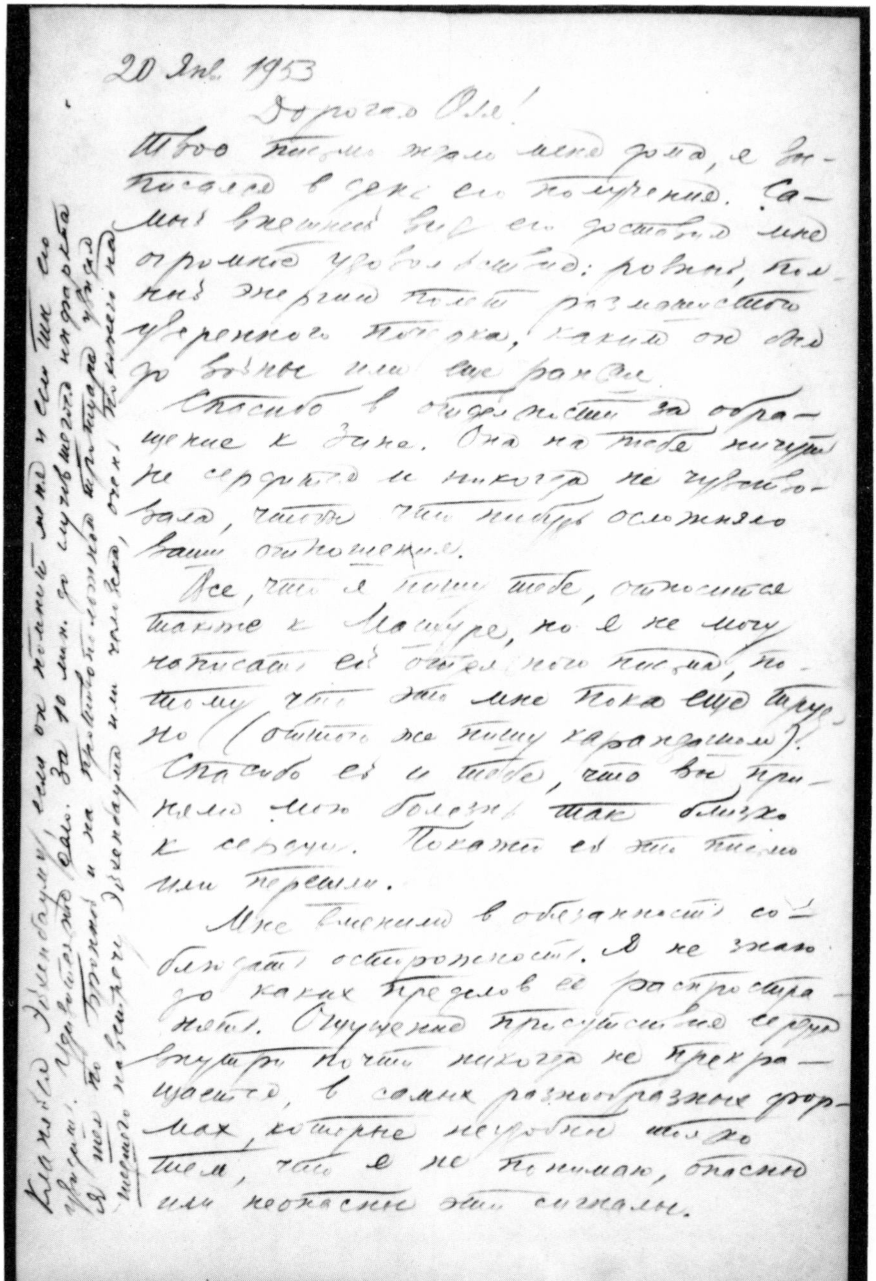

20 Янв. 1953

Дорогая Оля!

[handwritten letter text in Russian cursive]

First page of a letter from Boris Pasternak to Olga Freidenberg,
dated January 20, 1953

17-XI 54

Боря, родной мой, у вас письмо такое белое, но оно совершенно потрясло меня каким-то этическим величием твоего духа. Ты так мудр, благороден и высок, так велико твое пониманье жизни и истории, что человек не может, читая тебя, не потрясаться. Слезами могу ответить тебе, не словами.

Ты можешь говорить то и так, как оно эмоционально лежит в животе невысказанных дум, еще не доверенных событий. Когда называл Ба тебе повивальной бабкой. Ты писатель и еще. Но разве я мо-

First page of a letter from Olga Freidenberg to Boris Pasternak,
dated November 17, 1954

I wish you a complete recovery. I cannot tell you how distressed I was by your illness. And how I love you, how dear you are to me.

Mashura's husband showed stomach cancer in his X rays, but my love for him made me refuse to accept the diagnosis and I believed my optimism was capable of changing it. Just imagine, it worked: faith proved more reliable than X rays. He just has an ulcer.

My best love. Greetings to Zina and Lyonya. I join them in their concern for you with all my soul. Take care of yourself.

Yours,
OLYA

DIARY

I am used to all sorts of hardships; I have suffered everything. Yet, unable to die, I remain among the living.

Everyone knows by this time that it is forbidden to engage in scholarly research. To introduce original ideas, to cite or make references to scholarly works, to pose genuine problems, is the equivalent of being caught in a political crime.

I am ready for anything, even that. Long ago I reconciled myself to never being published; I have suffered defeat in the principal struggle of my life. But I still want to write. I have accumulated a vast amount of material. It must be organized. Before me lies a grandiose undertaking: to write a book generalizing all the knowledge and ideas I have amassed in a lifetime of intellectual labor. It is to be called *Image and Concept*, and in it I want to demonstrate that a concept is an image transformed and that life renews itself from within. I wish to show that concept and image are not to be separated and that poetry arises out of concepts. Greece speaks with me and to me; I understand her idiom. Never, anywhere, does it become conceptual. So poetry was just emerging in ancient Greece.

The catastrophe is that I am no longer equal to such a task. My time for creative endeavor has run out. Old age has destroyed my soul before my body. I am mortally tired.

Leningrad, May 27, 1953

Dear Borya,

I think of you often. I inquired of Alexander back in April about your health but got no answer. One can hardly expect letters to get lost these days. I don't know what to think.

Our city has become provincial. Everything that is vital, that speaks, acts, and thinks, is straightway transferred to Moscow. No ideas or activi-

312

ties are left. "Provincial" is an ancient word of bad repute; eventually
Rome was caught in it as in a flagon, and all her energy evaporated. Here
it manifests itself in petty-mindedness, in travesties of law suits and cari-
catures of social incongruities, as in *The Death of Tarelkin,** in the tearing
up of apartments for fundamental repairs with or without temporary
asylum offered to the occupants. In how many ways have our writers
lampooned provincialism, from *The Inspector General* to *Poshekhonye*!†
But it basically should be depicted faceless and blind, or at least indifferent to and ignorant of the term "life." I can't tell you how depressed I am
by this funereal provincialism! Our house is at present being torn up
without asylum being offered us. Everything is being smashed, ripped,
reduced to rubble, in a most stupid and senseless way. This absence of
reason and purpose in respect not to philosophy, literary criticism, and
epistemology but to toilets and flues is insufferable.

I may sound petty, but my life is so mixed up that I no longer understand what is petty and what is not.

Mashura has come upon misfortune. Pavel, her husband, had an operation for a stomach ulcer and came through it well. Then they let him get
peritonitis, and his heart, which was not supposed to "hold out" (he had
had angina pectoris and a coronary), refused to give up. And so he
endured lingering torture. In the end he died, of course. Without the
operation he might have lived several years more.

What can I tell you about myself? I accomplished a good deal this
winter. But I write with a heavy heart, unevenly, repetitiously, going off
on tangents. People, circumstances, and the epoch have robbed me of
faith in my own resources. My life was to have justified my being born of
such a mother and father. But my stubbornness and loathing for oppor-
tunism have kept me from winning social position. I do, however, take
pleasure at the age of sixty-three in facing the years of my life and
justifying to them what I have done.

For the past few years I have been working on the aesthetics of antiquity. Greek tragedies are my material. The antique chorus presents
special problems arising from dialects and the archaic quality of thought,
images, and expressions. Few there are among us now who know Greek
tragedies better than I do or can lecture on them better. For the last ten
years I have worked with my pupils only on the tragedies and Plato's
Symposium, the alpha and omega of classical literature.

I have made some interesting discoveries. I would stake my soul on the

* A comedy (1869) by Alexander Vladimirovich Sukhovo-Kobylin (1817–1903).
† Probably a reference to *Bygone Days in Poshekhonsk* (1887–1889) by Mikhail
Evgrafovich Saltykov-Shchedrin (1826–1889).

truth of them. The main thing is that I could have made them only by pursuing the path I chose. In this lies my "justification."

I spent the summer near Terioki, in the academic paradise of Komarovo, where for a room with a veranda I paid 4,000 rubles! Physically I am "okay," as they say these days—mentally, too, though I am terribly exhausted spiritually. I want to say "mortally," "irreparably," for there is a limit to all things. As far as my stomach is concerned, sometimes it is better, sometimes worse; this may be connected with an ulcer, but I am not going to take any treatments. Things could be worse.

Love.

Yours,
OLYA

Moscow, July 12, 1953

Dear Olya,

I can't believe my eyes that at last I am writing to you. Thank you, but please don't write me such marvelous letters. It isn't pleasant to think myself a beast for leaving them unanswered day after day.

Faust, my own writing, etc., are no excuse: my basic vileness remains evident. It is by my own free will, or rather because of my extreme egotism, that now, to a greater extent than ever before, I sacrifice everything else for the sake of two or three works that, after my heart attack, cannot be put off.

I must die as myself, not as a remembrance of myself (as you yourself wrote). I must finish the novel and another thing or two; not that I *must*—the expression is wrong—but that I want to, want to with indomitable will. How do I feel? As happy as can be, for the simple reason that a feeling of happiness must accompany my efforts if what I have planned is to succeed—that is an absolute prerequisite. According to some predetermined pattern, the feeling of happiness comes back to me from what I have written, as in a kind of manufacturing process: the tangible return on an original investment.

I have sent off the proofs of both parts of *Faust*, and I completely rewrote, with an entirely new interpretation, at least a tenth of this veritable river of verse—600 pages!—led on by my curiosity as to whether I could permit myself the luxury and the daring, taking no account of the hours spent day and night, of giving birth to a *Faust* that would appeal to both the mind and the imagination, a *Faust* that would occupy a place in space as a solid body, not as a force, a *Faust* in accord with my own present judgment and feeling.

I found what you said in your letter about Greek tragedy and Greek choruses very important. How hard I sought for something from the classical world in the trimeters and choruses of Act III, Part 2! And in the netherworld rituals of Act V. Ah, what a pleasure it was to struggle with expressing all that, so that it sang, breathed, lived! Both Goethe and I did best with the most difficult, elusive, and intractable parts: the Greek netherworld of Act III and the contemporary, Christian afterworld. I think the book will come out in the fall, and the threat of your having to read it grows and is borne down upon you by this boastful letter.

I haven't told you a thing. You see how eagerly I press you for the pardon I seek, cramming it in monstrous haste into a single sentence covering the entire letter, a haste evident even in my handwriting, which may give you concern as to whether or not I have fallen ill again.

All my love to you. I felt Mashura's loss deeply. I didn't know her husband well, but I knew him to be a good man. I liked his manner, his mind, his masculine optimism and equanimity. If I can, I will write her soon. Forgive me. I am writing even to you in a sort of transparent fashion, without feeling what I am saying. I have been living with you and your letter all this time, but passively; actively I have plunged with odious greed into my work to the exclusion of everything else.

All my love.

Yours,

BORYA

Moscow, December 30, 1953

Dear Olyusha,

Happy New Year! Why haven't I written you? As a consequence of my fundamental baseness, of course. But there are other reasons as well. We have got to meet and live together for a while. Only in such circumstances does an exchange of news come naturally. But it's not the news that is of consequence; it's the clearing up of our philosophical stand as we chat about this and that. Another reason I haven't written is because everything is going well—more or less—and to write when things are going well is very like boasting, or *is* boasting.

Nothing has basically changed with me except the one thing, the most important thing in the lives of all of us. The daily and indiscriminate disappearance of names and people has stopped, the fate of the survivors has improved, and some have returned.

Everything good you predicted for me in the near future, after the heart attack, began to materialize toward the end of summer. I think I wrote you about it. I succeeded in revising both parts of that monstrous colossus *Faust* to my satisfaction. The satisfaction I felt after turning in the proofs unfortunately grew as I awaited the appearance of the book and created the illusion that in this translation I had achieved something significant in the sense of its being an almost touchable, tangible whole and a well-ordered system of thought, as well as being something new, palpable, instantly revealed. Now *Faust* is out. I see that I was wrong; my intuition deceived me. But I am not disappointed. My misconception of the inner essence was the price I paid for success in another aspect—in achieving a natural flow of form and language without which the reading of a text of nearly 600 pages of lyrical verse would have been impossible. I strove for this from the outset, and I achieved it.

I have finished the novel in the roughest, most superficial draft, a bare telling of the story, still without the epilogue I have in mind, and I have written a dozen or so new poems. It is foolish of me to tell you all this. Of what import is the mere enumeration of facts? You can, however, conclude from it that I am well and in good spirits.

Of late Zina has had frequent liver attacks, so we canceled our New Year's party. Yesterday and the day before she was in great pain, but she is better today.

All the above is just an extended introduction to the one important thing, to my request that at the first opportunity, in early January, you write me about yourself and Mashura, how both of you are doing and what's new. Please give her my best wishes and greetings for the New Year. All my love.

Yours,
BORYA

Leningrad, December 27, 1953

Borya dear, where is *Faust*? I didn't dare inflict on you a relative's effusions, but I had the urge to let go a broadside of joyful exclamations. The fact is that, without knowing anything about how your work on *Faust* was progressing, I had been waiting for the final result for years and had accumulated on my desk a heap of notes marked "Faust." That means I was getting ready to write you about it. And suddenly—your announcement that it is already at the printers!

Happy New Year! Happy New *Faust*! But where is it?

Many kisses,
OLYA

Beloved cousin, my own dear Olyushka,

Just think, what a coincidence! I wrote you a letter this morning, deliberately dull and ordinary so as not to oblige you to write a long answer. My lack of enthusiasm for my *Faust* and all my remarks are sincere, well-founded, and remain in force. I took the letter when I went out for a walk and forgot to mail it. I meant to send it off this evening. Suddenly your postcard arrived, so full of warmth and love that it changed the whole tone of our conversation.

I will send you *Faust* tomorrow, but believe me, I am finished and done with it—it is a thing of the past. I am not at all impatient about it; you need not even read it. I beg you not to write me at length about it, and give it no thought. Now pray don't think I am just putting this on, being coy and coquettish.

I made an effort in my first letter to assure you, without entering into details or giving evidence, that all goes very well with me. Even earlier, when things were at their worst, I staked out for myself an independence for which I might have paid a terrible price at any moment. Now I can lay claim to this independence with significantly less risk. But that is not the source of my well-being. It has many causes, some real, some imagined. Outwardly nothing has changed. My time has not yet come. I have no intention of writing rubbish just to have it published. What I am writing now, which comes closer and closer to what I think and feel, is not for publication yet.

Thanks for the postcard. Love.

Yours,

BORYA

As you will have gathered from my first letter, I wasn't even going to send you *Faust* so as not to trouble you. How can I explain it? These are elementary things, from elementary physics. *Faust*, I myself, my works and my joys, all require air if they are to exist, take on meaning, and be set in motion. They are unthinkable in a vacuum. But there is no air as yet. Still, I manage to find happiness without air. Do try to understand me.

[Inscription in Goethe's *Faust*:]

To my dear cousin Olya,
so talented, clever, and courageous

From Borya

For the new year 1954

December 31, 1953

Dear cousin Olechka,

This is a warning in answer to your telegram, a warning to spare you an unnecessary expenditure of time and energy, to spare you an unnecessary "pea in your shoe," as the late Tsvetayeva used to say. I am writing you a third letter as well to tell you how secret and dual my life is, how dispersed, how full of contradictions. I have been supremely happy in recent months, yet I despair when I see how impotent this inner state is to influence the outer state. Though I am writing you a third letter about this, I still have not been able to explain anything.

Please don't suffer for me; don't think I am a victim of injustice, that I have not received my due. It is surprising that I remained whole during the purges. You cannot imagine the liberties I allowed myself! My future was shaped in precisely the way I myself shaped it. I foresaw a great deal and, more important, rejected much of it. I foresaw a great deal, but I did not store up enough patience to last me to the end. As I wrote you, my time is still far off.

You must realize that *Faust* is not the main thing. There are other things that outweigh it in importance—the novel, the completion of the novel, new poems for it, a new state of mind. This inner world is of vast significance; the outer world signifies nothing.

I am aware that there is a lot that is good in the translation. Need I tell you that this work is an integral part of my life, that it was written with my heart's blood at a time when people were being thrown into prisons, camps, etc., a time of horror, of guilt, and of loyalty? But this, too, is not the main thing.

Last summer I revitalized the text by pouring into the proofs my last store of living water. My revisions—whole new pages (and a great many of them)—left me for good when I sent the proofs back; not a trace of them remained with me, and so great was the haste in which I worked that I didn't remember a word of the new text. Only now have I seen the results, and in spite of everything I must say there are not more than a dozen lines in the whole book whose rigidity continues to shock me. They could easily have been rewritten, but I lacked the courage to depart freely from the letter of the original. As for the rest, it all looks and sounds just as I wanted it to; it has taken the form I dreamed of.

What disappoints me is something else. Above and beyond a good translation, Goethe needs to be reconsidered, and reassured, by means of an inspired introduction and commentaries. These are lacking. How many times did I offer my services! But how could so responsible an ideological task be entrusted to an uninitiated non-Party person like myself? I could have paraphrased the contents in succinct, lively, accessible prose, I could have pointed out the undeniable oddities of the original and its moral inconsistencies, things that now remain unidentified and unexplained, and I could have made *an honest and eager* attempt to find an explanation for them. No doubt my efforts would have thrown additional light on the revelations made by the translation itself. Ah, how unnecessarily free we were in our youth, when we had neither the knowledge nor the skill to accomplish anything.

Pray don't write me a long letter; don't bother to make an elaborate, complex analysis. You know how I value and love your letters—that's not the point. Don't spoil the satisfaction that you may receive from a few of the pages by being weighed down by a wearisome and imaginary obligation to answer, to repay. Don't torment yourself by making hurtful comparisons and saying how great this is and how small the appreciation. I cannot tell you about all the covert, unofficial appreciation fortune has bestowed upon me undeservedly; it always comes so unexpectedly, but to speak of it would be silly and immodest. I could give you the most fantastic, unbelievable examples, but they involve other people, and I have no right to divulge their secrets.

Forgive me. Why should I write all this? I don't know the rules of proper communication.

All is well with me, Olya.

Yours,
BORYA

Leningrad, January 6, 1954

Dear Borya,

I was just about to answer your two letters as they deserve—especially the second, which overwhelmed me with its brotherly love and sincerity (I reached out to you so, and how my spirit was raised up!)—when *Faust* arrived.

You really ought to be happy, to enjoy the highest, the only true satisfaction earth can offer. And how many times you thought all was over with you!

When the creative spirit is struck barren, it is by the hand of God. It brings a pause for the restoring of strength, without which there could be no rhythm. When you fell silent, how much remained for you to do! How much lay ahead!

Faust is a monument to your glory. I took up the book in professional hands, I looked into it, and understood.

But why should it have been *Faust*? Why should you have needed *Faust* after your own writings and after Shakespeare?

I am amazed to find your strength overflowing at the age of sixty-four. You emerged from prison not pale of face but robed in ermine, erect in your pride as an artist, radiating the splendor of fullness and proportion.

I bear no love for the homeland of Purishkevich and the Third Department.* I am sick to death of an aching stomach and nausea, which is a strain on the heart. My head goes round and I vomit, disgustingly innocent of being pregnant. For years I have not spoken out to you because of Shpekin.†

But when I took up your book I thought, This has the feel of culture, this is its tangible manifestation. This is a treasure created here and now, not by the hand of man but by the shed blood of Russian culture. Nothing can wash it away.

The door opened, you entered, you stayed. That is the whole story.

Here there can be no talk of taste and schools. Of whether you represent the past or the present, Surkov or Isakovsky, Burliuk‡ or the bourgeois writers—or Alexander Alexandrovich Smirnov. These contemporary Russian writers will break their teeth on *Faust* because it is broader (for Russian intellectuals) than Shakespeare or Pasternak. This is the first Russian Goethe, to say nothing of the first East German Goethe. It is a political fact. For those who are blind and for those who see. The language is superb—natural, precise, concise, full of life. Simplicity of form is joined to the fullness of Goethe's wisdom, and, as in any mature work of art, one easily loses oneself in its depth. There is a beautiful play of irony and jest, giving the reader an insight into medieval German life. All is color and movement. The sentiments (so numerous) and the endings of each part are sharply accentuated. Enchanting is the music of the verse.

You cannot but be in good spirits. You have been given the happiness not only of being great but also of becoming great. You have been given the joy of self-fulfillment.

I haven't finished reading it yet, but one thing is clear: you have changed the nature of translation, transforming it from a stranger dressed up in a Russian caftan into a fellow countryman with whom one com-

* The Third Department was the czar's own secret police during the last century of imperial Russia. Vladimir Purishkevich was a right-wing political figure during the years preceding World War I and the February Revolution of 1917.

† The name used by Olga and Boris for the censor of correspondence.

‡ Alexei Alexandrovich Surkov (1899–): Soviet poet and literary activist. Mikhail Vasilevich Isakovsky (1900–1973): Soviet poet. David Davidovich Burliuk (1882–1967): avant-garde Russian poet and artist.

municates without the feeling of being away from home. How bitter to realize that Mama will never see it! How she would have loved it!

Your inscription in the book surprised and wounded me. How much better to have left out that appraisal, coming so unnaturally from a cousin's lips. You are an incorrigible littérateur.

Much love.

Yours,
OLYA

I am sure you will receive official recognition.

Leningrad, March 18, 1954

Borya,

In April they are performing your *Hamlet* at the Alexandrinka.* Don't you want to hear how you sound? The fact that they are staging it is very significant. You might come for the dress rehearsal or the first night. I can find out the exact date. You could stay with me, poor little orphan.

Freindlich, a talented actor, will play Hamlet; he was very good as Khlestakov. I'm sure you would be pleased. Love.

Yours,
OLYA

Moscow, March 20, 1954

Dear Olyushka,

My sincere thanks for the postcard. I know about that performance; Kozintsev, the director, has been in correspondence with me and also invited me to Leningrad. I will not come. I have to and I want to finish the novel, and until it is finished I am a fantastically, maniacally unfree man. Take this, for example.

In the April issue of the journal *The Banner* they are going to publish ten of my poems from the novel *Zhivago*, most of them written this year. I have been reading them to friends and they bring me great pleasure. They might be not ten but twenty or thirty, if I allowed myself to go on. It is much easier to write them than it is to write prose, but only prose brings me closer to the absolute; it is this that supports me and determines my life, my behavior, etc., and creates an inner, spiritual edifice, one story of which is dedicated to what would otherwise be the meaningless and shameful occupation of writing poetry. I long to throw off the

---

* The play was directed by Grigory Mikhailovich Kozintsev (1905–   ), an outstanding director of Soviet theater and film.

yoke of prose and work in a field to which I am better suited and in which I can better express myself.

Or another example. Outside of Zina's untouchable savings, my resources have become temporarily too thin to cover my current expenses. Again the blame must be put on the unfinished novel, which gives me no time to assert myself, take necessary measures, seek aid from publishers, etc.

Because of my preoccupation with the novel I don't bother to argue when people say foolish things, and for want of time I agree with everyone, and at editors' requests I make changes in new editions of my translations that ought not to be made.

So you see what a misfortune this novel is, and how necessary it is that I free myself of it as soon as possible. For the same reason I am writing you in haste, for which I ask your forgiveness.

I haven't yet thanked you for your generous sentiments, for your kind letter about *Faust*. It was that very letter I wanted and had no time to warn you not to write. How trusting you are if you imagine anyone will appreciate this translation or even take any notice of it (I am referring to the hopes you expressed in your letter). I never have and never could count on any such thing.

Now to speak of something else, much more important. If you know any of the participants in the performance, convey to them my gratitude and best wishes for success. Let them not think, if I do not come forward, remain silent, and fail to communicate with them, that I have too high an opinion of myself, that I am indifferent to them, and that their work means nothing to me. Sometimes I write letters with enforced haste and suffer the consequences: they offend by sounding as if I were grudgingly and perfunctorily fulfilling a duty. I fear I have offended Kozintsev in this way.

Well, Olga dear, you see I have written you a monstrously stupid letter, repeating "the novel, the novel, the novel," over and over again. But I do love you, and how I long to see and talk to you! This will come about, is sure to come about—you'll see.

All my love.

Yours,

BORYA

Moscow, April 2, 1954

Dear Olyushka,

They sent me the *Hamlet* playbill that is already on display in your town. I am delighted, but there is a grammatical mistake. It reads: "In

Pasternak Translation"; it ought to read: "In Pasternak's Translation." I wrote Kozintsev about it in a polite, unassuming way, asking that they correct it in subsequent playbills, i.e., that they put my name in the possessive case. If you have any friends in the theater or anyone working on the production, do me the favor of reminding them of my request. See that someone checks on its being carried out. If that makes your life difficult or you feel uncomfortable about it, or if you have no connections, then forgive me and forget it.

All my love.

Yours,
BORYA

Leningrad, April 3, 1954

Dear Borya,

I did what you requested, but I cannot vouch for the printers' interest in grammar. I will see when the bill for the first performance, on April 11, is up. The very best actors are engaged. I will be at the first night and write you my impressions. Everyone here, including the public, feels that you have slighted us.

May we meet on paper soon!

Yours,
OLYA

Moscow, April 4, 1954

Dear Olya,

Answer one thing: have they corrected my name on the playbills ("Pasternak's")? This triviality probably astounds you, given my apparent indifference to everything else concerning the performance. But life comes back to you in bits and crumbs from all directions. One cannot keep up with it. I have already heard one opinion held by the actors of a Moscow theater now on tour in Leningrad—rivals, and not well-wishers. They praised Polonius and the ghost and found Hamlet too active and optimistic, expressing nothing of the tragedy. But such is the translation. The poor actors! They will bring me more gossip.

All my love.

Yours,
BORYA

Leningrad, April 10, 1954

The mistake has been corrected. Tomorrow is the opening. I can't wait. Will send you an account. I'm writing on the way from the theater to the post office, my hands full of sausage, frankfurters, and buns for my friend. So long until the day after tomorrow.

Yours,

OLYA

Moscow, April 12, 1954

Beloved Olyushka,

Thank you for keeping me informed of events so quickly and enthusiastically. I've heard very good opinions of the performance. Livanov, my good friend, who was to have played Hamlet at the Moscow Art Theater fifteen years ago, often goes to Leningrad. Recently he was there with his wife (both friends of Cherkasov*), and they asked him and Kozintsev to be allowed to see the dress rehearsal. They were refused. Lili Brik† has left here to go to the opening. It's a theatrical event, and opinions will be varied and contradictory. Don't suffer for me, as I always admonish you. I must rush off to an evening of Hungarian poetry. In the April issue of *The Banner*, several of my poems from the novel will appear. On the 16th there will be a discussion of *Faust* (my translation) at the Writers' Union. So far these things seem unimportant to me; so far they don't touch me. If only I can save my strength for the big issues ahead and not go to pieces over all this preliminary nonsense. How much more there is to do and say! Here's a big kiss for you, Olga dear.

Yours,

B.

Leningrad, April 11, 1954

Dear Borya,

The performance was magnificent, but without Shakespeare. They staged *Hamlet* as a contemporary, realistic, psychological drama. When I read in the paper that Hamlet demonstrates "distorted social relations" and that Kozintsev's goal is to "create a hero defending the people's aspirations toward a rational life, free of falsehood, violence, and the

* Nikolai Konstantinovich Cherkasov (1903–1966): Leningrad actor.

† Lili Yurevna Brik (1892–1978): wife of the formalist critic Osip Maximovich Brik (1888–1945), hostess of an avant-garde salon and close companion of Mayakovsky.

oppression of man by man," I was prepared to see in Hamlet a popular democrat or a precursor of the Decembrists. There is some of that in the play—a pantomime display of the simple folk, an uprising led by Laertes in the dress of a ship's master, with a torn white blouse. But it is no more than "an approximation of our contemporary life." In an effort not to be routine, the theater showed considerable innovation in interpretation and staging. It began with a prologue. Darkness. A clock on a tower strikes, a clock with mechanical medieval figures. In the depths of the stage there is a tomb before which Hamlet is kneeling. People gather round him respectfully. They love Hamlet, are drawn to him. He bestows gifts on the beggars.

Claudius is small, red-haired, pale; he is vain. He looks at himself in a pocket mirror. Gertrude is a beautiful woman, not pompous but with a touch of arrogance. Polonius is, as always, stout and cunning. Laertes is a rogue. Ophelia appears in her final scene without flowers and garlands, in a sumptuous velvet cape that she later casts aside.

Everyone is natural, true to life, without affectation. There are no throne scenes. The king and queen, like contemporary lovers, are drawn to each other, grope for each other's hands, exchange glances, walk together. "Gonzago" is played in the garden, from the stage of a carnival cart. The ghost appears on the tower parapet; he is corpulent, bareheaded, kindhearted, very human. And what about Hamlet?

He is played by a clever, intellectual actor with a wide range of gifts. I have never seen the role of Hamlet worked out in such detail (certainly not by the talentless Kachalov*). The external image is as simple as possible—a black costume that might be made of sacking, no "headgear" or curls. A high forehead, a tall, spare figure, thin legs. Sharp, sarcastic, and cunning toward his enemies, otherwise kind and affectionate. Rather touching. In the scene with his mother he is not brusque, and after seeing the ghost he is tender, sorrowful, and soft, like a character from Chekhov. Forgetting about the play, I watched him as though he were "alive," as though I were living his life, the life of a friend. The thought never occurred to me, Wherein lies this tragedy? Does one think of tragedy when one is serving tea to a friend who has had "an unhappy life"?

Ophelia was played by a talented young actress who won fame as Juliet in a performance at the Children's Theater. Graceful, youthful, completely natural in intonation and movement—almost too much so, too "everyday"—with a plain face, no trace of poetry. The best of them all

---

* Vasily Ivanovich Kachalov (real name Shverubovich; 1875–1948): a leading actor of the Moscow Art Theater.

was Horatio. I have never seen such sincerity, achieved with such simple, modest means. Oh yes, Rosencrantz and Guildenstern. Two handsome gentlemen foppishly dressed, without the usual truckling and knee bending. There is no Fortinbras. Accordingly there is no splendid philosophical image. What is *Hamlet* without Fortinbras? Maupassant had a way of revealing the whole meaning of the meaning (I wrote that accidentally, but I'll let it stand) in the last sentence. That is Fortinbras: a second version, simpler, but real, genuine, and a man of action. He is eternal youth, life in spontaneous flow and accomplishment. He has got to appear at the end of the play. When Hamlet dies, Fortinbras appears. Otherwise life would end on this earth. How much Hamlet takes away with him!

Wherein lies the drama of Hamlet's life? In his living for life (If you can say that), in his taking the responsibility for it on himself, building significance into it early and late, boring his way like an earthworm through layer upon layer of its meaning. Hamlet's weariness is measureless. Fortinbras's life is made simpler by the absence of world-weariness. How he illuminates Hamlet's epilogue! How filled he is with Shakespeare's magnificent optimism! There is, of course, no place for this in Kozintsev's "bourgeois drama." All the famous monologues are deliberately "toned down" to the flatness of real life. "To be or not to be" fails to touch us because it is delivered against a background of muted organ music coming from backstage. Many of the puzzles in *Hamlet* are ironed out, everything is perfectly clear. The setting for the "gallery" scene is replaced—naturally—by an interior. Hamlet's room is shown. In the middle stands a huge Nike on a pedestal, without a head (fittingly); a shelf above an antique bas-relief holds an enormous scroll—an ancient manuscript! This is where the dialogue with Polonius takes place. "Words, words, words" is spoken as Hamlet half sits on the table or the arm of a chair, noisily leafing through countless pages. The playing of the recorders following "Gonzago" is turned melodramatically into a "theatricalized show," with dances, shouting, and horseplay.

And how much is deleted! Gone are Shakespeare's metaphors and aphorisms. Gone the verse. Actors speak their lines as in ordinary conversation. If ours were not such a bright and glorious epoch, I would say that such antagonism to verse, rhythm, passion, and temperament could be engendered only by an epoch that splits the individual in two and rips out his entrails, an epoch that tramples poetry in the dust and spits on the human spirit. Tell me this: if we hide rhythm and meter as we would hide a stain on our ancestry, why should we write in rhythm and meter? Let us always speak as we do at the dinner table.

You will count it exaggeration by one near of kin (I believe you call it "emotional generosity") if I say that no two writers have ever enjoyed greater intellectual affinity than you and Shakespeare. All the things for which you have been so cruelly hounded and harassed are "Shakespearean." And on reading Shakespeare I am amazed to find so much that is "Pasternakian," what your critics call futurism and Khlebnikovism:* Shakespeare's images and metaphors, the many levels of thought, the conjugation of events in all tenses and aspects simultaneously, the conversion of particulars into universals, the enormous scale of his poetic thinking. Amazing, too, is Shakespeare's use of anachronisms. He holds in his hand the thread of past and present. How splendidly, as in *Caesar* and *Antony*, does he address remarks directly to us, tearing through the fabric of time. Just as a painter like Holbein, say, can sit the Meyer family at the dinner table with the Virgin Mary and God. How puerile are these demands for "modernity" and "realism"! It's like demanding that the elephant have a trunk. One might think there was such a thing as art that was not modern or real, such a thing as a colt nurtured by a boa constrictor.

I left before the end. Not because it was boring. But the actors had already reached their "peak" and had nothing more to offer. Art is expectation. When there is no more to expect all is over. Like love.

I walked home happy with the freshness of the evening. And I had my own shades beside me: Mama, Uncle Leonid, Lyonya. *Hamlet* is not only theater—it is also youth, family, and that spirituality by which we live and move and have our being without noticing it.

Your name is known to the entire civilized world. When the murmuring, shuffling playgoers took their seats, filling the orchestra, the parterre, and all the balconies, jostling one another, stepping on one another's toes, how keenly then was I aware of the importance of the moment! Every playbill testified to your greatness—buy one and marvel at its tangibility! The curtain went up and your language sounded from the stage, your life achievement made manifest on the stage, *Hamlet* in Borya's translation!

But I felt no personal pride. History has gobbled up my family.

Forgive me for being tiresome. And for heaven's sake don't think you must answer this. I write you out of necessity. Don't deprive me of this right, and don't constrain me with stupid conditions. I know you are a good boy and a model citizen, but very busy and sick to death of pen and

---

* Velimir (Viktor Vladimirovich) Khlebnikov (1885–1922): an innovative Russian poet of the futurist movement.

ink. Your feeling that you must answer sometimes keeps me from talking to you, and you have no idea how much I need to talk to you.

Much love. I hope you are fine and that your work is going well.

Yours,

OLYA

I just learned that the finale of *Hamlet* goes like this: the dead lie in darkness, the sky is brightly lit, and there, high against it, stands Nike on her pedestal. No comment needed, as they say.

Moscow, April 16, 1954

Dear Olya,

I am answering you instantly upon having read your talented, diverting, long, and perceptive letter, and at a most inappropriate moment: it is 7 P.M., and at 7:30 there is a discussion of my *Faust* at the Writers' Club, to which I am going. I wept reading your lines. Dear friend, see if in the next week or two you can get issue 4 of *The Banner* (it is already out here). With two or three exceptions, all the poems are new. You will be pleased to see something simple, natural, and unlike the rest of the stuff appearing in our journals. They aren't to blame, of course—it's the "system" that catches them and drags them down. The words "Doctor Zhivago" have now made their appearance on a contemporary page—like a hideous blot!

All my love, dear one.

I am annoyed that they have attached Marshak* to me. Why?

Yours,

B.

Moscow, July 12, 1954

Dear Olyushka,

Are you alive? What are you doing? How is your health? I am more than a swine, I am a wretch and a scoundrel (if they are worse than a swine) for having got off with a short note in answer to your long, detailed analysis of the *Hamlet* premiere. It was a marvelous letter, offering a whole world of ideas, rivaling *Hamlet* in depth and trenchancy. And now when I hear or read anything about the production, it is not Shake-

---

* Samuil Yakovlevich Marshak (1887–1964): children's writer and translator of English poets.

speare or the Alexandrinka or Leningrad that comes to my mind, but your letter.

I fear you don't know how much I love you and don't feel my kiss on your cheek. But if I should give up my dogged devotion to work (now become a habit), what would be left of me?

For a few liberal months last winter we enjoyed a breathing spell, in the sense that friends spoke out more readily and more sensibly and it became more interesting to go out and see people. There came a break in that wearisome voyage, captainless and rudderless, on a shoreless sea of our own making; something resembling fresh, life-giving air was wafted our way, enveloped us, and restored form and outline to our lives. It became easier to work. By its very existence this element of definiteness, be it but a promise of definiteness, made it possible to know where one begins and ends, what one wants, why one should have such strange wants, and what one should do about them.

Even then I held myself aloof from such trifling changes, allowing myself to cherish no hopes. But it was a relief to find circumstances bearing more resemblance to reality. Now I am again immersed in fathomless freedom and solitude. I want to finish the novel and believe I will. Nothing prevents me from doing so. I am well and feeling fit. Last winter the dacha we rent from the Literary Fund was overhauled and turned into a palace. Running water, a bath, gas, three new rooms. I find it embarrassing to live in such grandeur. It doesn't suit my rank; I am ashamed of my huge study with its parquet floor and central heating. I am working. I don't know how to rest and enjoy myself, but how dull and talentless are the rough drafts I am making for the final part of the book! You can imagine the extent of my horror and despair if I have allowed myself to put aside the daily stint so as to indulge my constant desire to be with you. But I will not tempt God. You see, I have somewhat unburdened my heart to you without being explicit in any way. Is that not cause for satisfaction? And then fate has been so kind to me. Yet how immense is the difference between what I could and ought to have done had there been some sort of fusion and identification with the world about me and what I have done without this fusion.

Every summer, each time hoping it will come off, I invite you to visit us. I will not repeat it now, but my wish is stronger than ever.

Please give my love to Mashura. These are not empty words, not an unfeeling cliché. Often scenes of our distant childhood pass before my mind's eye, never more vividly than they do this burning hot summer, with the grasshoppers hopping into the house. Again I see it all, not only with the heat, the sounds, and the smells of those days but also with a feeling that their sultriness and dull reality have already been touched by the liberating and refreshing breath of the future. Oh, Olya, Olya, just as I long to see you, I long to see the girls again, and not merely because of ties of kinship but also because of the increased knowledge of the world it would bring. Breadth of vision, your achievements, their travels.

All my love.

Yours,
BORYA

Leningrad, July 17, 1954

Borya, dear friend,

What a miracle! Every day I am with you in my thoughts, writing to you. Finally, when I resolve to take up my pen and write a letter already overlong in gestation, that moment your envelope arrives, in which everything is foreseen and already said. Well, of course, I am neither alive nor well—your question went straight to the mark.

How very stupidly it all came out: as soon as you wrote "see if you can get a copy of *The Banner*," I fell silent. I already knew the reviews. My silence was, as it were, an opinion (not, of course, in your eyes, but in mine). Therefore I dared not ask how the discussion of *Faust* went, even though that interested me exceedingly.

The fact is I considered it unpardonable of me to talk to you before seeing *The Banner*. And besides, I had a bout of stomach trouble that everyone thought was cancer (everyone, that is, but me; I couldn't believe in an illness so serious that it would free me from the double burden of existing and growing old). In short, I now conceal it, live with it, survive it. But it snatches me out of the current of life, destroying the fixed regime I had perforce adopted.

To continue: since critics have stopped lambasting the journals, people have stopped subscribing to them. I had to go to the library. In the meantime Satan sank his teeth into the instep of my left foot, forcing me to hop about on one leg. The result: bed, a surgeon, telephone calls, advice, indignation, admonitions, etc., etc. The diagnosis? It proved to be as lame as my leg—out of sympathy, I suppose. In a word—idiocy, a complete waste of time. I haven't been out of the house since the Creation and have spent this Sahara of a summer shut up in a box with the sun blazing in on me.

And just fancy: I enjoyed it! With a free conscience I accepted a papal indulgence permitting me to break with the outer world.

Now you understand with what boundless gratitude I read your letter.

It came as an angel of liberation. Mythology is silent as to who drew out the nails that set Prometheus free. It was you. Now I have the right to send this letter without having seen *The Banner*.

Ah, dear friend, at this point I fall at your feet and extol you! All that man bears in his heart and longs to give expression to, you, as its external manifestation, its embodiment in the flesh, have defined for him and for those around him. Forgive me for repeating myself, but I must tell you again and again that in you our family barque has ventured so far out on the open sea that even I (through you) have been able to extend my capabilities to the uttermost. No precision instrument could achieve your precision of definition (if things without limit or within limit need to be defined). Have I ever told you what it means for a person to experience the singular joy of recognizing his *kinship* (literally that) to art? It is a joy that throws him down and to one side, like a shadow. It is of this I am speaking. I am, if you like, referring to those "declarations" of our youth that we called "our last will and testament," remember? (oh, you do, you do!—your memory retains everything forever). Well, then, that is the answer to our familial charades, the answer to why I avoided you, withdrew from you, felt a distance between us of almost railroad dimensions, felt it well-nigh impossible to board the train and go to you in Moscow, to allow my fingers to touch your life, why I loved you above all else in this world, why I found no words to convey how two-in-one you are to me— you who judged me in the light of integral calculus, expressing then and expressing always that part of me which is called my human self. Never has there been anything I couldn't confide to you—and one cannot say that about many people, only about one person. What happiness that my birth certificate testifies to my being your cousin! It is almost unbelievable. Now I have the right to tell you this, and what is more, I can do it while there is still time.

The Greeks were fools to believe that the gods die. Only people die and are resurrected.

Not to speak of the universal significance of poetry, the rhythm alone of yours is sufficient to provide a complete picture of our family. When Mother was incapable of reaching out to you with a clear mind, I would read your verse to her, and the rhythm of your thoughts revealed so much grandeur, so much that was near and dear to her, that the tears streamed down her cheeks and she sat there shaken—and proud. It was truly the feeling we call kinship, the most important feeling, one that is an integral part of the biology of our birth.

I want to tell you about a trifling thing. Recently the Academy of Sciences has published much about Father's being the inventor of motion pictures (and so has an encyclopedia). I am not yet able to go out, so I haven't seen any of these publications. Motion pictures, mind you! They keep writing to me and asking for his photograph. There were many such "preinventors." Most of their blueprints and models have been lost. What, then, is the historical evidence? In Father's case just a few sentences from his unpublished *Memoirs*, the very existence of which no one might ever have discovered. How accidentally they survived! Through revolution, civil war, blockade, death, and turmoil; through Sasha's hands and Sasha's fate. In the dust and rubble of the family clutter, overrun with rats, they lay more securely guarded by the armor of history than in the pantheon of *len* and *stal.**

Impotent, defenseless thought flashing by in the innocence of youth without ever reaching fruition, creative thought though it was, came to the fore, entered the history of technology, and bore witness to the inventor.

Is there not great consolation in this? Is it not testimony to the vast warehouses of immortality in which the great and the true never decay or lose their luster?

Oh, do keep on working and working. You are a king; your name is already engraved in stone. You take after Uncle Leonid in that you eschew repose, yet even he rested at times. Fatigue leads to disillusion; a thought is fresher after rest. But this is elementary; forgive me the truism.

I will write you when I am able to get out. I am glad you are now enjoying some of the comforts of life. I don't like Stone Age Russian dachas.

Much love,

OLYA

Moscow, July 21, 1954

Dear Olyusha,

Again I have no way of repaying you for your wonderful letter, so strong and youthful. Don't go out searching for *The Banner*; I am sending it to you. And don't think of writing in response and troubling yourself with an analysis of the poems. There is no reason to think you will admire them. I am sending them as a curiosity—whole pages in which there is no mention at all of *len* and *stal*. Then, too, it has been a great joy for me to see the sacramental words "Doctor Zhivago" in print.

They are a part of what I wrote last summer (a few were done earlier). Suddenly, after the hospital, the sanatorium, the anxiety, the limitations, a

---

* Ill-disguised substitutes for Lenin and Stalin.

thing occurred not provided for by my strict regime: I was engulfed in a wave of happiness that opened my eyes and sharpened my ears, and it was then that I ran through the whole of *Faust* for a last time before it was sent to the printers and wrote these pieces and a few others.

Thanks awfully for the letter. All my love.

Yours,

BORYA

Leningrad, July 27, 1954

Dear Borya,

Forgive me. I'm writing in great haste. I'm going away, have to take treatments. My health is slipping like a run in a stocking.

Thanks most of all for taking the trouble of sending the journal; as for the "contents," that goes without saying. I know you don't send it to get my opinion, and what could my opinion give you? This is not an opinion, merely an expression of feelings whose ambivalence I mentioned to you in my last letter. Once again I discover a biographical affinity with your poems, an unutterable understanding of them, as well as of the "iconostasis," the barrier separating the sacred from the profane (in the classical sense). And this leads me to something basic, the most basic thing: art does not tolerate an attitude of familiarity, and no birth certificate awards privileges. I have always revered the artist in you with whom I could not be on free and easy terms precisely because I was a relative.

So now, as if we were strangers. No one can appreciate more than I can what it means to see those two words* in print. It's amazing how it happens: the door is shut tight, then the day comes when a chink appears in it, and suddenly—the words in print.

In one brief line you succeed in giving a complete portrait of your hero. That is not nearly so simple as it appears at first glance.

I seem to have found much that is new in your verse—a new you, so to speak. I find your logic new, your entire language new and reaching out to great simplicity, real texture, finely chiseled thought. And yet for some inexplicable reason I also find that no other cycle of poems has ever brought you so close to your youthful beginning, to your *Twin in the Clouds*, as if you had advanced in a circle and when you reached the point of furthest departure (maturity) from your timid start, you found yourself only two steps away from your youth. If this is true (I may be talking nonsense), it is good. It is good when the artist is tied like a

---

* The words "Doctor Zhivago."

balloon to his childhood and youth, when he "speaks himself" (as the Greeks would have put it), remains one with his original, essential self.

These poems have been out for some time, but it is never too late to congratulate and bestow a kiss. You emanate great faith, you are living a great life.

I am taking leave of you for a long time. I expect to stay on the Karelian Isthmus until late autumn. I love to see the everlasting rain falling on a forest of silent firs. They stand in such close ranks, so tall, so many, so alike, all silent, that they create the impression of a different order of height, dignity, and unassailable nobility. There have been times when, driven to despair by human beings, I sought spiritual asylum among the trees and thought, How kind they are—they do not torment, do not intrigue or use violence, just quietly live and grow beside me.

Forgive me for being such a bore of late. Don't hold it against me; you know what is in my heart. I am exceedingly tired, exceedingly discomfited. I have expressed my thoughts eccentrically because of the pressure I am under. They have no form; they resist being expressed as water resists being poured out of a narrow-necked bottle—the more you tip it, the greater the blockage. I loathe my style. It is like Aseyev's early poems: high-toned, evasive, with pretentions to being original. I have offended your taste more than once, but be assured I have offended my own as well.

I have much work to do. I must finish one thing and begin another, but my foot demands rest, for which I must take a holiday. Fancy the bother!

This is what you call writing in haste.

Much love. Take care of yourself and be happy.

Yours,

OLYA

Oh yes, I have forgotten to offer you two choice morsels following on the "theatrical departure" of Kozintsev's staging of *Hamlet*.

(1) One of my pupils asked her little son what he made of the performance. "Oh," he replied quite seriously, "Hamlet put up a fight for the good strong family. I understood everything."

(2) My neighbor asked me: "Tell me, Olga Mikhailovna, what was that bird without a head (the Nike of Samothrace) doing in Hamlet's room? There was no one I could ask. Everybody was wondering why there should be a man-sized bird there without a head."

This adieu is final.

OLYA

Moscow, July 31, 1954

Dear Olya,

A few breathless words to reach you as you pack hastily, or perhaps to fly after you as you speed on your way. I know what you had in mind when you spoke of the pressure under which you were writing and the pretentiousness of your style. This is sheer calumny. Anyone who has ever written is familiar with the curse of unfinished thoughts and the consequent inability to give them exact expression. I might have left your letter unanswered this time, but I feel constrained to defend you from your own attacks.

And then, several coincidences. In passing you mentioned a name at the end of your letter—remember whose? ("Aseyev's early poems.") I broke with that circle and, even more, with the whole milieu, but this past winter several of them so touched me with the warmth and sincerity of their declarations that I gave in and, incidentally, visited Aseyev and his wife. The three of us spent an evening together and I recited from memory all my new poems, some of which appear in *The Banner*. One of the Aseyevs wept (I don't remember which one), but she said to her husband, "It's as if the veil had been taken off *My Sister, Life*." Exactly your own opinion.

One other thing. At the same time your letter arrived, there was one from the daughter of Marina Tsvetayeva (who hanged herself in 1941). The daughter has spent eighteen years in exile, in Turukhansk. We are very close, very good friends; I saw her as a little girl in Paris in 1935. She is very intelligent, writes brilliant letters, and is a most unfortunate woman. But she hasn't lost her spirit or sense of humor despite her endless trials. So I wanted to forward her letter to you, since you are somewhat alike and are neighbors in my heart; she, too, is unjustly severe with herself, and expecting heaven knows what. But it would be indiscreet of me to forward it. Yes, Olechka, all is well. It is well even to be sorrowful. All my love.

Yours,

BORYA

Leningrad, November 4, 1954

Dear Borya,

There are rumors here that you have been awarded the Nobel Prize. Are they true? If not, then why the rumors?

I suppose my question is stupid, but how can I help asking it? I will wait impatiently for a postcard from you. Take care of yourself.

Yours,

OLYA

Moscow, November 12, 1954

Dear Olyushka,

How happy your every line, the very sight of your handwriting makes me!

The same rumors are circulating here. I am the last one they reach. They come to me third-hand, after everyone else. "Poor Borya!" you are probably thinking. "What an unreal, sorry existence, with no one to turn to and no place to which he can go to find out the truth!"

You cannot imagine how strained my relations with officialdom are and how terrifying it is to have attention drawn to me. On the least provocation they assume the right to ask me questions about my basic views, and there is no force on earth that can compel me to answer such questions in the way everyone else does. And the stronger, the happier, the more fruitful and wholesome my life becomes (as it has of late), the more strained become our relations. It is expedient that I live secretly and withdrawn.

I feared more than hoped that the rumors were true, though the prize would bring with it an obligatory trip abroad to receive it, and that would mean making a break into the wide world, exchanging views, etc. But I could not possibly go as the mechanical doll others become when they are "let out." And yet I have to think of the lives of my loved ones, of my unfinished novel, and of how to keep my position from becoming even more precarious. Ah, me! The Babylonian captivity. But the Lord seems to have shown mercy; the danger seems to have passed.

Evidently my candidacy was proposed and received definite and wide support. This has been reported in French, Belgian, and West German papers; there are those who have seen and read the reports. So they say.

Later it was announced by the BBC (I'm only telling what I was told) that my name was proposed, but, knowing our ways, the committee sought the Soviet government's approval; to which request said government responded by asking that Sholokhov's name* be substituted for

---

* Mikhail Alexandrovich Sholokhov (1905–   ): Soviet novelist.

mine. When this was rejected, Hemingway was nominated, and he will probably receive the award. Some say, however, that the question is not yet settled. Of course this is only gossip, but widespread gossip.

I am happy to be but a nominee for an honor extended to such men as Hamsun and Bunin, and to be placed side by side, if only through a misunderstanding, with Hemingway.

One thing I am proud of: not for a moment has there been any interruption in the even flow of hours devoted to my simple, anonymous, unpublished life of labor.

There is indeed a guardian angel watching over me. That is what matters. Praise and glory to my angel.

All my love, dear Olya.

Yours,

BORYA

P.S. Forgive me for the haste you must detect in my tone. Never am I free of the presentiment of approaching evil, of preordained catastrophe. It does not deter me. Without undue anxiety and paralyzing fear, I know that I must hurry and be always on the alert.

I am working well. And here's an interesting item: Zina has luxuriously converted the dacha for winter habitation, so I am spending the winter in Peredelkino.

Leningrad, November 17, 1954

Borya dear,

Your letter was indeed a hurried one, yet it revealed the epic greatness of your spirit to an astonishing degree. Anyone who reads you must be astonished by your wisdom, nobility, loftiness, and profound understanding of life and history. I can reply only in tears, not in words.

You are a past master at expressing what lies, like an embryo, in the womb of unspoken thoughts and unborn events. Plato would have called you a midwife. You are in fact a writer. Could I have produced your tight formulations or those obedient words bringing order out of a chaos of facts and ideas? I long to write you about a thousand things. I find myself tempted to discuss the shifting of continents, Asia moving on Europe, hydroelectric power plants in Assurbanipal, the subway to the university, slabs of malachite and fluorescent light in pitch blackness. The devil only knows what thoughts seethe in the bottle they are corked up in.

I rejoice for you. I had known of correspondence schools; now I know of correspondence coronations. That is the best outcome for you. The bitterness, of course, remains. One wants to believe that the sun is shining in the south, even if the snow is falling outside my window. I am so proud of you and of our elders! Remember my predicting that you would soon receive "official recognition"? I heard the whir of wings in the air but didn't know from whence they came. You'll admit that even at such a distance from you I sometimes see things first—you'll admit it, that is, if you're not the most swinish of swine.

Dearest friend, never has dynamite led to such happy consequences as your candidacy for the throne of Apollo. What if in Peredelkino you are accomplishing your feat in solitude and seclusion? Somewhere typesetters are supporting their families on the wages they receive for setting up your name in all the languages of the world. You are giving work to men in Belgium and Paris. Presses are humming, pages are being folded, the smell of ink fills the air, while you are having breakfast with Zina in Peredelkino or are complaining of the bars of your golden cage. It is unity of time and action, if not unity of place.

I am made proud and happy by your lofty optimism. Father Zosima* dwells within you and shares with you the light of eternity. Ah, how well Dostoyevsky puts it: when everyone awaits the miraculous "assumption" of Father Zosima, his body rots and gives off the stench of corruption faster than the bodies of the sinful. Faith is sorely tempted. Even Alyosha turns away from his master. Transcendence achieved through putrefaction! Light and revelation through "the days of our life" and our body's disintegration!

Do you not see the great significance of your life in Peredelkino and in the bars, above and beyond which, far, far away, people are talking about the unalloyed you, the unseen you? This, then, is how our fate is determined, without our knowing it.

Dear brother (to address you in the style of Father Zosima), I am laughing and crying at once. There is a confession I have wanted to make to you for a long time. I have suffered a great loss, an irreparable loss. I have lost my own self.

Yes, yes, I am dead. I have withered and wasted away from lack of oxygen. M. Bonnivard† has never been a model for me, though tourists are enchanted by his place of residence. Had I been Byron I would never have used the expression "chainless mind"; he was unacquainted with reality.

I guess I've said all there is to say about me.

Mashura came to see me yesterday. She's an odd one—in three dimen-

* Saintly monk in Dostoyevsky's novel *The Brothers Karamazov* (1880).
† Hero of Byron's *Prisoner of Chillon* (1816).

sions. She made me promise to convey her greetings, her love, her most tender affection. But that's like using another's love letters to declare your feelings. Horribly naïve. Why shouldn't she say it herself? I shrink from such a commission.

Since I've run on so long, let me add one more thing, though it has little to do with this letter. Don't tell Zina, but in her place I would never have forgiven me that winter evening when she and Lyonya came to say good-by before leaving for Moscow. It was a day of great perturbation for her. You know all about it, of course. You heard monstrous things about my "hospitality," and they were all correct. A friend of mine once said, "Never judge people, especially Soviet people." Zina thought I was a miserable coward; really I am quite brave, but at that time the force of circumstances outweighed my personal feelings. I have wanted to tell you this for some time. Subjectively, Zina is right.

Best love. Let me know if something crystallizes for you.

Yours,
OLYA

CHAPTER X

[Inscription in Olga Freidenberg's manuscript of *Image and Concept:*]

I must begin with the same old thing: the prisonlike conditions in which this book was written. I have no access to
works of scholarship. I have had to rely solely on my memory
in writing this book. I am isolated from the ideas of contemporary scholars. Pupils and friends alike turned away from
me. I was deprived of my university audience. Under the
circumstances I decided to synthesize my thirty-seven years of
research and, having done so, to fall silent forever.

Passers-by! Pause before this work and pray for learning!

OLGA FREIDENBERG
March 20, 1954

[From the correspondence between Boris Pasternak and M. A. Markova
(Mashura)]

Leningrad, June 23, 1955

Boryushka,

I consider it my duty to inform you that on the 24th Olga will be taken
to the hospital. She has been seriously ill for a long time. You knew of
this; a young man* came to her from you and she told him she was too ill
to see him. None of you made any response to this, and how much that
would have meant to her in her loneliness! If you wish to hear more about
her, my telephone is A1-88-45 and my name is Maria Alexandrovna Mar-

---

* Vyacheslav Vsevolodovich Ivanov, son of the Russian writer Vsevolod Ivanov (1895–
1963) and prominent Soviet linguist, called on Olga at the request not of Boris Pasternak but of his elder son, Zhenya.

kova (Mashura, if that name means anything to you). It would be best to call at about midnight.

I hope you are well and may God spare you the loneliness I have suffered.

MASHURA

Moscow, June 26, 1955

Dear Mashura,

Thank you for thinking of writing me. The letter was just brought to me at the dacha from town. I was completely unaware of the things your postcard told me. I did not send anyone to Olya in Leningrad; this is the first time I have heard of it, and I have no idea what it refers to. Perhaps the man was sent by Alexander and Irina, but even so I know nothing about it. Presently I will tell you about the solitude and isolation in which I live so that you will not see things in a false light.

I have always felt uneasy about Olya's stomach complaint and have long been quite alarmed. I don't know whether her friend who lives in the same house and recently lost a daughter is still alive. Some member of Alexander's family who visited Leningrad told us about her, from which we gathered that Olya's intimacy with this woman supported her in her loneliness and made it more endurable.

I have always answered Olya's letters immediately. Even if she were not so gifted and intelligent and I did not love her and you so well, all the same you are the voices of the life I have lived, a life for which I am deeply grateful—grateful for the whole of it, from beginning to end, in minutest detail. That is why I took your comment that you are Mashura, "if that name means anything to you," with a smile, as a mild little joke. It was Olga who, by passing on to you my inquiries and regards, confirmed just how much the name means to me.

Lately I have stopped writing to people, and I avoid seeing even those near and dear to me, even my older son and my brother Alexander (which explains why I knew nothing about the young man who went to Leningrad and the news he brought back about Olga's worsening illness). I do this not because I am conceited and put on airs, not because of some imaginary and completely nonexistent fame, but because I am working very hard this year, more particularly this summer, to complete a long work I would not want to leave unfinished. It is the second book of the novel whose first book you read in part (which is further proof that the name Mashura does indeed mean something to me). I remember your comments well. You were not alone in your disapproval of it. Most people dislike the novel and raise objections to it. I could count on the fingers of one hand the number of those who do like it.

If I add that it is a work of love, which will never, or only in the distant future, see the light, that it is not motivated by pressing needs, or publishers' deadlines, and is not a source of income—on the contrary, I write it with no hope of material reward, spasmodically, with prolonged interruptions, at the expense of commissioned work—if you take all these factors into consideration, you will understand that such a work of love can be accomplished only by cutting myself off from everybody and everything for the time being. It has nothing to do with conceit.

But enough of this. I understand the threat presented by Olya's type of illness. But so many times have I seen a gathering storm pass over that in this case, too, I have hope for a joyful outcome. Please send me the address of Olga's hospital and tell me whether I can write her there, and also keep me posted as to the state of her health by mailing cards to our town address.

Give her a kiss from me and tell her about me if you see her. Talk to doctors and tell me their opinion. Thank you for giving me your telephone number, but I cannot call you from here and I rarely go to town.

Love to you. I am well and working very hard, but I am appalled by the mediocrity and diffuseness of my manuscript (more than 600 pages!). This, however, is not a tragedy—that is, the disappointment is not enough to spoil my mood. I am well, full of inner strength, and so happy I fear to acknowledge it.

Yours,
BORYA

Leningrad, July 2, 1955

Dear Boryushka,

I just left Olya after a doctors' consultation. She is still in the hospital. The doctors are not hopeful. Her condition is critical; she is in a state of collapse. She doesn't eat, doesn't drink, and often doesn't want to talk. She has grown alarmingly weak.

Among other things I am worried about the fate of her works, her manuscripts. Her wish was that after some time they should be brought out under her name. I don't know what to do with them. The difficulty is aggravated by the fact that the apartment is locked and she holds the key. She herself is prepared for the worst and seems to have forgotten all about the work of a lifetime.

None of us can or dares bring this matter to her attention and ask for instructions. An authoritative influence is needed and quickly. Please advise me what to do; I have no one but you to turn to.

MASHURA

Moscow, July 6, 1955

Dear Mashura,

How sad and, judging by your word, inevitable this is! But the grief lies only in the threat of impending loss, nothing else. Don't create additional worries for yourself by racking your brains to solve insoluble problems.

Olya is a professor at the university; even with the most extreme apostasy on her part, her membership in that corporation makes it responsible for her works and her memory. I don't mean to say that I believe in the benevolence of her colleagues, but even if you or I wanted to do something, we could do it only within the limits set by the university. In any case, the initiative and the last word belong to it, whether you intercede or not. Olya had and still has admiring pupils; it cannot be that no one will support her now. It is for them to defend her works, not you.

You may be surprised that I write about this so callously, as if my main purpose were to hold myself aloof and do nothing. This is not entirely true. It would be easy for me to make my recent illness an excuse, copying the manner of those who hide anything sad or upsetting from me and urge me not to attend funerals for fear they will disturb my equanimity. That would be despicable. My reserve (I did not rush to Leningrad on receiving your first postcard) is the result of having a heap of other demands on my time added to those I have already told you about, these others connected with the staging of my plays this year at two Moscow theaters, the Maly and the Moscow Art Theater. So long as my heart gives me respite, the pull of life is stronger than I am; I cannot resist it, cannot withdraw and refuse to take part in it.

In passing let me say something else. I hope you will allow me at my first opportunity to forward some money to you, not for Olya or for the expenses incurred by her illness, but for you personally, so that your hands will be untied to give of your time—which is costly—to this sad circumstance. Such an opportunity presented itself yesterday or the day before, but that was before I received your card, and so the money is spent; I missed the chance. I do believe, however, that another is in the offing.

You must wonder at my letters. No doubt you find me an unfeeling brute, indifferent to Olya and her fate, serenely burying her alive. Oh,

Boris Pasternak

Boris Pasternak

A sketch of Aunt Asya and Olya by Leonid Pasternak.
On the back, in Boris Pasternak's hand (1956): "Aunt Asya and Olyushka,
both already deceased"

how mistaken you are! It is only that I am prepared for anything, so long
and so deeply have I reflected on my own end and that of all I hold dear.
What can we do about it?

The only thing we can do, faced as we are with so many heartbreaking
moments and so vast a loss of precious human life, is to pour all of our
love into the making and molding of the living, into useful labor and
creative effort.

Love.

Yours,

BORYA

Perhaps we are too hasty in lamenting our friend, so noble in character,
so rich in gifts, and so dearly beloved? God is merciful; all may yet turn
out for the best, and perhaps we shall have reason for unexpected rejoicing.

[Telegram; Leningrad, July 7, 1955]

OLYA DIED TODAY—MASHURA

[Telegram; Moscow, July 7, 1955]

THIS BLOW FELL SOONER THAN EXPECTED. POOR OLYA. I JUST POSTED LETTER
EXPRESSING FAINT HOPE. ANSWER WHEN YOU HAVE TIME. THANK YOU FOR
EVERYTHING. LOVE—BORYA

Leningrad, July 10, 1955

Dear Boryushka,

I received your letter when I got back from the funeral. The funeral
made a very painful impression on me. I could not avoid asking the
university for assistance in procuring a burial plot and placing an obituary
notice in the newspaper. Believe it or not, I received no response—not a
word from a soul! About anything! All was passed over in complete
silence. Poor Olya!

I buried her in the Bogoslovskoye Cemetery, but not in the Academy
plot, which was inaccessible. In a few days I will place a headstone with
an inscription on it and, if there is enough money, have a fence put
around the grave.

Her apartment has been sealed for three days; who sealed it I do not
know, probably the house management. What will happen to it in the
future is also unknown. She apparently left no will. Copies of old ones are

in the apartment. Her pension for the last two months is lost because she did not collect it, wanting the money to accumulate to pay for the dacha to which she intended going when she got out of the hospital. I have spent all the money that was left in the apartment on funeral expenses and paying necessary bribes. I know she had a savings account, but I don't know to whom it is bequeathed and where her bankbook is.

Poor Olya! How she wished (she always said so) that her hard-earned money should go to people she loved. She never expected catastrophe to overtake her so suddenly; she thought she would put her affairs in order when she came home from the hospital. In this, as in everything else in her life, she was unfortunate. Her possessions will go either to people she did not intend should have them (if the first will is not voided) or to the state. Incidentally, the post-mortem showed she died of chronic hepatitis and dystrophy of the liver. She was afraid of cancer and was sure she had it.

How dreadful to lose all my relatives so quickly! To you and Alexander I am a parvenu, although Olya did not think so; I don't even know your families or they me, though I still write to you as to a brother about his sister. She dreamed so of seeing you!

I did not quite understand what you meant in your letter about my "hands being untied" to give time to Olya.

First of all, you probably think I am still employed, but at sixty-two one does not get work easily, although I have tried very hard (285 rubles a month is not enough to live on). Secondly, I did everything out of love for Olya. If you are offering to help me as a cousin, I will accept it simply and with gratitude, but if you want to pay me for my labor, you will offend me deeply and undeservedly, intensifying my grievous loss. For the last four or five years she and I were very close, as you know—spiritually close.

Remember our childhood, my summer vacations spent at your dacha, "Raika," with Grandmother? How far away it seems, and how unlike our present relations!

I will notify you of any new developments in Olya's affairs. I do beg you not to break with me completely; only three of us are left, you know.

Yours,
MASHURA

Moscow, July 19, 1955

Dear Mashura,

I am answering you in a frightful hurry, I am exhausted by too much work, all of it urgent. It will be like this for a long time to come—always, I fear. Thanks for the letter. How sad I am made by our loss, sadder even than I had expected.

Don't take unforeseen circumstances to heart. Olya was the keeper of family traditions, of letters and mementos, some of which may relate to my immediate family. I hasten to tell you this in a few words. I personally do not keep heirlooms, archives, collections of any kind, including books and furniture. I do not save letters or draft copies of my work. Nothing piles up in my room; it is easier to clean than a hotel room. My life resembles a student's.

When something is dear to me, it is dear to me not necessarily in *my* hands, but in anyone's hands, or better—in no one's hands, but in living memory or in history; dear to me are all memories, everyone's past, and very, very dear is the place occupied in the history of modern art by my father, a remarkable artist. This sort of preservation isn't contrived; you don't have to push it or worry about it. If it doesn't come about of itself, no effort from the outside will achieve it.

I am glad you spoke about the money. I wrote you that I missed my last opportunity and will seize the next. Although I cannot say exactly when it will come, surely it will be within the month. How can you not be ashamed of writing such foolish things as that you are a parvenu to us (Who is this "us"? My wife and I? Alexander and I? Someone else and I?) and that there are only three of us left? Ah, if you only knew how much simpler, broader, gayer life is! What three? What parvenu? What Alexander? I don't live by such things, but by work. Taking from life and giving back to it.

I must stop unexpectedly. Expect more to follow. Take care of yourself. Love.

Yours,
BORYA

Leningrad, August 31, 1955

Dear Boryushka,

Only today Mila and I got back; we had been on vacation. I was not home when your money order came. Many thanks. I also received a letter from Petukhova (forwarded to me at the dacha). I have already answered. It told me that a second will was found, according to which everything without exception goes to R. R. Orbeli.*

The legatee seems to have expressed a wish that the paintings by Uncle Leonid and Braz be given to a museum. Do you approve? Olya once expressed the same wish. If you want to write to Orbeli, I will give you her address.

She also has the manuscript of Olya's book, which she wants to put away for the time being as a means of saving it. If you are interested, write and I will keep you informed.

Thank you again.

MASHURA

Leningrad, February 26, 1956

Dear Borya,

Here it is, more than six months since I last wrote you. Orbeli has now received inheritance rights. She has succeeded in placing a big cast-iron model of Uncle Misha's linotype machine in the Moscow Polytechnical Museum. It is now being shipped there. His portrait by Braz will hang in the Leningrad Museum of Communications, to which Olya earlier gave a great many of his inventions. Orbeli is trying to place Uncle Leonid's paintings in the Russian Museum, but she wants them to be on display and not relegated to the storerooms. If they tell her this is impossible, that there is no room to hang them at present, then she will keep all the canvases with her for the time being and continue her efforts. Such are her plans.

She wishes to communicate with you and get your advice. I will give her your address.

That is all the news that might interest you. If you have any questions, ask me and I will answer at once.

Take care of yourself, Borya dear.

MASHURA

Moscow, September 30, 1956

Dear Mashura,

Thank you for your warm letter. Don't think I have forgotten you or am indifferent to Papa's or Olya's memory. It is simply that I am busy with something all the time. I feel that those who remain can best honor

---

* Rusudan Rubenovna Orbeli: daughter of Olga's Gymnasium teacher Olga Vladimirovna Nikolskaya. She was Olga Freidenberg's executrix.

the memory of the dead by engaging in intense and productive activity of a sort they who are gone would approve of. I also think it unnecessary to try to arrange their affairs here.

Thank you for responding so quickly to the news about me, news of which I myself was ignorant. It's true that my fate is now being decided, but at such a great distance from me that I cannot influence it or even know anything definite about it.

I don't doubt but that it will bring me misfortune, and for that reason I don't talk about it to the family; I don't want to distress them.

I am well and happy. My mood is excellent but a bit strange, as if I were living on the moon or in a fourth dimension.

Love to you, dear cousin, and thank you again.

Yours,
BORYA

[In 1956, nearly forty years after the Revolution, Pasternak wrote a poem commemorating those who had suffered at its hands. It is quite possible that Olga Freidenberg would have been among those to whom the poem, "Soul," is addressed.]

SOUL

My mournful soul, you, sorrowing
For all my friends around,
You have become the burial vault
Of all those hounded down.

Devoting to their memory
A verse, embalming them,
In torment, broken, lovingly
Lamenting over them,

In this our mean and selfish time,
For conscience and for quest
You stand—a columbarium,
To lay their souls to rest.

The sum of all their agonies
Has bowed you to the ground.
You smell of dust, of death's decay,
Of morgue and burial mound.

My beggarly, dejected soul,
You heard and saw your fill,
Remembered all and mixed it well
And ground it like a mill.

Continue pounding, and compound
All that I witnessed here
To graveyard compost, as you did
For almost forty years.

Translated by
Lydia Pasternak Slater

ДУША

Душа моя, печальница
О всех в кругу моем!
Ты стала усыпальницей
Замученных живьем.

Тела их бальзамируя,
Им посвящая стих,
Рыдающею лирою
Оплакиваю их.

Ты в наше время шкурное
За совесть и за страх
Стоишь могильной урною,
Покоящей их прах.

Их муки совокупные
Тебя склонили ниц.
Ты пахнешь пылью трупною
Мертвецких и гробниц.

Душа моя, скудельница,
Все, виденное здесь,
Перемолов, как мельница,
Ты превратила в смесь.

И дальше перемалывай
Все бывшее со мной,
Как сорок лет без малого
В погостный перегной.

Index

Freidenberg, Olga *(cont.)*
    nesses, 34, 56–58, 88, 186, 214,
    220, 224, 257, 276, 279–80,
    300–1, 329, 331, 339–41, 344;
    Izvestia attack on, 157–58;
    language study, xiv, 38, 85;
    Leonid Pasternak on, xv, 90;
    reflections on own life, 80, 312;
    and Lifshitses, xiv; literary
    theory, 90, 145–46, 198, 215,
    250, 259, 264–68, 282–83,
    294–95, 326; refusal to retract
    works, 162–63; and brother
    Sasha, xiv; views on Soviet life
    and art, xv, 271–73, 303–4;
    students, 219, 227, 244–45;
    suppression of works, xv, xx,
    84–85, 119, 157–58, 162–65;
    university career, xv, 146, 280,
    295, 305; struggle with univer-
    sity, 193, 252, 257–59, 279,
    339; university studies, xiv,
    54–57; and Zina Pasternak,
    309. Works: "Heroines of the
    Blockade," 227; *Image and
    Concept*, xv, 311, 339; *Lectures
    on the Theory of Folklore*, 226;
    *Myth and the Literature of
    Antiquity*, xv; "The Novel,"
    119; "Origin of the Epic Simile
    Based on Examples from *The
    Iliad*," 259; *Origin of the Lyric*,
    261; "*Palliata*," 244; *Poetics of
    Plot and Genre (Procris)*, *see*
    separate entry; "The Plot
    Semantics of *The Odyssey*,"
    145; dissertation on *Life of
    Thecla*, xiv, 57, 71–72, 74, 76;
    "Theophrastus," 197–98, 204;
    "Three Plots," 145; translation
    of Frazer's *Golden Bough*, 71–
    72
Freindlich, 320
Friche, V. M., 126

Froman, Mikhail, 91
Futurism, xvii, 326

GAIMK (Academy of the History of
    Material Culture), 55, 107
Galerkina, Beba, 244
Gatchina, 104
Genikes, Sonya, 189
Georgian Lyrics (trans. Pasternak),
    157
Georgian SSR, xx, 173
German invasion of Russia, 201–4.
    See also Leningrad blockade
Ghirlandaio, 92
Ginsberg (Olga's colleague), 148
Glavlit (censorship bureau), 165
Glion (Switzerland), 34, 39
"Glow on the Horizon" (Pasternak),
    201
Goethe, Johann Wolfgang von, xix,
    52; *Faust*, 272, 274, 276, 281–
    82, 313–14, 319
Gogol, Nikolai, 80, 201; *The
    Inspector General*, 312
Golden Bough, The (Frazer), 71–72
Gorky, Maxim, 104
Gorlovsky (director, LIFLI), 147,
    153
Gospels, xx, 255
Grabar, Igor, 247
Greek Lyric Poetry (Bowra), 261
Gukovsky, G. A., 211
Gumilev, L. N., 140

"Hamlet" (Pasternak), 287
Hamlet (Shakespeare), 74, 183–88,
    190–93, 257, 321–26
Hamsun, Knut, 135, 336; *Hunger*,
    135; *Victoria*, 257
Harassment by government authori-